The State of the South African State: Capacity, capability and ethics

EDITED BY

Sandy Africa, Na'eem Jeenah
and Musa Nxele

MAPUNGUBWE
INSTITUTE FOR STRATEGIC REFLECTION (MISTRA)

First published by the Mapungubwe Institute for Strategic Reflection (MISTRA) in 2025

142 Western Service Road
Woodmead
Johannesburg

ISBN 978-1-991274-03-8

© MISTRA, 2025

Production and design by Jacana Media, 2025
Cover design: Hothouse
Text editor: Terry Shakinovsky
Copy editor: Lara Jacob
Proofreader: Ali Parry
Indexer: Ali Parry
Designer: Sam van Straaten
Set in Stempel Garamond 10.5/15pt

Please cite this publication as follows:
MISTRA. 2025. *The State of the South African State: Capacity, capability and ethics.* Sandy Africa, Na'eem Jeenah and Musa Nxele (eds). Johannesburg: Mapungubwe Institute for Strategic Reflection

Contents

SECTION ONE:
FRAMING THE ISSUES

SECTION TWO:
CRITICAL THEMES IN THE EVOLUTION
OF THE POST-APARTHEID STATE

SECTION THREE:
RESPONSES AND SOLUTIONS

Contents

About the Contributors

Amanda Gouws is Distinguished Professor of Political Science at the University of Stellenbosch where she holds a SARChI Chair in Gender Politics. Her research focuses on women and citizenship, women's representation, women's movements and gender-based violence, in which she has published widely. She was a Commissioner for the South African Commission for Gender Equality (2012–2014). She has authored several books and articles in her research areas. Her most recent is *Feminist Institutionalism in South Africa: Designing for Gender Equality* (Rowman and Littlefield, 2022).

Brian Levy teaches at the Luskin School of Public Affairs at the University of California, Los Angeles. He received his PhD in Economics from Harvard University. He was Professor of Practice at the School of Advanced International Studies, Johns Hopkins University (2012–2023), and the founding Academic Director of the Nelson Mandela School of Public Governance at the University of Cape Town. He worked at the World Bank (1989–2012), where his work focused on interactions between governance and development. He has published widely on the interactions among institutions, political economy and development policy, including *Working with the Grain: Integrating Governance and Growth in Development Strategies* (Oxford University Press, 2014).

Eddie M. Rakabe is a Senior Researcher in the Political Economy faculty at the Mapungubwe Institute for Strategic Reflection (MISTRA). He holds an MA in Economic Development from the University of Johannesburg. Before joining MISTRA, Rakabe worked for the Financial and Fiscal Commission heading up its fiscal policy division, as a Lead Economist at the National Research Foundation for South Africa's SKA bid, and as a Senior Economist in the local and provincial finance policy units of the National Treasury. Rakabe's research interests include public finance, informal and rural economies, market concentration, and making markets work for the poor.

Garth le Pere is Visiting Professor in the Political Studies Department at the University of Pretoria. He holds an MA, an MPhil and a PhD in Political Science from Yale University. He was the founding Executive Director of the Institute for Global Dialogue, where he served for 12 years. His areas of research and publications include international political economy, political philosophy, public policy, multilateral trade and emerging markets, South African foreign policy, and the politics of Europe, Africa and the Middle East.

Joel Netshitenzhe is the Executive Director of the Mapungubwe Institute for Strategic Reflection (MISTRA). He has an MSc degree in Financial Economics, a postgraduate diploma in Economic Principles from the University of London, and a diploma in Political Science from the Institute of Social Sciences in Moscow. He is a board member of the Development Bank of Southern Africa (DBSA) and Life Healthcare Group. Netshitenzhe served as a member of the African National Congress (ANC) National Executive Committee (1991–2022) and is currently a member of the National Executive Committee of the ANC Veterans League. He also served as a member of the National Planning Commission (2010–2015).

Laurence Caromba is a Researcher in the Humanity faculty at the Mapungubwe Institute for Strategic Reflection (MISTRA) and an Associate Researcher in the Department of Politics and International Relations at the University of Johannesburg. He holds a PhD in Political Science from the University of the Free State, and an MA in Political Science from the University of Pretoria. Before joining MISTRA, Dr Caromba was a lecturer at the University of Johannesburg and Monash South Africa. His publications focus on African politics and security, and he is writing a book on cyber operations and online propaganda as tools of foreign policy.

Lungisile Ntsebeza is a Senior Research Scholar and Emeritus Professor in African Studies and Sociology at the University of Cape Town. He holds a PhD from Rhodes University and an MA from the University of Natal. His work experience includes being a Professor of African Studies and Sociology at the University of Cape Town, Acting Director of the Programme for Land and Agrarian Studies at the University of the Western Cape, and Senior Research Specialist at the Human Sciences Research Council, and has held several research chairs. He has several publications on the political economy of land in Africa, and on traditional leadership to his credit. His current research interest is youth and education in South Africa, with specific reference to early childhood development.

Mabutho Shangase is a Senior Lecturer in the Department of Political Studies and International Relations at North-West University, South Africa. He also served in the South African government at national level for many years. Shangase holds a PhD in African Studies from the University of Edinburgh, an MA in Development Studies from the University of the Witwatersrand, and an MBA in Public Services Management from Aston University in the UK. His research interests include public policy in the post-apartheid state, state autonomy and regional integration. He has published on these topics and is a regular commentator on political affairs.

Mark Heywood is a social justice activist and writer, currently involved in several campaigns on issues such as access to sufficient food and health care services, and works as a Senior Researcher, focusing on activism and civil society, at the Nelson Mandela School of Public Governance at the University of Cape Town. He holds an MA in African Literature from the University of the Witwatersrand. He co-founded and led several successful NGOs and social movements, including the Treatment Action Campaign, SECTION27 and Corruption Watch. He recently founded a new organisation, the Justice and Activism Hub (JAH).

Michael Sachs is an Adjunct Professor at the Southern Centre for Inequality Studies at the University of the Witwatersrand. He holds an MSc in Economics from the University of London (SOAS) and an MA in Public Administration (International Development) from Harvard's Kennedy School of Government. He worked for many years in public policy in South Africa. He is a former head of the budget office at the National Treasury. Before that, he was based at the national headquarters of the African National Congress (ANC) where he coordinated economic policy and led the party's research agenda.

Musa Nxele is Academic Director at the Nelson Mandela School of Public Governance at the University of Cape Town, where he teaches the political economy of policymaking and development. He holds a PhD in Economics from the Université de Paris 1 Panthéon-Sorbonne, a PhD in Development Policy and Practice from the University of Cape Town, a Master of Research in Globalisation and International Economics from the Université de Paris 1 and the École Normale Supérieure de Cachan, and a Master of Commerce in Economic Development from the University of Cape Town. Before joining academia, he worked in investment banking and industrial development consulting. His research focuses on the nexus between governance and development, with a particular interest in the role of capital in national development policy.

Na'eem Jeenah is a Senior Researcher in the Humanity faculty at the Mapungubwe Institute for Strategic Reflection (MISTRA) and an Associate Researcher in the Department of Politics and International Relations at the University of Johannesburg. He holds an MA in Social Sciences from the University of the Witwatersrand. Jeenah is a former Executive Director of the Afro-Middle East Centre (AMEC). He is currently Deputy Chair of the Denis Hurley Peace Institute and an Advisory Board Member of the World Congress for Middle East Studies. He has written and edited numerous articles and books on the Middle East, feminism and South African politics, among other topics.

Richard Meissner is an Associate Professor in the Department of

Political Sciences at the University of South Africa (UNISA). He obtained a PhD in International Politics from the University of Pretoria. Before joining UNISA, he served as a Senior Researcher at the Council for Scientific and Industrial Research's Water Centre (2010–2021). He specialises in water politics and governance, local government water security, green and ecological infrastructure, and transboundary river basin governance and politics.

Sandy Africa is Director of Research at the Mapungubwe Institute for Strategic Reflection (MISTRA), and a Research Associate in the Department of Political Sciences at the University of Pretoria (UP). She holds a PhD in Management from the University of the Witwatersrand. Prior to joining MISTRA, she was the Deputy Dean for Teaching and Learning in the Faculty of Humanities at UP. She worked as a senior official in the security cluster for the post-apartheid government. Thereafter, she joined academia and taught public policy and international relations. Her research interests include security sector governance, especially in post-conflict countries.

Shanil Haricharan is an academic at the Nelson Mandela School of Public Governance at the University of Cape Town. He holds a PhD from Stellenbosch University and an MBA from the University of Cape Town. He served as a Senior and Principal Technical Advisor on governance and administration in the National Treasury's Technical Assistance Unit and the Government Technical Advisory Centre. He is a board member of the Coalition for Humanity (South Sudan), the Pan-African Collective for Evidence, the Human Rights Media Centre, and the Descendants Art Institute. His research focuses on leadership behaviours, democratic governance, organisational behaviour, emotional and social intelligence, institutional reform, and employee well-being within Africa's public sector.

Steven Friedman is Research Professor in the Faculty of Humanities at the University of Johannesburg. He holds a PhD in Literature from Rhodes University. He has published several studies on South Africa's transition to democracy and his current work focuses on the theory and practice of democracy. He is the author of several books, numerous book chapters and journal articles. His most recent book, *Good Jew, Bad Jew: Racism, Anti-Semitism and the Assault on Meaning* (Wits University Press, 2024), discusses the use of ostensibly anti-racist language to justify racism. He is also a media commentator on the development of South African democracy and the author of a weekly column for subscribers, 'Against the Tide'.

Yacoob Abba Omar is the Director of Operations at the Mapungubwe Institute for Strategic Reflection (MISTRA). He obtained a PhD in Sociology from the University of the Witwatersrand in 2017. He was Head of Strategy and Communications at the Banking Association South Africa (BASA), and, before that, he served the South African government as Ambassador to Oman (2003–2008), Ambassador to the United Arab Emirates (2008–2013), and Head of Corporate Affairs at Armscor in the Ministry of Defence. Dr Omar is a *Business Day* columnist, serves on the Executive Committee of South Africa's National Planning Commission, is Chair of the Board of the South African National AIDS Council (SANAC), and is a board member of Business Arts South Africa. A specialist in scenarios, Dr Omar has facilitated numerous scenario development exercises, including two country scenarios for the Office of the South African Presidency.

Acronyms and Abbreviations

ACHPR	African Commission on Human and People's Rights
AfCFTA	African Continental Free Trade Area
AG	Auditor-General
ANC	African National Congress
ANCWL	African National Congress Women's League
APLA	Azanian People's Liberation Army
APRM	African Peer Review Mechanism
ARV	Antiretroviral
AsgiSA	Accelerated and Shared Growth Initiative for South Africa
AU	African Union
AZAPO	Azanian People's Organisation
BC	Black Consciousness
BEE	Black Economic Empowerment
BELA Act	Basic Education Laws Amendment Act
BRIC	Brazil, Russia, India, China
BRICS	Brazil, Russia, India, China, South Africa
BRT	Black Republic Thesis
CALS	Centre for Applied Legal Studies
CAR	Central African Republic
CBAM	Carbon Border Adjustment Mechanism
CEO	Chief Executive Officer
CEPD	Council for Economic Planning and Development (Taiwan)
CGE	Commission for Gender Equality
CIT	Corporate Income Tax
CLaRA	Communal Land Rights Act
CLTP	Communal Land Tenure Policy
CoG	Centre of Government
CoGTA	Cooperative Governance and Traditional Affairs
CONTRALESA	Congress of Traditional Leaders of South Africa
COSATU	Congress of South African Trade Unions
CPSA	Communist Party of South Africa
CRT	Critical Race Theory

CSIR	Council for Scientific and Industrial Research
CST	Colonialism of a Special Type
CTOP	Choice on Termination of Pregnancy Act
DFA	Department of Foreign Affairs
DGs	Directors-General
DHA	Department of Home Affairs
DIRCO	Department of International Relations and Cooperation
DLA	Department of Land Affairs
DME	Department of Minerals and Energy
DMRE	Department of Mineral Resources and Energy
DoE	Department of Energy
DPLG	Department of Provincial and Local Government
DPME	Department of Planning, Monitoring and Evaluation
DPSA	Department of Public Service and Administration
DRC	Democratic Republic of the Congo
DRDLR	Department of Rural Development and Land Reform
DSD	Department of Social Development
DTI	Department of Trade and Industry
DTIC	Department of Trade, Industry and Competition
DWS	Department of Water and Sanitation
DWYPD	Department of Women, Youth and Persons with Disabilities
EAF	Energy Availability Factor
ECD	Early Childhood Development
EI	Emotional Intelligence
EPB	Economic Planning Board (Korea)
ERRP	Economic Reconstruction and Recovery Plan
EU	European Union
FOSAD	Forum of South African Directors-General
G20	Group of 20
GBV	Gender-Based Violence
GBVF	Gender-Based Violence and Femicide
GDP	Gross Domestic Product
GEAR	Growth, Employment and Redistribution (strategy)
GNU	Government of National Unity
HoD	Head of Department
HoPS	Head of Public Service
HRM	Human Resource Management
IBSA	India, Brazil, South Africa
ICJ	International Court of Justice

IFP	Inkatha Freedom Party
IMF	International Monetary Fund
IPID	Independent Police Investigative Directorate
JMC	Joint Monitoring Committee on Improvement of Quality of Life and Status of Women
JSC	Judicial Services Commission
JSCD	Joint Standing Committee on Defence
JSCI	Joint Standing Committee on Intelligence
JSE	Johannesburg Stock Exchange
LMCF	Leadership and Management Competency Framework
M&E	Monitoring and Evaluation
MECs	Members of the Executive Council
MERS	Microeconomic Reform Strategy
MFMA	Municipal Finance Management Act
MINCOMBUD	Ministers' Committee on the Budget
MINCOMPLAN	Ministerial Committee on Planning
MINMECs	Ministers and Members of the Executive Council
MITI	Ministry of International Trade and Industry (Japan)
MK	Umkhonto weSwize
MONUSCO	United Nations Organization Stabilization Mission in the Democratic Republic of the Congo
MSF	Médecins Sans Frontières
MTDP	Medium-Term Development Plan
MTEF	Medium-Term Expenditure Framework
MTSF	Medium-Term Strategic Framework
NAM	Non-Aligned Movement
NDP	National Development Plan
NDR	National Democratic Revolution
NEC	National Executive Committee
NEDLAC	National Economic, Development and Labour Council
NEPAD	New Partnership for Africa's Development
NERSA	National Energy Regulator of South Africa
NGM	National Gender Machinery
NGO	Non-Governmental Organisation
NHI	National Health Insurance
NIA	National Intelligence Agency
NICOC	National Intelligence Coordinating Committee
NICs	Newly Industrialised Countries
NIS	National Intelligence Service
NLC	National Land Committee

NPA	National Prosecuting Authority
NPC	National Planning Commission
NPG	New Public Governance
NPM	New Public Management
NPO	Non-Profit Organisation
NSG	National School of Governance
NT	National Treasury
NUM	National Union of Mineworkers
NUMSA	National Union of Metalworkers of South Africa
OCM	Optimum Coal Mine
OECD	Organisation for Economic Co-operation and Development
OHCHR	United Nations Office of the High Commissioner on Human Rights
OSW	Office of the Status of Women
OUTA	Organisation Undoing Tax Abuse
PAC	Pan Africanist Congress
PALAMA	Public Administration and Leadership Academy
PAMA Bill	Public Administration Management Amendment Bill
PARI	Public Affairs Research Institute
PAYE	Pay As You Earn
PCAS	Policy Coordination and Advisory Services
PCC	Presidential Coordinating Committee
PFMA	Public Finance Management Act
PIT	Personal Income Tax
PLAAS	Programme for Land and Agrarian Studies
PMDS	Performance Management and Development System
POA	Programme of Action
PR	Proportional Representation
PSA	Public Service Act
PSA Bill	Public Service Amendment Bill
PSC	Public Service Commission
RDP	Reconstruction and Development Programme
REFIT	Renewable Energy Feed-in Tariff
REIPPPP	Renewable Energy Independent Power Producer Procurement Programme
SACP	South African Communist Party
SACU	Southern African Customs Union
SADC	Southern African Development Community
SADF	South African Defence Force

SADPA	South African Development Partnership Agency
SADTU	South African Democratic Teachers Union
SAFA	South African Football Association
SAHRC	South African Human Rights Commission
SALGA	South African Local Government Association
SAMDI	South African Management Development Institute
SANAC	South African National AIDS Council
SANCO	South African National Civic Organisation
SANDF	South African National Defence Force
SAPS	South African Police Service
SAQA	South African Qualifications Authority
SARS	South African Revenue Service
SASA	South African Schools Act
SASS	South African Secret Service
SAWEA	South African Wind Energy Association
SDGs	Sustainable Development Goals
SCOPA	Standing Committee on Public Accounts
SETAs	Sector Education and Training Authorities
SGB	School Governing Body
SMS	Senior Management Service
SOE	State-Owned Enterprise
SONA	State of the Nation Address
SSA	State Security Agency
TAC	Treatment Action Campaign
TLGFA	Traditional Leadership and Governance Framework Act
TKLA	Traditional and Khoi-San Leadership Act
TRC	Truth and Reconciliation Commission
TVET	Technical and Vocational Education and Training
UDF	United Democratic Front
UN	United Nations
UNFCCC	United Nations Framework Convention on Climate Change
VAT	Value-Added Tax
VLDP	Value-Based Leadership Development Programme
VMMC	Voluntary Medical Male Circumcision
WDI	World Development Indicators (World Bank)
WEF	Water-Energy-Food
WNC	Women's National Coalition
WOW	Who Owns Whom
WTO	World Trade Organization
ZAR	Zuid-Afrikaansche Republiek

Acknowledgements

MISTRA is deeply grateful to the three co-editors of this volume – Dr Sandy Africa, Na'eem Jeenah and Dr Musa Nxele – for their attempts to ensure that this book would be of the highest possible intellectual quality and would cover the topic as comprehensively as possible. They were ably assisted by MISTRA Associate Researcher, Njabulo Zwane. MISTRA's Finance Manager, Lorraine Pillay, made sure that while the contributors tried to hold the state to account, MISTRA's books, too, would provide balance for this research project. Thanks are also due to MISTRA's former Director of Research, Professor Susan Booysen, who guided and oversaw a major part of this project, and to Dr Laurence Caromba for his early work on it. Gratitude also goes to MISTRA's Executive Director, Joel Netshitenzhe, for overall strategic leadership of the project as well as his meticulous reading and reviewing of the text.

MISTRA's heartfelt thanks go to the various chapter authors for their careful research and writing. In addition, MISTRA thanks the various scholars who participated in the Reference Group for this project; the peer reviewers whose critical comments helped ensure that each chapter would meet high standards of research and be as up to date as possible; and Terry Shakinovsky for editing the manuscript and overseeing the publication process. Terry worked with an efficient team from Jacana Media, which also deserves our thanks for ensuring the publication and distribution of this book.

Intellectual endeavours of this magnitude are not possible without substantial financial resources. MISTRA's fundraising team worked hard to get the resources necessary for this book to be published. The Oppenheimer Memorial Trust (OMT) deserves our special thanks for its financial support of this project. We also thank the other donors who support the Institute and make its work possible. They are:

- Batho Batho Trust
- Consulate General of India, Johannesburg
- Embassy of the People's Republic of China, South Africa
- Department of Science, Technology and Innovation
- Department of Home Affairs
- Discovery Central Services
- Friedrich Ebert Stiftung (FES)
- Millennium Trust
- Social Justice Initiative
- Standard Bank
- Transnet
- Yellowwoods.

Preface

The political, economic and social life of any modern country and society is profoundly shaped, and its development guided, by the state and its numerous institutions – irrespective of the nature of that state. Three decades into its democratic experience, the South African state has made remarkable strides in its efforts to change South African society for the better. But it has also faced several challenges that have frustrated its proclaimed objective of building a democratic and inclusive society. South Africa's challenges stem, in part, from a weakness of state capacity – primarily to design and implement effective programmes to achieve the country's constitutional imperatives. This includes restructuring the state to meet its goals, ensuring that the necessary skills have been secured for successful implementation, and developing robust monitoring and evaluation mechanisms to track progress and make improvements where necessary.

Looming large in recent years, the revelations of 'state capture' have cast a shadow on the integrity of the state as a whole, and certain of its branches more specifically. This has affected its legitimacy in the eyes of society, as well as its standing in the rest of the world. At the same time, the shift towards coalition politics – increasingly at the local/municipal level in recent years, and at national and provincial levels after the 2024 elections – has significantly complicated the nation's political landscape. The state has also struggled to cope with several crises, including the Covid-19 pandemic and its economic and social impacts; an electricity supply crisis spanning more than a decade; low and unsustainable economic growth; rising unemployment; deteriorating service delivery; breakdowns in infrastructure across sectors; a global rise in food and energy prices; and increasingly severe conflicts globally and regionally. These developments have stretched and strained the limits of South Africa's state capacity and exposed deep-seated and systemic problems.

The National Development Plan (NDP), adopted by government in 2012 as a long-term development blueprint for the state, identified two goals for the country by 2030: eradicating poverty and drastically reducing inequality. These goals were established after the NDP identified the country's main 'developmental challenges' as poverty, inequality and unemployment. The Statement of Intent issued by the Government of National Unity (GNU), formed after the May 2024 elections, identifies the same challenges and goals. There is widespread agreement that, because of the various challenges faced by the state in the past decade and a half, the objectives of the NDP will not be realised by 2030. Furthermore, months after the formation of the GNU, debates continue to rage about the new government's efficacy and sustainability, casting even greater doubt on the ability of the state to tackle its developmental challenges effectively.

This volume assesses the South African state three decades into its democracy, and a year after the formation of the GNU. It examines the state within a long-term historical context, but with a specific focus on events and trends that have become prominent since 2014.

This book builds on earlier MISTRA projects, particularly *Essays on the Evolution of the Post-Apartheid State; 20 Years of South African Democracy: So where to now?*, the 'Macro-Social Report', and the two Indlulamithi Scenarios projects – 2030 and 2035. With a focus on state capacity, capability and ethics, this volume advances MISTRA's transdisciplinary research agenda, provides an up-to-date evaluation of the South African state and provides recommendations for course correction.

It seeks to answer the following core research question: 'What is the current capacity of the South African state to develop and implement effective public policy, conduct efficient and service-oriented governance, and effectively address the problems plaguing the South African nation?'

In attempting to answer this core question, it also considers several secondary research questions:

- How far has the post-colonial state gone in meeting its objective of overcoming the legacy of apartheid and transforming the erstwhile racist and exclusionary state?

- What have been the manifestations of contemporary state weaknesses or failures, and what have been the effects on various aspects of South African life, including economic development, infrastructure, social cohesion and political stability?
- What possible reforms or interventions could help strengthen the state?
- Is the ideal of a 'developmental state' still viable in light of South Africa's weakened state capacity?

The book targets a general audience comprising policymakers, academics, the broader research community, civil society organisations, journalists, and political, economic and social commentators. Furthermore, it is hoped that specific organs of state, as well as political parties, will use the research to guide their policy formulation and practical programmes. MISTRA wishes to thank the authors, peer reviewers and the broader family of partners who have variously contributed to the making of this volume.

Professor Sibusiso Vil-Nkomo
Chair, MISTRA Board of Governors

ONE

Introduction: Reading the state – hope or despair?

Sandy Africa, Na'eem Jeenah
and Musa Nxele

Any attempt at theorising and assessing the state – or a particular state – at the end of the first quarter of the twenty-first century will be a daunting task, not least because the polycrisis that grips the world has created multiple uncertainties impacting the global order. Globally, economic inequality is rapidly increasing, with the poorest 50 per cent of the world's population sharing just 8 per cent of total income; the impact of the Covid-19 pandemic had cost approximately $82 trillion by 2024; and there are signs of significant reversals in some of the UN's Sustainable Development Goals (SDGs), such as subjective well-being, access to vaccination, reduction in poverty and improved employment rates (Chancel et al., 2022; Yunnan and Park, 2020). Recurring pandemics and mental health crises; climate change and its devastating effects; growing pressure on resources such as water; an increasing number of military conflicts; a genocide in the Middle East and its attendant challenges to international law; and several other economic, environmental, geopolitical, social and technological crises, compound

1

the situation which has been described as a global polycrisis (Whiting and Park, 2023).

The South African state is impacted by these uncertainties, in addition to facing its own peculiar challenges. There is a widespread sense among the population that the state is failing in its duty to improve the lives of all its citizens, and this has fuelled a growing polarisation along ideological, humanitarian and political lines (Carothers and O'Donohue, 2019; Matlosa, 2023). The country is in the grip of a 'middle-income trap', a term coined by the World Bank to describe countries which have struggled to break out of a low-growth equilibrium, and to transcend their status as middle-income countries in order to attain high-income status (Gill and Kharas, 2015).

TOWARDS A FRAMEWORK TO ANALYSE THE STATE OF THE SOUTH AFRICAN STATE

The title of this book carries a dual meaning that serves as a framework for analysing the South African state. On the one hand, '*The State* of the South African State' refers to the current conditions or state of affairs within the government and its institutions, capturing the empirical and contextual realities of governance in South Africa. These include how the state operates; its power dynamics; political settlements that govern its functioning (including coalitions); and the institutional cultures within its structures. On the other hand, the title also addresses the *form* of the '*The State*' as an institutional entity, examining its structure and operations and the rules that govern its operations. This aspect of the definition focuses on structural and functional elements, and how these determine the effectiveness of the state in managing the state of affairs. The state's effectiveness is, in large part, determined by its capacity, capabilities and ethics. Capacity includes elements such as the architecture and configuration of its branches and institutions, the availability of resources, and the foundational rules and processes that enable governance, while capability focuses on how effectively these capacities are used, including the strategic direction of the state, its ability to implement policies, and its ability to respond to challenges. Ethics refers to the commitment of the state and its functionaries to the constitutional values of justice, fairness, equality and the common good, and a commitment to redressing past injustices. Using this understanding, this book attempts to provide a holistic analysis of the South African state's strengths, weaknesses and potential for renewal. Such an analysis connects the structural elements of the state with societal outcomes, thereby deepening our understanding of both the causes and effects of governance challenges in South Africa.

Given the global and domestic challenges confronting South Africa, it is appropriate to ask whether the state of the South African state gives us hope or despair. The truth probably lies somewhere in between.

Many of the challenges that democratic South Africa has faced in its three decades have to do with a combination of the state's (and society's) ethical foundations, issues of capacity and capability. This volume offers analyses of these challenges by examining the dynamic tensions between state capacity, capability, ethics, exploitation, capture and corruption – all features of the South African state in different ways and at different times.

Reflecting on 30 years of South African democracy, and particularly the democratic South African state, the state's dual nature becomes apparent — its potential for progress and its risk of regression. The dynamic tension in South Africa between these potentials demands a path into the future that upholds democracy and justice while addressing deep-seated governance issues.

THE THREE-DECADE EVOLUTION OF THE DEMOCRATIC SOUTH AFRICAN STATE

The democratic South African state has developed through several phases in the past three decades.

The first phase, from 1994 to 1999, presided over by South Africa's first democratically elected president, Nelson Mandela, was characterised by immense optimism, and even euphoria, which gripped a large part of the country's citizenry, parliamentarians and new government officials as they anticipated the realisation of constitutional ideals and electoral promises (Bawa, 2005). There was much talk of the role of the new South African state in the process of reconciliation after the destruction wrought by apartheid, of nation-building, inclusion and redressing the injustices of the past. As the new state – with its executive, legislative and judicial branches and new institutions to protect the citizenry – was being reimagined and transformed, the constitutionally mandated Government of National Unity devoted much of its attention to this discourse. Established after the first democratic elections in 1994, the government initiated the implementation of the Reconstruction and Development Programme (RDP), a social-democratic programme meant to improve the conditions of the most marginalised in society and meet a baseline of the socioeconomic needs of the population. The quasi-judicial Truth and Reconciliation Commission (TRC) began its work in 1996, expecting to reveal gross human rights abuses that had taken place in the apartheid era, allow citizens to find closure on those matters, and reconcile the nation. Government attention was also focused on nation-building and reconciliation, with society being mobilised for this agenda; transformation charters were developed for many sites of social endeavour – from business to sports. Several laws were passed or amended and policies were adopted to achieve democratic objectives.

The euphoria and hope were bolstered by South Africa's 1993 interim Constitution, and, later, the final Constitution of the Republic of South Africa, adopted in 1996. Both promised societal transformation, improved rights – including the progressive realisation of socioeconomic rights, and, in general, the realisation of 'a better life for all' through the deep transformation of South African society. The democratically elected Parliament of South Africa engaged in its tasks with vigour, hoping to spearhead the ongoing process of fundamental change. Parliament's transformation was mandated, in part, by the Interim Constitution and its restructuring began immediately upon the swearing-in of the first democratic parliament.

Within two years of the first elections, however, cracks began to show in this optimism as the imperatives of macroeconomic balance slowed down the realisation of RDP objectives. In 1996, the RDP, which had been a product of broad consultation among political groups and civil society before 1994, was replaced by the macroeconomic Growth, Employment and Redistribution (GEAR) strategy. This was drawn up by a small technical committee and emphasised macroeconomic balance against the backdrop of high levels of debt, low rates of investment and the expectations of global economic players in an era of emergent neoliberalism. Although taking place in the 1994–1999 first phase, these developments marked the start of the second phase, overlapping with the first.

Apart from these macroeconomic changes, the state underwent transformation of institutions in its three branches. Within the executive, institutional transformation and restructuring (see Booysen, 2011: 406) focused on building and reinforcing the state machinery and its capacity to deliver on its mandates. Much of this transformative work had begun in the first phase and was intensified in the second phase, symbolised by the restructuring of the Presidency which was undertaken with the objective of optimising state operations.

This second phase, from 1996 to 2008, also focused on establishing a macroeconomic framework, beginning with the adoption of GEAR. While this strategy was liberal (some would argue it was neoliberal) (Narsiah, 2002), government and the governing party regarded it as 'developmental', and South Africa, it was said, aspired to be a 'developmental state' (Buhlungu et al., 2006). The macroeconomic efforts to 'balance the books' had made some progress by the turn of the century; focus then shifted to microeconomic interventions, starting with the introduction of the Microeconomic Reform Strategy (MERS) in 2002. As efforts to increase economic growth intensified, it became clear that there were many constraints. This led to the adoption, in 2006, of the Accelerated and Shared Growth Initiative for South Africa (AsgiSA), which sought to address those constraints. Between 2002 and 2008, South Africa experienced several positive economic trends, such as high rates of economic growth (especially between 2004 and 2007), a decline in unemployment rates, stable prices and a reduction in public debt. However, while poverty was reduced, inequality increased. Furthermore, certain agencies of the state, especially in the security cluster, were increasingly affected by factional battles within the ANC, which were fought using state resources (Booysen, 2011: 359–360).

The third phase began in the period 2008–2009. To address South Africa's economic and social challenges, government set up a National

Planning Commission (NPC), which included several individuals from outside of state structures. It drafted a National Development Plan (NDP) (National Planning Commission, 2012) that provided a vision for the country in 2030 and detailed interventions required to attain it. However, efforts at implementation were insufficient to meet the objectives set out in the NDP. There were new promises about governance that would result in a closer connection between the state and the people, a greater redistribution of wealth, the eradication of poverty, and a reduction in inequality and unemployment. Poverty, inequality and unemployment were the three 'developmental challenges' confronting South Africa, according to the NDP. There was an expectation that earlier approaches would be replaced by a more caring, welfarist one that would ensure that all citizens' needs would be met (Buhlungu and Ellis, 2013). Little of that materialised. Instead, when the NDP was published in 2012, the state had already descended into a form of kleptocracy; economic growth had become pedestrian; unemployment had increased; the provision of services had deteriorated; and both poverty and inequality had increased. State-owned enterprises, in particular, became targets for corruption, and public utilities degraded and failed under the weight of corruption, maladministration and incompetence (Zondo, 2022). The era of state capture had taken hold, and it sought to blur the lines between the executive, legislature and judiciary in a manner that would serve the kleptocratic elite.

Once the state capture project was exposed, there was huge civil society mobilisation against it, with the media playing a crucial role in continually exposing wrongdoing. Within the state itself, there were also pockets of opposition, resulting in battles within the government, between ANC Members of Parliament and within entities such as the South African Revenue Service (SARS). The judiciary played an activist role, as the South African judiciary occasionally has done since 1994 (see Chapter 14), and the Office of the Public Protector was key to investigating and exposing state capture machinations, effectively forcing President Zuma to establish a commission of inquiry into the phenomenon.

The South African state is yet to recover from the era of state capture. Even though there have not been definitive reversals of the harm done during that period, it is possible to talk about the onset of a fourth phase from around 2019/2020. This phase had its beginnings in the 2018 government, formed after President Zuma was forced to resign. It set itself the task of tackling corruption and restoring trust in government (Von Holdt, 2019). The Zondo Commission and its report went a long way in uncovering the activities of those who had captured the state; many agencies of the state have since been restructured and new personnel appointed (e.g. in the National Prosecuting Authority (NPA), SARS, South African Police Service (SAPS) and the State Security Agency (SSA) and other intelligence services, and some parts of the state have managed to weed out corrupt elements and chart a path to recovery. The systems of patronage that had been established will likely take years to fully root out and some factional battles will continue to be fought within the state. The task of uprooting the legacy of corruption is made more difficult by the fact that it and the patronage networks that sustained it did not start during the period of state capture but earlier, in the 1990s (Booysen, 2011), though they deepened considerably and became systemic within government in this period. Neither the government nor the state have broadly charted a new institutional course that would eliminate the corrupt practices of the past.

While small, incremental successes may be seen, the Covid-19 pandemic and the lockdowns associated with it worsened the situation, ravaged the economy, increased unemployment, delayed infrastructure and other programmes, and provided further opportunities for corruption. There has also been much criticism of the government's lack of decisiveness in addressing the weaknesses. As importantly, and more defining of the fourth phase, it is characterised by attempts to initiate and entrench a series of structural economic reforms to address many of the developmental problems faced by the state and the nation, especially the high rates of poverty and unemployment and the huge income inequality. Several of these reforms have reached a stage where they have become irreversible and will bear fruit by around 2026. Whether they will successfully address the country's main developmental challenges remains to be seen. The fourth phase also includes the formation in 2024 of a coalition government called the Government of National Unity (GNU), less than a month after the national elections in May that year.

South Africa faces paradoxical policy challenges, such as the persistent need for racial and class transformation alongside the imperative for capital-rich, job-creating investment. This paradox has given rise to a range of narratives, from calls for 'radical economic transformation' to advocating for inclusive economic growth. However, none of these narratives has successfully reconciled the inherent contradictions. Some narratives challenge the Constitution for both legitimate and opportunistic reasons, while others aim to construct a more inclusive future.

STRUCTURE OF THE BOOK

Beyond this Introduction, the book is divided into three distinct parts.

The first section on 'Framing the Issues' consists of three core chapters that seek to rethink basic conceptual tenets about the effectiveness of the state. Yacoob Abba Omar's 'Conceptualising the theory of the state' (Chapter 2) references classical theory and critical theory but takes a fresh look at the concept through a distinctly South African lens. In Chapter 3, Joel Netshitenzhe, while looking at global experiences and strategies including those of the so-called Asian Tigers, critiques the South African experience of development planning and makes recommendations for how to improve the functioning of the South African state, particularly the centre of government. The third framing chapter, by Musa Nxele (Chapter 4), identifies a key flaw in democratic South Africa's strategies for realising the principles laid out in the Constitution, and offers suggestions for a different way forward.

This section is followed by 'Critical Themes in the Evolution of the Post-Apartheid State', in which the authors assess key areas of state functioning and delivery and highlight some of the challenges it faces. Michael Sachs (Chapter 5) uses the lens of taxation to shed light on the question of the sources of state capacity and their relationship to society. His chapter focuses on the building and evolution of the state's fiscal and institutional capacity, treating taxation as foundational to broader state development. Looking at the issue of state capture, Mabutho Shangase (Chapter 7) focuses an ethical lens on the state. He argues that any explanation of state capture requires a concomitant interrogation and understanding of state autonomy and ideational approaches to policymaking.

Steven Friedman's chapter (Chapter 14) deals with the judiciary – not only as an important branch of the state but as the South African state's 'most valuable asset', which, he argues, was critical in enhancing the state's legitimacy and in resolving conflicts that might have caused serious harm to the state. He cautions, however, that though the judiciary enjoys high legitimacy among more vocal sections of the population, this is not the case with the majority, and therefore that extending its legitimacy is a critical and immediate task. An often-overlooked structure within the state machinery in South Africa is that of traditional leadership, an especially important consideration because it is sometimes (erroneously) referred to as the 'fourth branch of the state'. Lungisile Ntsebeza's chapter (Chapter 10) examines the tensions arising within state and society because of the recognition and granting of powers to unelected traditional leaders in the South African democratic system.

In her contribution, Amanda Gouws (Chapter 12) examines women's representation and feminist institutionalism – the effort to 'get women into the state' – and assesses the extent of success in promoting gender equality through the state since the advent of democracy. In what should be a critical issue regarding both state capacity and capability, she includes an assessment of the National Gender Machinery as a vehicle for promoting feminist institutionalism in the state. Shanil Haricharan (Chapter 6) continues the discussion about state capacity and capabilities with a focus on the question of the professionalisation of the South African public service. In particular, he examines various factors that impact senior government managers' capacity to embrace transformational leadership and uphold public values.

Two chapters examine specific service delivery issues (and crises). Laurence Caromba (Chapter 8) addresses the vexed question of South Africa's energy crisis and the much-discussed just energy transition. The impact of loadshedding on the South African economy, he points out, was about the same as that of the 2008–2009 financial crisis. To address the crisis, he calls for reform of the institutional rules that surround energy policy, among other measures. Richard Meissner (Chapter 9) looks at the equally vexed issue of water access by citizens. He reflects on the South African state's capability to supply water services and evaluates which governance model might best explain how South Africa is attempting to fulfil its hydro-social contract.

With an eye on the work of specific government departments, Garth le Pere and Na'eem Jeenah (Chapter 13) assess South Africa's foreign policy, and in Chapter 11, Sandy Africa subjects the country's security services to scrutiny. Le Pere and Jeenah examine South Africa's foreign policy dilemma in attempting to balance its national interest against its claimed internationalism, including its role in Africa. They also consider several related themes: institutional and diplomatic challenges; multilateral, trade and economic diplomacy; peace and security; and development aid. Africa provides an overview of the pre-1994 transition and its role in the creation of the post-apartheid security system. She also examines the major security challenges and contradictions faced by the state over the past 30 years, reflecting also on the context of geopolitical shifts and how they influenced South Africa's security decisions.

In the final section, 'Responses and Solutions', the authors focus on how to make the state more responsive to the needs of the people it is meant to serve. Reflecting on the fact that, 30 years into democracy, the South African state still faces serious challenges with service delivery and with translating policy into implementation, Eddie Rakabe (Chapter 15) argues that state capacity to deliver is dependent on its organisational configuration. His chapter explores the possibilities of reorganising the state delivery machinery to improve inter- and intra-organisational interfaces for a sustainable, efficient, effective and accountable public service. Mark Heywood and Brian Levy (Chapter 16) discuss civil society responses to state policy and practice, by focusing on campaigns of the Treatment Action Campaign. They argue that civil society can, in different contexts, play both the role of pressuring the state to respond to citizens' demands, and cooperating with the state to enhance service delivery.

The Conclusion (Chapter 17) reflects on the cumulative contribution of the various chapters considering the current, unique moment that South Africa and, especially, the South African state, faces, with its developmental challenges deepening, a unique national coalition government facing opportunities and pitfalls, and continental and global contexts that pose additional challenges. The Conclusion considers possible future trajectories for the South African state considering this context.

CONCLUSION

The publication of this volume coincides with the thirtieth anniversary of South Africa's establishment as a post-apartheid, democratic state. It also follows the country's 2024 national and provincial elections which resulted in the formation of a national multi-party coalition government. This political arrangement, referred to as a Government of National Unity (GNU) by the political parties who are part of the coalition, came about because electoral support for the African National Congress (ANC), which had been the governing party from 1994, plummeted to only 40 per cent in the 2024 general elections. Although the parties had been forced to scramble for coalition partners once it became clear that there were no outright winners, ANC president Cyril Ramaphosa characterised the outcome of the elections as an expression of the will of the people, in his inaugural speech that followed his election as president of the Republic by Parliament (The Presidency, 2024):

> The people have spoken loudly that they choose peace and democracy over violent, undemocratic and unconstitutional methods... The voters of South Africa did not give any single party the full mandate to govern our country alone. They have directed us to work together to address their plight and realise their aspirations.

The implications of a national coalition government for the state and its effectiveness will emerge over time. Political coalitions at local government level have been a feature of the South African landscape for more than a decade, and are a reflection that operating within the structures of the state, even when policy positions differ, remains a preferred option for major political actors.

REFERENCES

Allinder, S.M. and Fleischman, J. 2019. 'The world's largest HIV epidemic in crisis: HIV in South Africa'. *Centre for Strategic and International Studies*, 2 April, https://www.csis.org/analysis/worlds-largest-hiv-epidemic-crisis-hiv-south-africa, accessed 8 October 2024.

Bawa, A.C. 2005. 'South Africa's young democracy, ten years on'. *Social Research: An International Quarterly*, 72(3), vii–xviii.

Bongmba, E.K. 2004. 'Reflections on Thabo Mbeki's African Renaissance'. *Journal of Southern African Studies*, 30(2), 291–316.

Booysen, S. 2011. *The African National Congress and the Regeneration of Political Power*. Johannesburg: Wits University Press.

Buhlungu, S., Daniel, J., Southall, R. and Lutchman, J. (eds). 2006. *State of the Nation: South Africa 2005–2006*. Cape Town: HSRC Press.

Buhlungu, S. and Ellis, S. 2013. 'The trade union movement and the Tripartite Alliance: A tangled history', in Buhlungu, S. and Tshoaedi, M. (eds), *COSATU'S Contested Legacy: South African Trade Unions in the Second Decade of Democracy*. Cape Town: HSRC Press.

Buthelezi, L. 2021. 'SA lost R1.5 trillion to corruption in five years and continues to bleed - report'. *News24*, https://www.news24.com/fin24/sa-lost-r15-trillion-to-corruption-in-five-years-and-continues-to-bleed-report-20210623, accessed 19 August 2024.

Carothers, T. and O'Donohue, A. (eds). 2019. *Democracies Divided: The Global Challenge of Political Polarization*. Washington D.C.: Brookings Institution Press, https://www.jstor.org/stable/10.7864/j.ctvbd8j2p, accessed 2 September 2024.

Chancel, L., Piketty, T., Saez, E. and Zucman, G. 2022. *World Inequality Report 2022*. United Nations Development Programme, https://wir2022.wid.world/www-site/uploads/2021/12/WorldInequalityReport2022_Full_Report.pdf, accessed 14 August 2024.

Dahl, R.A. 1961. *Who Governs? Democracy and Power in an American city*. New Haven: Yale University Press.

Dolley, C. and Ellis, E. 2024. 'Police and business turn the screws on extortion mafia terrorising SA'. *Daily Maverick*, https://www.dailymaverick.co.za/article/2024-08-24-police-and-business-turn-the-screws-on-extortion-mafia-terrorising-all-corners-of-sa/, accessed 2 September 2024.

Evans, P. 2006. 'Building a 21st-century developmental state: Internal structure, state-society relations and organizational culture'. Policy Coordination and Advisory Services (PCAS), The Presidency, Republic of South Africa.

Gill, I.S. and Kharas, H. 2015. *The Middle-Income Trap Turns Ten.* World Bank Group, https://documents1.worldbank.org/curated/en/291521468179640202/pdf/WPS7403.pdf, accessed 2 September 2024.

Gramsci, A. 1975. *Prison Notebooks: Volume I.* New York: Columbia University Press.

Grindle, M.S. and Hilderbrand, M.E. 1995. 'Building sustainable capacity in the public sector: What can be done?'. *Public Administration and Development*, 15(5), 441–463.

Hobbes, T. 1651. *Leviathan.* London: Andrew Crooke.

Judicial Commission of Inquiry into State Capture. 2022. *Final Reports, Judicial Commission of Inquiry into Allegations of State Capture, Corruption and Fraud in the Public Sector including Organs of State*, https://www.statecapture.org.za/, accessed 8 October 2024.

Kalina, M., Makwetu, N. and Tilley, E. 2024. '"The rich will always be able to dispose of their waste": A view from the frontlines of municipal failure in Makhanda, South Africa'. *Environment, Development and Sustainability*, 26(7), 17759–17782.

Khan, M. 2010. 'Political settlements and the governance of growth-enhancing institutions', https://eprints.soas.ac.uk/9968/1/Political_Settlements_internet.pdf, accessed 13 September 2022.

Leftwich, A. 2010. 'Beyond institutions: Rethinking the role of leaders, elites and coalitions in the institutional formation of developmental states and strategies'. *Forum for Development Studies*, 37(1), 93–111.

Levy, B. 2014. *Working with the Grain: Integrating Governance and Growth in Development Strategies.* New York: Oxford Academic.

Levy, B., Hirsch, A., Naidoo, V. and Nxele, M. 2021. *South Africa: When Strong Institutions and Massive Inequalities Collide.* Carnegie Endowment for International Peace, https://www.jstor.org/stable/resrep30023.1, accessed 14 August 2024.

MacKinnon, C.A. 1989. *Toward a Feminist Theory of the State.* Cambridge, Mass.: Harvard University Press.

Matlosa, K. 2023. 'Global trends and impact of democratic recession: Hard choices for the Global South'. *South African Journal of International Affairs*, 30(3), 337–355.

Migdal, J.S. 1988. *Strong Societies and Weak States: State-Society Relations and State Capabilities in the Third World.* Princeton, N.J.: Princeton University Press.

Narsiah, S. 2002. 'Neoliberalism and privatisation in South Africa'. *Geojournal*, 57(1), 29–38.

National Planning Commission. 2012. *National Development Plan 2030: Our Future - Make it Work.* South African Government, https://www.gov.za/

sites/default/files/gcis_document/201409/ndp-2030-our-future-make-it-workr.pdf, accessed 2 September 2024.

National Treasury. 2024. *2024 Budget Review Consolidated Spending Plans, Chapter 5,* https://www.treasury.gov.za/documents/National%20Budget/2024/review/Chapter%205.pdf, accessed 19 August 2024.

Netshitenzhe, J. 2011. 'South Africa: The path towards a developmental state'. SANPAD Thematic Conference on the Developmental State.

Netshitenzhe, J. 2024a. 'A strategic overview of Election 2024'. MISTRA, https://mistra.org.za/wp-content/uploads/2024/07/ELECTION-REVIEW-WORKING-PAPER-Final-1915.pdf, accessed 22 October 2024.

Netshitenzhe, J. 2024b. 'Organisational underpinnings of National Development Planning: Interrogating democratic South Africa's experience'. MISTRA, https://mistra.org.za/wp-content/uploads/2024/04/Underpinnings-of-National-Planning-MISTRA-Working-Paper-final.pdf, accessed 20 October 2024.

Pareto, V. 1935. *The Mind and Society.* New York: Harcourt, Brace and Company.

Rawls, J. 1971. *A Theory of Justice: Original Edition.* Cambridge, MA: Harvard University Press.

Roberts, B. and Gordon, S. 2022. 'South Africans have low trust in their police. Here's why'. *The Conversation,* 28 March, http://theconversation.com/south-africans-have-low-trust-in-their-police-heres-why-178821, accessed 2 September 2024.

Ryan, C. 2024. 'The water mafias are taking over'. *Moneyweb,* 26 August, https://www.moneyweb.co.za/news/south-africa/the-water-mafias-are-taking-over/, accessed 2 September 2024.

Sapire, I., Tshuma, T. and Herholdt, H. 2024. *Spotlight on Basic Education Completion and Foundational Learning: South Africa.* Paris: United Nations Educational, Scientific and Cultural Organization, https://unesdoc.unesco.org/ark:/48223/pf0000389034, accessed 8 October 2024.

Sen, A. 2001. *Development as Freedom.* New York: Alfred A. Knopf.

Skocpol, T. 1979. *States and Social Revolutions: A Comparative Analysis of France, Russia, and China.* Cambridge: Cambridge University Press.

Skocpol, T. 1985. 'Bringing the state back in: Strategies of analysis in current research', in Rueschemeyer, D., Evans, P.B. and Skocpol, T. (eds), *Bringing the State Back In.* Cambridge: Cambridge University Press, pp. 3–38.

Smith, A. 1776. *An Inquiry into the Nature and Causes of the Wealth of Nations.* Ireland: W. Strahan; and T. Cadell, in the Strand.

Sobuwa, Y. 2024. 'Is HIV the leading cause of death in South Africa?'. *Health-e News,* 26 September, https://health-e.org.za/2024/09/26/is-hiv-the-leading-cause-of-death-in-south-africa/, accessed 8 October 2024.

Spivak, G.C. 1988. 'Can the subaltern speak?', in Nelson, C. and Grossberg, L. (eds), *Marxism and the Interpretation of Culture.* Basingstoke: Macmillan.

Statistics South Africa. 2023. 'GDP declines in the fourth quarter', https://www.statssa.gov.za/?p=16162, accessed 19 August 2024.

Stephan, H.J. and Power, M. 2012. *The Scramble for Africa in the 21st Century: From the Old World to the New*. Cape Town: Renaissance Press.

The Citizen. 2017. 'R250bn lost to state capture in the last three years, says Gordhan'. *The Citizen*, 12 September, https://www.citizen.co.za/news/south-africa/r250bn-lost-to-state-capture-in-the-last-three-years-says-gordhan/, accessed 19 August 2024.

The Presidency. 2024. 'Address by President Cyril Ramaphosa on the occasion of the Presidential Inauguration, Union Buildings, Tshwane', https://www.thepresidency.gov.za/address-president-cyril-ramaphosa-occasion-presidential-inauguration-union-buildings-tshwane, accessed 28 October 2024.

Tilly, C. 1985. 'War making and state making as organized crime', in Rueschemeyer, D., Evans, P.B. and Skocpol, T. (eds), *Bringing the State Back In*. Cambridge: Cambridge University Press, pp. 169–191.

Trading Economics. 2024. 'South Africa - Public Spending On Education, Total (% Of GDP)', https://tradingeconomics.com/south-africa/public-spending-on-education-total-percent-of-gdp-wb-data.html, accessed 8 October 2024.

United Nations Office of Legal Affairs. 1999. Treaty Series 1761: *No. 3802. Convention on Rights and Duties of States adopted by the Seventh International Conference of American States. Signed at Montevideo, December 26th, 1933*. United Nations, https://www.un-ilibrary.org/content/books/9789210596800s003-c002/read

Von Holdt, K. 2019. 'The political economy of corruption: Elite-formation, factions and violence'. SWOP Working Paper 10, https://www.researchgate.net/publication/334112574_The_political_economy_of_corruption_elite-formation_factions_and_violence_Acknowledgements, accessed 2 September 2024.

Weber, M. 1946. 'Politics as a vocation', in Gerth, H.H. and Wright, M.C. (eds), *From Max Weber: Essays in Sociology*. New York: Oxford University Press.

Whiting, K. and Park, H. 2023. 'This is why "polycrisis" is a useful way of looking at the world right now'. World Economic Forum, https://www.weforum.org/agenda/2023/03/polycrisis-adam-tooze-historian-explains/, accessed 8 October 2024.

World Bank Group. 2024. *Government Expenditure on Education, Total (% of Government Expenditure*. World Bank Open Data, https://data.worldbank.org/indicator/SE.XPD.TOTL.GB.ZS?most_recent_value_desc=true, accessed 8 October 2024.

Yunnan, C.C. and Park, A. 2020. 'Inside the global quest to trace the origins of COVID-19 – and predict where it will go next'. *Time*, 23 July, https://time.com/5870481/coronavirus-origins/, accessed 2 September 2024.

Zondo, R.M.M. 2022. *Judicial Commission of Inquiry into State Capture*, https://www.statecapture.org.za/site/files/announcements/673/OCR_version_-_State_Capture_Commission_Report_Part_1_Vol_I.pdf, accessed 2 September 2024.

Section One

Framing the Issues

TWO

Conceptualising the South African state

Yacoob Abba Omar

INTRODUCTION

The South African state has been the focus of many conceptual debates, from analyses by intellectuals associated with anti-colonial, nationalist resistance in the 20th century, to conceptualisations associated with the liberal tradition of political thought. Intellectual debate about the nature of the South African state has continued vigorously even after the transition to democracy in 1994. Theories of the South African political economy and the state have varied from characterising the country as a case of 'colonialism of a special type', as an example of settler colonialism, or as racial capitalism, by South Africa's liberation-oriented intellectual tradition. In public policy discourse, the framing of the South African state as a developmental state has been increasingly mainstreamed, begging the question of the roots of this conceptualisation.

This chapter aims to trace this intellectual journey from its roots in the liberation struggle to the 2000s. It was at this point that both public policy within government and political discourse, especially within the African National Congress (ANC), began to be framed around the concept of the developmental state. At the same time, there were attempts to examine contemporaneous alternative notions of the South African state and its political economy. The chapter attempts firstly to establish the challenges faced when theorising or conceptualising the state. This entails highlighting some theoretical approaches appropriate for consideration in developing a conceptual framework of the South African state. The chapter then provides a brief genealogy of debates around the South African state and their current manifestations. It concludes by arguing that the South African state is best seen as a postcolonial state with a developmentalist orientation, typically dealing with the heritages of the colonial and apartheid period while attempting to assert its hegemony over society.

THEORETICAL ISSUES

Thinking on the postcolonial state has drawn from a plethora of theories, schools and conceptual contributions. Two forms of the state have dominated the postcolonial landscape: the developmental state and the neopatrimonial state. The term neopatrimonialism was coined by Eisenstadt (1973), building on Weber's theory of patrimonial domination, to describe rule based on administrative and military personnel responsible only to the ruler. It describes a situation where patrimonial and rational-bureaucratic forms co-exist and are interlaced. Schlichte (2018: 55) argues that 'we can observe many practices, such as clientelism, and large-scale and petty corruption' in neopatrimonial states which 'legalist political science conceives as deviant behaviour' that would impede state-building. It is, however, equally plausible to consider them as 'part and parcel of state formation in North America and Europe, too, including piracy, organized crime, vote and office buying, as well as systemic corruption'.

Mkandawire provides an effective riposte to the uncritical use of 'neopatrimonialism' in describing African states, arguing that it (Mkandawire, 2015: 36):

… simply undermines internally driven change by occluding the real problems: corruption, vertical and horizontal inequality, ethnic and gender discrimination, weak state capacity, wrong ideas, political chicanery, and the machinations of the many external actors who seek to exploit Africa in some form or other.

He calls for 'more concrete studies of the African continent and an approach that enjoys a healthier relationship with the empirical world than the procrustean concept of neopatrimonialism does'.

The concept of 'developmental state' debuted in Johnson's (1982) seminal work on East Asian developmental states, and Japan in particular. He distinguished the 'developmental orientation' of such a 'plan rational' state from both the 'plan ideological' state of the Soviet-type command economies and from the 'regulatory orientation' of typical liberal or social-democratic states. Johnson argues that a key aspect of Japan's developmental trajectory was the power and autonomy of its elite bureaucracy, found especially in the Ministry of International Trade and Industry (MITI) and the Finance Ministry (Johnson, 1982: 63).

The developmental state framework places particular emphasis on the role of a technically capable, networked elite. Johnson highlights the presence, in developmental states, of agreed policy goals, with plans crafted mainly by the bureaucratic elite, rather than by elected officials. He describes Taiwan's model as one where 'the politicians reign and the state bureaucrats rule' (1982: 65). Building on this, Evans' (1995: 102) notion of 'embedded autonomy' refers to the affinity of the state's relationship with the private sector and the intensity of its involvement in the market. Writing on 'developmental authoritarianism', Singh and Ovadia (2018: 1042) point out:

Growing authoritarianism notwithstanding, the ability of political elites at the apex of power to generate a consensus or 'political settlement' is the glue that holds together the relationships between contending elites – and between states and social forces – that consequently provides an enabling environment for national elites to secure political stability and policy consensus over the trajectory of development planning.

Notwithstanding the impulse towards centralisation, Castells (1992: 56) regards a state as developmental when its legitimacy is based on its ability to promote and sustain development, which includes high growth rates and structural change in the productive system, both domestically and in its interactions with the international economy. For a developmental state, then, economic growth is not a goal but a means (Castells, 1992: 56–57). Mkandawire (1997: 36-38) expands on this, arguing that the developmental state had to have social commitment which ensured its autonomy, would not be used for predatory purposes, and would be able to represent key social interests in the country. Such a state would politically weaken those 'existing social forces, interests, customs and institutions which have held back development', and which continue to oppose modernisation (Evans, 1995: 90).

Regarding developmental states' economic role, Chang (2002) and Bresser-Pereira (2019), among others, argue that early industrialised countries used a range of industrial policies to promote development. Bresser-Pereira (2019: 39-43) identifies four developmental state models at the time of their industrial revolutions:

- the 'original central developmental state' of early industrialisers, such as France and England;
- the 'latecomer central model that were not colonies', such as the United States and Germany;
- the 'independent peripheral model' of countries that had been colonies, but which caught up with industrialised countries or became middle-income countries, with Japan being the exemplar, copied later by Taiwan, Singapore and South Korea, then Malaysia and Indonesia, and then China and Vietnam; and
- the 'national-dependent peripheral model' of countries that 'did achieve the capitalist revolution but, after the deep foreign debt crisis of the 1980s, lost some of their national autonomy and started growing at a very slow pace', including Brazil and Mexico.

He also identifies a fifth model, which emerged after the Second World War: the 'welfare developmental state (Bresser-Pereira, 2019: 39). Chang (2010) expands the definition of the developmental state to include not only the pro-corporate developmental states of the East-Asian model, but also the 'left-wing Scandinavian "developmentalist welfare state"', whose legitimacy depends on reaching its social equity objectives through, *inter alia*, welfare policies and generally active government intervention. The relationship between developmental and democratic practices occupies the minds of many scholars in this field. Evans' (1995) notion of 'embedded autonomy' shows that democracy is reconcilable with development. Mkandawire (2012: 2) describes 'democratic developmental states' as 'developmental (in the sense that they facilitate and promote economic growth and structural transformation), democratic (in the sense that they derive their legitimacy through popular participation and [the] electoral process) and socially inclusive' in that they pursue social policies which ensure equitable entitlements for citizens, and so ensure inclusion in societal affairs.

I will argue that South Africa displays features of the national-dependent peripheral and welfare developmental models, and, at certain moments in its history, has possessed a lead agency which helped integrate the business, labour and governmental elites around a common set of socioeconomic goals.

SOVEREIGNTY AND LIMITED STATEHOOD

Theoretical approaches to the postcolonial state have often differed over three central concepts: sovereignty and statehood; the relationship between state and civil society; and the inheritances of a postcolonial state. This leads to a consideration of the notions of 'weak' or 'limited' statehood. The ascendancy of a single political authority which embodies sovereignty was never inevitable and was the product of intense rivalry and struggles with other formations – be they the gods, nature or representatives of specific class, ethnic or tribal interests.

Colonial rule never quite achieved the total dominance of territories that colonial powers desired. Mamdani (1996) argues that the postcolonial state has to contend with its dual heritages of precolonial state formation as well as that created through the colonial legacy, while Mbembe (2001: 24–25) points out: 'African regimes have not invented what they know of government from scratch. Their knowledge is the product of several cultures, heritages and traditions, of which the features have become entangled over time.' Chatterjee (2012: 47), drawing on the Indian experience, argues that there are two aspects to contemporary politics: contest over the sovereignty of the state, often taking the form of insurgent movements; and claims on governmental authorities over services and benefits, impacting on the very nature of the state. Mamdani (2021) argues that in the face of competing forms of political authority, legitimacy and power, the postcolonial nation state found itself in crisis. Contests over national belonging became central to the violence of the postcolonial state, often mimicking the violence of the colonial state.

Börzel et al. (2018) help develop an understanding of 'limited statehood', which can be applied to developed, advanced democracies as well as so-called 'fragile' or 'failed' states. They argue that 'areas of limited statehood ... constitute those parts of a country in which central authorities (governments) lack the ability to implement and enforce rules and decisions and/or in which they do not command a legitimate monopoly over the means of violence' (Börzel et al., 2018: 6). The ability to rule hierarchically is not confined to states, but many non-state actors do so too – from warlords to local chiefs (Börzel et al., 2018: 9), and, increasingly, organised crime which can take multinational, national or regional forms.

To wrap up this treatment of the evolution of conceptions of the state and their relevance to the South African state, the following can be emphasised:

- According to Marxian notions of the state, a central tenet is that the state must act autonomously in relation to other social forces. This is made possible by an apex-level 'political settlement', which ensures maximum possible societal inclusivity, especially through a multiclass agreement on policy goals.
- The national-dependent peripheral model requires the state to be located in the context of an array of contending global, regional and domestic forces which limit the extent to which its writ is inscribed across the land.
- While several scholars refer to the correlation between developmental

states and democracy, emphasis has been placed on the extent of hegemony achieved, especially by the bureaucratic elite, and on the legitimacy this elite enjoys due to its success in meeting the needs of society generally.

- The technical capacity of this elite and its organisation within what is termed a lead or pilot agency, is critical for the achievement of the goals of the state. The bureaucratic elite acts in its role as a regulator of the economy, but also, as importantly, in addressing non-competitive aspects of the market, such as infrastructure as a common good.

EVOLUTION IN THINKING AROUND THE SOUTH AFRICAN STATE

Intellectuals and activists opposed to the colonial and apartheid South African state articulated a rich array of approaches before the notion of the developmental state was arrived at in the early 2000s. More recently, that notion has been challenged. A notable contribution to the depiction of the South African state in the early 1930s was the Black Republic Thesis (BRT) (also referred to as the Native Republic Thesis). Moses Kotane, Secretary-General of the Communist Party of South Africa (CPSA) from 1939 to 1978, explained that it 'in essence means a bourgeois republic … (which) must necessarily presuppose a democratic workers' and peasants' republic …' (SACP, 1962a). Jordan writes: 'It projected a bourgeois-democratic alliance under the leadership of the working class', and argues that 'the land question, the national question and capitalist power were integrally linked' (1988: 123). There were fears that the BRT would be used by traditional leaders in the ANC for narrow, ethnic objectives, or that it would encourage anti-white attitudes. Greenstein, however, argued that CPSA members could not appreciate the potential of the BRT since they did not recognise that concerns about land were widespread and manifested in very localised forms, relating to 'specific territories rather than to indigenous rights in the abstract' (1997: 9).

'African Claims in South Africa', adopted by the ANC at its 16 December 1943 conference, proved another early milestone in the evolution of the national question. It proclaimed that 'the African people in the Union of South Africa urgently demand the granting of full citizenship rights such as are enjoyed by all Europeans in South Africa'. The 'Bill of Rights' contained in 'African Claims' listed the 'Full Citizens Rights and Demands', which called for, *inter alia*, 'The right of every child to free and compulsory education'; 'the establishment of free medical and health services for all'; and 'a substantial and immediate improvement in the economic position of the African'. This approach found its way into the Freedom Charter, adopted in 1955, which made important pronouncements about democracy and sovereignty, e.g. that 'no government can justly claim authority unless it is based on the will of all the people', and 'that only a democratic state, based on the will of all the people, can secure to all their birthright without distinction of colour, race, sex or belief'.

Proponents of the Colonialism of a Special Type (CST) theory argue that adopting a historical perspective means seeing South Africa (until 1994) as a colonial state. CST was the basis of the SACP's 1962 programme titled 'The Road to South African Freedom' and is described by Nyawuza as 'the situation where the colonizer and the colonized reside "side by side" in the same territory, which has been the case since 1910 when Britain granted political power to the whites in South Africa who used it to further oppress the black majority' (1990: 48). Laying out this thesis in 1962, in 'The Road to South African Freedom', the SACP proposed that CST require a two-stage process, first to a national democratic society and, second, to socialism. The immediate goal of the first stage was 'to unite all sections and classes of oppressed and democratic people for a national democratic revolution [NDR] to destroy White domination' (SACP, 1962a).

Hudson captures the genesis of the concept of 'national democracy', arguing that the possibility of 'transitional social structures', which reflect the 'interests not of any one particular class, but of the widest strata of population of the newly-free nations' (1986: 18), led to the concept of 'national democracy' being introduced in the Marxist-Leninist world. It was intended 'to designate that category of ex-colonial (and dependent) countries which could be identified as engaged on a non-capitalist path of development in opposition to imperialism and towards national autonomy'. The ANC officially adopted the goal of a National Democratic Revolution (NDR) in 1969 at its conference in exile in Morogoro, Tanzania (Filatova, 2012), after which NDR became the guiding principle of the dominant wing of the national liberation movement.

The CST and NDR concepts were not uncontested. Critics argued that the two-stage approach effectively separated struggles against racism from struggles against capitalism. This critique emerged from two quarters: the left, initially based in White liberal universities, with some of the activists there becoming involved in the incipient trade union movement, and a multi-racial group of socialists associated with the emerging Black Consciousness (BC) movement. In the 1970s and 1980s, analysts used 'racial capitalism' to describe the racially oppressive system of exploitation in contrast to the CST approach, with some suggesting that it referred to a strategic orientation to be adopted against the system being fought. Legassick, a leading voice of the Marxist Workers Tendency of the ANC, punted the idea of racial capitalism, trying to convince the ANC to reorient towards a socialist revolution without going through the first stage of the NDR (Legassick and Hemson, 1976). Wolpe (1975), who was associated with the ANC and SACP, criticised the CST/NDR for failing to account for class relations, the modes of production, and the historically contingent relationship between class and race. Alexander (1979) criticised the ANC for failing to adequately theorise the nation and racial/national difference. He focused on the possibility that the Black middle class would facilitate the co-option of the movement, emphasising the need for working-class leadership of the national liberation struggle.

The Black Consciousness (BC) tradition, which emerged in the late '60s and early '70s, distinguished itself from that of the ANC/SACP by emphasising racial domination and the centrality of a Black political subject. As BC matured over the years, it inserted class, capitalism, exploitation and the need for socialism into its analysis (Reddy, 2009). This fusion was embodied in the Azanian People's Organisation (AZAPO), founded in 1979 as a merger of various Black Consciousness organisations. Netshitenzhe (2012: 26), in his evaluation of the CST theory, argued that post-apartheid South Africa is characterised by an internal metropolis that is integrated into the global economy, and which should be leveraged for inclusive growth and development, and the colony which is marginalised from the economic mainstream.

The Tripartite Alliance, which included the ANC, SACP and the Congress of South African Trade Unions (COSATU), committed to the NDR after the attainment of democracy in 1994. The more recent forms of racial capitalism considered below, as well as a reconsideration of the contributions of BC and the Pan Africanist Congress (PAC), challenge this approach, especially when looked at through the experiences of the vast number of unemployed and poverty-stricken Black Africans.

POST-1994 EVOLUTION OF THE SOUTH AFRICAN STATE

In May 1996, the new South African Constitution was adopted after years of negotiations begun under the F.W. de Klerk presidency to 'normalise' politics away from the repressive measures of most of the 20th century. Wilson captures what was achieved (1996: 4–5):

> In the context of negotiations between two competing nationalisms (Afrikaner and Africanist), the constitution became the only viable political blueprint to bridge the chasm between the seemingly incommensurable political positions... in the end constitutionalism replicated elements of other nationalist narratives.

The ANC came to power in 1994 with the stated objective of transforming South African society and the Reconstruction and Development Programme (RDP) was to be the strategy which ensured that. The genesis of the RDP lay in the cementing of the electoral pact between the ANC and COSATU. Marais (2011: 105) argues that COSATU wanted its Reconstruction Accord to be adopted by the ANC:

> ... as a government programme once it assumed power. In return, COSATU would campaign for an ANC victory. The

accord would eventually mature into the Reconstruction and Development Programme, which formed a central plank in the ANC's 1994 election campaign.

In his preface to the document, President Nelson Mandela wrote: 'In preparing the document, and in taking it forward, we are building on the tradition of the Freedom Charter.'

Karriem and Hoskins (2016) argue that the RDP Office, established in 1994 to exercise a coordinating role and located in the Presidency, was understaffed, which limited its ability to coordinate and lead government programmes. In 1996, the RDP Office was closed, leaving the state without a strategic oversight agency. During its brief existence it represented the concentration of a number of technically astute former anti-apartheid activists who could draw on the experience of bureaucrats who had been serving in the state machinery prior to 1994. Given the shared sense of purpose this combination of mandarins represented, the RDP Office could have been similar to the pilot agencies of the Asian developmental states, such as MITI in Japan.

Karriem and Hoskins (2016: 6) note:

The closure of the social democratic-oriented RDP office signalled the shift to the market-oriented GEAR macroeconomic programme, with government coordination now overseen by the Ministry of Finance (specifically the Treasury), which was more concerned with maintaining fiscal discipline than promoting broader developmental goals.

The Growth, Employment and Redistribution (GEAR) programme was formulated in the wake of a call made by President Mandela in February 1996 at the opening of the parliamentary session. He urged South Africa's public and private sectors to develop and implement 'a national vision to lift us out of this quagmire'. Capital responded to Mandela's call by proposing a strategy called 'Growth for All', while the major union federations contained their proposals in a document called 'Social Equity and Job Creation'. Government was criticised for recruiting a select group of economists to draft GEAR, with little input from the ANC's allies. Natrass (1999: 85) argued that GEAR and Growth for All were both located within a neo-classical economic growth theory but 'move beyond this by including a Keynesian concern for investor confidence and by positing an active and redistributive role for the state'.

Mbeki described GEAR as a response to South Africa's fiscal crisis in 1995/1996. Marais takes a contrarian view, arguing that 'GEAR was a dramatic element of a longer narrative of restructuring that dates back to the halting efforts of the apartheid regime in the early 1980s and which now arcs forward beyond GEAR. It formed part of an evolving process that has not yet run its course' (Marais, 2011: 105–106).

Jacob Zuma was elected in 2007 as president of the ANC on the back of support from an unwieldy alliance of the trade union movement, the SACP, and a range of elements in the ANC and civil society. His election was meant to herald the end of neo-classical and orthodox economic thinking. Zuma's installation as president of the country in 2009 ushered in a group of ministers who were keen to place the blame for the continued unemployment of millions of people, a dysfunctional education system and all the other ills the country was facing on the Mbeki administration, and especially on GEAR. Cabinet appointments in 2009 reflected the disparate alliance which had brought Zuma to power.

This quickly manifested itself in different visions for economic growth. The New Growth Path, which was drawn up by the Department of Economic Development (2011), and the National Development Plan, which was released in 2012 and fell under the Minister in the Presidency, jostled for attention. The Industrial Policy Action Plan, initially drawn up in 2013 by the Ministry of Trade and Industry, reflected the Medium-Term Expenditure Framework three-year cycles – but with a claimed ten-year economic outlook. However, these various plans soon caved under the effect of the corruption presided over by the Zuma administration, which saw grand-scale looting of the state's coffers through what came to be termed 'state capture'.

To sum up, the experience of government planning in the first 20 years of South Africa's democracy suggests that when there has been a reasonable level of alignment within the leadership structures of government, as was the case during the period of the RDP and GEAR, government can play a leading role in directing economic development. In the case of the RDP, alignment was assisted by the Tripartite Alliance – the ANC, COSATU and the SACP – being involved in the formulation of RDP policies, notwithstanding the reservations of Marais and others. In the case of the GEAR macro-economic strategy, there is no doubt that it was able to make an impact because of the technical astuteness of the team around Mbeki, his firm leadership and the quality of the leadership in the lead departments implementing GEAR.

CURRENT DEBATES AROUND SOUTH AFRICA'S STATE AND POLITICAL ECONOMY

It is noteworthy that much of the conceptualising around the developmental state in South Africa emanates from the ANC, since the release of its 1998 document titled 'The State, Property Relations, and Social Transformation, A Discussion Paper Towards the Alliance Summit' and its economic transformation policy document, prepared for the 2017 policy conference. Its 2020 policy document states that 'by 2000 the ANC had adopted the concept of the developmental state to frame its approach to governance' (2020: 73).

The ANC combined the notion of a developmental state with Sen's view (Sen, 1999) that the 'freedom of citizens to attain socioeconomic well-being is of primary moral importance, and that freedom of citizens to attain this well-being is to be understood in terms of people's capabilities' (ANC, 2020: 172). Acknowledging the turmoil of state capture experienced during the Zuma administration, the ANC added the descriptor 'ethical', giving rise to the notion of 'an ethical, capable, developmental state' (ANC, 2022: 135).

Endorsing the idea of South Africa as a developmental state, Swilling et al. (2023: 523) point out that in the first decades of democracy a political settlement formed which endorsed the economic policies of the Ministry of Finance, which acted as the kind of pilot agency found in developmental states. This settlement cemented an alliance between key elements of Mbeki's Cabinet, White business leaders, the first generation of BEE beneficiaries, and a core group of state bureaucrats within government and state-owned enterprises (SOEs). 'Up until 2002, when the "developmental state" narrative was adopted by the ANC and the government, this coalition strongly favoured the privatisation of SOEs, inflation targeting and fiscal restraint' (Swilling et al., 2023: 524).

By the beginning of the 21st century, the ANC's view of the NDR and the developmental state was being challenged by many strands of thinking, such as critical race theory (CRT) and a revised racial capitalism approach. Steyn (2001: xxxi–xxxii), for example, argued that CRT alerts us to the efforts of 'South Africans … intent on dissociating the country from its racialized legacy', leading to the 'mould of liberal colour blindness… If we prematurely banish it [race] from our analytical framework, we serve the narrow interests of those previously advantaged'. For Modiri, CRT can be conceptualised as a potentially transformative genre by showing that despite democratic constitutional changes, 'racism and White privilege are continually reproduced institutionally and within social relations' (2012: 435). Furthermore, it lifts the veil on the hypocrisy of 'the celebratory narratives of "post"-apartheid South Africa ("the rainbow nation") … colour-blindness and … the demise of apartheid by exposing the ongoing racial subordination, social misery and suffering and exploitation experienced by blacks in their daily lives' (Modiri, 2012: 436).

More recently, the racial capitalism approach has been revived, especially in addressing why South Africa has not been able to register levels of development, increase employment for Blacks, address poverty and reduce inequality. This renewed focus was in the context of the 2015 #Fees Must Fall movement which saw a new generation of scholars seeking to explain the lack of progress since 1994, especially for the Black working class and the growing army of unemployed. One example is Clarno's (2017) *Neoliberal Apartheid*, where he compares the Palestine/Israel and South African experiences, emphasising the need to understand racial capitalism with the kindred concept of settler colonialism. The latter emphasises the control of land via dispossession and settlement, the use of racial projects to dehumanise 'native' populations; and the state as a 'racialized structure of settler domination' that enables dispossession (Clarno, 2017: 5).

Mabasa (2022) uses racial capitalism to understand the co-constitution of Marxism and decolonial politics, straddling multiple approaches and arguing that colonial capitalism, which emerged from pre-existing racism, shaped the development of capitalism. His notion of racism is broadened to include other modes of social differentiation, while rooting colonial racism in the political economy of capitalism itself. Ndlovu-Gatsheni (2020: 190) also links racial capitalism to colonialism, defining the former as the central 'economic extractive technology' of the latter. He argues that the emergence of Black insurgency in the democratic era should be understood in relation to this period's racial capitalist context (Ndlovu-Gatsheni, 2021: 63). Other South African writers straightforwardly invoke the term to signal the enemy: Hlatshwayo (2018) argues that racial capitalism is what workers struggle against, while Gillespie and Naidoo use racial capitalism to explain how racism is a strategy to maintain profitability: '… outsourced black workers, Marikana, the privatization of education at the moment of racial democratization, the black township itself' (2019: 235).

Rudin (2022: 23) sees an inversion in how racial capitalism is deployed:

> There are now considerably more poor South Africans than ever before. That they remain Black is but a convenient opportunity for the Black rich to cry racism, as the battle cry of their own self-enrichment…Those of us who endorse historical materialism popularise the now ahistorical term 'racial capitalism', denoting exclusive White wealth at the expense of Black poverty.

Madlingozi (2019: 123–124) explains this form of distinguishing two groups of Black people as 'an anti-black bifurcated societal structure' where 'white people and the black middle class are governed through a system of liberal democracy', and there is the 'other side' where 'patronage, appropriation, and repression remain politics *du jour*'. Labelling this as neo-apartheid constitutionalism, he notes that this is consistent with the Pan Africanist Congress's historical perspective which rejected the discourse of incorporation pursued by the ANC and advocated for the 'complete overhaul of the present structure of society' (Sobukwe, 1959: 196). He similarly cited Biko who argues that unless the totality of White supremacy is destroyed, democratisation and transformative constitutionalism would simply lead to a situation where Black elites are 'extracted' from the Black world into the White world (Biko, 1996: 21).

Apart from these alternative frameworks offered by contemporary writers, the notion of South Africa as a developmental state continues to be debated, with some arguing that the country does not resemble a developmental state at all. Matisonn (2024: 18) argues that disagreements among Cabinet ministers, the inability to implement a series of compacts between government, business and labour, and the lack of urgency among bureaucrats 'about development actually including the poor' are contributory factors. He suggests that '(p)rioritising three or four sectors, reaching agreements with stakeholders in which every member of the government is required to be in lockstep will move South Africa many steps forward towards a developmental state' (Matisonn, 2024: 28).

Burger describes South Africa as a 'social investment state' rather than a developmental state, due to its emphasis on investment in human development and on enabling people to participate in skilled and thus better-paying jobs (Burger, 2014). At a superficial level, this may be true, given that total government expenditure on education is among the highest items in the budget. A total of R1.4 trillion was allocated for the three-year period from 2023 for higher and basic education and for the sports, arts and culture function, representing, on average, 18 per cent of the annual budget directed to human development. However, a 2024 study by the Department of Higher Education and Training on the skills gap in South Africa 'highlights the lack of foundational, technical, soft, and cognitive skills in the South African labour force', and concludes that given that 'certain segments of the population face greater barriers to accessing quality education and training opportunities, the cycle of disadvantage persists, exacerbating existing inequality' (Department of Higher Education and Training, 2024: 45).

For Ukwandu (2019) the following factors have stymied South Africa's evolution to a developmental state:

- The lack of 'a shared mutual goal of eliminating poverty, provision of jobs and development for the majority of citizens' (Ukwandu, 2019: 53).
- A paucity of skills 'exacerbated by the affirmative action of the ANC-led government and the cadre deployment of the party' (Ukwandu, 2019: 53).
- Government's intervention in market processes which occurs more through regulation than direct participation (Ukwandu, 2019: 55).
- The absence of a 'leading government department that is in charge of economic formation and implementation' (Ukwandu, 2019: 54).
- Inability of the South African government to enforce the high savings rate that was an important feature of Asian developmental states (Ukwandu, 2019: 55).

In a similar vein, Laubscher (2007: 16) argues 'there is no national consensus or hegemonic project on which all sectors of society are focused, and for which everyone is willing to make sacrifices'. He argues that unlike other developmental states, South Africa is not focusing exclusively on achieving high economic growth because 'there is an equal focus on the redistribution of wealth because of decades of exclusion and marginalisation'.

Alternative depictions of the South Africa state are being formulated on a regular basis. Bond (2002: 35) sees South Africa as a 'class-compromise non-developmental democratic state' which cannot be regarded as a developmental state in the classic Asian sense. Laubscher (2007: 21) suggests that South Africa finds itself in the company of countries pursuing a so-called 'third way', that is, the search for an alternative to an uncontrolled free market economy and to a fully socialistic system.

On the credit side, Laubscher (2007: 16) points out that certain elements of a developmental state are present in South Africa, such as 'the development programme for the motor industry, the pursuit of mineral enrichment, the pressure of the financial sector to extend financial services to low-income groups, and the current comprehensive industrial policy'.

CONCLUSION

It is tempting to generously conclude that South Africa should be seen as a developmental state in the making. However, there is little evidence to suggest that; in fact, quite the opposite.

Developmental states have been characterised by a national consensus – whether through coercion, such as in the case of the South Korean generals, through centralised control over the levers of power as in China, or through democratically derived consensus, as was the case in Malaysia, Singapore and possibly India. However, there is little indication of a shared set of values and national objectives in South Africa. This chapter pointed out that there was such a moment in the immediate aftermath of the 1994 elections, through the consensus achieved around the RDP and Mandela's leadership. While Mbeki's microeconomic strategy, GEAR, and later the Microeconomic Reform Strategy (MERS) and Accelerated and Shared Growth Initiative for South Africa (AsgiSA), could have laid the basis for the take-off of the South African economy, they stumbled at the altar of the politics that ushered in the corrupt era of the Zuma administration. This saw critical resources being diverted and key institutions being undermined, rendering the state rudderless.

It was thus unable to reach the second key ingredient of a developmental state: an apex-level 'political settlement', consisting of an agreement across sector and class, which committed the majority of South Africans to a particular set of goals. Such an agreement ensures maximum possible societal inclusivity, especially through a multiclass agreement on policy goals. South Africa is a classic example of limited statehood, whereby the various elements of the state show differential levels of capacity and efficacy, and, therefore, ability to impact on their specific domains. This engenders an erratic centre which, at rare moments, is able to play a leading role in the economy, and, at others, is too weak to provide even basic guarantees, such as the provision of water.

As a national dependent peripheral model, the South African state has to be located in the context of the various forces which limit the extent to which its writ extends across the land. These include global forces such as the world economy and the eroding of institutions by international crime syndicates, to domestic role players intent on challenging the state's sovereignty. The antidote to this weakening could be the extent of hegemony achieved, especially by the bureaucratic elite, and the legitimacy it could enjoy from successfully meeting the general needs of society. Such an exercise requires a high level of technical capacity, and the confidence to manage relations with the various social forces. This would enhance the state's role as a regulator of the economy which can direct investment into non-competitive parts of the economy, such as infrastructure.

REFERENCES

African National Congress (ANC). 1943. 'African Claims in South Africa by Dr Xuma, ANC Conference, 1943'. South African History Online, https://sahistory.org.za/archive/african-claims-south-africa-dr-xuma-anc-conference-1943, accessed 10 June 2025.

African National Congress (ANC). 1998. 'The State, Property Relations and Social Transformation. A Discussion Paper Towards the Alliance Summit'. *Umrabulo*, 5, 3rd quarter.

African National Congress (ANC). 2017. '5th National Policy Conference: Economic Transformation Discussion Document', https://www.anc1912.org.za/wp-content/uploads/2022/08/National-Policy-Conference-2017-Economic-Transformation.pdf, accessed 10 June 2025.

African National Congress (ANC). 2020. *Umrabulo: NGC2020 Special Edition*, https://www.ancpl.org.za/wp-content/uploads/2020/11/2020-UMRABULO-SPECIAL-EDITION-draft-121120201.pdf, accessed 30 June 2025.

African National Congress (ANC). 2022. 'Umrabulo Policy Document', https://docs.google.com/viewerng/viewer?url=https://www.anc1912.org.za/wp-content/uploads/2022/05/Umrabulo-Policy-Document-18th-May-2022.pdf

Alexander, N. (No Sizwe). 1979. *One Azania, One Nation: The National Question in South Africa.* London: Zed Press.

Biko, S. 1996. *Steve Biko: I Write What I Like. A Selection of His Writings.* Randburg: Ravan Press.

Bond, P. 2002. *Unsustainable South Africa: Environment, Development, and Social Protest.* London: Merlin Press.

Börzel, T.A., Risse, T. and Draude, A. 2018. 'Governance in areas of limited statehood: Conceptual clarifications and major contributions of the handbook', in Risse, T., Börzel, T.A. and Draude, A. (eds), *The Oxford Handbook of Governance and Limited Statehood.* Oxford: Oxford

University Press, pp. 3–18.

Bresser-Pereira, L.C. 1998. Paper presented at the UNU-AERC Workshop on Institutions and Development in Africa, UNU Headquarters, Tokyo, 14–15 October.

Bresser-Pereira, L.C. 2019. 'Models of the developmental state'. *Cepal Review*, 128 (August), 1–13.

Burger, P. 2014. 'How suitable is a "developmental state" to tackle unemployment, inequality and poverty in South Africa?', *Econ3x3*, 1–8.

Castells, M. 1992. 'Four Asian Tigers with a Dragon Head: A comparative analysis of the state, economy and society in the Asian Pacific Rim', in Henderson, R. and Applebaum, J. (eds), *State and Development in the Asian Pacific Rim*. London: Sage Publications.

Chang, H.-J. 2002. *Kicking Away the Ladder*. London: Anthem Press.

Chang H-J. 2010. 'Institutions and economic development: Theory, policy and history'. *Journal of Institutional Economics*, 7(4), 2011, 473–498, https://www.cambridge.org/core/journals/journal-of-institutional-economics/article/institutions-and-economic-development-theory-policy-and-history/483B04277F72313E9080AA3264997A93, accessed 30 June 2025.

Chatterjee, P. 2012. 'After Subaltern Studies'. *Economic and Political Weekly*, XLVII(35), 44–49.

Clarno, A. 2017. *Neoliberal Apartheid: Palestine/Israel and South Africa after 1994*. Chicago, IL: University of Chicago Press.

Department of Economic Development. 2011. *The New Growth Path: Framework*. Cape Town: Government Printing Works.

Department of Higher Education and Training (DHET). 2024. *Identification of Skills Gaps in South Africa: A Technical Research Report*, https://lmi-research.org.za/wp-content/uploads/2024/04/LMI-1-11-C2A-Technical-ID-SkillGapSA-WEB.pdf, accessed 10 June 2025.

Department of Trade and Industry. 2013. *Industrial Policy Action Plan: Economic Sectors and Employment Cluster: IPAP 2013/14 – 2015/16*. Pretoria.

Eisenstadt, S.N. 1973. *Traditional Patrimonialism and Modern Neopatrimonialism*. Beverly Hills: Sage Publications.

Evans, P.B. 1995. *Embedded Autonomy: States and Industrial Transformation*. Princeton, NJ: Princeton University Press.

Filatova, I. 2012. 'The lasting legacy: The Soviet theory of the National Democratic Revolution and South Africa'. *South African Historical Journal*, 64(3), 507–537.

Gillespie, K. and Naidoo, L. 2019. 'Between the Cold War and the fire: The student movement, Ant assimilation, and the question of the future in South Africa'. *South Atlantic Quarterly*, 118(1), 226–239.

Greenstein, R. 1994. 'The study of South African society: Towards a new agenda for comparative historical inquiry'. *Journal of Southern African Studies*, 20(4).

Greenstein, R. 1995. *Genealogies of Conflict: Class, Identity and State in Palestine/Israel and South Africa.* London: Wesleyan University Press.

Greenstein, R. 1997. *Genealogies of Conflict: Class, Identity and State in Palestine/Israel and South Africa.* London: Wesleyan University Press.

Hlatshwayo, M. 2018. 'Building workers' education in the context of the struggle against racial capitalism: The role of labour support organisations'. *Education as Change*, 22(2), 1–24.

Hudson, P.J. 1986. 'The Freedom Charter and the theory of national democratic revolution'. *Transformation*, 1(1).

Johnson, C.A. 1982. *MITI and the Japanese Miracle.* Bloomington: Stanford University Press.

Jordan, P. 1988. 'The South African Liberation Movement and the making of a new nation', in Van Diepen, M. (ed.), *The National Question in South Africa.* Amsterdam: Brill.

Karriem, A. and Hoskins, M. 2016. 'From the RDP to the NDP: A critical appraisal of the developmental state, land reform, and rural development in South Africa'. *Politikon*, DOI: 10.1080/02589346.2016.1160858

Laubscher, J. 2007. 'South Africa is developing a false identity'. *Business Day*, 20 April, https://www.businesslive.co.za/bd/, accessed 10 June 2025.

Legassick, M. 2017. 'The Marxist workers' tendency of the African National Congress', in Webster, E. and Pampallis, K. (eds), *The Unresolved National Question: Left Thought under Apartheid.* Johannesburg: Wits University Press, pp. 149–162.

Legassick, M. and Hemson, D. 1976. *Foreign Investment and the Reproduction of Racial Capitalism in South Africa.* London: Anti-Apartheid Movement.

Mabasa, K. 2022. 'Racial capitalism: Marxism and decolonial politics', in Ndlovu-Gatsheni, S.J. and Ndlovu, N. (eds), *Marxism and Decolonization in the 21st Century: Living Theories and True Ideas.* London: Routledge, pp. 228–247.

Macreconomic Research Group (MERG). 1993. 'Making democracy work: A framework for macroeconomic policy in South Africa. A report to members of the Democratic Movement of South Africa', https://archive.org/details/makingdemocracyw0000macr, accessed 10 June 2025.

Madlingozi, T. 2019. 'Social justice in a time of neo-apartheid constitutionalism: Critiquing the anti-black economy of recognition, incorporation and distribution'. *Stellenbosch Law Review*, 3(3).

Mamdani, M. 1996. *Citizen and Subject: Contemporary Africa and the Legacy of Late Colonialism.* Itaca: Princeton University Press.

Mamdani, M. 2021. *Neither Settler nor Native: The Making and Unmaking of Permanent Minorities.* Johannesburg: Wits University Press.

Marais, H. 2011. *South Africa Pushed to the Limit: The Political Economy of Change.* Cape Town: UCT Press.

Matisonn, J. 2024. 'Where is the *development* in SA's developmental state?

And where is the road to sustainable job creation?'. *New Agenda,* 92 (Special Issue), 17–31.

Mbembe, A. 2001. *On the Postcolony*. Berkeley: University of California Press.

Migdal, J. S. 1988. *Strong Societies and Weak States: State-Society Relations and State Capabilities in the Third World*. Princeton University Press.

Mkandawire, T. 1997. *Shifting Commitments and National Cohesion in African Countries*. New York: Uppsala.

Mkandawire, T. 2012. 'Building the African state in the age of globalisation: The role of social compacts and lessons for South Africa'. MISTRA Inaugural Mapungubwe Annual Lecture, University of the Witwatersrand, 29 March.

Mkandawire, T. 2015. 'Neopatrimonialism and the political economy of economic performance'. *World Politics*, 67(3), 563–612.

Modiri, J.T. 2012. 'The colour of law, power and knowledge: Introducing Critical Race Theory in (post-) apartheid South Africa'. *South Africa Journal of Human Rights*, 28, 405–436.

Natrass, N. 1999. 'Gambling on investment: Competing economic strategies in South Africa', in Maharaj, G. (ed.), *Between Unity and Diversity: Essays on Nation-building in post-apartheid South Africa*. Cape Town: David Philip Publishers.

Ndlovu-Gatsheni, S.J. 2020. 'African decolonization's past and present trajectories'. *Current History*, 119(817), 188–193.

Ndlovu-Gatsheni, S.J. 2021. 'Revisiting Marxism and decolonisation through the legacy of Samir Amin'. *Review of African Political Economy,* 48(167), 50–65.

Netshitenzhe, J.K. 2012. 'The state of the state in South Africa: Tenth Harold Wolpe Memorial Lecture – Cape Town 7 November 2012'. *The Socialist Correspondent,* 18, 2013, 21–25, https://www.thesocialistcorrespondent. org.uk/media/1094/issue18.pdf, accessed 30 June 2025.

Nyawuza. 1990. 'The road to the "Black Republic" slogan in South Africa'. *African Communist*, First quarter, https://www.sahistory.org.za/sites/ default/files/archive-files4/Acn12290.pdf, accessed 10 June 2025.

Randeria, S. 2007. 'The state of globalization: Legal plurality, overlapping sovereignties and ambiguous alliances between civil society and the cunning state in India'. *Theory Culture Society*, 24(1), DOI: 10.1177/0263276407071559

Reddy, T. 2009. 'Black Consciousness in contemporary South African politics', in Kagwanja, P. and Kondlo, K. (eds), *State of the Nation: South Africa 2008*. Cape Town: HSRC Press, pp. 84–103.

Risse, T., Börzel, T.A. and Draude, A. (eds). 2018. *The Oxford Handbook of Governance and Limited Statehood*. Oxford: Oxford University Press.

Rudin, J. 2022. 'Racial capitalism: Understanding South Africa before, during and after apartheid'. *New Agenda*, 85, 19–24.

Schlichte, K. 2018. 'A historical-sociological perspective on statehood', in Risse, T., Börzel, T.A. and Draude, A. (eds), *The Oxford Handbook of Governance and Limited Statehood*. Oxford: Oxford University Press, pp. 48–67.

Sen, A. 1999. *Development as Freedom*. Oxford: Oxford University Press.

Singh, J.N. and Ovadia, J.S. 2018. 'The theory and practice of building developmental states in the Global South'. *Third World Quarterly*, 39(6), 1033–1055.

Sobukwe, R. 1959. 'The State of the Nation on National Heroes Day 2 August 1959', in Karis, T. and Gerhart, G.M. (eds), *From Protest to Challenge: A Documentary History of African Politics in South Africa 1882–1964*. Johannesburg: Jacana Media, pp. 545–546.

South African Communist Party (SACP). 1962a. 'The Road to South African Freedom', in *South African Communists Speak*, pp. 284–320, https://www.sacp.org.za/sites/default/files/documents/south-african-communists-speak-documents-from-the-history-of-the-south-african-communist-party-1915-1980.pdf, accessed 10 June 2025.

South African Communist Party (SACP). 1962b. 'Towards the Black Republic', in *South African Communists Speak*, pp. 67–72, https://www.sacp.org.za/sites/default/files/documents/south-african-communists-speak-documents-from-the-history-of-the-south-african-communist-party-1915-1980.pdf, accessed 10 June 2025.

Steyn, M. 2001. *Whiteness Just Isn't What It Used to Be: White Identity in a Changing South Africa*. Albany: SUNY Press.

Swilling, M., Callaghan, N. and McCallum, W. 2023. 'Political settlements and the rebuilding of South Africa's state-owned enterprises', in Mohamed, S., Ngoma, A. and Baloyi, B. (eds), *Structures of the South African Economy*. Johannesburg: Mapungubwe Institute for Strategic Reflection.

Ukwandu, D.C. 2019. 'South Africa as a developmental state: Is it a viable idea?'. *African Journal of Public Affairs*, 11(2), 41–62.

Wilson, R.A. 1996. 'The Sizwe will not go away'. *African Studies*, 55(2), 1–20.

Wolpe, H. 1975. 'The theory of internal colonialism: The South African case', in Oxaal, I., Barnett, T. and Booth, D. (eds), *Beyond the Sociology of Development: Economy and Society in Latin America and Africa*, London: Routledge.

THREE

Development planning in democratic South Africa: Organisational underpinnings

Joel Netshitenzhe

INTRODUCTION

This chapter examines the institutional architecture appropriate for developmentalism in the South African context. It seeks to identify relevant lessons from global and domestic experiences in implementing strategic planning. The focus is on institutions tailored to craft development plans and ensure the coordination and integration of government operations.

The chapter focuses on professional, bureaucratic structures as distinct from political, executive oversight. Lessons are drawn from the experience of the Policy Coordination and Advisory Services (PCAS, also referred to as the Policy Unit) in the Presidency in South Africa, particularly during the 2000s. After an examination of how the PCAS sought to promote 'joined-up' government (Bogdanor, 2012), the question is posed of whether the mechanisms set up after the dissolution of the PCAS built on its experience.

The chapter proceeds from the view that effective development planning and implementation require a pilot agency at the centre of government that is 'responsible for long-term strategy and coordination of policy inputs, and staffed by a competent, mission-oriented professional bureaucracy, sufficiently insulated from the push and pull of special short-term interests' (Weiss, 2010: 11).

Two perspectives inform the treatment of these issues. Firstly, it is assumed that the South African government is seeking to establish a 'developmental state' that is shaped by the history and socioeconomic dynamics of South African society; and, secondly, that such a state is meant to have a planning regime that 'guides national economic development' (ANC, 2007: 5).

Debate continues to rage about whether national planning is still relevant in a world economy that is characterised by globalisation with widespread integration of global production processes, complex supply chains, and the dominance of the financial sector.

Mkandawire (2012) critiques arguments common in the 1990s that globalisation had rendered national planning irrelevant (Mkandawire, 2012: 6). His critique is echoed by Chimhowu et al. (2019) in their analysis of global trends in national planning, with the number of countries 'with a national development plan' doubling between 2006 and 2018 (Chimhowu et al., 2019: 80).

The chapter starts by briefly examining the current trends in, and discourse on, national planning as well as the notion of a developmental state. It then examines the application of these concepts in post-apartheid South Africa. The issue of macro-organisation of the state to meet planning and developmental objectives is interrogated, first generically, then in relation to South Africa. The chapter then looks at whether the Policy Unit had the attributes of a pilot agency; assesses relevant post-2009 institutional arrangements; and offers proposals on how these arrangements can be strengthened.

The chapter does not interrogate the content of South Africa's 'development plans' crafted since 1994; nor does it assess the appropriateness of such plans or their developmental impact. Further, the structures examined are those related to development planning, as distinct from ad hoc organisational interventions.

CURRENT TRENDS IN NATIONAL PLANNING

National development planning has been an important instrument used by many states to achieve economic growth, industrialisation and an improved quality of life for their populations. This planning has entailed the active involvement of the state 'to coordinate national development efforts or, at least, to coordinate national investment planning to ensure complementary investments' (Chimhowu et al., 2019: 79). Theories and practices have differed from country to country, with varied approaches to the roles of the state, the private sector and citizens.

While the developed economies of Europe and North America employed economic planning to attain high levels of industrialisation, more centralised approaches were adopted by socialist countries such as the erstwhile Soviet Union. From the middle of the 20th century, newly independent states in Asia and Africa sought to use national development planning to catch up. But it is the success of what came to be known as the developmental states of East Asia that caught universal attention for the fast pace at which they were able to industrialise, grow, modernise and improve social well-being (Weiss, 2010: 7). While attention has focused on the unique geopolitical environment in which many of these states embarked on their development journeys – leveraging a supportive environment among allied global powers that included foreign direct investment, technology transfer and market access – this does not detract from the endogenous factors that propelled their rise.

National planning had, by the turn of the 21st century, largely fallen out of favour – though it did not completely disappear – with the fall of the 'socialist world' and the emergence of neoliberal economics, popularly referred to as the Washington Consensus (Weiss, 2010: 3) and characterised by the reduced role of the state in the economy. Mkandawire (2012) attributes this retreat from national planning to the argument that globalisation had 'closed the window for state intervention' (Mkandawire, 2012: 6), and considers this 'the bogeyman evoked in minatory terms to silence any demands for restraining the market' (Mkandawire, 2012: 28).

However, national planning is now back in vogue. Chimhowu et al. (2019) refer to work done by the Strategic Network on New National Planning (University of Manchester) which 'shows that the number of countries with a national development plan has more than doubled – from 62 to 134 – between 2006 and 2018, and that nearly 80 per cent of the global population now lives in a country with a national development plan of one form or another' (Chimhowu et al., 2019: 76).

Weiss (2010) attributes the increasing role of the state to the 2008–2009 global financial crisis. However, Chimhowu et al. (2019) establish a correlation between 'new national planning' and several factors: planning requirements by some multilateral institutions for bailouts of Highly Indebted and Poor Countries; the systematic state interventions required to meet the United Nations Millennium Development Goals of 2000 and Sustainable Development Goals of 2015; and a response to 'processes of economic globalization, national sovereignty and democratic governance' (Chimhowu et al., 2019: 77, 81).

If the 2008–2009 global financial crisis forced even neoliberal states to intervene more intensely in the economy, the Covid-19 pandemic put this trend on steroids (MISTRA, 2021: 30). Good examples include current industrial and broader economic policy developments in the United States of America. Combined with geopolitical considerations and efforts to deal with global warming, the pandemic spurred the US administration to introduce numerous policies in pursuit of re-industrialisation, de-risking and practices such as re-shoring, friend-shoring and near-shoring of production sites. 'Bidenomics' is the popular appellation attached to this policy, and it includes growing the economy '"from the bottom up and middle out" through public investments, empowering workers, and promoting competition' (Hanauer, 2023). The Inflation Reduction Act in the US is characterised as 'the most significant legislation to combat climate change in [US] history, and one of the largest investments in the American economy in a generation' (US Department of Treasury Factsheet, 2023). In addition, the Chips and Science Act aims to (US White House Factsheet, 2022):

strengthen American manufacturing, supply chains, and national security, and invest in research and development, science and technology, and the workforce of the future to keep the United States the leader in the industries of tomorrow, including nanotechnology, clean energy, quantum computing, and artificial intelligence [AI] while restricting access to such technologies by China and other US rivals.

There are, of course, debates about whether the rise of national planning implies the emergence of a new form of developmentalism. Certainly, the context in which 'the current generation of national development planning practices is emerging' (Chimhowu et al., 2019: 77) is new, and the epistemologies that underpin the practices are varied. Of relevance to this chapter is the consensus that strategic planning is once more infusing economic policy and praxis in many parts of the world. South Africa needs to assess its own approaches, taking this reality into account.

MACRO-ORGANISATIONAL UNDERPINNING OF NATIONAL PLANNING: THE DEVELOPMENTAL STATE

In this section, the macro-organisational architecture appropriate for national planning is examined, using the concept of a developmental state as a frame of reference.

Concept of a developmental state

The category of a developmental state, as a macro-organisational instrument to attain high rates of growth and development, has been applied largely to some East Asian countries 'to explain the riddles of growth and development trends of such magnitude and consistency that countries have climbed from one rung of industrial and socioeconomic development to another within one generation – qualitatively bridging the gap between themselves and the most developed countries' (Netshitenzhe, 2011: 2). This is because, traditionally, developmental convergence within and across countries is quite slow. As such, the science of social development had to devise novel categories to explicate a relatively new phenomenon in the dynamic of 'the relationship between the state, the citizen and the market' (Netshitenzhe, 2011: 2).

How was such rapid development possible? In citing East Asian newly industrialised countries as 'archetypical empirical cases' of developmental states, Evans (2006) identifies their unique characteristic as a distinctive organisational structure of the state and how it related to society. It had the 'capacity for coherent collective action' and was embedded among social partners, especially business, while maintaining autonomy from these elites – what is referred to as embedded autonomy. These states had political vision and the will to provide guidance and reduce uncertainty. Because of the state's distinctive role, these countries were able 'to transform their position in the global hierarchy of nations during the late 20th century' (Evans, 2006: 11). The newly industrialised countries (NICs) moved 'so far so fast', Weiss (2010) argues, because there was a 'non-ordinary factor [that] consisted in the role of the state' (Weiss, 2010: 7).

Mkandawire (2012) and Evans (2006) also underline social compacting among the main social players in the economy: the state, business, labour and civil society. Mkandawire specifically rejects the argument that developmental states are by definition authoritarian, arguing that (Mkandawire, 2012: 2):

we are talking about 'democratic developmental states': developmental (in the sense that they facilitate and promote economic growth and structural transformation), democratic (in the sense that they derive their legitimacy through popular participation and electoral process) and socially inclusive (in the sense that they pursue social policies that ensure equitable entitlements of all their citizens to ensure that their capacities and functioning are adequate for a decent inclusion in societal affairs).

In this context, leadership by the state in the planning process should not take the form of top-down dictation but should rather be characterised by 'collaborative rationality' and 'social deliberation' (Chimhowu et al., 2019: 77). Evans (2006) further argues that, in the

21st century, embeddedness 'based primarily on ties with industrial elites no longer makes sense and building more encompassing synergistic ties to civil society becomes essential; [and] therefore, "thick democracy" becomes a key part of any growth strategy' (Evans, 2006: 41). In other words, taking into account the varied and at times contradictory interests of all classes and strata, including the working class, is critical: developmentalism and embedded autonomy are not merely about compacting with investors and managing elite market concerns.

Evolution of South African discourse on a developmental state – a brief outline

Internationally, the concept of a developmental state emerged *post facto* in analyses of the impressive achievements of states that had consistently achieved high rates of growth and development in relatively short periods. Drawing from this experience, South Africa has, *a priori*, expressly set out to become a developmental state. As Weiss (2010: 2) observes:

> South Africa has set itself the unusual and challenging goal of becoming a developmental state. In principle, this is a unique and noble enterprise: unique in so far as no state has ever self-consciously set out to become a Developmental State; and noble in so far as such a project draws inspiration from the experience of certain countries that achieved *shared* growth – growth with equity. Predatory states have appeared in abundance; developmental states are a much rarer breed.

While developmental planning had, in one form or another, always been part of African National Congress policy discourse, serious and focused attention to the concept of a developmental state started to feature in its documents only during the decade of the 2000s, as elaborated on below. The main reason for this is that, after a decade of democracy, there was one question that had started to bother policymakers more intently: why was the South African economy not growing at the same high rates as Malaysia's and Singapore's, for instance? And what lessons could South Africa learn from these and other experiences?

Debate in South Africa in the early 1990s had centred on issues such as the balance between growth and redistribution, and between state and private ownership of the commanding heights of the economy. Seminal documents such as *Ready to Govern* (ANC, 1992), which set the framework for the post-1994 democratic government, did refer to the 'ultimate responsibility' of the state – working with business, labour and other civil society organisations – to plan, coordinate and guide the economy 'towards a sustainable economic growth pattern'. It was envisaged that 'a developmental state' would be in charge of the provision of public goods (ANC, 1992: 18). The Reconstruction and Development (RDP) White Paper, the 1994 blueprint for such a path, saw the RDP Office as a catalyst for change but also recognised that serious planning would succeed only if all of the state was being repurposed towards developmental ends (RDP Office, 1994: 18). That was besides the contestation within the Presidency and across government around the role and powers of the RDP Office, which was dissolved in 1995.

By 1998, the ANC had started more expressly to refer to the concept of a developmental state, but it was meant more as 'the kind of state whose character is developmental' rather than a strict definition of such a state or its unique attributes (ANC, 1998: 12).

Only in the mid-2000s did the ANC and the South African government comprehensively apply themselves to the concept of a developmental state. This is elaborated more clearly in the ANC *Strategy and Tactics* document (ANC, 2007: 37) where the attributes of such a state were articulated: strategic orientation; capacity to lead in defining a common national agenda and in mobilising all of society; organisational capacity; and technical capacity. This would be combined with 'the best traditions of social democracy' (ANC, 2007: 13). While the notion of a developmental state assumes requisite state capacity, capability and efficiency, the National Development Plan adopted in 2012 expressly refers (presumably for emphasis) to a 'capable' developmental state that is able to play a developmental and transformative role; a public service that is professional; and a clear role for state-owned enterprises (NPC, 2012: 71).

By the latter half of the 2000s, South Africa had thus embraced the ambition to become a developmental state. But all this was undermined in the following decade by massive corruption and state capture which caused the degradation and hollowing out of the South African state (Godinho and Hermanus, 2018: 9). Beyond this, South Africa has had to contend, since 1994, with the nature, composition and mobility of capital in the context of both its colonial history and globalisation. This has limited the extent to which capital can be mobilised for a national development project.

The generic instruments of medium- and long-term planning within the post-apartheid government are found in multiple iterations such as the RDP (1994); Growth, Employment and Redistribution strategy (GEAR, 1996); Microeconomic Reform Strategy (MERS, 2002); Accelerated and Shared Growth Initiative for South Africa (AsgiSA, 2006); New Growth Path (2011); and the National Development Plan (NDP, 2012). The current Economic Reconstruction and Recovery Plan (ERRP, 2020), while informed by the objectives and general content of the NDP, identifies the interventions required to recover from the ravages of the Covid-19 pandemic and place the country on a higher growth and development trajectory. Related to these is the Medium-Term Expenditure Framework (MTEF), a three-year rolling budgeting process introduced in 1997, which was later followed by the generic Medium-Term Strategic Framework (MTSF) introduced in 2004, which outlines the five-year programme of government informed by the electoral mandate, and is reviewed annually. The MTSF was replaced in 2024 by the Medium-Term Development Plan (MTDP). This chapter, however, focuses on the organisational underpinnings of development planning rather than the content, form and impact of these plans.

MICRO-ORGANISATIONAL UNDERPINNINGS OF NATIONAL PLANNING: THE CASE FOR A PILOT AGENCY

If a developmental state is the macro-organisational foundation of successful economic planning, as witnessed in East Asia, a pilot agency within this state is its micro-organisational underpinning.

According to Weiss (2010: 11), a critical element in the success of the NICs in East Asia was:

> the creation of a *pilot agency* responsible for long-term strategy and coordination of policy inputs, and staffed by a competent, mission-oriented professional bureaucracy, sufficiently insulated from the push and pull of special short-term interests. East Asia's pilot agencies – Japan's MITI [Ministry of International Trade and Industry], Taiwan's CEPD [Council for Economic Planning and Development], and Korea's EPB [Economic Planning Board] – famously undertook this coordination role during the postwar transformation of their economies.

In contrast, Weiss (2010: 13) argues, countries that had not been successful (not for lack of effort) did not have such organisational capacity.

> [W]hen looking to the much more 'mixed' development records of, say, Brazil and India or the countries of Southeast Asia and Latin America more generally, the difference lies not in the presence or absence of industry policies per se, but in the character and purposiveness of their bureaucracies, in the extent of their political cohesion and insulation, and in the manner of their public-private linkages.

The existence of such an agency does not imply that the polymorphous nature of government is eliminated. It is impossible to eliminate differing approaches and emphases in as large an institution as the state with its many ministries, departments and a raft of other agencies. What is required is that the central agency must develop a long-term vision and ensure that it becomes the organising framework within which all other state institutions operate.

Functionaries of the pilot agency should be insulated from special interests, and they should be among the best and brightest, appropriately remunerated, and have professional career-pathing. In other words, the authority that attaches to such an agency should derive not so much from the formal status it enjoys in the state hierarchy, but from the legitimacy that issues from its expertise, capacity and professionalism. Weiss opines that many of these bureaucrats should have 'an engineering background, since engineers are problem solvers and well placed to understand logistical and production-related issues' (Weiss, 2010: 19). Further, Evans argues that utilisation of the bureaucratic pipeline to source personnel was, in a number of these states, combined with lateral entry of experts from outside the state, helping to develop a web that had expertise and enjoyed confidence within political and broader societal environments (Evans, 1989: 129 – 146). The professionals in the pilot agency should have formal and informal lines of communication with both internal (state) and external (non-state) actors.

Sangweni (2007: 4–5), then chairperson of South Africa's Public Service Commission, underlines the importance of a professional public service in achieving such developmental goals, using the example of Japan:

> [The] organisational configuration of the Japanese public service not only allowed it autonomy and a lot of room to experiment and take risks without colliding with its parliament or public opinion, but was critical in making it the Developmental Juggernaut that was able to heave Japan off the ground with the trade-off being delivery on a grand scale. Its astuteness in managing relations with the private sector, harnessing public opinion behind it and mediating competing demands on government from various sectors of society were also its great assets.

Proceeding from the premise that a pilot agency is a vital micro-organisational instrument to drive planning and ensure effective monitoring and evaluation of implementation, where should such a structure be located and what kind of approach should guide its work? Further, how can 'institutional monocropping' – the imposition of uniform blueprints – be avoided, as cautioned by Evans (2004)? Beyond this, account also has to be taken of 21st-century complexities underlined by Evans (2006) such as the need for bottom-up democratic control, enhanced transparency and accountability as well as a deeper appreciation of societal preferences.

Central to these issues, as highlighted by the Organisation for Economic Co-operation and Development (OECD), is the inadequacy of traditional leadership approaches in government, often manifested through 'inter-ministerial bodies and standing committees, used as a way to level differences of opinion, rather than arbitration by the Head of Government' (OECD, 2015: 2). The OECD goes to the extent of arguing that the structure to ensure coherence should be 'in the same building as the Head of Government' – not even in the Treasury, as the core issue is not about monitoring the use of resources. This would allow for better accountability, especially on cross-cutting issues (OECD, 2015: 16).

In practice, as illustrated in Figure 3.1, new national planning entities are variously located in a strategic ministry, a planning agency or in the office of the head of government (Chimhowu et al., 2019: 82).

Figure 3.1: Ownership and drivers of national development plans

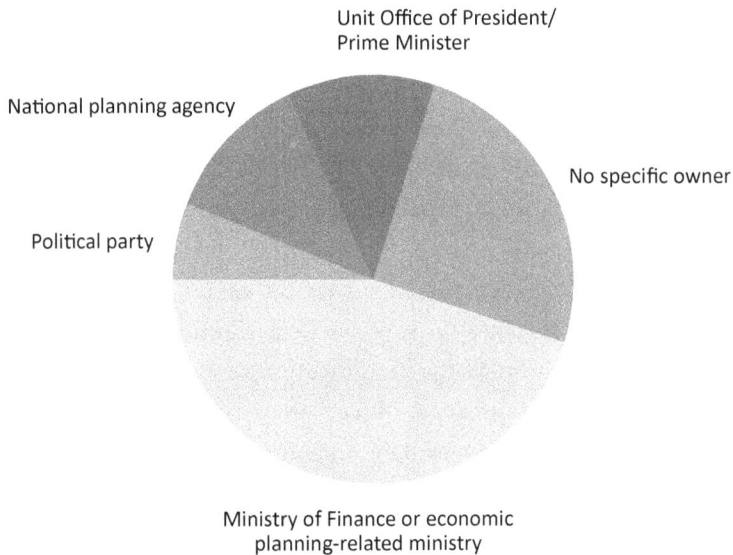

Unit Office of President/
Prime Minister

National planning agency

No specific owner

Political party

Ministry of Finance or economic
planning-related ministry

Source: Chimhowu et al. (2019)

Note: 24 of the 107 countries sampled (22.4 per cent) did not have a 'specific owner' for the planning entity, which the authors interpret as indicating a lack of seriousness.

In the mid-2000s, research by the Policy Unit in the South African Presidency also highlighted variegated approaches to the location of national planning structures across the countries it studied (PCAS, 2005):

- Brazil: Ministry of Planning, and Budget and Management;
- India: Planning Commission, chaired by the Prime Minister;
- South Korea: Ministries of Finance, Planning and Co-ordination; and
- Malaysia: Economic Planning Unit in the Prime Minister's Office.

These varied strategic locations for national planning, as well as for monitoring and evaluation, reflect the unique characteristics of each country and its government leadership, including efforts to balance interests between role players within the state and assert central authority (PCAS, 2007).

EVOLUTION OF MICRO-ORGANISATIONAL PLATFORMS OF PLANNING IN THE SOUTH AFRICAN STATE: TOWARDS A PILOT AGENCY

In this section, two categories of issues are dealt with: firstly, how the South African state broadly sought to improve its planning, integration and coordination capacities as it evolved beyond the 1994 democratic transition, and, secondly, the specific role played by the PCAS, which itself matured over time.

Gumede (2018: 5) defines coordination as entailing 'processes, systems and structures that have a role in the design and implementation of a policy', and planning as the identification of a sequence of actions required to achieve set strategic objectives. To this should be added integration, which entails ensuring joint action by the various actors in developing and implementing relevant plans and programmes.

Evolution of the centre of government

From its establishment in 1994, the RDP Office (a ministry within the President's Office) served as a kind of centre of government for 'policy development and implementation procedures', tasked with 'integrating the different organs of government, centrally, regionally and locally in a concerted drive towards the national goals of renewal' (RDP Office, 1994: 6). The understanding, according to President Nelson Mandela, was that this arrangement would be temporary, as the RDP Office's orientation and resource allocation would become integrated into the rest of government.

Jay Naidoo (2003), the minister responsible for the RDP Office, reminisced:

> We had an anticipation that the president's office in a sense would become a coordinator of an integrated effort. In the first instance that did work and it was the intention that that was only a temporary thing; that once you'd established a common policy framework and restructured both the budget and the civil service, the need to try to create a centralised, more integrated planning process would fall away.

As in most governments, formal responsibility for decision-making was assumed by structures such as Cabinet committees, Cabinet, and special executive or bureaucratic task teams and – in the initial years of the post-apartheid government – ministerial caucuses of the leading party in government. This is inadequate, as illustrated in the observation of OECD researchers (OECD, 2015: 6) that formal systems provide:

> very limited time or opportunity for the Head of Government to … intervene on key priorities (and perhaps the policy output being declared a success regardless of the outcome). This is because reporting systems that are ad hoc combined with no clear feedback loops can mean that the success or failure of an initiative is only apparent at the end of a budget cycle.

As illustrated in Figure 3.2, a head of government relies on a disjointed system of accounting.

Figure 3.2: Principal channels through which the head of government discusses policy issues

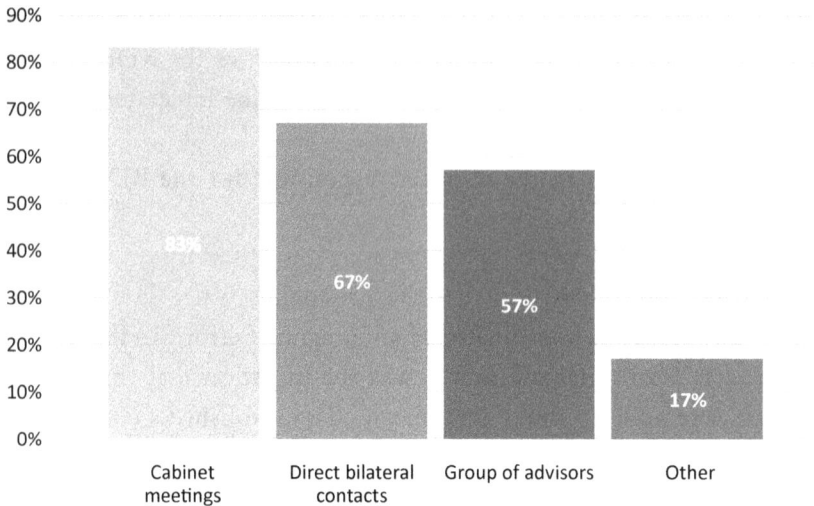

Source: OECD (2015)

It is precisely this kind of weakness, especially after the dissolution of the RDP Office, which occasioned complaints about the role of the President's Office in the hearings of the Presidential Review Commission. In its report, the Commission recommended that the President's Office should be strengthened to play a leadership role across government. However, the President's Office argued that the structure of the Office had to take into account the personality and interests of the incumbent (PRC, 1998: 47–54).

In essence, the Mandela presidency was seen as transitional and – as elaborated later – a unit was being set up in the Deputy President's Office, reflecting the 'prime ministerial' role that that office had assumed. This capacity was strengthened and appropriately located under the President's supervision in the post-Mandela era.

Broader weaknesses of the new democratic state also undermined its planning and integrative capacity. These weaknesses included its quasi-federal nature, poor executive-management interface, and a flat Cabinet structure. At the request of President Mbeki, reflections on these issues were conducted in 2005 by the PCAS in collaboration with the Forum of South African Directors-General

(FOSAD). Proposals from these reflections included, among others, a reconfiguration of the Cabinet committee system; a hierarchy in the executive with 'senior' (coordinating) ministers and a corresponding hierarchy among Directors-General; constitution of coordinating departments – Department of Public Service and Administration (DPSA), Department of Provincial and Local Government (DPLG), National Treasury (NT), National Intelligence Agency (NIA), Department of Foreign Affairs (DFA) and Department of Trade and Industry (DTI) – into a centre directly supporting the Presidency; and flexible application of 'subsidiarity' and 'asymmetry' in managing inter-governmental relations among the spheres (PCAS/FOSAD, 2005). Most of these proposals were not adopted or implemented as debate about their value was not resolved due to differing opinions; others were diffusely embraced or found later expression in the 2012 National Development Plan.

One area in which the democratic government seemed to be adept was the application of what it referred to as people-driven (and people-centred) development (Levin, 2018: 34). Besides campaigns to encourage popular agency and constitutionally mandated consultative processes, government set up presidential working groups and councils of consultation with various sectors (big business, Black business, agriculture, international investors, trade unions, women, youth, religious sector and higher education). In other words, the government did quite well in deliberative participation – some would argue to a fault, if not to paralysis!

Did the dissolution of the RDP Office (arguably a nascent pilot agency) imply the death of planning and coordinating capacity and the dispersal of points of control and authority?

Around the time that the RDP Office was being disbanded, a policy unit was being assembled in the Office of Deputy President Thabo Mbeki: a structure that, over the years, evolved into the PCAS. It is to this unit that the chapter now turns, primarily to examine whether it had evolved into a pilot agency in an emergent developmental state.

Examination of the PCAS experience: Evolution towards a pilot agency?[1]

When the second administration of democratic South Africa was formed after the 1999 elections, the putative Policy Unit migrated into the Office of the President. New senior bureaucrats were employed, including, in 2002, a new head of the unit (at the level of Director-General). This was aimed at improving coherence, coordination and integration within government, with the Presidency in the lead. The Unit 'was the main clearing house in the policy-making processes in South Africa. It undertook policy development and policy analysis, policy coordination and policy advice. The Policy Unit also conducted medium- to long-range planning, and government-wide monitoring and evaluation' (Gumede, 2018: 13).

With the broad objectives of the PCAS identified, the unit's team was given space to elaborate on the capacities it would require to carry out its mandate. According to Netshitenzhe (2008: 1), by 2008 it had streamlined its tasks and organisational establishment as follows:

- Ensure monitoring and evaluation (M&E) of implementation of government programmes to facilitate the achievement of the strategic agenda of government.
- Facilitate strategic and integrated policy planning across government, build partnerships with civil society and promote regional integration.
- Ensure alignment of cluster/departmental plans and programmes with national government priorities and the National Planning Framework.
- Provide strategic support to and leadership of the Forum of South African Directors-General (FOSAD) and its clusters.
- Provide strategic advice and support to the Presidency in the fulfilment of its mandate.

The PCAS also undertook scenario planning to help inform long-term strategic reflections and context-specific planning within

---

1   Declaration: the author was the head of the PCAS between 2002 and 2009 and a member of the first NPC; Profs Alan Hirsch and Vusi Gumede were senior members of PCAS staff.

government and among social partners.

Many of these functions had evolved with the growth and refinement of the unit's structures; by 2008, it had 54 members of staff. In addition to focusing on various sectors in line with Cabinet committees (economic, social, governance and administration, international relations and security), the unit also set up structures to deal with planning, monitoring and evaluation, and services to FOSAD, and assumed responsibility for specific cross-cutting issues such as youth, women, people with disabilities and children.

The PCAS was critical in bringing together clusters of Directors-General and the broader FOSAD, identifying the strategic agenda of the moment, and confirming Cabinet submissions and/or advising political principals on the content of these submissions. It also coordinated the councils and working groups of external partners that were set up to advise the President.

In addition to developing the Medium-Term Strategic Framework (MTSF) and other generic strategies, the unit also streamlined planning cycles across the spheres of government; and its head and sectoral coordinators took part, respectively, in the meetings of the Ministers' Committee on the Budget (MINCOMBUD) and technical meetings in which budgetary allocations were processed. Towards the end of the first decade of the 2000s, it had started to liaise with National Treasury (NT) in the drafting of, and feedback loop around, the MTSF and Medium-Term Expenditure Framework (MTEF), and to set up the structure of coordinating departments referred to earlier.

With regard to planning, in particular, the discourse around a developmental state had put the issue of a long-term vision and plan on the government's agenda. The 2007 study referred to earlier called for more attention to relevant 'technical competences required for national economic management'; 'effective processes of consultation and engagement with major sectors of the society'; and 'delineation of responsibilities ... between the planning function and the role of the head of state as well as of the office responsible' (PCAS, 2005: 40).

Regarding monitoring and evaluation, a government-wide M&E policy framework was developed and reports – starting with one on the functionality of departments – had started to flow to the political principals in the Presidency. The formal allocation of tasks and their implementation give a flavour of the capacities extant in the Policy Unit. However, what lent the PCAS the legitimacy and authority it enjoyed was the expertise of its bureaucrats; the deportment exhibited in relating to peers and political principals across government; the seniority of its leadership within the broader political terrain; and the President's support.

Though in many respects still fledgeling, the PCAS had acquired some of the critical attributes of a pilot agency. However, the state it was serving had some way to go before becoming developmental in the strictest terms. It still had to develop a long-term plan, and coordination and integration still needed improvement. Overall, based on the details of these developments, it can be argued that South Africa was well on its way to having a pilot agency and becoming a developmental state.

The post-2009 configuration at the centre of government

Under the fourth administration (2009–2014), there was an overhaul of the planning and integrative capacities within the Presidency. Ministers of Planning and of Performance Monitoring and Evaluation were appointed in 2009, and processes were initiated to build new long-term structures for planning and for monitoring and evaluation. With regard to planning, the proposal at first was to establish a Ministerial Committee on Planning (MINCOMPLAN) as well as a structure of external stakeholders (National Stakeholder Council on Planning) (Planning Ministry, 2009: 39), as reflected in Figure 3.3.

This was changed at the behest of the then president, in part premised on the argument that an intra-governmental planning commission would merely reflect the conceptual debates among Cabinet members. The NPC was thus subsequently conceptualised by the PCAS (2009: 3) and then formed as:

> … a body consisting of respected intellectuals, leaders and experts from outside of government appointed by the President. Commissioners should therefore be drawn from various sectors of society based on experience, knowledge and expertise in various fields such as labour, politics, business, finance,

Figure 3.3: Ministerial Committee on Planning

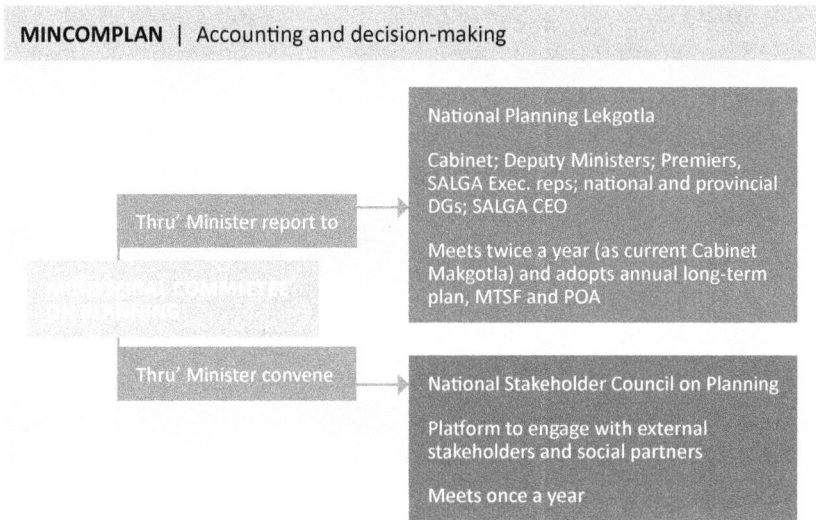

MINCOMPLAN | Accounting and decision-making

Thru' Minister report to →

National Planning Lekgotla

Cabinet; Deputy Ministers; Premiers, SALGA Exec. reps; national and provincial DGs; SALGA CEO

Meets twice a year (as current Cabinet Makgotla) and adopts annual long-term plan, MTSF and POA

Thru' Minister convene →

National Stakeholder Council on Planning

Platform to engage with external stakeholders and social partners

Meets once a year

Source: Planning Ministry (2009)

sociology, economics, science, technology and environment. The NPC will work under the guidance of the Minister in The Presidency to produce a long-term plan for South Africa with technical and administrative support from a Secretariat.

Against the backdrop of case studies cited earlier, South Africa's NPC is an institutional outlier in terms of planning responsibilities being allocated to experts from outside of government. Yet, given its successes, particularly the development of a widely embraced NDP, strategic research on specific themes, and its societal reach and legitimacy, it can be argued that the NPC configuration meets some of Evans' requirements for modern planning relating to 'thick democracy', 'bottom-up democratic control', and 'high levels of transparency [and] accountability' (Evans, 2006: 41, 45). However, the NPC lacks the kind of authority, access and influence that would be enjoyed by an in-house state planning agency.

The setting up of the NPC was accompanied by a number of changes in the configuration of structures for joined-up government in the Presidency. These were initially two ministers (Planning, and

Performance Monitoring and Evaluation) and later one ministry with a Department of Planning, Monitoring and Evaluation (DPME) and an NPC Secretariat largely subsumed under the department.

Compared to the monitoring and evaluation capacity the PCAS was setting up, a relatively large bureaucracy is located in the Monitoring and Evaluation section of the DPME, with expertise to deal with the minutiae of performance indicators. Besides a seeming lack of serious application to monitoring and evaluation reports over time by Cabinet, it is debatable whether part of the extensive capacity is of strategic value to high-level, generic monitoring and evaluation of outcomes and impacts, and how these are affected by ongoing efforts at implementation. What is critical is that two post-2009 negative developments detracted from much that had been built in the early 2000s. While there was some improvement and 'seniorisation' of the planning, and monitoring and evaluation functions – through the establishment of larger institutions and the appointment of ministers for work that was being done by bureaucrats – there were also critical reversals. Firstly, at a functional level, there was a weakening of critical PCAS functions such as coordination, integration and advisory services. As such, the polymorphous nature of government started to assert itself potently, with many ministries and departments acting as fiefdoms. Secondly, at macro-organisational and cultural levels, the worm of state capture ate at the core of the state, degrading generic state capacity, siphoning off resources, and destroying state-owned enterprises which form critical economic leverage for a developmental state (Godinho and Hermanus, 2018: 9).

In an attempt to address some of these weaknesses after the 2018 change in presidential leadership, the government set up the Policy and Research Services (PRS) branch in 2019. It was, according to The Presidency (2020: 34):

> tasked with the responsibility of providing policy support and advice to the Political Principals; to facilitate policy coordination in government through the Cabinet system and FOSAD, through providing technical support to the structures chaired by the President and the Deputy President; to influence the agenda

of Cabinet to ensure that Cabinet monitors the implementation of the seven priorities of government[;] and to implement a programme of action to unblock service delivery challenges.

By 2023, it was reported to have started some of this work while being further capacitated (The Presidency, 2023: 72).

How the PRS relates to the NPC and the broader DPME has not been fully clarified. When the announcement was made, Hirsch (2019) expressed some concern regarding the seniority of appointees and questioned whether the PRS would 'be able to assert its role in the [DPME's] shadow' (Hirsch, 2019).

A special intervention unit, Operation Vulindlela, was set up to focus on the transformation and modernisation of network industries such as digital communications, electricity, water and transport (The Presidency, 2024). This was done in order to identify and address challenges in relation to reforms required to realise the ERRP, and to accelerate implementation. The unit brings together officials from the Presidency and National Treasury, with some private sector support. The effectiveness of this unit speaks to the importance of a close working relationship between the Presidency and National Treasury in the planning and implementation regime.

The next section provides broad recommendations for how the centre of the South African government can be strengthened – in the manner of a developmental state with a pilot agency.

CONCLUSION: TOWARDS A PILOT AGENCY IN THE ERA OF RECONSTRUCTION AND RECOVERY

The South African economy has barely grown since the relatively idyllic era of the early 2000s. Even in that period, there was acknowledgement that the growth rate of around 5 per cent per annum, underpinned in part by high prices during the commodity super-cycle, was not sustainable. AsgiSA identified 'deficiencies in state organisation, capacity and strategic leadership impacting on delivery' as part of the binding constraints (PCAS, 2006: 7).

These and other constraints – currency volatility, skilled labour shortages, competition and regulatory burdens – have not yet been adequately addressed. Because the recovery from the devastation of state capture is painstaking and slow, deficiencies are currently worse than in the first decade of the 2000s. The 2022 NDP review attributes this, in some measure, to 'policy incoherence, … lack of capacity within the state to execute plans, [and] corruption' (NPC, 2023: 61).

The irony is that, in the first decade of the 2000s, an effective centre of government had been emerging, but there had not been a long-term vision and plan. Post-2009, the widely embraced NDP was adopted, but this was hardly implemented as state capture degraded state capacity. Currently, the centre of government seems to be dispersed in a clutter of structures: the NPC and its Secretariat, the monitoring and evaluation structure in the DPME, PRS and Vulindlela.

The central recommendation of this chapter, therefore, is that these entities should be rationalised, with a clear hierarchy and, for those that remain, a streamlined division of labour. A set of permutations relating to some of these structures is outlined hereunder.

On the NPC, Chang's proposal that it should either be re-oriented and strengthened 'into an "orchestrating body"' or be complemented 'with a co-ordinating body more specifically charged with inter-ministerial coordination' is eminently sensible (Chang, 2023: 29). As intimated earlier, a major drawback of post-2009 restructuring was the weakening of the coordination and integrative functions earlier undertaken by the PCAS.

While the PRS seems to mimic the erstwhile PCAS, the question is whether it should be a standalone entity or should also assume functions currently undertaken by the NPC Secretariat to enable a seamless continuum between planning, coordination and advisory services.

There are many functions that reside in the monitoring and evaluation section of the DPME which are quite critical for a centre of government: defining and monitoring performance indicators; an evaluation system which includes provincial counterparts; citizen-based monitoring; and special integrated initiatives such as Operation Phakisa (a DPME programme which brings together public and private sector stakeholders to address delivery constraints in an NDP area of priority).

A critical question, though, is whether all the detailed capacities and the large behemoth that the monitoring and evaluation section has become, belong in the Presidency.

Like any bureaucracy, the DPME now has an internal rhythm of its own and an impulse towards self-perpetuation. However, many elements of its detailed functions can be located elsewhere in government – across the departments of Public Service and Administration (DPSA), Cooperative Governance and Traditional Affairs (CoGTA) and the National Treasury. Related to this is the earlier observation about coordinating departments that should directly support the Presidency as the second ring of the concentric circles of the centre of government. Other coordinating departments that can be added are: Trade, Industry and Competition (DTIC), intelligence agencies in the National Intelligence Coordinating Committee (NICOC)[2] and International Relations and Cooperation (DIRCO). The monitoring and evaluation function in the Presidency would thus deal with high-level outcome and impact indicators.

What about Operation Vulindlela? The most logical approach to such an intervention and turnaround function would be to locate it in, and as a sub-unit of, a structure that combines the PRS, the NPC Secretariat, a restructured monitoring and evaluation entity, and Operation Phakisa.

Such changes have the potential to strengthen the centre of the South African government so it can galvanise and lead the state and, in turn, the rest of society to take the country to a higher trajectory of growth and development – as envisaged in the ERRP and, broadly, the NDP. There may be other effective permutations in the detail, but the fundamental principle is that all the functional capacities of an effective pilot agency (straddling planning, coordination and integration, monitoring and evaluation, as well as advisory services) should be rationalised and strengthened within the Presidency as the centre of government. These proposals are posited with consideration for the fact that re-ordering state institutions is not an easy or narrow

---

2   The NICOC brings together all the intelligence agencies, including those in the police and the military.

technical undertaking. As Leftwich and Hogg (2007: 10) warn:

> State-building is not simply a matter of the technical design and
> erection of the architecture of the state. Effective state-building
> has almost universally been a matter of complex political processes
> involving the interaction of often rival or competing leaders and
> elites (in both democratic and non-democratic contexts) who
> recognise that a greater public good can be achieved, for all, by
> establishing a new and inclusive set of institutions of rule rather
> than by clinging to the old and remaining in conflict.

Questions have been raised about the many 'external' advisory
bodies currently supporting the Presidency: are there too many cooks
who may spoil the broth of reconstruction and recovery? 'Thick
democracy', as espoused by Evans – which essentially is about social
compacting – largely renders this concern moot, as long as the pilot
agency is sufficiently capacitated to coordinate and process such
interactions, and is appropriately embedded within, and autonomous
in relation to, all the social partners (Evans, 2006: 41).

REFERENCES

African National Congress (ANC). 1992. *Ready to Govern: ANC policy
guidelines for a democratic South Africa*. As adopted at the National
Conference, 31 May.

African National Congress (ANC). 1998. *Alliance Summit Discussion
Document: The State, Property Relations and Social Transformation - A
Conceptual Framework*.

African National Congress (ANC). 2007. *Building a National Democratic
Society* [*Strategy and Tactics of the ANC*]. As adopted by the 52nd National
Conference of the African National Congress, Polokwane, Limpopo
Province, 16–20 December.

Bogdanor, V. (ed.). 2012. *Joined-Up Government*. London: British
Academy Scholarship Online, https://doi.org/10.5871/
bacad/9780197263334.001.0001, accessed 15 December 2023.

Chang, H. 2023. 'South Africa at a crossroads: The need for a sustainable
structural transformation'. Presentation at the NSG master class,
20 November.

Chimhowu, A., Hulme, D. and Munro, L. 2019. 'The "New" national development planning and global development goals: Processes and partnerships'. *World Development*, 120 (August), 76, 77, 79, 80, 81 and 82.

Evans, P. 1989. 'The future of the developmental state'. *The Korean Journal of Policy Studies*, 4, 129–146.

Evans, P. 2004. 'Development as Institutional Change: The Pitfalls of Monocropping and the Potentials of Deliberation', https://gsdrc.org/document-library/development-as-institutional-change-the-pitfalls-of-monocropping-and-the-potentials-of-deliberation/, accessed 19 December 2023.

Evans, P. 2006. 'Building a 21st-century developmental state: Internal structure, state-society relations and organizational culture'. Presentation to Policy Coordination and Advisory Services, 2 August.

Godinho, C. and Hermanus, L. 2018. '(Re)conceptualising state capture: With a case study of South African power company – Eskom'. Conference paper prepared for the Public Affairs Research Institute's 'State Capture and Its Aftermath: Building Responsiveness Through State Reform', 22–24 October, Johannesburg.

Gumede, V. 2018. 'Presidencies and policy in post-apartheid South Africa'. *Politeia,* 36(1), 5, 13.

Hanauer, N. 2023. 'Bidenomics is real economics'. *Time Magazine*, 8 December, https://time.com/6343967/bidenomics-is-real-economics/, accessed 16 December 2023.

Hirsch, A. 2019. 'South Africa has a new presidential advisory unit. Will it improve policy?'. *The Conversation,* https://theconversation.com/south-africa-has-a-new-presidential-advisory-unit-will-it-improve-policy-117128, accessed 21 December 2023.

Leftwich, A. and Hogg, S. 2007. 'The case for leadership and the primacy of politics in building effective states, institutions and governance for sustainable growth and social development'. Leaders, Elites and Coalitions Research Program (LECRP), November.

Levin, R. 2018. 'Building a people-centred, people-driven public service and administration culture in Africa for youth empowerment and development'. *Africa Journal of Public Sector Development and Governance*, 1(1), https://journals.co.za/doi/epdf/10.10520/EJC-1724a70445. 34, accessed 20 March 2024.

Mandela, N. 1994. 'President's Budget Vote Opening Address'. 18 August, http://www.mandela.gov.za/mandela_speeches/1994/940818_budgetopen.htm, accessed 20 December 2023.

Mapungubwe Institute for Strategic Reflection (MISTRA). 2021. 'Towards Reconstruction and Recovery: Assessing COVID-19 interventions and their impact in South Africa – March to October 2020'. MISTRA Research Report.

Mkandawire, T. 2012. 'Building the African state in the age of globalisation:

The role of social compacts and lessons for South Africa'. Mapungubwe Annual Lecture.

Naidoo, J. 2003. Interview with Padraig O'Malley, 14 April, https://tpy. nelsonmandela.org/footnotes/208-jay-naidoo-interview-by-padraig-omalley-14-april-2003, accessed 20 December 2023.

National Planning Commission (NPC). 2012. *National Development Plan*, https://www.nationalplanningcommission.org.za/National_Development_ Plan, accessed 15 June 2025.

National Planning Commission (NPC). 2023. *10 Year Review of National Development Plan (2012-2022)*, https://www.nationalplanningcommission. org.za/assets/Documents/Ten%20Year%20Review%20of%20the%20 National%20Development%20Plan_26%20September%202023.pdf, accessed 27 December 2023.

Netshitenzhe, J. 2008. 'Briefing Memo to Deputy President on the main functions of the Policy Co-ordination and Advisory Services'.

Netshitenzhe, J. 2011. 'South Africa: The path towards a developmental state'. SANPAD Thematic Conference on Developmental State.

Netshitenzhe, J. 2018. 'Public policy after Apartheid: The fortunes of the Reconstruction and Development Programme'. Public Affairs Research Institute (PARI) Keynote Lecture.

Organisation for Economic Co-operation and Development (OECD). 2015. 'Delivering from the centre: Strengthening the role of the Centre of Government in driving priority strategies'. Draft Discussion Paper.

Planning Ministry in The Presidency. 2009. 'Draft Green Paper on National Strategic Planning'.

Policy Coordination and Advisory Services (PCAS). 2005. 'Strategic National Development Planning in South Korea, India, Brazil, Malaysia (with consideration the experience of Chile and Tunisia)'. Report for Policy Coordination and Advisory Services Unit of The Presidency. Prepared by Mike Muller.

Policy Coordination and Advisory Services (PCAS). 2006. 'Presentation of a summary of the Accelerated and Shared Growth Initiative – South Africa'.

Policy Coordination and Advisory Services (PCAS). 2007. 'Presentation on planning function in government'.

Policy Coordination and Advisory Services (PCAS). 2009. 'Memo on the National Planning Commission'. Unpublished text.

Policy Coordination and Advisory Services (PCAS) and Forum of South African Directors-General (FOSAD). 2005. 'Capacity and Organisation of the State (Author's recollection)'.

Presidential Review Commission (PRC). 1998. 'Developing a Culture of Good Governance: Report of the Presidential Review Commission on the Reform and Transformation of the Public Service in South Africa'.

Reconstruction and Development Programme (RDP) Office. 1994. 'White

Paper on Reconstruction and Development: Government's Strategy for Fundamental Transformation'. Government Gazette.

Sangweni, S. 2007. 'It does not matter what slant or take you have on the developmental state – at the end of the day a strong, coherent and astute public service is critical'. Speech delivered at the Developmental State Seminar on 19 October.

The Presidency. 2020. 'Annual Report 2019/2020'.

The Presidency. 2023. 'Annual Report 2022/23'.

The Presidency. 2024. 'Programmes: Operation Vulindlela', https://www.stateofthenation.gov.za/operation-vulindlela/summary-of-operation-vulindlela, accessed 20 March 2024.

United States of America (US) Department of Treasury Factsheet. 2023. 'How the Inflation Reduction Act's tax incentives are ensuring all Americans benefit from the growth of the Clean Energy Economy', https://home.treasury.gov/news/press-releases/jy1830#:~:text=The%20Inflation%20Reduction%20Act%20modifies,proportion%20of%20qualified%20apprentices%20from, accessed 22 December 2023.

United States of America (US) White House Factsheet. 2022. 'CHIPS and Science Act Will Lower Costs, Create Jobs, Strengthen Supply Chains, and Counter China', https://www.whitehouse.gov/briefing-room/statements-releases/2022/08/09/fact-sheet-chips-and-science-act-will-lower-costs-create-jobs-strengthen-supply-chains-and-counter-china/, accessed 15 December 2023.

Weiss, L. 2010. 'Transformative capacity and developmental states: Lessons for South Africa'. Public lecture prepared for Policy Analysis Unit/Centre for Africa's Social Progress, Human Sciences Research Council, Pretoria, 18 February.

FOUR

Missed development: South Africa's unrealised middle economy

Musa Nxele

INTRODUCTION

South Africa, renowned for its progressive Constitution – often humorously regarded as one of its most successful mid-1990s exports – poses a critical question: how well does the structure of the economy reflect the constitutional vision? This is not merely a legal or philosophical query; it goes to the heart of the country's social contract. The Constitution commits the state to build a society founded on dignity, freedom and equality (Liebenberg, 2010; Republic of South Africa, 1996). That commitment cannot be realised without an economy that enables people to generate value, exercise agency and access opportunity – preconditions for meaningful socioeconomic inclusion.

This chapter argues that South Africa has failed to meet that constitutional mandate. It begins, in the first of six sections, by clarifying what the Constitution demands of the economy; not simply redistribution, but an enabling structure for dignity and opportunity. In the next section, it examines the nature of the post-apartheid political settlement, showing how elite bargains and institutional compromises shaped the evolution of the state's economic role. The third section analyses how South Africa's economy has hollowed out, despite growth episodes and fiscal expansion — with a shift towards service sectors, stagnant productivity and an eroded industrial core.

The fourth section unpacks the rise of elite rentierism, which occurs when both public and private actors extract value without building productive capacity (Bhorat et al., 2017; Chipkin and Swilling, 2018). The fifth section outlines the 'missing middle' across key dimensions: firm structure, employment, financial access, skills development and state capability. The final section sets out the implications for state strategy. It argues that South Africa must move beyond surface-level transformation tools and refocus on building a middle-strong, opportunity-rich economy through ethical leadership, smart industrial policy and institution-building (Hausmann et al., 2008; Mazzucato, 2021).

The chapter concludes by returning to the Constitution – not as a symbolic backdrop, but as a living mandate. It proposes that rebuilding the middle is not only a matter of economic strategy but of national purpose and moral responsibility.

THE CONSTITUTION AND THE UNFINISHED PROJECT OF ECONOMIC TRANSFORMATION

The Constitution is more than a set of fundamental legal-political rules; it is the bedrock of the country's economic thought and orientation. It prioritises human dignity as a national objective, striving for a society in which every individual derives dignity by contributing, exchanging and building value (Fredman, 2008; Liebenberg, 2010).

Constitution-building was part of and an outcome of the broader political settlement between the powerful actors negotiating the transition, including big business, which had become entrenched economic players. As argued by Levy et al. (2021), South Africa's political settlement rested on five distinct deals. The first was between the (overwhelmingly White) economic elite and the country's new political leadership. It included commitments to the rule of law (notably the protection of private property) and economic transformation, notably through the Black Economic Empowerment (BEE) policy. The second was within the new political elite within the African National Congress (ANC), with its differing ideological orientations, levels of public spiritedness, and regional, ethnic and economic interests. The first non-elite promise was of upward mobility: a commitment to promote the interests of new, predominantly Black, middle-class insiders; a wider promise that education, skills, jobs and the end of racial discrimination would make upward mobility accessible to the broader population; and equal rights before the law. The third deal was a promise to reduce extreme poverty through a redirection of public resources and services. This middle bargain was most dependent on the first inter-elite deal: if transformation of the economic elite had been built on capability development and long-term productive investment, it may have delivered broader, durable opportunities.

Former Deputy Chief Justice Dikgang Moseneke argues that, despite the democratic dividends of the transition, the country has failed to dismantle structural inequality. He locates this failure in the political settlement that enabled democracy (Moseneke, 2018: 7). He argues that the Constitution's negotiators avoided confronting structural inequality, leaving socioeconomic rights reliant on state transfers rather than productive restructuring.

This absence of a social pact on a productive and inclusive economy was a far-reaching omission, given the deeply embedded inequality at the start of the transition. Moseneke (2018: 7) continues: 'I am simply observing the plain fact that an existing and insular economic arrangement survived the transfer of political power. This simply meant ownership of productive assets … and management prowess by and large remained unaltered.'

Although a stern defender of the Constitution, Moseneke is blunt about its limitations as a blueprint for structural change. Normative legal standards, he argues, do little to instruct the state on how to overcome structural economic inequality and associated low growth. 'The normative standards tell us little about how to achieve inclusive economic growth in a way that overcomes structural economic inequality and resultant low growth' (Moseneke, 2018: 8). In response to these questions, Moseneke emphasises that economic transformation must centre on productive capabilities: shifting contestation towards skills, entrepreneurship, innovation and continual learning. Similarly, former President Kgalema Motlanthe described transformation as rooted in the values of industry and effort – mobilising a broad cross-section of talent to drive development (Turok, 2014). Jordan (2014) echoes this idea, arguing that transformation should foster an emergent Black capitalist class independent of White capital, with a bias towards productive investment and growth. This, Jordan contends, would link the Black working class and the productive elite through shared interest in a dynamic, inclusive economy. But if this was the vision, what has actually happened in the 30 years since democracy?

ECONOMIC HOLLOWING AND THE EROSION OF OPPORTUNITY IN POST-APARTHEID SOUTH AFRICA

Despite extensive policy reform and institutional development since 1994, South Africa remains one of the most structurally unequal economies in the world. The foundations of exclusion – in asset ownership, skills, employment, spatial access and wealth – have not been overturned. In some cases, the disparities have deepened. The Gini coefficient, already extremely high in 1993 at 0.63, has remained persistently so, recorded at around 0.65 in 2019 – among the highest globally (World Bank, 2022). Wealth inequality is starker still: the top 10 per cent of earners control more than 85 per cent of the country's wealth (Chatterjee et al., 2022; Orthofer, 2016). Official unemployment rose from around 20 per cent in 1994 to 33 per cent in 2025 (Stats SA, 2025a), with young Black South Africans most affected. Meanwhile, labour market segmentation and educational inequalities continue to reproduce racial and class divisions. Although school enrolment has expanded, the quality of learning outcomes remains sharply stratified, and access to high-skill employment remains racially skewed (Spaull and Jansen, 2019). The economy has not served as a vehicle for mobility and opportunity at scale.

The founding democratic government faced formidable challenges, constrained by limited strategic choices. The economy, marked by structural concentration and inefficiency, exhibited minimal and unstable growth. Prolonged periods of upheaval had eroded investment levels, leading to a significant reduction in government revenue while expenditures surged. A paramount objective of government was to address the stark divisions within the nation. Initially, the ANC advanced a vision of economic transformation centred on redistribution and social justice. The Reconstruction and Development Programme (RDP), adopted as government policy in 1994, outlined an ambitious framework for meeting basic needs, building human capabilities, democratising the economy, and promoting employment-led growth (ANC, 1994; Marais, 2011). However, these ambitions were constrained by a profound recession, rising public debt, the stipulations of the political settlement and shifting global conditions following the end of the Cold War. Facing capital flight, investor anxiety and a collapsing fiscal position, the ANC gradually pivoted towards pro-business reforms. The introduction of GEAR (Growth, Employment and Redistribution) in 1996 formalised this shift, anchoring policy in macroeconomic stabilisation and trade liberalisation as preconditions for future growth (Padayachee and Van Niekerk, 2019; Terreblanche, 2002). This strategic reorientation prioritised fiscal discipline and market confidence, even as social inequalities persisted.

The journey towards economic rejuvenation seemed promising at the turn of the millennium, significantly propelled by the global demand for commodities. Yet the nation missed crucial opportunities for structural transformation essential for sustained prosperity. Figure 4.1 demonstrates that, instead of building in the middle, the economy shifted towards a service-based structure, with significant growth in finance, tourism and telecommunications accompanied by a hollowing out of both industrial manufacturing and skilling. This shift to services was not accompanied by the necessary expansion of productive investment and capability development for comprehensive structural transformation (Andreoni and Tregenna, 2021). The result was a consumption-led services boom, weakly embedded in the productive economy and poorly positioned to generate inclusive or resilient growth.

Figure 4.1: Sectoral composition of GDP in South Africa, 1990–2022

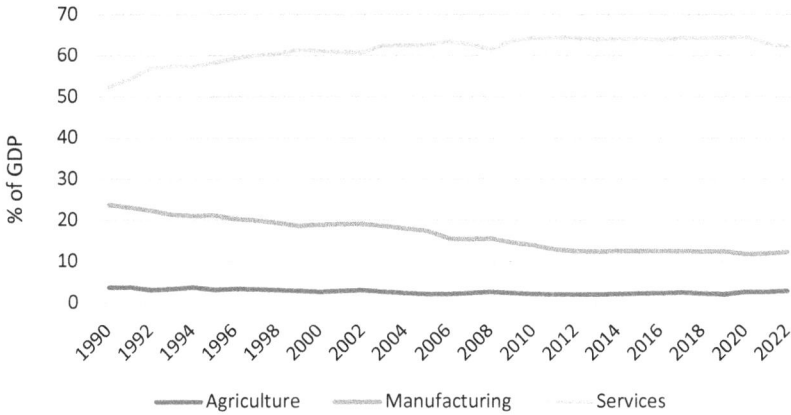

Source: World Bank, World Development Indicators (2024); value added by sector (% of GDP), indicators NV.AGR.TOTL.ZS, NV.MNF.TOTL.ZS, NV.SRV.TETC.ZS

South Africa's peak performance came in 2007, with GDP growth exceeding global averages and the country rising in international competitiveness rankings (Stats SA, 2017). Yet the momentum proved fleeting. Anticipated benefits from commodity rents failed to materialise in the form of reinvestment or diversification. The mining sector – long a foundation of employment and exports – faced declining returns, disrupted by prolonged uncertainty over nationalisation, policy reversals and inconsistent regulation (Andreoni et al., 2021). At the same time, South Africa recorded the lowest labour force participation rate among middle-income countries since 2008 (World Bank, 2021). This placed the country in a structurally weak position, with only a fraction of its population gainfully employed – a stark mismatch between demographic potential and economic absorption.

As the economy shifted towards skill-intensive services, the trade union landscape also changed. Traditionally rooted in the manufacturing and mining sectors, unions increasingly found their base in white-collar employment. This shift mirrored the changing composition of the workforce and the hollowing out of the productive base. Consolidation across unions allowed broader representation, but it left a critical gap in advocacy for the middle: for the development of artisanal skills, productive work and industrial upgrading. The result was a high-skilled, low-productivity economy – a configuration that pushed up the public and formal sector wage bill without strengthening productive foundations. South Africa's public wage-to-GDP ratio is now one of the highest among its peers, crowding out investment and undermining efforts to build middle-strong economic capacity (Bhorat et al., 2017; IMF, 2023).

Figure 4.2: South Africa's gross fixed-investment growth relative to the middle-income country group

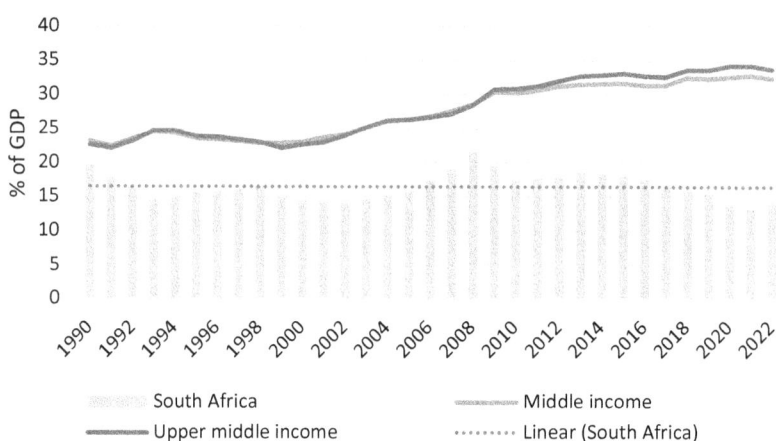

Source: World Bank, World Development Indicators (2025a); gross fixed capital formation (% of GDP), indicator NE.GDI.FTOT.ZS

Figure 4.2 shows that fixed investment has been persistently lower than that of comparator middle-income countries. Rather than reinvesting resource rents or growth dividends into future productivity, South Africa's capital formation stagnated. This has limited the expansion of infrastructure, productive firms and value-adding capabilities. Combined with the earlier erosion of state-owned enterprises (SOEs) and strategic sectors, the economy has been unable to generate new centres of dynamism.

The cumulative effect has been an economy progressively hollowed out – one marked by the erosion of manufacturing jobs, deepening socioeconomic divides and the disappearance of productive anchors. This hollowing has coincided with state-led infrastructure decline,

Figure 4.3: Unemployment and growth, 1991–2022

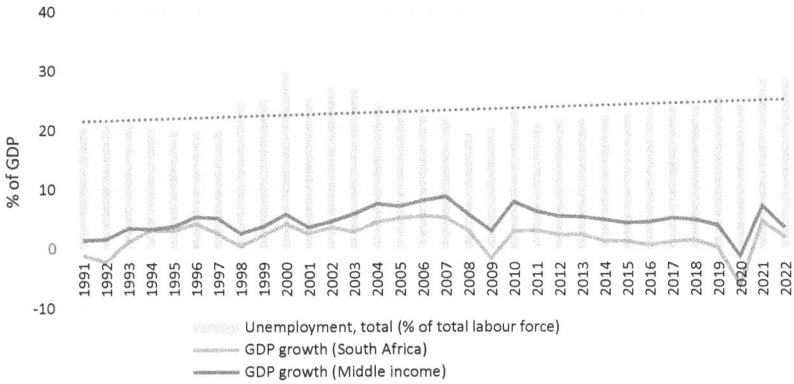

Source: World Bank, World Development Indicators (2025b); indicators: unemployment, total (% of total labour force), indicator SL.UEM.TOTL.ZS, and GDP growth (annual %), indicator NY.GDP.MKTP.KD.ZG

energy crises and escalating debt burdens on a narrow tax base. Despite rising government expenditure, public investment has failed to deliver a meaningful stimulus, highlighting the weakness of South Africa's fiscal multiplier (IMF, 2023; World Bank, 2022). The result is illustrated in Figure 4.3: persistently low growth and structurally high unemployment, despite successive macroeconomic shifts. Overall, the 30 years of democracy have delivered an economy characterised by high unemployment, low growth and missed opportunities to expand a middle-strong, opportunity-rich structure.

SOUTH AFRICA'S RENT SPACE AND THE ROLE OF THE STATE

The interplay between political elites and economic actors has shaped South Africa's growth trajectory. Pritchett's et al.'s (2018) 'deals space' framework highlights how negotiated access to rents and regulatory advantages determines economic outcomes. In South Africa, this dynamic has skewed towards rentiers (export-oriented firms reliant on state-granted privileges, e.g. mining) and powerbrokers (domestic firms dependent on regulation, e.g. finance, telecoms). These groups dominate the economy, while workhorses (competitive domestic firms) and magicians (innovative exporters) remain scarce (Table 4.1).

Table 4.1: The JSE rents space, 2018

	Regulatory rents	Market competition
Export-oriented	Rentiers 29 firms c.R531 billion	Magicians 28 firms c.R392 billion
Domestic market	Powerbrokers 153 firms c.R3.7 trillion	Workhorses 67 firms c.R2.0 trillion

Source: Typology adapted from Pritchett et al. (2018). JSE-listed company data from JSE. Computations by the author.

Notes: Regulatory rents: derived from some discretionary action of government (e.g. licensing, tax advantages, market exclusivity, and government tenders). Rentiers: natural resource firms exporting to world commodity markets. Powerbrokers: firms catering to the domestic sector, operating under government regulation and contracts. Workhorses: firms operating in competitive markets that serve the domestic economy. Magicians: firms operating in competitive markets and serving the export market.

The framework highlights the inherent risk of growth being driven primarily by rentiers and powerbrokers. In contexts dominated by a strong ruling party, political leaders may be able to enforce credible commitments – ensuring that deals are honoured and growth-oriented. However, under limited access conditions, growth accelerations often favour actors who rely on discretionary state support: rentiers, who benefit from resource-based or politically negotiated access to global markets, and powerbrokers, who dominate heavily regulated domestic sectors. Growth led by these groups can entrench elite capture and reinforce patronage networks. Rather than broadening opportunity, such patterns of growth may reproduce closed, exclusionary political settlements. In this way, rentier- and powerbroker-led growth can both fuel and frustrate transformation – by strengthening already dominant actors at the expense of those capable of generating new, competitive and inclusive economic value.

Regulatory rents are defined as those derived from discretionary actions of the state – including licensing (e.g. mining rights), firm-specific tax advantages, market exclusivity or even strategic inaction. Table 4.1 classifies all 371 JSE- and AltX-listed companies in 2018 into the rents space matrix, using their capital marketisation as a proxy for medium to large firms in South Africa. While this is a limited measure, the snapshot reveals a striking skewness towards rentiers and powerbrokers. Rentiers are primarily mining firms; powerbrokers include financial services, telecommunications, construction and real estate. Workhorses — such as food, beverages and retail – are fewer, while magicians are mostly technology and software firms. Although this skewness raises concerns about dependency on regulatory rents, it also shows that the state has had ample space to steer private capital into more productive, capability-building directions. Instead, sectors like finance have flourished in ways that have not supported industrial development or the emergence of middle-strong firms and markets. A broader classification using the Who Owns Whom (WOW) dataset – a comprehensive registry of both listed and unlisted firms – suggests a similar pattern: formal businesses are largely concentrated in domestic, regulation-dependent sectors, with only limited presence in capability-intensive export markets.

Continuing with the same proxy to assess the evolution of the rents space, Table 4.2 tracks the registration periods of listed firms by rents space category. The pattern shows a clear decline in the registration of productive, competitive firms. Many of the largest listed firms – particularly workhorses and magicians – were established before 1994. Since then, most new entries fall within the powerbroker quadrant, followed by rentiers. The competitive end of the rents space – workhorses and magicians – has remained the thinnest and most stagnant.

The challenge has been to secure a form of state leadership capable of charting a more transformative path. Transformation is essential to maintaining the political settlement, just as investment is essential to economic growth, and therefore to the sustainability of transformation itself. In scenarios where these imperatives reinforce one another, transformation becomes investment-inducing, while a more inclusive economy offers a stable and expanding market. Redressing South Africa's difficult political and economic legacy requires a productive economy that generates new, capability-based rents – through entrepreneurship, enterprise development and skills expansion.

The inter-elite bargain embedded in the political settlement

Table 4.2: The rents space periodised according to ANC presidential terms

Type of firm	Era	No. of firms registered (periodised)	Market value (Rm)
Powerbrokers	Pre-1994	77	2,282,500
	Nelson Mandela era	25	931,174
	Thabo Mbeki era	25	290,567
	Jacob Zuma era	25	134,902
Rentiers	Pre-1994	13	105,690
	Nelson Mandela era	3	154,032
	Thabo Mbeki era	11	239,997
	Jacob Zuma era	2	31,500
Workhorses	Pre-1994	47	1,907,812
	Nelson Mandela era	12	36,434
	Thabo Mbeki era	6	19,764
	Jacob Zuma era	2	1,394
Magicians	Pre-1994	19	351,454
	Nelson Mandela era	2	13,500
	Thabo Mbeki era	4	11,611
	Jacob Zuma era	3	15,058

Source: Compiled by author with data from the Johannesburg Stock Exchange (JSE)

– to integrate new elites into key economic sectors – has partly devolved into corrosive rent-seeking. This is in large part because the transformation project was not designed with embedded requirements for productivity or capability-building, beyond the use of 'set-asides'. As highlighted by Coleman (2017b), Levy et al. (2021), Nxele (2023) and others, the transformation agenda has become a contest over access to rents, generating new regulatory frameworks that facilitate access but do little to encourage productive cooperation or long-term investment. As a result, the racial-class transformation initiative has failed to align with sustained investment growth. The political economy is now marked by credible commitment problems: short-term corporate and political interests continue to crowd out long-term, mutually reinforcing strategies. This has entrenched a dysfunctional relationship between transformation and investment – fuelling low growth, persistent inequality and high unemployment (Nxele, 2022).

ELITE SYMBIOSIS AND INSTITUTIONAL DECLINE

In 2018, former Deputy Finance Minister Mcebisi Jonas described South Africa as a middle-income country trapped in a cycle of high inequality and low growth. He pointed to the rising share of asset income relative to wages, declining fixed-capital formation as firms increasingly invested abroad, a structural shift from low-skilled industries to high-skilled services, and the corrosive effects of state capture – all reinforcing a trajectory of exclusion and stagnation.

This pattern has not persisted in spite of post-apartheid elite bargains; it has been reinforced by them. Rather than catalysing structural transformation or building in the middle, those bargains have allowed economic power to consolidate at the top, contributing to the hollowing-out dynamic at the heart of the current crisis.

Adding to this analysis, Bell et al. (2018) argue that South Africa's challenge of class transformation has been inseparable from the failure to achieve structural transformation. The economy has remained overly reliant on capital-intensive and resource-based industries – in stark contrast to other middle-income countries that have reallocated resources into more dynamic, labour-intensive sectors. They contend that meaningful structural transformation requires sustained investment in productive capacity, including the expansion of Black entrepreneurship and the implementation of deliberate strategies for upgrading skills to broaden economic participation.

This situation highlights the significance of 'patient capital', or long-term investments from development finance institutions, as essential for aligning with industrial policy and enabling the entry of new productive firms. Such capital is pivotal to structural transformation, laying the foundation for a more inclusive and resilient economy (Nxele, 2023).

Predatory elites, big capital and institutional decay
In contrast to the need for patient, long-term investment, Coleman (2017a) identifies two elite groupings that have entrenched the economic and institutional decline in South Africa. The first is an emerging predatory elite aligned to political power, whose access to

state resources has driven widespread institutional erosion and rent extraction. The second is established big capital, which Coleman argues is more extractive than patriotic – reinforcing, rather than challenging, patterns of exclusion and underinvestment. Crucially, he contends that these elites operate in a symbiotic relationship. The most credible challenge to their dominance, he suggests, lies not within the market or the state, but in progressive civil society.

The emerging predatory elite, closely tied to state power, has focused on accumulating wealth through public resources. This group embeds itself within the ruling party, Cabinet and key state institutions, using access to procurement systems, state-owned enterprises and subnational governance to secure rents. Their methods range from semi-legal arrangements – such as creating businesses to exploit insider access – to outright illegal activity. The result is not merely opportunistic corruption, but a systematic threat to development, as documented in the Public Protector's 2016 report on state capture (Public Protector, 2016). That investigation showed how internal party competition became a contest for control over tenders and patronage networks, displacing developmental priorities with factional rent-seeking (Coleman, 2017a; Jonas, 2018; Public Protector, 2016).

In an interview with Ben Turok (Turok, 2014), former President Kgalema Motlanthe argued that some emerging Black business elites should not be seen as patriotic entrepreneurs, but rather as rent-seekers. These actors, he suggested, had been incorporated into an existing business class whose voice and interests remained shaped by historically dominant capital. Despite organising under platforms such as the Black Business Council, their main policy proposals focused on 'set-asides' – quotas for government tenders — reflecting, in Motlanthe's view, an inability to compete with the established corporate sector (Turok, 2014: 19). He further argued that, in practice, once such tenders are awarded, the work is often subcontracted back to the same established (White) corporates, with little to no transfer of skills or capabilities.

This dynamic reflects a broader failure by the state to create legitimate pathways for accumulation, fostering conditions for populist mobilisation around the idea that 'it is our turn to eat'. Coleman

(2017b) argues that the post-apartheid political settlement contained within it the seeds of both the predatory elite and parasitic big capital. By focusing on Black Economic Empowerment (BEE) as a vehicle for elite inclusion, the state neglected the wider South African population excluded from the formal economy. This raises serious questions about governance ethics and legitimacy, and points to the need for a transformation model that offers sustainable, productivity-based routes out of poverty. As Khan (2006; 2010) argues, anti-corruption efforts are only effective when tied to inclusive economic strategies that generate viable accumulation opportunities for new actors. The core challenge lies in the failure to restructure the economy – a failure that continues to block credible, legitimate pathways to development.

Coleman argues that established big business does not serve as a counterweight to the emerging predatory elite, but rather functions in a symbiotic relationship with it. Historically, under colonialism and apartheid, big business tolerated authoritarian state power in exchange for economic benefits – most notably, access to cheap Black labour. That pattern, Coleman suggests, persists through informal alliances between large corporations and the political elite. As such, big capital is not a force for restraint or transformation. He further challenges the position advanced by Chris Malikane – adviser to former Finance Minister Malusi Gigaba – that the rise of a tender-based Black capitalist class could form the basis of a 'patriotic bourgeoisie'. Malikane contended that, insofar as this class was confronting dominant White monopoly capital, it should be supported. He viewed public procurement as a more viable route to accumulation for Black business than BEE, and as a means to break dependency on established capital (Malikane, 2017: 5).

Coleman fundamentally diverges from Malikane's perspective. He draws a clear distinction between groups seeking to build productive capacity and those primarily engaged in rent-seeking – exploiting public resources for personal gain. The predatory elite, he argues, is not interested in building productive capability and is often associated with fronting. The deeper issue, Coleman insists, is not who owns capital, but how it behaves: 'The issue is to transform the character and behaviour of capital, not merely to change its colour' (Coleman,

2017b). Even Malikane concedes that neither elite faction offers a programme capable of advancing the interests of the Black and African majority, which remains overwhelmingly working-class.

Popular discontent, Coleman argues, has been actively channelled into populist ideologies that legitimise the predatory accumulation strategies of elite factions. Aligica and Tarko (2014) provide a theoretical framing of this dynamic as crony capitalism – an alternative rent-seeking order sustained by the unfalsifiable ideology of populism. Levy et al. (2021) empirically trace the rise of populism as a strategy to secure elite rents during South Africa's state capture period in the 2010s, when the rhetoric of empowerment masked deepening economic exclusion.

The main mechanism for accessing public funds has been corruption and the systematic weakening of institutions. Meanwhile, established big capital – which relied on parasitic accumulation under colonialism and apartheid – has continued those practices in new forms. Coleman (2017b) describes this as the financialisation of capital: extracting value from the domestic economy while diverting surplus abroad through dual listings, large offshore cash reserves, tax havens and repatriated profits. These behaviours have persisted even as big business has deracialised its senior workforce and co-opted a new Black elite – creating an illusion of change while avoiding substantive redistribution or productive reinvestment. As a result, elite interests on both sides have continued to extract value without building a new middle of productive firms, skills or institutional capability.

These dynamics have contributed directly to South Africa's hollowing out. Fixed investment has declined steadily, while de-industrialisation has deepened. The industrial sector – encompassing mining, construction, utilities and manufacturing – fell from over 40 per cent of GDP in 1980 to just under 30 per cent by 2008, with services comprising more than half the economy (Coleman, 2017b). This trend reflects the failure of industrial policy to counteract the structural shift away from production and capability development. The rise of elite accumulation without transformation has reinforced exclusion and stalled the emergence of a middle-strong, opportunity-rich economy.

FINDING AND FILLING THE MISSING MIDDLE

The state emerges as a crucial actor in driving the transformation envisioned by the Constitution. Businesses, by contrast, do not naturally undertake structural transformation due to their inherent incentives, market logics and the broader economic environment (Mazzucato, 2021; Paus, 2017). The drive to maximise shareholder returns often means that short-term profits are prioritised over long-term societal benefits – particularly when transformation requires upfront investment, lacks immediate returns or disrupts existing models. Faced with financial, regulatory and reputational risks, firms tend to respond to existing market demand rather than reshape markets or invest in uncertain innovation. Nor do they consistently internalise the social and environmental impacts of production, unless compelled by regulation or public pressure. These limits highlight the central role of the state in directing investment and shaping structural change.

Transforming the economy is an ethical imperative with profound implications for the state. It is not merely about improving outcomes, but about affirming the inherent dignity of every person – a principle embedded in the Constitution's vision of a just society. The state is guided by a set of ethical principles that include autonomy, beneficence, non-maleficence, justice, honesty, integrity, respect for persons and responsibility. These form a comprehensive normative framework for state action. On this basis, the state must provide diverse opportunities in education, employment and entrepreneurship; create conditions that support individual growth and societal welfare; and ensure fair and transparent allocation of opportunity. Ethical governance also requires inclusive implementation, a prioritisation of dignity and a commitment to sustainability. This framework mandates that the state move beyond redistribution alone to actively foster opportunity, capability and fairness as the basis for collective progress.

The strength lies in the middle

The fundamental flaw in strategies for achieving dynamism and an opportunity-rich economy has been the dearth of a focus on the middle. As a middle-income country, South Africa encounters the 'middle-income trap', a challenge common among its peers, where it can no longer compete in labour-intensive goods due to relatively high wages, nor in high-value activities due to low productivity (Gill and Kharas, 2015; Kharas and Kohli, 2011; Paus, 2017). This is exacerbated by the nation's multi-dimensional inequality, creating a divided economy with minimal upward mobility opportunities for those at the bottom who remain trapped in poverty. While the country debates the phenomenon of the 'missing middle' in relation to funding tertiary education fees (Garrod and Wildschut, 2021), the country suffers from a literal missing middle in the economy.

Moreover, South Africa's focus on formalism over practicality has stifled the informal economy's potential to inject dynamism and foster self-employment. Despite accounting for nearly 30 per cent of total employment and supporting millions of livelihoods, the informal sector contributes only about 6 per cent to GDP – reflecting structural constraints and policy neglect (Fourie, 2018; Rogan and Skinner, 2018). There's a critical distinction between the appearance of good institutions (mirroring colonial models) and their effectiveness (being fit for purpose to expand opportunity, agency, belonging and dignity). This dichotomy contributes to the country's division into 'first world' and 'third world' segments, not just spatially but in the lived realities of its people compared to the policies intended to govern them. True democracy should empower the people, and the reconstruction of South Africa ought to prioritise policies that empower rather than manage or accommodate through welfare programmes disconnected from sustainable empowerment. This realignment could address the literal and metaphorical 'missing middle' in the economy and society, overcoming one of the world's most opportunity-poor environments.

Narrow pathways: Why South Africa fails to build capability and mobility

The scarcity of the middle in South Africa spans various dimensions – as shown in Table 4.3 – including industrial structure, human capital, income and age participation. Structurally, South Africa's industrial sector is polarised between big businesses and small enterprises, with a noticeable void in the middle. This imbalance has resulted in an economy dominated by primary industries and a large tertiary sector, while the secondary sector – key for mass employment and economic diversification – remains small and is eroding (Andreoni and Tregenna, 2021). Furthermore, South Africa's historical overemphasis on formalism has privileged only those with means (Nxele, 2023), stifling the growth of a vibrant informal economy – which in many other middle-income countries functions as a middle range and a stepping stone to formal sector participation.

Table 4.3: South Africa's missing economic middle across key dimensions

Dimension	Bottom	Middle (missing)	Top
Population age	Children	Youth (high unemployment)	'Post-youth' and seniors
Income	Poor	'Middle class' (statistically poor)	Upper to rich
Enterprises	Informal and small	Medium enterprises (scarce)	Big business
Sector	Primary	Secondary (eroding)	Tertiary
Education and training	Basic education	TVETs and SETAs (overlooked)	Tertiary education
Financial services and access	Informal lenders	Medium financial services (?)	World class financial services

Source: Compiled by Author

Note: Stylised distribution across Bottom, Middle and Top categories. This illustrates persistent gaps in the middle section across sectors, age cohorts, institutions and income levels.

In the human capital development sphere, the democratic government rightly focused on reversing apartheid's educational exclusion. Yet, in doing so, it prioritised basic education (which still struggles with quality) and tertiary education (often equated with mass progress and higher income), while largely overlooking the middle segment – skills training colleges. This neglect has rendered Technical and Vocational Education and Training (TVET) colleges and Sector Education and Training Authorities (SETAs) secondary in the post-apartheid policy agenda, despite their pivotal role in workforce development.

While tertiary education is essential, the focus on university access has crowded out the vocational routes that are critical for broadening access to work. Skills colleges and SETAs – potential drivers of mobility and inclusion – have faltered due to weak collaboration between businesses, the state and educational institutions. Seen by businesses as a tax (in the case of SETAs) and by government as an outsourced responsibility, these institutions have missed a vital opportunity to expand practical skills and labour market readiness. The South African Qualifications Authority (SAQA) (2014) highlights this imbalance, noting that only 1.12 per cent of the working-age population holds a relevant N qualification – a stark indicator of the vocational sector's marginalisation.

This situation has led to the exclusion of the middle age range – particularly youth – from productive participation and ownership of the economy. Lacking viable paths to skill acquisition, a dynamic industrial 'middle', or a bridge between the informal and formal sectors, many young South Africans remain locked out. The most visible manifestation is South Africa's alarmingly high *official* youth unemployment rate: over 62 per cent of people aged 15–34 are unemployed, and over 40 per cent of those 25–34 (Stats SA, 2025b). The transition from education to employment is not a ladder, but a cliff – severing economic opportunity at a life-stage critical for mobility and social contribution. This rupture sets the stage for long-term exclusion and inter-generational poverty. The way the state treats individuals aged 15 to 45 – its productive core – is crucial to building an economy that is capable, inclusive and resilient.

This missing middle is also stark in income distribution. South Africa's statistical 'middle class' remains precarious and often poor. Visagie and Posel (2013) show that a large share of this group falls below meaningful thresholds for stability or wealth-building, due to high income volatility, low savings and exposure to shocks. The absence of a substantial and secure middle class undermines both social cohesion and aggregate demand – limiting domestic consumption, savings and investment, all of which are essential for inclusive growth.

The same hollowing is visible in the financial services sector. South Africa's financial system is dominated by large corporate institutions and a fragmented, informal lending ecosystem. The middle space – comprising mid-tier financial institutions that could support small businesses, working-class households and informal entrepreneurs – remains thin and underdeveloped. This gap distorts financial inclusion: while the elite have access to world-class financial services and the poor rely on informal lenders, those in between are often underserved. The absence of appropriate financial tools for the middle reinforces structural inequality, restricts entrepreneurial growth and impedes economic agency.

Opportunity-building deals: The ethical path to transformation

South Africa's economic vitality depends on bridging the void in its middle sector. This is not only an economic imperative, but a moral one. The task is to construct an economy that serves the whole population through structural transformation rooted in fairness, stewardship and shared prosperity.

A thriving, dynamic economy would also bridge the stark spatial divides between rural and urban areas, large cities and small towns. This kind of integration would catalyse new markets, enhance mobility and spread opportunity – reinforcing the social fabric rather than fragmenting it.

Table 4.4: Narrow paths of upward mobility in South Africa's opportunity system

	Capability building	**Capability eroding**
Productive	Skilled or educated entrepreneurs	Some tenderpreneurs
Unproductive	Does not exist	Most tenderpreneurs* Cadre deployment**

*Notes: *including large consulting firms; **significant share thereof*

In South Africa, the available pathways for moving up have been narrow and highly selective. As Table 4.4 shows, individuals who succeed typically do so via a handful of routes:
- Education and/or skills (productive, capability building)
- Tenderpreneurs (predatory, capability eroding)
- Public sector cadre deployment (based on political loyalty, potentially unproductive)

- Entrepreneurs (few, but productive)
- Crime (whether organised or ad hoc, sophisticated or basic, capability eroding).

Only a small subset of these genuinely builds capability and contributes to social value. Too often, upward mobility has relied on predatory or opportunistic routes – eroding public trust and deepening inequality. Tenderpreneurship and political deployment, in particular, have become dominant but damaging avenues: they offer access, but not productivity; enrichment, but not inclusion.

The real challenge is to expand the number and quality of capability-building pathways. Education, skills, technical entrepreneurship and productive investment must become the core avenues for advancement – not the exception. This is what it means to build a middle-strong economy; one that can generate employment, absorb human capital, and build institutional depth from the centre out.

Table 4.5: Business and the state: ethical routes and capabilities

	Limited access accumulation	Open access capacity and capability building
Socially embedded business (corporate strategy)	Credible deals (pockets of high investment and employment)	Society-wide, durable win-win Expanding economy, capability, capacity
Enclave accumulation (or extraction)	Enclave, unstable - state capture - downward economy - erosion of capability and capacity	Win-lose, stifled social policy Policy undercut by fronting and co-optation

Source: Author

Table 4.5 shows how the relationship between the state and business determines the direction of the economy. When the state is weak and access is limited, accumulation becomes elite-driven, extractive and unstable – as in the case of state capture and fronting. But where the state acts with strategic capability, and business is socially embedded, deals can become instruments of transformation. Credible, inclusive agreements – between public and private actors – are key to expanding the economy's opportunity base.

Echoing Jonas (2018), this requires a new consensus for inclusive growth, based on:

- a capable state that leads restructuring and decentralises economic power;
- a dynamic private sector committed to long-term investment;
- a strong civil society; and
- political leadership that prioritises national prosperity over elite gain.

While civil society has often risen to the challenge, both business and political elites have fallen short. South Africa's private sector has rarely taken on the long-term, inclusive investment role seen in successful industrialisers – and state institutions have not compelled it to.

This is why adopting a new framework of opportunity-building deals is critical. Such deals are not transactional, elite compacts – but structural partnerships aimed at capability, employment and inclusion. They are ethical in both aim and process: focused on dignity, sustainability and the expansion of real freedom.

Structural transformation and racial class transformation must be reconnected. Instead of empowerment defined only by ownership, we need empowerment through capability: skills, innovation, firm formation and productive employment (Pityana, 2015; Turok, 2014). Under visionary leadership, deals can become vehicles for serious capital investment, institutional renewal and human development (Nxele, 2023; Theobald, 2014).

As South Africa enters its fourth decade of democracy, the challenge is to move beyond stalled transformation narratives and invest in the middle – not only as a space, but as a strategy. Building the middle is the key to ending hollowing, restoring social mobility and realising the Constitution's vision of a dignified, inclusive and just society.

REFERENCES

African National Congress (ANC). 1994. *The Reconstruction and Development Programme: A Policy Framework*, https://www.sahistory.org.za/archive/reconstruction-and-development-programme-policy-framework, accessed 10 June 2025.

Aligica, P.D. and Tarko, V. 2014. 'Crony capitalism: Rent seeking, institutions and ideology'. *Kyklos*, 67(2), 156–176, https://doi.org/10.1111/kykl.12048

Andreoni, A., Mondliwa, P., Roberts, S. and Tregenna, F. (eds). 2021. *Structural Transformation in South Africa*. Oxford: Oxford University Press.

Andreoni, A. and Tregenna, F. 2021. 'The middle-income trap and premature deindustrialization in South Africa', in Andreoni, A., Mondliwa, P., Roberts, S. and Tregenna, F. (eds), *Structural Transformation in South Africa*. Oxford: Oxford University Press.

Bell, J., Goga, S., Mondliwa, P. and Roberts, S. 2018. 'Structural Transformation in South Africa: Moving Towards a Smart, Open Economy for All'. CCRED Working Paper No. 9/2018, Centre for Competition, Regulation and Economic Development (CCRED), https://ssrn.com/abstract=3269732, accessed 6 April 2025.

Bhorat, H., Buthelezi, M., Chipkin, I., Duma, S., Mondi, L., Peter, C., Qobo, M., Swilling, M. and Toxopeüs, M. 2017. *Betrayal of the Promise: How South Africa is Being Stolen*. State Capacity Research Project, https://pari.org.za/wp-content/uploads/2017/05/Betrayal-of-the-Promise-25052017.pdf, accessed 6 April 2025.

Chatterjee, A., Czajka, L. and Gethin, A. 2022. 'Wealth inequality in South Africa, 1993–2017'. *The World Bank Economic Review*, 36(1), 19–36, https://doi.org/10.1093/wber/lhab012, accessed 6 April 2025.

Chipkin, I. and Swilling, M. 2018. *Shadow State: The Politics of State Capture*. Johannesburg: Wits University Press.

Coleman, N. 2017a. 'Do we have to choose between a predatory elite and white monopoly capital?' (Part One). *Daily Maverick*, 21 April, https://www.dailymaverick.co.za/opinionista/2017-04-21-do-we-have-to-choose-between-a-predatory-elite-and-white-monopoly-capital-part-one/, accessed 6 April 2025.

Coleman, N. 2017b. 'On the side of the Angels or the Predators? Big business and its role in the current crisis' (Part Two). *Daily Maverick*, 26 April, https://www.dailymaverick.co.za/opinionista/2017-04-26-on-the-side-of-the-angels-or-the-predators-big-business-and-its-role-in-the-current-crisis-part-two/, accessed 6 April 2025.

Edigheji, O. 2010. *Constructing a Democratic Developmental State in South Africa: Potentials and Challenges*. Cape Town: HSRC Press.

Fourie, F. (ed.) 2018. *The South African Informal Sector: Creating Jobs, Reducing Poverty*. Cape Town: HSRC Press.

Fredman, S. 2008. *Human Rights Transformed: Positive Rights and Positive Duties*. Oxford: Oxford University Press.

Garrod, N. and Wildschut, A. 2021. 'How large is the missing middle and what would it cost to fund?'. *Development Southern Africa*, 38(3), 484–491. DOI: https://doi.org/10.1080/0376835X.2020.1796594

Gill, I.S. and Kharas, H. 2015. 'The middle-income trap turns ten' (English). Policy Research Working Paper No. WPS 7403, World Bank Group, http://documents.worldbank.org/curated/en/291521468179640202/The-middle-income-trap-turns-ten, accessed 6 April 2025.

Hausmann, R., Rodrik, D. and Velasco, A. 2008. 'Growth diagnostics', in Serra, N. and Stiglitz, J. (eds), *The Washington Consensus Reconsidered: Towards a New Global Governance*. Oxford: Oxford University Press.

Hirsch, A., Levy, B. and Nxele, M. 2021. Politics and Economic Policymaking in South Africa since 1994, in Oqubay, A., Tregenna, F. and Valodia, L. (eds), *The Oxford Handbook of the South African Economy*. Oxford University Press, pp. 66–90, https://doi.org/10.1093/oxfordhb/9780192894199.013.4

International Monetary Fund (IMF). 2023. *South Africa: 2023 Article IV Consultation-Press Release; Staff Report; and Statement by the Executive Director for South Africa*. International Monetary Fund, https://www.imf.org/en/Publications/CR/Issues/2023/06/06/South-Africa-2023-Article-IV-Consultation-Press-Release-Staff-Report-and-Statement-by-the-534271, accessed 6 April 2025.

Jonas, M. 2018. 'Locating state capture within a broader theory of change'. *South African Journal of Social Science and Economic Policy*, 70, 12–16.

Jordan, P. 2014. 'Towards a more inclusive capitalism'. *ANC Today*, 14(23), 13–16, https://www.anc1912.org.za/anctoday/towards-a-more-inclusive-capitalism, accessed 6 April 2025.

Khan, M.H. 2006. 'Governance and anti-corruption reforms in developing countries: Policies, evidence and ways forward'. G-24 Discussion Paper Series, No. 42, United Nations Conference on Trade and Development, https://unctad.org/system/files/official-document/gdsmdpbg2420064_en.pdf, accessed 6 April 2025.

Khan, M.H. 2010. 'Political settlements and the governance of growth-enhancing institutions'. Research Paper Series on Governance for Growth, School of Oriental and African Studies (SOAS), University of London, https://eprints.soas.ac.uk/9968/, accessed 10 June 2025.

Kharas, H. and Kohli, H. 2011. 'What is the middle income trap, why do countries fall into it, and how can it be avoided?' *Global Journal of Emerging Market Economies*, 3(3), 281–289, DOI: 10.1177/097491011100300302

Levy, B., Hirsch, A. and Woolard, I. 2014. *South Africa's Evolving Political Settlement*. ESID Working Paper No. 51. Manchester: Effective States and Inclusive Development Research Centre (ESID), University of Manchester, https://www.effective-states.org/wp-content/uploads/working_papers/final-pdfs/esid_wp_51_levy_hirsch_woolard.pdf, accessed 6 April 2025.

Levy, B., Hirsch, A., Naidoo, V. and Nxele, M. 2021. *South Africa: When Strong Institutions and Massive Inequalities Collide*. Carnegie Endowment for International Peace, https://carnegieendowment.org/2021/03/18/south-africa-when-strong-institutions-and-massive-inequalities-collide-pub-84063, accessed 6 April 2025.

Liebenberg, S. 2010. *Socio-Economic Rights: Adjudication under a*

Transformative Constitution. Cape Town: Juta.

Malikane, C. 2017. 'Concerning the current situation'. 7 April, https://drive.google.com/file/d/0B8WLisEA3WalT2lnbjFrM1M2cW8/view?resourcekey=0-eZS1Db6ucEiMexQnwjq5aA, accessed 25 February 2024.

Marais, H. 2011. *South Africa Pushed to the Limit: The Political Economy of Change*. London: Zed Books.

Mazzucato, M. 2021. *Mission Economy: A Moonshot Guide to Changing Capitalism*. London: Allen Lane.

Mazzucato, M., Qobo, M. and Kattel, R. 2021. *Building state capacities and dynamic capabilities to drive social and economic development: The case of South Africa*. UCL Institute for Innovation and Public Purpose, Working Paper 2021-09, https://www.ucl.ac.uk/bartlett/public-purpose/wp2021-09, accessed 6 April 2025.

Moseneke, D. 2018. 'Was it all in vain? – South Africa'. *South African Journal of Social and Economic Policy*, 69, 6–9.

Nxele, M. 2022. 'Crony capitalist deals and investment in South Africa's platinum belt: A case study of Anglo American Platinum's scramble for mining rights, 1995–2019'. *Review of African Political Economy*, 49(173), 20–41, https://doi.org/10.1080/03056244.2022.2098009, accessed 6 April 2025.

Nxele, M. 2023. 'Not about rules, but about good deals: The political economy of securing inclusive capital investment and transformation in South African mining'. PhD thesis, University of Cape Town, https://open.uct.ac.za/items/70566ad5-a5f3-4ad0-893e-e8fe73c2218b, accessed 6 April 2025.

Orthofer, A. 2016. 'Wealth inequality in South Africa: Evidence from survey and tax data'. REDI3x3 Working Paper 15, https://www.redi3x3.org/sites/default/files/Orthofer%202016%20REDI3x3%20Working%20Paper%2015%20-%20Wealth%20inequality.pdf, accessed 6 April 2025.

Padayachee, V. and Van Niekerk, R. 2019. *Shadow of Liberation: Contestation and Compromise in the Economic and Social Policy of the African National Congress, 1943–1996*. Johannesburg: Wits University Press.

Paus, E. 2017. 'Escaping the middle-income trap: Innovate or perish'. Asian Development Bank, https://www.adb.org/publications/escaping-middle-income-trap-innovate-or-perish, accessed 6 April 2024.

Pityana, S. 2015. 'BEE in review: More than box-ticking required'. *South African Journal of Social and Economic Policy*, 58, 16–17.

Pritchett, L., Sen, K. and Werker, E. 2018. *Deals and Development: The Political Dynamics of Growth Episodes*. Oxford: Oxford University Press.

Public Protector. 2016. *State of Capture*. Report No. 6 of 2016/17, https://www.saflii.org/images/329756472-State-of-Capture.pdf, accessed 6 April 2025.

Republic of South Africa. 1996. The Constitution of the Republic of South Africa, https://www.gov.za/documents/constitution-republic-south-africa-1996, accessed 6 April 2025.

Rodrik, D. 2008. 'Understanding South Africa's economic puzzles'. *Economics of Transition*, 16(4), 769–797.

Rogan, M. and Skinner, C. 2018. 'The size and structure of the South African informal sector 2008–2014: A labour-force analysis', in Fourie, F. (ed.) *The South African Informal Sector: Creating Jobs, Reducing Poverty*. Cape Town: HSRC Press.

South African Qualifications Authority (SAQA). 2014. *Towards assessment of the impact of the South African National Qualifications Framework (NQF): Data and information highlights from the 2014 study*, https://www.saqa.org.za/wp-content/uploads/2023/02/Impact-study-report-final.pdf, accessed 6 April 2024.

Spaull, N. and Jansen, J.D. (eds). 2019. *South African Schooling: The Enigma of Inequality – A Study of the Present Situation and Future Possibilities*. Cham: Springer.

Statistics South Africa (Stats SA). 2017. *The ups and downs of gross domestic product*, https://www.statssa.gov.za/?p=9181, accessed 6 April 2025.

Statistics South Africa (Stats SA). 2025a. *Quarterly Labour Force Survey Q1:2025*, https://www.statssa.gov.za/publications/P0211/Media%20Release%20QLFS%20Q1%202025.pdf, accessed 13 May 2025.

Statistics South Africa (Stats SA). 2025b. 'South Africa's Youth in the Labour Market: A Decade in Review', https://www.statssa.gov.za/?p=18398, accessed 16 May 2025.

Terreblanche, S. 2002. *A History of Inequality in South Africa, 1652–2002*. Pietermaritzburg: University of Natal Press.

Theobald, S. 2014. 'The good and the bad in empowerment deals: A shareholder's perspective'. *South African Journal of Social and Economic Policy*, 53, 22–24.

Turok, B. 2014. 'The role of emerging black business: An interview with Kgalema Motlanthe'. *South African Journal of Social and Economic Policy*, 53, 16–20.

Visagie, J. and Posel, D. 2013. 'A reconsideration of what and who is middle class in South Africa'. *Development Southern Africa*, 30(2), 149–167, https://doi.org/10.1080/0376835X.2013.797224

World Bank. 2021. *Benchmarking Labour Legislation and Enforcement in South Africa*. Washington, D.C.: World Bank, https://documents1.worldbank.org/curated/en/099715108182237686/pdf/P172175088141700108c54071df2c525986.pdf, accessed 6 April 2025.

World Bank. 2022. *Overcoming Poverty and Inequality in South Africa: An Assessment of Drivers, Constraints and Opportunities*. Washington, D.C.: World Bank.

World Bank. 2024. 'World Development Indicators', Washington, D.C.: The World Bank, https://databank.worldbank.org/source/world-development-indicators, accessed 9 April 2025.

World Bank. 2025a. 'World Development Indicators', Indicator: 'Gross fixed capital formation (% of GDP)' (NE.GDI.FTOT.ZS), Washington, D.C.: The World Bank, https://data.worldbank.org/indicator/NE.GDI.FTOT.ZS?locations=ZA, accessed 9 April 2025.

World Bank. 2025b. 'World Development Indicators', Indicators: 'Unemployment, total (% of total labour force)' and 'GDP growth (annual %)', Washington, D.C.: The World Bank, https://databank.worldbank.org/source/world-development-indicators, accessed 9 April 2025.

Section Two

*Critical Themes in the Evolution
of the Post-Apartheid State*

FIVE

The tax state and state capability in South Africa

MICHAEL SACHS

INTRODUCTION

How should we think about the sources of state capacity and its relationship with society? There are three perspectives that help frame these questions. One approach is to consider the capacity of state agencies to execute policy choices effectively. In this view, the state is capable of formulating and executing policy to regulate or transform society. The challenges include recruiting and deploying skilled personnel, building ethical and effective public services, and developing robust bureaucratic capacity.

Another approach is to ask how society holds the state to account. According to this perspective, a state with sufficient institutional and fiscal capacity is able to translate a democratic mandate into effective executive action, with office bearers held accountable for their use of common resources. The challenges concern the strengths of political institutions and civil society actors, and their abilities to ensure that state agencies adhere to collective choices or constitutional imperatives.

A third perspective centres on the interactions between the state and society. Social and political institutions of society evolve in a dialectic with state regulation. Strengthening state capacity often depends on the 'coproduction' of public goods, as government administrators build synergies with private or social actors (Ostrom, 1996). To build and sustain capacity, state agencies must be autonomous but also embedded within progressive social forces (Evans, 1995). From this perspective, the question of state capacity revolves around how the state interacts and collaborates, especially with elite actors in civil society.

The objective of this chapter is to use the lens of taxation to shed light on these questions. The focus is on the building and evolution of the state's fiscal and institutional capacity, treating taxation as foundational to broader state development. In the development of the modern state, the ability to levy taxes is foundational to a broader set of state functions, catalysing the creation of a Weberian bureaucracy (Besley and Persson, 2009; 2013; 2014). The 'power to tax' is rooted in the social contract or implicit 'fiscal constitution' which underpins modern states (Brennan and Buchanan, 1980). The connection between taxation and representation is believed to have given rise to modern democratic institutions and the rule of law (North and Weingast, 1989). Today, taxation plays a central role in sustaining the power of states and shaping their ties to society (Brautigam, 2008).

The exercise of tax powers has also shaped market structures and the private economy. Early modern states curated and directed capital accumulation, playing a central role in sparking the transition to a new, capitalist economic order (Bonney, 1995). A critical marker of this transition was a shift from a 'domain state', in which royal households' personal asset holdings generated revenue for the government, to a 'tax state', which 'bleeds' capitalist accumulation through taxation and debt (Musgrave, 1992; Schumpeter, 1918). Through this process, the modern capitalist state became a 'poor state', structurally dependent on capital accumulation to sustain its income (Goldscheid, 1925; Przeworski and Wallerstein, 1988).

This chapter describes South Africa's contemporary 'tax state' and considers three explanations for its highly developed institutional and fiscal capacity. First, South Africa has a 'world-class' national tax authority, more effective than other developing nations, which – until it was assaulted by the state capture project – stood out as a centre of excellence (Smulders, 2014). Second, effective tax collection reflects the structure of the underlying economic base and its associated corporate and market institutions. South Africa's economic peculiarities map strongly onto its tax performance. Third, the state's capacity to tax developed in the context of colonialism, racial domination and the extraction of mineral rents. I treat these three approaches not as competing explanations but as interconnected aspects of the same phenomenon. Each sheds light on the character of South Africa's tax institutions, and together they form an important foundation for understanding the future of the tax system.

The next section gives an overview of the salient features of South Africa's national tax system. I recount the story of the South African Revenue Service (SARS) in the democratic era, from its zenith in the early 2000s to its nadir in the period of state capture and its subsequent rehabilitation. The subsequent section considers the relationship between taxation and economic structure, looking at the foundation of taxation in the structure of industries, labour markets and finance. The chapter then turns to the political economy of tax institutions, focusing on the explanations offered by Lieberman (2003). The conclusion asks what the analysis might tell us about the future of tax capacity in democratic South Africa.

FEATURES OF SOUTH AFRICA'S TAX SYSTEM

As new nations emerged from colonial domination in the 1960s, Kaldor asked about the prospects for state development in his paper 'Will underdeveloped countries learn to tax?' (Kaldor, 1962). Half a century later, despite decades of development effort and capacity building, Besley and Persson (2014) gave a negative answer to Kaldor's question in their paper 'Why do developing countries tax so little?'. The power to tax, by most accounts, remains deficient in the developing world. As Brautingam (2008: 3) explains:

Few developing countries have yet succeeded in creating tax systems with high levels of both capacity and consent. Their tax systems are often regressive, distortionary and lack legitimacy. Tax administration is usually weakened and characterised by extensive evasion, corruption and coercion. In many cases, overall tax levels are low, and large sectors of the informal sector escape the tax net entirely.

South Africa is an exception to this characterisation. Despite concerns about 'state failure' or institutional erosion in other government domains, the South African state's capacity to collect tax revenue remains among the highest in the developing world. Figure 5.1, illustrating the relationship between income levels and tax collection as a share of GDP, shows that higher-income countries tend to collect more tax because rising national income is associated with a broadening of the tax base. This relationship between GDP per capita and taxation is well known, as illustrated by the regression line in Figure 5.1.

On the other hand, there is considerable variation between countries, indicated by the vertical distance from the line. For instance, although Sweden's income per capita is about the same as that of the USA, Sweden taxes nearly 35 per cent of its GDP, compared to about 20 per cent in the USA. South Africa is also a high-tax country relative to its national income, sitting far above the regression line. Its tax-to-GDP ratio is on par with several more developed countries, including the United Kingdom.[1] No countries at South Africa's development level have a higher collection rate, although several Eastern European and two Caribbean nations come close. Brazil is also close to South Africa, but all other developing-country members of the G20 – China, India, Indonesia, Mexico and Türkiye – collect significantly lower shares of their GDP in taxes.

From the perspective of state capacity, it is not only the amount of revenue collected but the composition of taxes that matters. 'The relationship between taxes and development across countries is driven by a stark variation in tax *structure* across countries' (Kleven et al.,

---

1   Note that the tax-to-GDP ratio in Figure 5.1 excludes social security contributions, an issue which is discussed below.

Figure 5.1 GDP per capita and tax-to-GDP ratio

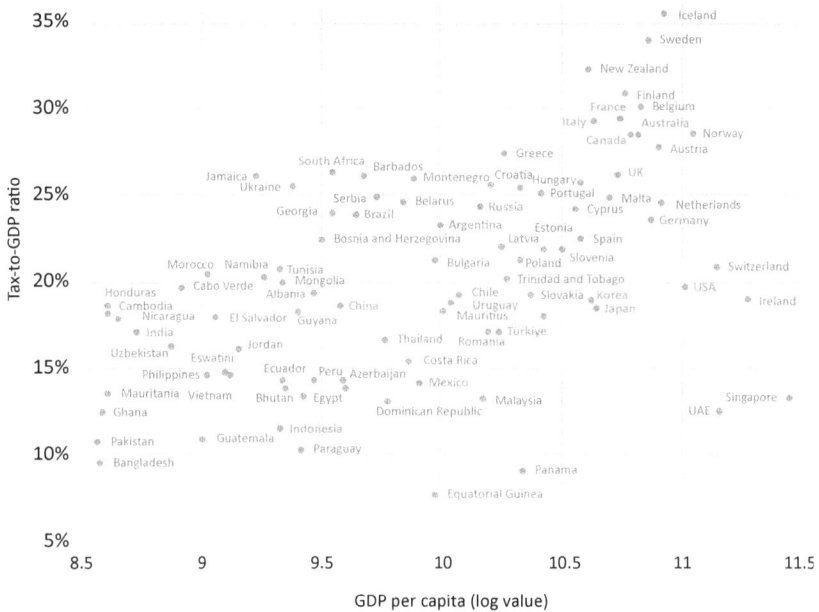

Source: UNU-WIDER Government Revenue Dataset (GRD), 2023 version; IMF World Economic Outlook, April 2024; author's calculations

Notes: Shows general government tax revenue, excluding social security contributions. GDP per capita reflects purchasing power parity in international dollars. Data has been averaged between 2015 and 2019. G20 countries are highlighted in bold.

2016: 223 – emphasis in original). Taxes on income are particularly important, and scholars often use personal income tax (PIT) revenue as a proxy for fiscal capacity (Andersson, 2023). This is because direct taxes like PIT are far more complex to collect since they require a valuation of taxpayer incomes. Many developing countries rely on trade taxes such as tariffs, which are easy to verify and enforce at borders. Direct income taxes are more difficult to collect and concentrate revenue extraction on high-income groups. This progressive structure contrasts strongly with the regressive incidence of tariffs and other consumption taxes, such as VAT. Therefore, income tax collection implies not only effective tax administration, but also suggests that problems between the state and high-income groups have largely been surmounted (Lieberman, 2003).

Figure 5.2 shows the level and composition of tax collection across a range of high- and middle-income countries ranked by % of GDP collected in direct income taxes on people and corporations (i.e. the sum of PIT and corporate income tax, CIT). South Africa is in the ranks of the most industrialised economies, making it unique among developing countries. South Africa collects about 5 per cent of its GDP in corporate income tax, on par with Australia; only Norway and Malaysia collect more.

Figure 5.2: Taxes and social contributions by tax type in selected countries

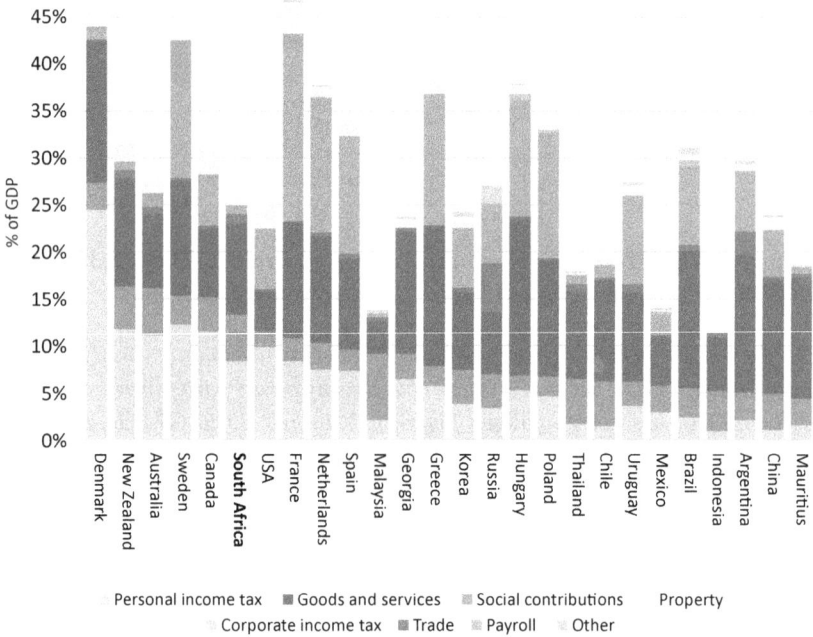

Source: UNU-WIDER Government Revenue Dataset (2023)

South Africa strongly focuses on income taxes, which amount to about half of its tax collection, while consumption taxes on goods and services (such as VAT, fuel levies and excise) account for the other half. This balance between tax instruments is absent in most developing countries, which rely primarily on consumption taxes. In Brazil, taxes on consumption account for almost 65 per cent of tax revenue, compared to less than a quarter from income taxes.

This picture is reinforced by comparative studies of fiscal incidence in developing countries, which find that South Africa's tax structure makes a larger contribution to reducing income inequality than in other middle- and low-income countries (Goldman et al., 2021; Inchauste and Lustig, 2017). The same studies find that payroll taxes and social security contributions are a less progressive part of the South African system, while consumption taxes — such as VAT, fuel levies and excise — are neutral and distributed proportionally across the population (Goldman et al., 2021; Inchauste and Lustig, 2017).

Figure 5.3 illustrates South Africa's tax-to-GDP ratio increasing substantially in the final 30 years of White rule, from about 12 per cent in 1960 to more than 20 per cent by 1990. Until about 1975, most of this increase is explained by rising income taxes, whereas taxes on consumption (and production) increase substantially thereafter. The overall tax burden continued to increase in the democratic era, albeit at a slower pace, with the rise balanced across direct and indirect taxation.

Greater detail of the evolution of the composition of taxes over the last 30 years is shown in Figure 5.4. Here, I classified taxes levied by national, provincial and local governments along the lines suggested by Piketty and others (Piketty, 2014; Saez and Zucman, 2019). Broad-based taxes on consumption increased towards 10 per cent of GDP over this period. Sales taxes were replaced by VAT in the early 1990s, and while VAT collection remains comparatively low, VAT has proven buoyant, with fuel levies, import tariffs and excise all raising significant additional revenue from indirect taxes. Direct income taxes now account for about 15% of GDP. There has been a large and sustained increase in revenue from personal income tax, which has been offset by the dramatic fall in corporate income tax collections following the 2008–2009 global financial crisis. Taxes on capital income and wealth have continued to stagnate – probably reflecting lower profitability after the unwinding of the global commodity super-cycle and the subsequent stagnation in per capita income growth since.

Figure 5.3: Tax-to-GDP ratio in South Africa, 1960–2023

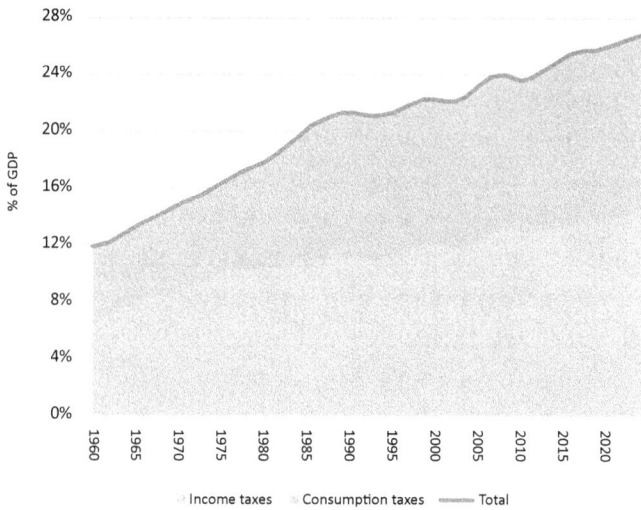

Source: SARB Quarterly Bulletin, author's calculations

Note: Quarterly values are smoothed using an HP filter. Income taxes are 'Current taxes on income, wealth, etc' as defined in the National Accounts. Consumption taxes are 'taxes on production and imports, as defined in the National Accounts.

Figure 5.4: Tax types in South South Africa, 2000–2023

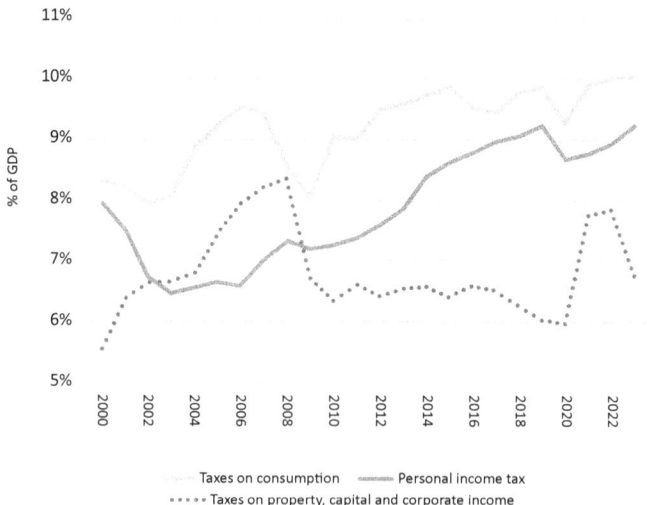

Source: Author's calculations based on National Treasury (Budget Review Table 2) and SARB Government Financial Statistics data

Note: Taxes on consumption include VAT, fuel levies, excise, import duties, provincial taxes and stamp duties. Taxes on property, capital and corporate income include corporate income tax, local government taxes, mining royalties, estate duty, securities taxes and transfer duty.

Another important feature of the South African tax system is its high degree of centralisation. The Constitution assigns most broad and buoyant tax instruments (including income tax, value-added tax, sales taxes and customs duties) to the national sphere of government. While property taxes are assigned to local government, provinces may only impose taxes and levies outside these constitutional assignments, limiting the provincial revenue base. National collections account for over 70 per cent of taxes, amounting to 24 per cent of GDP in 2019 (Figure 5.5). These revenues fund provincial governments, which themselves collect only 0.3 per cent of GDP in tax revenue. Local government property rates are the only significant tax revenue that are not collected at the centre, amounting to about 1.2 per cent of GDP. Local government operations are overwhelmingly funded by user charges and transfers from the centre. A large share of user charges finances the purchase of bulk water and electricity, and most of this revenue funds the national utilities that supply these goods.

Figure 5.6 shows the high concentration of market income and taxation in the most affluent decile of the population.[2]

In summary, South Africa is an unusually well-developed tax state in the developing world. Its tax-to-GDP ratio is an outlier among countries with a similar level of national income, and the composition of government revenue is also more consistent with high-income countries. Taxation has increased markedly over the last 60 years relative to national income, with income taxes accounting for an increasing share. Most of the increase in the tax burden took place before the transition to democracy, but the tax burden has continued to increase over the past 30 years. South Africa's tax system is also very centralised. The extreme inequality of income and consumption opportunities means that tax collection is strongly concentrated on the

---

2 Figure 5.6 should be taken as broadly indicative rather than precise as it is drawn from a paper analysing household income and expenditure surveys and does not estimate corporate income tax.

Figure 5.5: Revenue sources by sphere of government, 2019

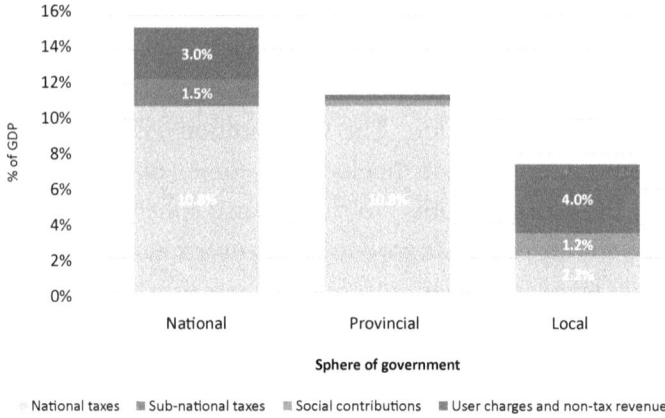

Source: Author's calculations based on SARB Government Financial Statistics data and National Treasury Division of Revenue tables

Figure 5.6: Share of taxes paid by income groups

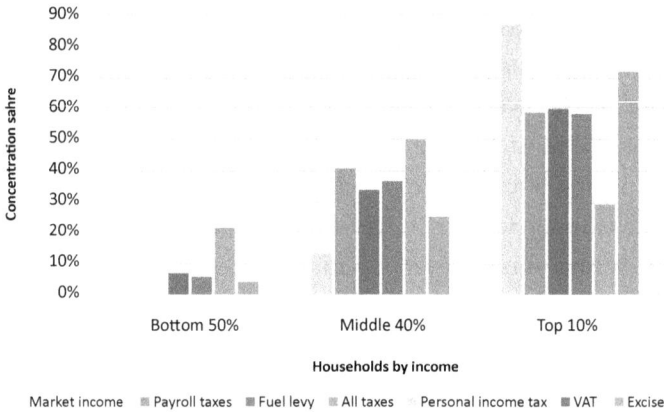

Source: Author's calculations based on Inchauste et al. (2015) Appendix Table A3.4

Note: Estimates are based on the 2010/11 Income and Expenditure Survey and show the percentage share of taxes collected from the population ordered by market income as well as the distribution of market income.

most affluent 10 per cent of households, who contribute about 70 per cent of government tax revenue.

BUILDING (AND REBUILDING)
A WORLD-CLASS TAX AUTHORITY

Tax collection is a pervasive and potentially contradictory relationship between the state and citizens, and tax administration is at the centre of this relationship. About 6 million citizens and 1 million firms file tax returns each year, and about 500,000 vendors are registered for VAT (SARS, 2023). The quality of relations between taxpayers and the revenue administration is a vital pillar of the social compact between citizens, businesses and the state.

Many believe that South Africa's strong tax capacity is explained by the high service standards of the South African Revenue Service (SARS), due to professional staff, ethical leadership and effective administrative systems. The discussion about tax capabilities has closely tracked the agency's fortunes from its outstanding performance in the first two decades of democracy, through its disruption during the state capture period, to its revitalisation under new leadership in the past five years. Changes in the quality of leadership and the structure of the organisation are assumed to drive shifts in the rate of revenue collection.

Statistics from the OECD and the World Bank confirm the 'world-class' status of South Africa's tax authority. The World Bank's (now defunct) 'Doing Business Index' – claiming to measure the administrative and compliance burdens of paying taxes for a medium-sized firm – scores South Africa far above most developing countries and on par with the OECD average (World Bank, 2020).

Table 5.1 shows various measures of tax capacity drawn from the OECD's tax administration reports based on surveys filed by tax administrators. For every 100 rand it collects, SARS uses about 64 cents to fund its own operations, below the average for even advanced economies. This could be seen as indicative of SARS' efficient use of resources. On the other hand, it might be interpreted as reflecting a below-average budget.

Two factors make SARS a global outlier. First, South Africa has a highly centralised tax system, collecting 86.7 per cent of all government revenue compared with the global average of about 61 per cent. The second factor is the amount of personal income tax that is paid after withholding taxes through pay-as-you-earn (PAYE) systems. On both these scores, SARS has among the highest scores in the world. In the developing world, there are two other outliers to rival SARS' performance on these scores – Kenya and Peru – but both agencies collect about 15 per cent of GDP, against the 25 per cent collected by SARS. The combination of these factors makes SARS truly exceptional in the developing world.

On many other measures, however, the high level of capability we can see at SARS is widely distributed. For instance, all tax returns are filed electronically in Brazil, Argentina, Kenya and Peru. Indeed, tax agencies in high-income countries routinely score lower for digital filing than those in the developing world. SARS' only obvious poor score is for the number of timeous payments, which might indicate deficiencies in administration or, alternately, a reluctance to pay for whatever reason on the part of the taxpaying public.

The roots of South Africa's modern tax administration go back to the First World War, but SARS was created as an independent agency only after the transition to democracy in the 1990s. Before this, revenue administration was a line function within the Department of Finance. The 1996 Katz Commission ensured that tax administration reforms and steps to broaden the tax base, especially for corporations, occurred through a cooperative and consultative process in which tax experts and industry advisors were given considerable scope to shape the implementation of reforms (Lieberman, 2003). The commission proposed the modernisation of tax administration based on the principles of autonomy and parliamentary oversight (Davis, 2022).

The combination of ethical and visionary SARS leadership, an effective policy reform programme and strong political support led to dramatic improvements in efficiency and effectiveness and generally improved compliance (Lieberman, 2003; Smith, 2003). The number of companies registered as active taxpayers was a particularly important feature of the programme and underpinned a broader increase in rates

Table 5.1: Tax administration indicators

	South Africa	Brazil	Emerging and developing economies	Emerging Europe	High-income economies	Average
Recurrent cost of collection (% of collection)	0.64	0.52	0.76	0.89	0.73	0.77
Revenue collected by tax administration (% of all govt revenue)	86.7	59.4	61.6	65.8	58.3	61.1
Percent of PIT withheld and subsequently paid	97.3	81.4	75.7	84.2	81.6	80.4
Percent of returns that are e-filed						
PIT	99.0	100.0	96.3	74.9	84.0	84.8
CIT	99.8	100.0	97.1	97.3	90.0	93.8
VAT	91.3	100.0	96.4	96.7	94.6	95.6
Percent of payments made electronically						
By number	89.0	72.6	75.2	85.5	90.6	84.9
By value	91.8	85.1	83.1	87.8	91.9	88.2
Percent of returns filed on time						
PIT	62.0	101.7	75.6	87.3	92.8	86.4
CIT	20.7	-	69.6	78.1	84.8	78.0
VAT	50.9	-	75.8	89.3	87.6	85.1
Percent of payments received on time						
PIT	42.2	90.3	70.6	81.9	88.3	81.4
CIT	33.7	91.3	76.7	86.9	89.7	85.0
VAT	96.7	95.9	87.2	89.3	96.8	91.8
Total tax administration FTEs	9,644	12,718	58,305	8,876	21,793	29,377
% staff working on HQ functions	8	6	17	14	15	15
% staff with bachelor's degree	27	81	58	32	37	42
% staff with master's or higher	4	1	12	40	21	23
% staff with 10 years or more service	74	89	62	71	65	66
% staff with 20 years or more service	32	56	38	43	42	41

Source: OECD Tax Administration data (2023): Data tables

Note: Scores are the average of reported data for the years 2018–2021.

of tax collection (Davis, 2022; Smith, 2003). The pressure in the early years of democracy to raise tax rates was offset by the broadening of the tax base as the new agency acted to simplify and extend its systems of tax administration.

Hausman and Zikhali (2016) attribute these impressive results to the autonomy given to SARS. As a 'public entity', SARS was exempted from civil service rules and pay scales, and management had the 'freedom to hire, pay, and reorganise' (Hausman and Zikhali, 2016: 56). SARS' creation brought direct tax collection (personal and corporate) into the same structure as customs and excise for the first time. Reforms to functions that dealt directly with taxpayers were critical for improving outcomes and broadening the tax base. These front-office functions were separated and decentralised to improve responsiveness to taxpayers, enabling SARS to centralise and streamline the back-office work of tax administration and organisational support. Under apartheid, SARS management had been, like all of central government, a Whites-only enterprise. Autonomy allowed the new SARS leadership to promote Black talent to the top of the organisation while also retaining previous skilled personnel and strengthening middle management. Rather than disrupting tax administration at the critical juncture of a new South Africa, the transformation was connected to a spirit of cohesion and strengthened camaraderie across the whole organisation (Hausman and Zikhali, 2016).

However, as the second Zuma administration took office in 2014, plans were afoot to replace the SARS leadership and undertake a root-and-branch restructuring of the agency. SARS' enforcement operations had increasingly encountered 'politically exposed persons' linked to the governing party and often with business ties to illicit and criminal economies. The agency became the target of the 'state capture' project (see Chipkin and Swilling, 2018) initiated by the president, who had 'unfettered' powers to appoint the SARS Commissioner (Davis, 2022: 180). He appointed Tom Moyane, who lacked knowledge or experience in tax administration and who 'arrived at SARS without any integrity' (Davis, 2022: 182). Moyane's actions disrupted, degraded and defenestrated the agency (Davis, 2022; Nugent, 2018).

The result, according to a SARS internal analysis in 2021, was a loss of morale and the resignation of critical staff. Moyane's restructuring was particularly disruptive for enforcement operations such as the large business unit, compliance data analysis, and litigation. Apart from these technical disruptions, the broader political context led to a collapse of public trust and confidence, which some claim had a negative impact on voluntary tax compliance (Davis, 2022: 186).

Many scholars (including Davis, 2022; Hausman and Zikhali, 2016; Nugent, 2018; Smith, 2003) reached strong conclusions about the impact of administrative changes on rates of tax collection. Some claim Moyane's reforms led directly to a fall in tax collections. In my view, these claims are not well supported because they fail to sufficiently account for the economic drivers of tax collection during the same period.

The few studies of the 'compliance gap' in South Africa that have been done with respect to PIT and VAT (Dare et al., 2019; Ueda and Thackray, 2015) do not find evidence of an unusually large gap. However, these studies do not track changes in compliance over time, which is, in principle, difficult. Short-term changes in tax collection rates always reflect a complex combination of factors, including tax policy, tax administration and macroeconomic shifts in the nominal value of the tax base (Sachs, 2021: 18–21). As far as I know, there are no reliable measures of changes in the rate of tax compliance in South Africa, and the evidence that Moyane's tenure coincided with a drop in compliance remains largely anecdotal.

ECONOMIC INSTITUTIONS, TAX POTENTIAL AND DEVELOPMENT

In the heyday of development economics, Kaldor (1963) proposed that a country's tax potential be determined by four factors: administrative competence, real income per head, the level of inequality and the structure of employment and production. Having reviewed the first two, I now turn to the economic base for high levels of taxation in South Africa.

Theory suggests that as markets deepen and urbanisation proceeds, corporate structures become more sophisticated and financial deepening extends the reach of banks. This means that there are increased opportunities for the state to collect taxes at a reasonably low cost and without disrupting production. Besley and Persson (2013) provide a framework for understanding the relationship between taxation and the development of economic systems, in which there is a dynamic interaction between economic, political and fiscal development. I do not attempt a full consideration of these dynamics in the South African context but merely report on how contemporary economic structures tend to correlate with high levels of taxation.

Table 5.2 provides a few comparative indicators of these structures. The first and most obvious feature of South Africa's economy is its extreme levels of inequality, whether measured by income or property ownership. The concentration of national income in the top 10 per cent most affluent households is far larger than even Brazil's. As Kaldor (1963: 10) suggests:

> It is the highest income groups that offer the highest potential yield to the tax collector … As between two countries with the same real income per head, the accustomed standard of living of the bulk of the population will evidently be lower in the country in which a larger share of total incomes accrues to a minority of wealthy individuals; and it will be this county that has the higher taxation potential.

From a purely administrative view, the concentration of income tends to reduce the number of individual taxpayers. Kaldor associated inequality with concentrated ownership of property, which, if immovable like residential or industrial assets, is easy to tax and difficult for the owner to evade taxes. Since Kaldor's articulation, the financialisation of wealth must have significantly attenuated this factor, as global capital can exploit its own mobility. But his insight remains valid, at least for concentrated ownership of land, buildings and mineral resources, which remain immovable.

Moreover, very high levels of market concentration in South Africa mean the bulk of South Africa's private income flows through large corporations; official statistics estimate that very large businesses account for 62 per cent of formal sector turnover (StatsSA, 2019). For most of the 20th century, South Africa was an economy dominated by large overlapping corporate structures, where state-enforced control of Black labour existed together with extensive social regulation of White labour and where capital and workers were channelled and concentrated into this structure.

Table 5.2: Selected indicators of economic structures

	South Africa	Brazil	High	Upper middle	Lower middle	Low	Source
Gini coefficient	63.2	52.7	32.3	40.1	38.3	39.3	(a)
Top 10% share of income	50.5	41.4	24.8	31.2	30.0	30.5	(a)
Informal output (% of official GDP)*	27.3	38.8	19.9	35.8	37.8	38.6	(b)
Self-employment (% of total employment)	15.0	32.4	13.6	31.2	54.9	75.4	(b)
Employment outside the formal sector (% of total employment)	31.3	37.0	26.9	42.9	71.4	82.6	(b)
5-bank asset concentration	99.0	80.5	84.4	78.6	73.1	87.0	(a)
Received wages into an account (% of wage recipients, age 15+)	77.8	67.5	87.0	64.4	34.0	30.5	(c)
Bank branches per 100,000 adults	49.0	19.4	72.1	18.9	11.1	2.6	(d)

Sources:
(a) Author's calculations based on World Bank, World Development Indicators, average value between 2009 and 2023
(b) Author's calculation based on Elgin et al. (2021). Values are the average between 2014 and 2019
(c) Author's calculation based on Global Findex database, World Bank, https://www.worldbank.org/en/publication/globalfindex/Data#sec1
(d) Author's calculation based on Global Financial Development database, https://www.worldbank.org/en/publication/gfdr/data/global-financial-development-database
*Multiple indicators multiple causes model-based (MIMIC) estimates (see Elgin et al., 2021 for details)

As well as concentrating income generation, big firms and monopolistic industries concentrate employees and capital. Friedman (2003: 5) points out that firms 'are forced to establish sets of rules to govern their internal workings and to engage with government agencies in a variety of rule-bound interactions'. In large firms, relations between managers, shareholders and employees are embedded, which creates self-reinforcing incentives for tax compliance and the reporting of accurate information. In other words, it is difficult to sustain collusion that is required to evade tax payments, and as a consequence, Kleven et al. (2016: 255) propose that it is a stylised fact that the 'tax take across countries is positively related to the share of employees working in large firms'.

Effective and disciplined industrial bureaucracies also act as a third party on behalf of the tax authority, withholding taxes at the source of payment (Kleven et al., 2016). Historically, this capacity to withhold taxes and reconcile with the tax authority at the end of the year, as is the case in South Africa with pay-as-you-earn, has reduced the cost of enforcement and been an administrative prerequisite for the creation of high tax systems (Besley and Persson, 2013). A withholding tax such as PAYE allows the state to extract cash directly at the point that production is transformed into money and reconciles high taxation with the demands of capital accumulation.

This does not mean evasion and avoidance do not exist but rather that, for most of us, the question of compliance does not even arise: it is a condition of employment. Large firms are also critical to the implementation of an effective VAT system because they routinely collect and submit records of their transactions (Pomeranz, 2015) but there is surprisingly little evidence. This chapter analyses the role of third-party information for VAT enforcement through two randomised experiments among over 400,000 Chilean firms. Announcing additional monitoring has less impact on transactions that are subject to a paper trail, indicating the paper trail's preventive deterrence effect. This leads to strong enforcement spillovers up the VAT chain. These findings confirm that when taking evasion into account, significant differences emerge between otherwise equivalent forms of taxation. This chapter trail deters evaders and ensures that suppliers are enmeshed in a network of compliance where even a small firm's transactions can be independently verified by the counterparts with which it trades. VAT also, by virtue of its structure, creates a powerful pecuniary incentive for compliance, as each firm along the production chain must approach the tax authority independently for rebates that offset its tax bill.

The flip side of an economy dominated by large corporations is a relatively small informal sector, and South Africa is an outlier here as well (see Table 5.2). Almost by definition, an informal sector is difficult to tax (Besley and Persson, 2014). Informality narrows the tax base and creates opportunities for taxpayers to shift into cash-based transactions, thus raising the sensitivity of the tax base to tax rates. On the other hand, widespread taxation on production creates powerful incentives against informal businesses. For instance, the formal receipting required by VAT generates a cascade of formality along the production chain (Pomeranz, 2015).

This should remind us that, in South Africa, informality was actively suppressed in systems that sought to destroy African peasant agriculture, force people out of subsistence into a monetary economy, control every detail of the labour supply, and create spatially segregated labour reserves. These policies were at the heart of creating the unequal society which endures today, a society dominated by large firms and formalised transactions in which high levels of taxation can be sustained.

It is through taxation, then, that the state enforces legality and imposes formality as a basic requirement of raising tax revenue. In part, perhaps, the rise of the tax state in South Africa has contributed to the construction of an economic structure in which the informal sector is conspicuously small. But where the formal sector dominates production, we can expect to find a higher tax-to-GDP ratio, other things being equal.

THE POLITICAL PATH TO THE SOUTH AFRICAN TAX STATE

Economic factors can help explain an economy's tax potential, but sustained investment in fiscal capacities is required to realise this potential, and the decision to make such investments is a political choice (Besley and Persson, 2013). The opportunity to tax is not automatically transformed into high taxation; it is contingent on the political will to create a national tax system.

A national tax system requires an architecture of a tax policy, a set of clearly identified tax bases encoded into law and other durable institutions, and an administrative unit capable of extracting revenues at low cost. Each of these functions depends on the consent of privileged groups, because the effective and economical extraction of private resources depends, in part, on their cooperation. A high level of taxation depends on quasi-voluntary compliance; the state must establish some compact with taxpayers to build cooperative relationships which allow for the construction of effective tax institutions (Levi, 2008). This bargain needs to be policed and enforced, but once the social relationship between the state and taxpayers becomes adversarial rather than cooperative, the political conditions for a sustainable tax state are undermined. South Africa's experience vividly illustrates this connection between political settlement and fiscal development.

In 1910, Britain imposed a political settlement on South Africa, having succeeded in dividing and defeating all local resistance, Black and White, over the previous 30 years. The Union of South Africa was to be a unitary state in which White citizens would provide for each other – including the poor among them – and preside over Black subjects (Lieberman, 2003: 4)

Over the course of the 20th century, the South African state successfully mobilised the rich, corporations and a growing affluent middle class behind the common purpose of White supremacy to build the institutions of high taxation. The particular idiom of domination changed with the form of the state. When the infant Union government introduced income tax during the First World War, it relied on corporate support for the British King and Empire. Although the income taxes were new and untested, taxpayer cooperation was strong because 'white South Africans – particularly upper-income English speakers – viewed themselves as constituting a virtually European country with a sense of common, collective obligation, and the war efforts were interpreted as a collective responsibility' (Lieberman, 2003: 124–125).

A new excess profits tax was initiated in 1917, and by the end of the war, income tax collections had surpassed customs duties on which the pre-Union states had largely depended. The wartime government invested significant effort to expand the cadre of revenue bureaucrats but also ensured that 'attorneys and accountants' were mobilised behind the standardisation of the system.

The same racist and jingoist sentiments were mobilised during the Second World War to support new, special war taxes on firms and individuals, and tax rates were raised in each successive war budget, with the top marginal rate reaching 72.4 per cent. Tax collections trebled over the period. Lieberman quotes a Chamber of Mines official explaining that gold mining companies were 'prepared to bear as cheerfully as any other section of the community their full share of the demands that have to be made by the Government to enable this country to maintain a maximum contribution to the common cause' (Lieberman, 2003: 142). After the war, high levels of taxation were not reduced, and were used to finance the extension of social welfare programmes to Whites and to build infrastructure and other public assets.

In the early 1960s, major new investments in tax administration took place. The Department of Inland Revenue created a data processing section, installing a computer system in 1962 to calculate and issue assessments, record payments and maintain controls (Lieberman, 2003: 161) The following year, the pay-as-you-earn (PAYE) system was introduced, making firms responsible for withholding taxes on employee salaries and paying the money directly to the state. In the wake of the Sharpeville massacre, top marginal rates on personnel were increased from 50 per cent in 1960 to 60 per cent in 1972. Company taxes were hiked from 30 per cent in 1960 to 40 per cent in 1967 and to 50 per cent in 1987, at the height of the popular uprising against apartheid. Figure 5.3 illustrates the rapid increase in taxation of wealth and income as a share of GDP from the 1960s through to the 1980s.

The 1994 settlement created a new cooperative, integrating force that mobilised inter-class solidarity and a coherent elite programme, at least in its early years. The 1996 Constitution entrenched, reformed and extended the state's fiscal capacities. Provinces were created, but the tax system remained highly centralised, and as we have seen, the tax system was modernised, simplified and expanded again. As the tax base was broadened, upper-income groups – households, firms and organisations – were mobilised behind a project of inclusive nationalism which sought to reinscribe the culture of tax compliance. The Minister of Finance and the state more generally made strenuous efforts to establish a social contract with more affluent groups and build transparency around spending programmes. Strong public campaigns sought to sustain taxpayer morality.

It must be noted, however, that moral sentiments were not the only factors that sustained compliance. In return for more extensive taxation of current incomes, firms and large pools of capital gained access to global markets, allowing for a historic relocation of wealth out of South Africa (Ndikumana et al., 2020). The introduction of VAT in 1992 broadened the tax base, ensuring that the affluent and corporations would share the burden with the consuming middle and working classes. As the global commodity supercycle raised national income and asset prices after the turn of the 21st century, government moved to lower rates of income taxation. With these sweeteners, upper-income groups supported and cooperated fully with the democratic state's development of the tax base, just as they had done previously for the British Empire and the apartheid state.

CONCLUSION: PROSPECTS FOR THE TAX STATE IN SOUTH AFRICA

The process of state formation over the course of the 20th century gave rise to a deep and diverse set of institutions supporting taxation in South Africa. Once investments are made in a national tax system, it is widely assumed that they are difficult to reverse. Tax institutions are 'path dependent'. Enforcing high levels of taxation requires an institutional and administrative transition to modern taxes (Kleven et al., 2016), but once the transition has been made, the system becomes entrenched and self-sustaining. Levels of taxation have remained high, and the subsequent decades appear to have borne out this optimism. But is this conclusion premature? The rosy picture of South Africa's development has shifted, particularly in the wake of state capture.

The administrative capacity and capabilities concentrated in SARS are critical to sustaining the high-tax system. The existence of a professional and effective revenue collection authority reflects both a deep institutional capacity and the capability to apply it effectively, and is critical to ensuring that the tax system remains sustainable even in the face of future challenges. Tax administration operates at the core of a pervasive and potentially conflictual relationship between the state and upper-income groups. At the very least, habitual widespread tax compliance must be constantly maintained by audits and enforcement actions; without the attention that the tax administration devotes to this, it becomes vulnerable to erosion, and capabilities can degenerate.

If SARS is to sustain its credibility, it must again strengthen and secure its autonomy from the executive. At times, tax policy choices (made by politicians) may infuriate affluent and corporate elites, but this is a political problem in which tax collectors should not be implicated. Autonomy means protection from the political elite that, in South Africa, has strong roots in the cash economy and which is becoming increasingly interwoven with the illicit economy (see GIATOC, 2022). This will clearly be a tension in the system, especially where the majority are excluded from formal sector employment and capital accumulation, but have access to the tools of representative democracy and executive authority.

A second frontier of improved tax administration is international cooperation. South Africa has been subject to sustained capital flight, which has accelerated in recent decades (Ndikumana et al., 2020). While holding South African taxpayers close, SARS must also build its reputation on the global stage. Tax collection and enforcement are deeply embedded in bilateral and multilateral relations with other tax authorities. Like any form of international relations, there are always political risks that will need to be managed. As Davis (2022) suggests, building the state's capacity here requires continued investments in SARS, as well as in the capabilities of the Financial Intelligence Centre and the Reserve Bank. These functions are deeply embedded in the global institutions that govern capital flows, money laundering and 'terrorist' financing, and which are dominated by the West – thus also helping to reduce illicit financial flows that include base erosion and profit shifting by some large corporations.

Yet even strong administration, international cooperation and political foundations are only part of the story. The long-term durability of South Africa's tax system ultimately rests on its underlying economic structures. These economic structures – the bedrock of a high tax-to-GDP ratio – show little sign of shifting. We should expect the peculiarities of South Africa's economic structure to automatically push up the tax-to-GDP ratio, relative to its peers. To put it in terms Kaldor might have used: between two countries with the same real income per head, the tax potential is greater where a larger share of total incomes accrues to a minority of wealthy individuals and corporations; where the informal, subsistence and self-employed sectors account for a lower share of employment and value-creation; where firms are large and concentrated in well-developed corporate monopolies.

At the same time, these very economic structures – and the institutional matrix they support – fundamentally limit the scope for further expansion of taxation. The concentration of tax revenue from a small share of the population imposes a relatively higher burden, creating natural ceilings to further extraction. While an effective tax state must have secured the cooperation of high-income groups and built a supportive policy and administrative infrastructure, taxation also rests on a broader context of growth and development. In the past 15 years, South Africa's tax-to-GDP ratio has increased even as its GDP per capita has stagnated. If the country continues on this path – rising taxes without rising incomes – then the tensions and contradictions at the heart of any tax system could become increasingly destructive. Moreover, the division and rancour that once threatened the national compact could intensify. While path-dependent institutions are durable, the unfolding of history reminds us that even the tax state, so painstakingly constructed, remains vulnerable to broader political and economic fractures.

REFERENCES

Andersson, P.F. 2023. 'Fiscal capacity in non-democratic states: The origins and expansion of the income tax'. *Journal of Institutional Economics*, 19(3), 364–378.

Besley, T. and Persson, T. 2009. 'The origins of state capacity: Property rights, taxation and policy'. *The American Economic Review*, 99(4), 1218–1244.

Besley, T. and Persson, T. 2013. 'Taxation and development', in *Handbook of Public Economics*, Vol. 5. Elsevier, pp. 51–110.

Besley, T. and Persson, T. 2014. 'Why do developing countries tax so little?'. *Journal of Economic Perspectives*, 28(4), 99–120.

Bonney, R. (ed.). 1995. *Economic Systems and State Finance*. Oxford: Clarendon Press.

Brautigam, D. 2008. 'Introduction: Taxation and state-building in developing countries', in Brautigam, D., Fjeldstad, O.-J. and Moore, M (eds), *Taxation and State-Building in Developing Countries: Capacity and Consent*. Cambridge: Cambridge University Press.

Brennan, G. and Buchanan, J.M. 1980. *The Power to Tax: Analytical Foundations of a Fiscal Constitution*. Cambridge: Cambridge University Press.

Chipkin, I. and Swilling, M. 2018. *Shadow State: The Politics of State Capture*. Johannesburg: Wits University Press.

Dare, C., Du Plessis, S. and Jansen, A. 2019. 'Tax revenue mobilisation: Estimates of South Africa's personal income tax gap'. *South African Journal of Economic and Management Sciences*, 22(1).

Davis, D. 2022. 'Fixing SARS: An institution dismantled by state capture', in Mills, G., Jonas, M., Bhorat, H. and Hartley, R. (eds), *Better Choices: Ensuring South Africa's Future*. Johannesburg: Picador Africa.

Elgin, C., Kose, M.A., Ohnsorge, F. and Yu, S. 2021. 'Understanding Informality', C.E.P.R. Discussion Paper 16497, Centre for Economic Policy Research, London.

Evans, P.B. 1995. *Embedded Autonomy: States and Industrial Transformation*. Princeton, N.J.: Princeton University Press.

Friedman, S. 2003. *Sending Them a Message: Culture, Tax Collection, and Governance in South Africa*. Johannesburg: Centre for Policy Studies.

Gelb, S. 1991. 'South Africa's economic crisis: An overview', in Gelb, S. (ed.), *South Africa's Economic Crisis*. Cape Town and London: David Philip and Zed Books.

Global Initiative Against Transnational Organized Crime (GIATOC). 2022. 'Strategic Organised Crime Risk Assessment: South Africa'. Global Initiative Against Transnational Organized Crime.

Goldman, M., Woolard, I. and Jellema, J. 2021. 'The impact of taxes and transfers on poverty and income distribution in South Africa 2014/15'. Commitment to Equity (CEQ) Working Paper Series 106, Tulane University, Department of Economics, https://repec.tulane.edu/RePEc/ceq/ceq106.pdf, accessed 30 June 2025.

Goldscheid, R. 1925. 'A sociological approach to the problems of public finance', in Musgrave, R.A. and Peacock, A. (eds), *Classics in the Theory of Public Finance*. New York: St. Martin Press [u.a.].

Hausman, D. and Zikhali, P. 2016. 'Raising tax revenue', in Alam, A., Plangemann, K. and Mokate, R. (eds), *Making It Happen: Selected Case Studies of Institutional Reforms in South Africa*. Washington, D.C.: World Bank Group.

Inchauste, G. and Lustig, N. (eds). 2017. *The Distributional Impact of Taxes and Transfers: Evidence from Eight Low- and Middle-Income Countries*. Washington, DC, USA: World Bank Group.

Kaldor, N. 1962. 'Will underdeveloped countries learn to tax'. *Foreign Affairs*, 41, 410.

Kaldor, N. 1963. 'Taxation for economic development'. *The Journal of Modern African Studies*, 1(1), 7–23.

Kleven, H.J., Kreiner, C.T. and Saez, E. 2016. 'Why can modern governments tax so much? An agency model of firms as fiscal intermediaries'. *Economica*, 83(330), 219–246.

Levi, M. 2008. *Of Rule and Revenue*. Berkeley: University of California Press.

Lieberman, E.S. 2003. *Race and Regionalism in the Politics of Taxation in Brazil and South Africa*. Cambridge/New York: Cambridge University Press.

Musgrave, R.A. 1992. 'Schumpeter's "Crisis of the Tax State": An Essay in Fiscal Sociology'. *Journal of Evolutionary Economics*, 2(2), 89–113.

Ndikumana, L., Naido, K. and Aboobaker, A. 2020. 'Capital flight from South Africa: A case study'. PERI Working Paper Series WP 516.

North, D.C. and Weingast, B.R. 1989. 'Constitutions and commitment: The evolution of institutions governing public choice in seventeenth-century England'. *The Journal of Economic History*, 49(4), 803–832.

Nugent, R. 2018. *Final Report: Commission of Inquiry into Tax Administration and Governance by SARS*, https://www.thepresidency.gov.za/sites/default/files/2022-05/SARS%20Commission%20Final%20Report.pdf, accessed 30 June 2025.

Organisation for Economic Co-operation and Development (OECD). 2023. 'Tax Administration 2023: Comparative Information on OECD and Other Advanced and Emerging Economies'. OECD.

Ostrom, E. 1996. 'Crossing the great divide: Coproduction, synergy, and development'. *World Development*, 24(6), 1073–1087.

Peacock, A.T. and Wiseman, J. 1961. *The Growth of Public Expenditure in the United Kingdom*. Princeton University Press.

Piketty, T. 2014. *Capital in the Twenty-First Century*. Cambridge, Massachusetts: The Belknap Press of Harvard University Press.

Pomeranz, D. 2015. 'No taxation without information: Deterrence and self-enforcement in the value added tax'. *American Economic Review*, 105(8), 2539–2569.

Przeworski, A. and Wallerstein, M. 1988. 'Structural dependence of the state on capital'. *The American Political Science Review*, 82(1), 11.

Sachs, M. 2021. 'Fiscal Dimensions of South Africa's Crisis', Southern Centre for Inequality Studies Working Paper 5, University of the Witwatersrand.

Saez, E. and Zucman, G. 2019. *The Triumph of Injustice: How the Rich Dodge Taxes and How to Make Them Pay*. WW Norton & Company.

SARS. 2023. 'Tax Statistics, 2023'.

Schumpeter, J.A. 1918. 'The Crisis of the Tax State'.

Smith, L. 2003. 'The power of politics: The performance of the South African Revenue Service and some of its implications'. Institute for Development Studies; Centre for the Future State Research Summary #6.

Smulders, S. 2014. 'The transformation of the South African Revenue Authority in the post-apartheid era'. *Tax Talk*, 46, January 2–9.

Statistics SA (StatsSA). 2019. 'How Large Is the Small Business Footprint?', https://www.statssa.gov.za/?p=12264, accessed 15 May 2024.

Tanzi, V. and Zee, H. 2001. *Tax Policy for Developing Countries*. International Monetary Fund.

Ueda, J. and Thackray, M. 2015. 'Revenue Administration Gap Analysis Program–The Value-Added Tax Gap'. Fiscal Affairs Department, International Monetary Fund (IMF), Washington, DC.

Veblen, T. 1899. *The Theory of the Leisure Class: An Economic Study of Institutions*.

World Bank. 2020. 'Paying Taxes - Doing Business'. World Bank Group, https://archive.doingbusiness.org/en/data/exploretopics/paying-taxes, 14 April 2025

World Bank. 2023. World Development Indicators, https://databank.worldbank.org/source/world-development-indicators, accessed 1 February 2025.

SIX

Transformational leadership in the South African public service[1]: Challenges, strategies and reforms

SHANIL HARICHARAN[2]

INTRODUCTION

[I]nternal factors may be even more crucial in assessing one's development as a human being. Honesty, sincerity, simplicity,

---

1   Public service, or the public sector, refers to the administrative arm of the executive branch of the state. It is responsible for executing policies and delivering services in line with the nation's constitution. In this context it includes all three levels of government: national, provincial and local, as well as public entities, agencies and state-owned enterprises.

2   My sincere gratitude goes to those who offered insightful feedback on the chapter drafts: Director Renel Singh Dastaghir and Chief Director Lusani Madzivhandila at the Office of the Public Service Commission; Dr Sean Phillips, Director-General of the Department of Water and Sanitation; Eileen Meyer, former Chief Director of the National Treasury's Technical Assistance Unit; and Dr Sarah Meny-Gibert at the Public Affairs Research Institute (PARI).

humility, pure generosity, absence of vanity, readiness to serve others – qualities which are within easy reach of every soul – are the foundation of one's spiritual life. Development in matters of this nature is inconceivable without serious introspection, without knowing yourself, your weaknesses and mistakes.[3]

Nelson Mandela personified ubuntu, an African ideal valuing compassion, community, public service and ethical relationships (Kets de Vries et al., 2016; Mangaliso, 2001; Ogude, 2019). Public values are foundational principles for government's actions, citizens' rights and responsibilities, and expected behaviour of public servants (Bozeman, 2007; Pandey et al., 2016). Transformational leadership, as highlighted by Burns (1978) and Bass (1985), aligns with ubuntu and prioritises morality, vision, integrity and the empowerment of followers. Unlike transactional leadership, which focuses on rules, outputs and compliance (Bass, 1985; Burns, 1978; 2012), transformational leadership fosters ethical governance and democratic ideals – principles central to South Africa's post-apartheid reforms.

The aspiration for transformational leaders and ubuntu principles inspired the adoption of a democratic constitution in South Africa in 1996. The Constitution aimed to transition from an oppressive regime to a constitutional democracy based on democratic principles, social justice and fundamental human rights. The public service is expected to uphold essential public values, such as human dignity, equality, justice, human rights and freedom. The nascent democratic state made significant changes to the public administration system inherited from apartheid. The emerging democratic state implemented a variety of public service reforms in order to align public administration with the values and principles outlined in Chapter 10 (section 195) of the Constitution. These values include addressing people's needs; supporting public engagement in policymaking; promoting development-orientated public administration; accountability; professional ethics; and establishing effective human-resource

3   Taken from a letter Nelson Mandela wrote to Winnie Mandela in 1975 while incarcerated on Robben Island, published in *Conversations with Myself*, 2010: vii.

management and career development strategies.

The 1995 White Paper on the Transformation of the Public Service anticipated that the Senior Management Service (SMS), which consists of employees in the four highest ranks of the public service, would be proactive in addressing the challenges of change as inspirational 'leaders, visionaries, initiators, effective communicators, and decision-makers' (RSA, 1995: 3). Despite various human resource management (HRM) reforms and efforts to develop management and leadership capability and capacity, senior managers have faced challenges in fulfilling their leadership and managerial duties. In October 2022, Cabinet approved 'A National Framework Towards the Professionalisation of the Public Sector' to address this situation. The Framework aims to strengthen the public service's capacity to provide effective services, in accordance with constitutional values and the goals of the National Development Plan (NDP) 2030 (NPC, 2012). It emphasises the need to improve the skills, effectiveness and professionalism of public service employees while addressing the development needs within the SMS.

This chapter contributes to the discourse around the professionalisation of the South African public service, delving specifically into various factors that impact senior managers' capacity to embrace transformational leadership and uphold public values. It emphasises the need to create a new leadership and management culture characterised by visionary, public values-based, emotionally intelligent, ethical and self-reflective public leaders. This is critical to achieving the values and developmental goals outlined in the Constitution and the NDP.

THE CHALLENGES AND IMPACT OF PUBLIC INSTITUTIONAL REFORM IN SOUTH AFRICA

March and Olsen (1983) propose two rhetorical approaches to help understand public institutional reform: orthodox administrative theory and realpolitik. The first emphasises the need to restructure administrative structures and procedures to achieve economies of scale, efficacy and control over bureaucratic hierarchies. In the second, power struggles among various stakeholders, including politicians and bureaucrats, shape the process of reorganisation. Political elites empower themselves to create structures for their own benefit that can perpetuate their dominance. Understanding the influence of these discourses on South Africa's democratic state formation is crucial for grasping major changes in the public service and the obstacles it faces in terms of professionalism and transformational leadership.

ADMINISTRATIVE REFORM AND THE CHALLENGE OF BALANCING RULES AND VALUES IN SOUTH AFRICA'S PUBLIC SERVICE

Various factors influence public service reforms, including the shift from outdated, hierarchical and commanding governance models to more inclusive, people-centred and democratic values-based approaches. During this transition, managers must adopt strategies that prioritise public values and capabilities, aiming to enhance the value creation of public organisations through strategic transformation and efficient administration (Benington and Hartley, 2024; Dirani et al., 2020; Moore, 1995). The South African public service reform project aimed for a governance culture prioritising ethical behaviour, inclusivity, equality, social cohesion and democratic representation as alternatives to apartheid. Several administrative reform frameworks guided the efforts to achieve a coherent, representative, competent and democratic public service (RSA, 1995; 1997). South Africa has experimented with various public administration and management models, notably New Public Management (NPM) – despite its limitations (Hood and Peters, 2004; Osborne et al., 2013) in addressing the distinctive features of the public sector, particularly in a transition.

There have been significant strides in establishing a democratic state and reforming the public administrative system, but several concerns remain related to upholding constitutional values, public governance, leadership and service delivery (AGSA, 2021; RSA, 2022; Stewart, 2023; Von Holdt, 2023). The reforms have inadvertently strengthened certain aspects of the administrative orthodox culture, including the promotion of transactional leadership styles and an excessive focus on bureaucratic norms, and regulations. This, in turn, has promoted a culture of unquestioning compliance, which has failed to meet expected standards of efficiency and effectiveness in the provision of public services.

The Public Service Commission (PSC), a constitutional oversight authority responsible for advancing constitutional values and principles within the public service, reiterates that the primary goal of the public service is to advance human dignity, equality, rights and freedoms, as exemplified in the values of ubuntu. It highlights the need to balance regulatory compliance with core values amid a public service culture overly focused on rule adherence (PSC, 2024). It argues that simply enforcing rules or relying on template-driven management does not adequately uphold constitutional values and principles. The PSC acknowledges that policies, processes and systems govern the bureaucracy, but asserts that values and norms are equally important governance instruments: balancing rules and values is seen as crucial for fostering creativity, driving innovation and advancing human rights and freedoms. The Public Affairs Research Institute (Meny-Gibert, 2023) suggests that systemic corruption and factional politics create instability in the public administration and a sense of risk or uncertainty for officials, influencing the compliance culture in post-apartheid South Africa. In this context, public servants and managers typically adopt a cautious approach, prioritising adherence to rules and directives.

THE IMPACT OF POLITICISATION AND CORRUPTION ON PUBLIC SERVICE REFORMS

Party politics, political elites and power dynamics significantly impact public policy and administrative reform processes (Khan, 2019; Stewart, 2023; Von Holdt, 2023), influencing management and leadership behaviours, as well as public organisational culture (Carbone and Pellegata, 2020; Wu et al., 2015). Khan (2019) emphasises the importance of strong political and institutional capacity for organisational reforms to be successful. Unfortunately, the absence of these crucial elements in developing countries contributes to the state's failure to achieve its goals.

Public service reforms in South Africa have faced numerous

challenges, including state capture and corruption (Public Protector, 2016; RSA, 2022); mismanagement of public funds (AGSA, 2021); politicisation of public administration and a strained political-administrative relationship (Cameron, 2022; Naidoo, 2019); and governance instability and ineffective leadership (NSG, 2020; PSC, 2022; 2024). According to a South African Reconciliation Barometer (Lefko-Everett, 2023), a significant number of South Africans lack trust in the democratic system and national leaders, with 81 per cent of respondents believing these leaders show little concern for the well-being of citizens. Additionally, most South Africans (82 per cent) are concerned about the extent to which corrupt officials evade punishment, and are apprehensive about the extent of corruption and the absence of political will to address this issue (Lefko-Everett, 2023).

The Judicial Commission of Inquiry into Allegations of State Capture, Corruption and Fraud in the Public Sector (the Zondo Commission) (RSA, 2022) revealed political deals involving influential politicians, bureaucrats and business networks, including foreign actors. The Commission disclosed instances of state capture, institutional manipulation, fund misappropriation, law enforcement obstruction and democratic backsliding during Jacob Zuma's presidency. It also criticised Parliament's failure to hold the executive accountable, and declared the African National Congress's (ANC) 'Cadre Policy and Deployment Strategy' unconstitutional. This is an example of the ANC's strategy of appointing loyalists to influential positions within the public service to consolidate power within the state, utilising realpolitik rhetoric. While the ANC has argued that the strategy is a means of ensuring transformation and takes into account both merit and appreciation of the governing party's policies, this strategy has faced criticism for its negative impact on public values, morale, organisational culture and service delivery (Cameron, 2022; NSG, 2020; RSA, 2022; Sebake and Sebola, 2014). Zuma's administration crudely intensified this behaviour and gained control over important public institutions through state capture (Public Protector, 2016).

TRANSACTIONAL AND TRANSFORMATIONAL LEADERSHIP: CONTRASTING BEHAVIOURS AND IMPLICATIONS IN THE PUBLIC SERVICE

Senior public service managers should have proficiency in both leadership and management domains. The conventional understanding of administrative management is that it includes planning, budgeting, organising, staffing, directing, coordinating, reporting, controlling, establishing order and increasing efficiency within organisations (Kotter, 1988). Leadership, on the other hand, involves driving change, establishing direction, uniting people, motivating and inspiring them, embracing new visions and promoting innovation (Bennis, 2009; Denhardt and Denhardt, 2006; Yukl, 1994). It also entails enacting values, openness and reaching consensus on action. According to Van Wart (2011), a significant challenge to exceptional public leadership is the seamless integration of operational-managerial dimensions with visionary leadership functions.

Achieving optimal management or leadership performance requires matching a person's talents to their job demands and environment, including values, vision, personal philosophy, knowledge, competencies, life and career stages, and interests (Boyatzis, 2009: 752). External factors such as political, social, economic and environmental conditions, as well as an organisation's maturity, structure, systems and culture, also play a significant role. Boyatzis (2009) identified three distinct competency clusters that differentiate high-performing managers: social (empathy and organisational awareness); emotional (self-awareness and self-management); and cognitive (systems thinking and pattern recognition). These competencies, combined with expertise, experience and knowledge, contribute to management and leadership success. Emotional intelligence (EI), which includes emotional and social competencies, is crucial for leaders in decision-making, problem-solving, and adjusting to change (Goleman et al., 2002). It has the potential to positively influence transformational leadership, as both involve qualities such as self-awareness, empathy, teamwork, vision and relationship-building (Burns, 2012; Kim et al., 2023; Levitats et al., 2019; Pandey et al., 2016).

Leadership theory distinguishes between transactional and transformational behaviours. In the 20th century, the Weberian administrative orthodoxy strongly emphasised transactional leadership. Transactional behaviours are directive, task-orientated and production-driven. However, in the 21st-century public service landscape, it is essential to employ appropriate leadership approaches and practices. The transformational leadership approach has grown in popularity and now accounts for a large portion of the leadership literature (Dinh et al., 2014). Transformational behaviours prioritise people, consideration and support for them, and a focus on building relationships. Transformational leaders address matters that involve emotions, feelings and fundamental human values (Denhardt and Denhardt, 2006). Public service academics and practitioners have accepted the significance of transformational leadership, sparking research into public administrative leadership (Dinh et al., 2014; Kellis and Ran, 2013).

The concept of transformational leadership has evolved over time to encompass various related leadership models, including authentic (Gardner et al., 2011), ethical (Brown et al., 2005) and servant leadership (Greenleaf, 1977). These models emphasise key behaviours and practices, such as having a clear and inspiring vision, acting in accordance with one's values, supporting others' growth, embracing change and prioritising a positive work environment (Bass, 1985; Bass and Avolio, 1994; Bennis and Nanus, 1985; Burns, 2012; Goleman et al., 2002; Kouzes and Posner, 2003). Particularly in public service organisations, ethical and servant leadership models can enhance decision-making and employee behaviour (Brown et al., 2005; Daweti and Evans, 2017; Kim et al., 2023). Leaders who adopt these models showcase altruistic and public values-based behaviours (Pandey et al., 2016). This approach promotes ethical workplace culture and conduct, and pro-organisational qualities (Kim et al., 2023). It can also enhance motivation and morale for change within teams, organisations and communities (Vigoda-Gadot and Meisler, 2010). Public organisations that nurture transformational leaders can reap the benefits of these models, which emphasise qualities such as accountability, fairness, integrity, respect, trust and responsible citizenship (Brown et al., 2005).

Transactional leadership, in contrast, emphasises setting performance goals, monitoring progress, and implementing rewards or penalties based on individual achievements (Bass and Avolio, 1994). Transactional leaders employ a task-orientated and directive approach, expecting individuals to adhere to instructions and achieve objectives. This approach is compatible with conventional hierarchical management models and their corresponding traditional administrative leadership styles. Transactional leaders often adhere to established norms, maintaining the status quo. These models have greatly influenced public administration and human resource management (Cameron, 2022; Laloux, 2014; Vigoda-Gadot and Meisler, 2010).

The transactional leadership style is not unexpected, given that government leaders must work in a regulatory environment and ensure the consistency of administrative and regulatory procedures. This leadership style, termed dissonant leadership by Boyatzis and McKee (2005), is marked by commanding, pace-setting and discordant behaviours. It leads to conflicts and fosters negative emotions among employees, such as anger, fear, apathy or silence.

TRANSACTIONAL AND TRANSFORMATIONAL LEADERSHIP AMONG PUBLIC MANAGERS

Public managers in South Africa are required to embrace transformative constitutional values to effectively pursue the state's developmental agenda. This section examines their leadership and management behaviours in navigating the complex and changing landscape of the South African state and society.

The impact of transactional leadership in the public sector

Public servants and citizens in South Africa are dissatisfied with the leadership of public managers and political leaders, being primarily concerned about their overly transactional tendencies (AGSA, 2021; Haricharan, 2023; Haricharan and Wyley, 2013; Levin, 2009; NSG, 2020; Mokgolo et al., 2012). Public managers frequently display transactional leadership styles, which lack the transformative qualities of an inspiring vision, alignment with public values, self- and social awareness, and a willingness to challenge the status quo.

According to Bandura (1977), leaders' hierarchical positions and their modelling effect on followers' behaviour are key drivers that substantially influence employee conduct and workplace culture. A study in one provincial government revealed strong discontent among public servants with their senior managers' perceived incompetence, lack of visionary leadership, and behaviours such as indifference, indecision, authoritarianism and inconsistency (Haricharan, 2023). The behaviours of senior managers helped shape a 'bureaucratic culture' and a 'power culture' that prioritised hierarchical relationships, rank status and power disparities. Bureaucratic culture was characterised by rigid bureaucratic structures and lengthy administrative procedures; power culture by commanding management styles, centralised authority and indecision. These cultures had detrimental impacts on workplace social cohesion, motivation and productivity, leading to feelings of exclusion and discontent (Haricharan, 2023). Public servants instead expressed a strong preference for leaders who demonstrated values and behaviours such as openness, understanding, dependability and regard for others (Haricharan, 2023). They generally preferred decentralised authority and autonomy, agile and efficient systems, fair and constructive performance appraisals, coordinated planning, adequate resources, recognition and self-expression (Görgens-Ekermans and Roux, 2021; Haricharan, 2023; Sibonde and Dassah, 2021). They anticipated that these elements would enhance their well-being, promote growth and improve service delivery, leading them to prefer transformational leadership styles while senior managers exhibited transactional leadership behaviours. This highlights the challenge of balancing transformational leadership with transactional and rules-based approaches in a regulatory context.

These findings are consistent with earlier research. Levin (2009) discovered employees harboured resentment and unhappiness towards their supervisors. Many believed that managers were incompetent, had poor communication skills, and showed favouritism. Levin's study highlighted the negative effects of excessive micromanagement and autocratic decision-making. Similarly, Haricharan and Wyley's (2013) leadership transition study found that newly appointed top managers in national government faced heightened anxiety and difficulties due to a negative work environment characterised by discontent and conflict. The study indicated that both political and administrative leaders favoured transactional leadership styles. These styles prioritised tasks, authority and frenetic behaviours over building relationships, supporting and motivating employees and looking out for their well-being. Newly appointed senior managers were expected to make personal sacrifices in order to navigate their challenging work environments effectively and minimise the risks of failure (Haricharan and Wyley, 2013). This stress is often attributed to their relationships with their political principals in all three spheres of government.

In such a context, it is imperative to establish a technocratic bureaucracy that is depoliticised, and to prioritise the importance of emotionally intelligent competencies for all leaders, irrespective of their political or administrative duties. When political office bearers exhibit a strongly transactional style of leadership, senior managers are compelled to partially embrace this approach to respond effectively to their political principals and fulfil these leaders' expectations. An organisation's culture is fundamentally shaped by its leadership; it is challenging for senior managers to adopt a transformational leadership style when a minister consistently acts in an authoritarian way.

The impact of transformational leadership in the South African public sector

Some public managers in South Africa, despite the prevalence of transactional leadership styles, demonstrate transformational leadership through their visionary, democratic, ethical, empathic and service-oriented behaviours. Studies in South Africa's public sector have demonstrated the positive impact of transformational leadership practices on the management and delivery of public services (Görgens-Ekermans and Roux, 2021; Haricharan, 2023; Mokgolo et al., 2012; Sibonde and Dassah, 2021). Thus, managers with transformational leadership capabilities are effective in guiding their organisations and enhancing the quality of the services they offer.

The former CEO of Frere Hospital in East London, Dr Rolene Wagner, who successfully led the hospital's revitalisation from 2012 to

2018, exemplifies transformational leadership (Mpofana and Ruiters, 2019). A prestigious global award from the International Hospital Federation acknowledged the hospital's achievement and the dedication of the CEO and staff members to bringing about positive change through implementation of their patient-centric healthcare strategy (Timeslive, 2018). The CEO is widely recognised as an exceptional leader who embodies the Batho Pele principles of caring, inclusion and service, along with other qualities of transformational leaders.

Transformational leaders like Wagner are distinguished by ethical values, devotion to social justice, a passion for public service, and a focus on fairness and transparency. They achieve their goals by promoting cooperation and participation, assessing individuals' and teams' strengths and weaknesses, and committing to providing direction and support for personal growth. Such managers, though rare, create environments that facilitate the development of individual, team and organisational capabilities, which then have a positive impact on behaviours and cultures that align with public values. In this way, they create effective, significant systemic changes in their public organisations.

The synergistic relationship between transformational leadership and EI significantly influences the effectiveness of South African managers. Kotzé and Venter (2011) found a significant difference in EI scores between capable and ineffective middle-level managers. A study by Mokgolo et al. (2012) underscores the importance of transformational leadership among provincial government managers. It revealed that managers' lack of transformational leadership negatively impacted management and service delivery, resulting in community dissatisfaction. Mfikwe and Pelser (2017) found a relationship between senior managers' EI and their ability to make sound leadership choices and foster favourable workplace cultures. Haricharan (2022) applied the Goleman et al. (2002) EI model and found significant positive correlations between leadership performance and EI competence among provincial executive managers. Those with strong competencies in the four EI clusters – self-awareness, self-management, social awareness, and relationship management – tend to excel as leaders and positively influence their organisation's culture.

At local government level, Sibonde and Dassah (2021) found a significant connection between service quality and effective leadership in a municipality in the Western Cape. The study highlights the crucial role of effective communication, employee involvement in decision-making and prioritising employees' well-being. Similarly, Haricharan (2023) discovered that these behaviours significantly enhance employee motivation and have a strong correlation with EI within a provincial government, revealing the significant influence of transformational leadership on the culture of provincial governance, which in turn impacts employee morale, well-being and performance. According to Boyatzis and McKee (2005), transformational leaders play a crucial role in shaping organisational culture and creating a positive environment for employee growth and success.

PROFESSIONALISING THE PUBLIC SECTOR: CHALLENGES AND OBSTACLES IN PROMOTING TRANSFORMATIONAL LEADERSHIP

The sixth administration (2019–2024) prioritised professionalisation of the public sector in order to uphold constitutional values and achieve the NDP goals (NSG, 2020). It launched several initiatives, such as a framework for professionalising the public sector and the revision of the Public Service Amendment (PSA) Bill and the Public Administration Management Amendment (PAMA) Bill. The framework promotes Batho Pele principles and constitutional values while also incorporating HRM and administrative structural shifts. For example, the public service career framework emphasises meritocracy and ethical orientation, while the Nyukela Public Service SMS Pre-entry Programme improves the recruiting process and ensures top managers have the appropriate skills and qualifications.

Despite the forward-thinking nature of these endeavours, the government must address a number of gaps and outstanding challenges to effectively establish a capable state and implement the professionalisation framework. The success of the developmental change agenda depends on the SMS's capability and capacity, as well as the promotion of transformational leadership that aligns with constitutional values and principles. This section examines key concerns in this regard.

The negative impact of politicisation on the public service

While technical deficiencies and implementation issues contribute to the dysfunctionality of the South African public service, political and ideational impediments are the most significant (Cameron, 2022; Southall, 2007; Stewart, 2023; Von Holdt, 2010; 2023). The politicisation of the public service has a detrimental effect on senior managers' abilities to carry out their mandates, thus creating strained political-administrative relations, resulting in governance instability and a risk of corruption (Cameron, 2022; NSG, 2020; RSA, 2022). Politicisation shows itself in several ways, including the replacement of merit-based criteria with political ones in the selection, promotion and remuneration of public servants, and in the disciplinary procedures they face (Peters and Pierre, 2004). The National School of Government (NSG) stresses the problem of undue political influence in the selection of senior staff and management (NSG, 2020: 47).

Cadre deployment and other forms of political patronage by the ANC and other political parties contradict the professionalisation framework's goal of creating a fair and merit-based recruitment system. Incorporating political criteria into these processes leads to unfavourable consequences (RSA, 2022). Politicisation can undermine public trust in governance and administration, negatively affecting professionalism, morale and stability in senior management (Cameron, 2022; NSG, 2020). The Zondo Commission concluded that cadre deployment is a violation of government policies regarding the appointment of public servants. The Commission determined that the ANC's Deployment Committee potentially exerted influence over the selection of Directors-General, senior officials and judges throughout the Zuma administration. The Democratic Alliance's lawsuit challenging this practice was dismissed by the high court, though the party is taking the case on appeal (Seeletsa, 2025).

President Ramaphosa, chairperson of the ANC's Deployment Committee in that period, resisted pressure and maintained firm support for cadre deployment during the Zondo Commission hearings. Arguably, this practice contradicts his commitment to promote honesty, ethics and integrity in the public service, which he considers crucial for establishing a capable state (RSA, 2021: 14). In his 2024 State of the Nation Address (RSA, 2024: 2), he highlighted the substantial harm caused during state capture, echoing the Zondo Commission's warnings about the risk of corruption resulting from political interference (RSA, 2022). The proposed amendment to the PSA (RSA, 2023: 23) which would prohibit a head of department (HoD), or an employee directly reporting to an HoD, from holding office in a political party, whether in a permanent, temporary or acting capacity, is a commendable step in the effort to reduce the politicisation of the public service.

Challenges and reforms in public service management development and human resource management

South African public service training institutions and human resource management (HRM) policy reforms have failed to achieve the desired outcomes for establishing a professional public service corps (Cameron, 2022; Daweti and Evans, 2017). The NSG (2020) asserts that despite 26 years of democracy, there were no significant efforts to enhance public service professionalism.

CHALLENGES AND SUCCESSES IN PUBLIC SECTOR TRAINING AND LEADERSHIP DEVELOPMENT

The precursors of the NSG, the South African Management Development Institute (SAMDI) (1994–2006) and the Public Administration and Leadership Academy (PALAMA) (2006–2013), faced criticism for their inadequate training resources, poorly designed programmes, subpar training, unsatisfactory administrative performances, failures to cultivate capable senior managers, as well as the fact that government departments did not fully use their services. National public training institutions have experienced major challenges in aligning their development strategies with the public sector reform agenda (McLennan and Orkin, 2009). Notably, a few provinces created institutions and programmes aimed at leadership development which have yielded positive results, such as the Leadership Academy of the Western Cape's Education Department, the Gauteng City Region Academy's leadership webinars and the Value-Based Leadership Development Programme (VLDP) of the Western Cape government.

REFORMING COMPETENCY FRAMEWORKS TO PROMOTE TRANSFORMATIONAL LEADERSHIP AMONG SENIOR MANAGERS

The SMS Competency Framework, including the Leadership and Management Competency Framework (LMCF) and associated development programmes, has not produced the expected enhancements in management and leadership effectiveness. They are crucial for recruiting managers and developing transformational leaders, yet they fail to explicitly define the necessary transformative capabilities and behaviours for senior managers, and need significant reform. Key elements are absent, such as the emotional, social and ethical qualities, guided by public values, essential for effective transformational leadership. Daweti and Evans (2017) argue that the NSG and its predecessors emphasise individualistic, vertical development rather than collaborative, peer and social learning.

The PSC (2024) indicates that the Competency Framework is restrictive, as it limits the assessment of the SMS to generic factors and overlooks the technical dimensions of the trainees' roles. It asserts that training and development programmes should promote a more value-driven approach for the SMS and public servants. Additionally, the PSC report underscores the importance of reviewing the SMS Handbook to ensure its consistency with the objective of empowering the SMS.

The NSG Professionalisation Framework (2020) acknowledges that the SMS Competency Framework does not fully align with the competency requirements for the leadership and governance needed to build a developmental state. It proposes revising competency instruments to incorporate skills, indicators and behavioural qualities across three dimensions: economic, political and technical/functional. It presents general proposals but lacks specificity in management and leadership development, failing to address the SMS's leadership challenges directly. It also fails to specify the leadership styles, strategies and capabilities necessary for constructing a developmental state, highlighting a recurring limitation of public training institutions. The framework focuses on strategies and measures for recruiting and training new entrants, but existing public servants and managers must also be skilled and engaged in behavioural change initiatives. A comprehensive, evidence-based approach is essential, rather than the implementation of incremental changes to the competency framework and training programmes.

THE LIMITATIONS OF FORMAL TRAINING AND THE IMPORTANCE OF EXPERIENTIAL LEARNING FOR LEADERSHIP DEVELOPMENT

Formal training constitutes a minor aspect of leadership development (Van Wart, 2011). Short training courses focusing on technical skills and cognitive competence in challenging public service environments are unlikely to change leaders' behaviours or produce lasting workplace outcomes (Day et al., 2014).

Behavioural adaptation for effective leadership development requires integrating adult learning theory, reflection and experimentation, continuous practice, coaching and methods like experiential and social learning (Kolb, 1984; Rainey and Kolb, 2014). Experiential learning platforms that emphasise behavioural and attitudinal changes in social contexts enhance leadership development (Kolb, 1984; Yeganeh and Kolb, 2009). Managers can enhance their emotional intelligence by leveraging experience and exerting focused effort, which will result in exceptional leadership performance (Goleman and Boyatzis, 2008). These emotional intelligence competencies enable managers to become aware of the negative effects of the 'sacrifice cycle' in the public sector (Boyatzis and McKee, 2005). Betancourt and Vivier (2021) propose an integrated leadership approach in their South African study which incorporates experiential, situational, affective and relational competencies. Additional research is necessary to explore these dimensions within a comprehensive framework aimed at professionalising the public sector.

CONCERNS WITH THE PERFORMANCE MANAGEMENT AND DEVELOPMENT SYSTEM (PMDS)

The Performance Management and Development System (PMDS), which has drawn heavy criticism from across the public sector, is another major issue that impacts senior managers' performance and leadership styles (Cameron 2022; Daweti and Evans, 2017; McLennan and Orkin, 2009; Sing 2012).

Public servants and managers have raised concerns about the legitimacy and fairness of the system's application (Haricharan, 2023). They demand that the SMS take a more proactive role in system administration, guaranteeing fair recognition and rewards for achievement and preventing system 'gaming' (Cameron, 2022), rather than applying the system punitively or solely for compliance (Haricharan, 2023). Punitive actions, or those meant only to elicit compliance, illustrate transactional leadership practices, which in turn reinforce orthodox administrative behaviours. The 2024 PSC report reflects on the PMDS and recommends a thorough review of the system. It suggests that 'performance assessments should be done through regular inspections or evaluations of units rather than through individual staff assessments' (PSC, 2024: 155).

Strengthening public institutional structures for effective governance and leadership

In the 21st century, public organisations must transition from transactional, hierarchical approaches to governance practices focused on the well-being of citizens. Effective public governance must embody collaborative, networked and relational institutional arrangements, along with responsiveness, accountability, inclusivity and transparency. South Africa's Constitution requires this transformation as a response to historical alienation and dehumanisation. The institutional structures of the South African government are frequently viewed as inflexible, poorly coordinated, centralised, lacking in resources and bureaucratic, resulting in entrenched power dynamics and bureaucratic cultures (Haricharan, 2023). Further transformation is needed due to post-apartheid South Africa's incoherent strategies, structural deficiencies, political interference, state capture and corruption.

The centre of government (CoG), a crucial element in the architecture of the public service, demands attention. The national CoG departments include the Department of Public Service and Administration (DPSA), the NSG, National Treasury, Department of Cooperative Governance and Traditional Affairs (CoGTA), Department of Planning, Monitoring and Evaluation (DPME), and the Presidency. They play a crucial role in ensuring policy coherence, cohesion and coordination. The Governance and Administration Cluster, which brings them together, has been ineffective in fulfilling its policy coordination mandate (TAU, 2009). Collaboration among these departments is crucial for the success of the professionalisation framework and the advancement of government-wide transformational leadership capabilities and behaviours. It is critical to align the DPSA's professional development frameworks with the NSG's capacity-building programmes. A strong CoG will improve the coordination of human resource management and leadership development initiatives. Working collaboratively with the PSC, it will help strengthen measures for developing SMS leadership skills and a professional public service.

The Public Service Amendment Bill 2023 is a crucial reform instrument, proposing changes to the roles and responsibilities of both the executive and senior managers. A notable development is the establishment of the Head of Public Service (HoPS). The PSC supports the Bill while noting specific limitations, especially that Clause 4 lacks a clear definition of the creation and functions of the HoPS (RSA, 2023). The clause adds functions for the Presidency's Director-General, to whom Directors-General report on operational, organisational and administrative matters. Varying positions within government regarding the HoPS highlight the necessity for coherence among key players and a unified leadership position from CoG departments, amid management instability and political interference in administration.

CONCLUSION

The democratic South African state enacted various reforms to restructure the public service, aiming to establish an accountable, inclusive and people-centred service aligned to constitutional values and principles. Three decades later, the trajectory of public institutional reform, shaped by orthodox administrative theory and realpolitik, has reinforced a culture of compliance and transactional leadership. This raises concerns regarding governance, corruption, political interference, management and service delivery. Trust in the democratic system and national leaders has declined, and immediate action is necessary to address the numerous governance and leadership challenges and restore public confidence.

Evidence from the South African public service indicates that transformational leadership, defined by visionary, ethical and service-orientated behaviours, is essential for promoting public values, enhancing employee motivation, morale and well-being, and ultimately cultivating effective and inclusive institutions. Public servants express dissatisfaction with managers' transactional leadership styles, which prioritise hierarchical rank and neglect their well-being. This approach creates a negative culture and climate, diminishing motivation, productivity and social cohesion.

President Ramaphosa's administration introduced initiatives and reforms to professionalise the public sector. To restore trust in government services, the professionalisation framework strives to address capacity development inadequacies while also improving management and leadership competence. Nevertheless, challenges persist in the areas of human resource management, the politicisation of the public service, management and leadership development, and collaboration between critical national departments. The success of the professionalisation framework and a capable state depends on addressing these and other issues. Evidence-based and novel approaches are required in leadership development with an emphasis on public values, experiential learning, behavioural adaptation and the cultivation of emotional and social competencies.

Addressing corruption requires strong political will and sincere intentions. Transformational leadership approaches can enhance the public service's ability to combat corruption and unethical conduct. These approaches can shift behaviours, enhance public value creation, and build trust in public institutions aligned with constitutional values.

Enhancing the PSC oversight and leadership is essential for ensuring accountability and upholding constitutional values. Comprehensive institutional reform and capacity building are essential to address challenges and foster transformational leadership in the South African public service.

South Africa has one of the world's best role models for promoting transformational leadership and establishing a trusted and effective democratic state. It is essential to draw inspiration from Nelson Mandela's leadership style which emphasised personal qualities like integrity, authenticity, humility and dedication to service. These attributes are crucial for promoting transformative leadership and ubuntu.

REFERENCES

Asamoah, K. and Yeboah-Assiamah, E. 2019. 'Ubuntu philosophy for public leadership and governance praxis'. *Journal of Global Responsibility,* 10(4), 307–321, https: //doi.10.1108/JGR-01-2019-0008

Auditor-General of South Africa (AGSA). 2021. *Consolidated General Report on National And Provincial Audit Outcomes*. Pretoria: AGSA.

Bandura, A. 1977. *Social learning theory*. Englewood Cliffs, NJ: Prentice Hall.

Bass, B.M. 1985. *Leadership and Performance Beyond Expectations*. New York: Free Press.

Bass, B.M. and Avolio, B.J. 1994. *Improving Organisational Effectiveness Through Transformational Leadership*. Thousand Oaks: Sage Publications.

Benington, J. and Hartley, J. 2024. 'The cloud of unknowing: The theory and practice of public value in times of extremity', in Cook, B.J. (ed.), *Challenges to Public Value Creation: Authority, Process, and Complexity,* Cham: Springer Nature Switzerland, pp. 57–76.

Bennis, W.G. 2009. *On Becoming a Leader*. 4th edition. New York: Basic Books.

Bennis, W.G. and Nanus, B. 1985. *The Strategies for Taking Charge*. New York: Harper and Row.

Betancourt, D.S. and Vivier, E. 2021. 'The relevance of contemplative studies and practices for improving participatory urban governance'. *Politikon*, 48(4), 607–624, https://doi.org/10.1080/02589346.2021.1995271

Boyatzis, R.E. 2009. 'Competencies as a behavioral approach to emotional intelligence'. *Journal of Management Development,* 28(9), 749–770.

Boyatzis, R. and McKee, A. 2005. *Resonant Leadership*. Boston: Harvard Business Press.

Bozeman, B. 2007. *Public Values and Public Interest: Counterbalancing Economic Individualism*. Washington, D.C.: Georgetown University Press.

Brown, M.E., Treviño, L.K. and Harrison, D.A. 2005. 'Ethical leadership: A social learning perspective for construct development and testing'. *Organizational Behavior and Human Decision Processes*, 97, 117–134.

Burns, J.M. 1978. *Leadership*. New York: Harper and Row.

Burns, J.M. 2012. *Leadership*. Open Road Media.

Cameron, R. 2022. *Public Sector Reform in South Africa 1994–2021*. Bingley, UK: Emerald Publishing Limited

Carbone, G. and Pellegata, A. 2020. *Political Leadership in Africa: Leaders and Development South of the Sahara*. New York: Cambridge University Press.

Daweti, M. and Evans, R. 2017. 'Leadership constructions and discourse interfaces in the public service in South Africa'. *African Journal of Public Affairs*, 9(8), 151–171.

Day, D.V., Fleenor, J.W., Atwater, L.E., Sturm, R.E. and McKee, R.A. 2014. 'Advances in leader and leadership development: A review of 25 years of research and theory'. *The Leadership Quarterly*, 25, 63–82.

Denhardt, R.B. and Denhardt, J.V. 2006. *The Dance of Leadership: The Art of Leading in Business, Government and Society*. New York: ME Sharpe.

Dinh, J.E., Lord, R.G., Gardner, W.L., Meuser, J.D., Liden, R.C. and Hu, J. 2014. 'Leadership theory and research in the new millennium: Current theoretical trends and changing perspectives'. *The Leadership Quarterly*, 25, 36–62.

Dirani, K.M., Abadi, M., Alizadeh, et al. 2020. 'Leadership competencies and the essential role of human resource development in times of crisis: A response to Covid-19 pandemic'. *Human Resource Development International*, 23(4), 380–384, https://doi.org/10.1080/13678868.2020.1780078

Gardner, W.L., Cogliser, C.C., Davis, K.M. and Dickens, M.P. 2011. 'Authentic leadership: A review of the literature and research agenda'. *The Leadership Quarterly*, 22, 1120–1145.

Goleman, D. and Boyatzis, R. 2008. 'Social intelligence and the biology of leadership'. *Harvard Business Review*, 86(9), 74–81.

Goleman, D., Boyatzis, R. and McKee, A. 2002. *Primal Leadership: Realizing The Power of Emotional* Intelligence. Boston, MA: Harvard Business School Press.

Görgens-Ekermans, G. and Roux, C. 2021. 'Revisiting the emotional intelligence and transformational leadership debate: (How) does emotional intelligence matter to effective leadership?'. *SA Journal of Human Resource Management*, 19(0), a1279, https://doi.org/10.4102/sajhrm.v19i0.1279

Greenleaf, R.K. 1977. *Servant Leadership: A Journey into the Nature Of Legitimate Power and Greatness*. New York, NY: Paulist Press.

Haricharan, S.J. 2022. 'Is the leadership performance of public service executive managers related to their emotional intelligence?'. *South African Journal of Human Resource Management*, 20(0), 1773, https://doi.org/10.4102/sajhrm

Haricharan, S.J. 2023. 'Leadership, management and organisational implications for public service employee wellbeing and performance'. *SA Journal of Human Resource Management*, 21(0), a2080, https://doi.org/10.4102/sajhrm.v21i0.2080

Haricharan, S.J. and Wyley, C. 2013. 'Facilitating effective leadership transitions in the South African public service'. Paper delivered at the 9th International Conference on Public Administration, Cape Town, 1 November 2013.

Hood, C. and Peters, G. 2004. 'The middle aging of new public management: Into the age of paradox?'. *Journal of Public Administration Research and Theory,* 14(3), 267–282, Doi: 10.1093/jopart/muh019

Kellis, D.S. and Ran, B. 2013. 'Modern leadership principles for public administration: Time to move forward'. *Journal of Public Affairs*, 139(1), 130–141.

Kets de Vries, M.F., Sexton, J.C. and Ellen III, B.P. 2016. 'Destructive and transformational leadership in Africa'. *Africa Journal of Management*, 2(2), 166–187.

Khan, M. 2019. 'Knowledge, skills and organizational capabilities for structural transformation'. *Structural Change and Economic Dynamics*, 48, 42–52.

Kim, J., Kang, H. and Lee, K. 2023. 'Transformational-transactional leadership and unethical pro-organizational behavior in the public sector: Does public service motivation make a difference?' *Public Management Review*, 25(2), 429–458, https://doi.org/10.1080/14719037.2021.1974714

Kolb, D.A. 1984. *Experiential Learning: Experience as the Source of Learning and Development*. Englewood Cliffs, N.J.: Prentice-Hall.

Kotter, J. 1988. *The Leadership Factor*. New York: Free Press.

Kotzé, M. and Venter, I. 2011. 'Differences in emotional intelligence between effective and ineffective leaders in the public sector: An empirical study'. *International Review of Administrative Sciences*, 77(2), 397–427.

Kouzes, J.M. and Posner, B.Z. 2003. *The Leadership Challenge*. 3rd ed. San Francisco: Jossey-Bass.

Laloux, F. 2014. *Reinventing Organisations*. Brussels: Nelson Parker.

Lefko-Everett, K. 2023. 'South African Reconciliation Barometer Survey: 2023 Report'. Institute for Justice and Reconciliation, Cape Town, South Africa.

Levin, R.M. 2009. 'Transforming the public service to support the developmental state'. *Journal of Public Administration*, 44(4.1), 943–968.

Levitats, Z., Vigoda-Gadot, E. and Vashdi, D.R. 2019. 'Engage them through emotions: Exploring the role of emotional intelligence in public sector engagement'. *Public Administration Review,* 79, 841–852, doi: 10.1111/puar.13113

Mandela, N. 2010. *Nelson Mandela: Conversations with Myself*. London: Macmillan.

Mangaliso, M.P. 2001. 'Building competitive advantage from ubuntu: Management lessons from South Africa'. *Academy of Management Perspectives*, 15(3), 23–33.

March, J.G. and Olsen, J.P. 1983. 'Organizing political life: What administrative reorganization tells us about government'. *The American Political Science Review*, 77(2), 281–296.

Mbigi, L. 2005. *Ubuntu: The Spirit of African Transformation Management.* Randburg: Knowledge Resources.

McLennan, A. 2007. 'The academic/practitioner interface in public administration: The early years – 1990 to 2000'. *Service Delivery Review*, 6(1), 40–46.

McLennan, A. and Orkin, M. 2009. '"That elusive value": Institutionalising management development for developmental government'. *Journal of Public Administration* 44(si-1), 1027–1045.

Meny-Gibert, S. 2023. 'Input on the Public Service Commission Report: Public Service Reform Towards Professionalisation: A PSC Perspective'. Public Affairs Research Institute, Johannesburg.

Mfikwe, N.M.G. and Pelser, T.G. 2017. 'The significance of emotional intelligence and leadership styles of senior leaders in the South African government'. *Management: Journal of Contemporary Management Issues*, 22(2), 115–126.

Mokgolo, M.M., Mokgolo, P. and Modiba, M. 2012. 'Transformational leadership in the South African public service after the April 2009 national elections'. *South African Journal of Human Resource Management*, 10(1), 1–9.

Moore, M. 1995. *Creating Public Value: Strategic Management in Government.* Massachusetts: Harvard University Press.

Mpofana, M. and Ruiters, G. 2019. 'New public management, quick fixes and policy churn in South Africa'. *Administratio Publica*, 27(4), 178–196.

Naidoo, V. 2019. 'Transitional politics and machinery of government change in South Africa'. *Journal of Southern African Studies*, 45(3), 575–595.

National Planning Commission (NPC). 2012. *National Development Plan 2030. Our Future: Make it Work.* Pretoria.

National School of Government (NSG). 2020. *National Framework Towards the Professionalisation of the Public Sector.* Pretoria.

Newman, M.A., Guy, M.E. and Mastracci, S.H. 2009. 'Beyond cognition: Affective leadership and emotional labor'. *Public Administration Review*, 69(1), 6–20.

O'Boyle, E., Humphrey, R.H., Pollack, J.M., Hawver, T.H. and Story, P. 2011. 'The relation between emotional intelligence and job performance: A meta-analysis'. *Journal of Organizational Behavior*, 32, 788–818.

Ogude, J. 2019. *Ubuntu and the Reconstitution of Community.* Indiana: Indiana University Press.

Osborne, S.P., Radnor Z. and Nasi, G. 2013. 'A new theory for public service management? Toward a (public) service-dominant approach'. *The American Review of Public Administration*, 43, 135, DOI: 10.1177/0275074012466935

Pandey, S.K., Davis, R.S., Pandey, S. and Peng, S. 2016. 'Transformational leadership and the use of normative public values: Can employees be inspired to serve larger public purposes?'. *Public Administration*, 94(1), 204–222, doi:10.1111/padm.12214

Pedersen, D. and Hartley, J. 2008. 'The changing context of public leadership and management. Implications for roles and dynamics'. *International Journal of Public Sector Management*, 21(4), 327–339.

Peters, B.G. and Pierre, J. 2004. *Politicization of the Civil Service in Comparative Perspective: The Quest for Control.* London: Routledge Studies in Government and Public Policy.

Public Protector. 2016. *State of Capture.* Report No. 6 of 2016/17.

Public Service Commission (PSC). 2022. *Report on the Investigative Analysis into the Enablers and Inhibitors of Job Performance of the Senior Management Service in the Public Service.* Pretoria.

Public Service Commission (PSC). 2024. *Public Service Reforms Towards Professionalisation: A Public Service Commission Perspective.* Pretoria.

Rainey, M.A. and Kolb, D.A. 2014. 'Organisation leadership: Leading in a learning way', in Jones, B.B. and Brazzel, M. (eds), *The NTL Handbook of Organization Development and Change: Principles, Practices, and Perspectives.* San Francisco, CA: Wiley, pp. 329–347.

Republic of South Africa (RSA). 1995. 'White Paper on the Transformation of the Public Service Notice 1227 of 1995'. Pretoria: Government Printers.

Republic of South Africa (RSA). 1997. 'White Paper on Transforming Service Delivery Notice 1459 of 1997'. Pretoria: Government Printers.

Republic of South Africa (RSA). 2003. 'Towards a ten-year review'. Pretoria: The Presidency.

Republic of South Africa (RSA). 2010. 'SMS Handbook'. Pretoria: Department of Public Service and Administration.

Republic of South Africa (RSA). 2014. 'Twenty-year review South Africa 1994–2014'. Pretoria: The Presidency.

Republic of South Africa (RSA). 2021. 'State of The Nation Address by President Cyril Ramaphosa'. National Parliament, Cape Town.

Republic of South Africa (RSA). 2022. 'Judicial Commission of Inquiry into Allegations of State Capture, Corruption and Fraud in the Public Sector including Organs of State. Part 1'. Pretoria: The Presidency.

Republic of South Africa (RSA). 2023. 'Public Service Amendment Bill'. Pretoria.

Republic of South Africa (RSA). 2024. 'State of The Nation Address by President Cyril Ramaphosa'. Cape Town City Hall.

Sebake, B. and Sebola, M. 2014. 'Growing trends and tendencies of corruption in the South African public service: Negative contribution to service delivery'. *Journal of Public Administration*, 49(3), 744–755.

Seeletsa, M. 2025. 'DA's "poor" appeal on cadre deployment dismissed as ANC welcomes ruling'. *The Citizen*, 7 May, https://www.citizen.co.za/

news/south-africa/courts/da-cadre-deployment-appeal-high-court-anc, accessed 15 June 2025.

Sibonde, A.H. and Dassah, M.O. 2021. 'The relationship between employee motivation and service quality: Case study of a selected municipality in the Western Cape province, South Africa'. *Africa's Public Service Delivery and Performance Review*, 9(1), 12.

Sing, D. 2012. 'Human resource challenges confronting the senior management service of the South African public service'. *Public Personnel Management*, 41(2), 379–388.

Southall, R. 2007. 'Introduction: The ANC state, more dysfunctional than developmental?', in Buhlungu, S., Daniel, J., Southall, R. and Lutchman, J. (eds), *State of Nation: South Africa*. Cape Town: HSRC Press.

Stewart, P. 2023. 'Class dynamics, a declining ANC and the failure of policy implementation'. *Politeia*.

Technical Assistance Unit (TAU). 2009. 'Review of the Functioning of the Governance and Administration (G&A) Cluster project'. Technical Assistance Unit, National Treasury, Pretoria.

Timeslive. 9 October 2018. 'East London hospital to get global excellence award'. *Timeslive*, https://www.timeslive.co.za/news/south-africa/2018-10-09-east-london-hospital-to-get-global-excellence-award/, accessed 20 November 2023.

Van Wart, M. 2011. *Dynamics of Leadership in Public Service: Theory and Practice*. New York: ME Sharpe.

Vigoda-Gadot, E. and Meisler, G. 2010. 'Emotions in management and the management of emotions: The impact of emotional intelligence and organisational politics on public sector employees'. *Public Administration Review*, 70(1), 72–86, https://doi. org/10.1111/j.1540-6210.2009.02112.x

Von Holdt, K. 2010. 'Nationalism, bureaucracy and the developmental state: The South African case'. *South African Review of Sociology*, 41(1), 4–27.

Von Holdt, K. 2023. 'Elite formation, factions and violence in the political economy of corruption', in Buthelezi, M., Vale, P. and Von Holdt, K. (eds), *State Capture in South Africa: How and Why It Happened*. Johannesburg: Wits University Press.

Weyer, J. 2002. 'Importance of leadership capacity versus competence: A case study'. *Australian Journal of Management and Organizational Behaviour*, 5(1), 117–128.

Wu, X., Ramesh, M. and Howlett, M. 2015. 'Policy capacity: A conceptual framework for understanding policy competences and capabilities'. *Policy and Society*, 34(3–4), 165–171.

Yeganeh, B. and Kolb, D.A. 2009. 'Mindfulness and experiential learning'. *OD Practitioner*, 41(3), 8–14.

Yukl, G. 1994. *Leadership in Organisations*. Englewood Cliffs, N.J.: Prentice Hall.

SEVEN

State autonomy and state capture in South Africa: A conceptual critique

MABUTHO SHANGASE

INTRODUCTION

'State capture' has become the dominant term for describing systemic corruption and misgovernance in South Africa (Chipkin et al., 2018; Myburgh, 2017; Olver, 2021). Originally an obscure political science concept, it now permeates public discourse, referring primarily to the period after the African National Congress's 2007 elective conference, where corruption escalated dramatically (Bloomberg, 2017, cited in Chipkin et al., 2018). The World Bank (2000) defines state capture as illicit efforts to influence laws and policies for private gain, diverting public institutions from their intended functions (Dávid-Barrett, 2023). Crucially, it entails the erosion of state autonomy – whereby corporations or other actors co-opt state institutions for their own benefit (Innes, 2016; Skocpol, 1985).

In South Africa, state capture peaked between 2012 and 2018 under President Jacob Zuma, whose alliance with the India-originating

Gupta business family and other private interests, redirected political decision-making away from formal state structures (Bhorat et al., 2017; Chipkin et al., 2018). The looting of state-owned enterprises (SOEs) like Eskom and Transnet, alongside the weakening of oversight bodies, exemplified this systemic collapse (Van Niekerk et al., 2022). Despite the 2022 report of the Zondo Commission, which implicated over 1,500 individuals and recommended prosecutions, the National Prosecuting Authority (NPA) has secured few convictions, fuelling public disillusionment (Corruption Watch, 2025; Cruywagen, 2024).

The Zondo Commission did have the effect, however, of further popularising the term 'state capture' in public discourse. Yet the term has often been applied indiscriminately, overshadowing deeper structural issues like the extent of state autonomy – the state's capacity to act independently of private or partisan interference (Von Holdt, 2019).

While corruption has been extensively documented (Chipkin, 2013; Lodge, 1998), the erosion of state autonomy remains understudied. Corruption in South Africa is not merely criminal but also institutional, serving as a mechanism for elite accumulation (Bhorat et al., 2017; Von Holdt, 2019). Surveys indicate widespread public belief in its pervasiveness: 59 per cent of South Africans think most people are involved, while 62 per cent fear reprisals for exposing it (Gordon and Pienaar, 2025).

Amid these narratives of corruption, governance failure and state capture, discourse about state autonomy has been close to non-existent. Instead, the narrative of state capture has dominated the South African public discourse at least for the past decade, with no indications of how state autonomy has been compromised. To put it even more bluntly, the concept of state autonomy has been starkly missing in South Africa. This chapter seeks to address that gap.

THE CONCEPT OF STATE CAPTURE IN THE SOUTH AFRICAN CONTEXT

Debates around state capture in South Africa have been murky as they tend to merge concepts of the state and the phenomenon of corruption. While these conversations do not directly refer to the concept of state autonomy, they do imply that there has never been an autonomous state in South Africa. Some reductionist commentary argues that, by design, the state is captured. This claim is not only aimed at the modern state, but at the capitalist state in general. Some commentators, in arguing for the inextricability of the state from corruption and capture, go as far as to excavate the scandals of Paul Kruger during the last decade of the Zuid-Afrikaansche Republiek (ZAR) (Heydenrych, 2017). In another instance, Seale (2017) contends that, in effect, state capture occurred through organisations such as the Broederbond before 1994. Consequently, the flawed assertion of the state being inherently captured has gained popularity (Van Wyk, 2018). Gordon and Pienaar (2025: 10) opine that 'apartheid was a system managed by a powerful elite who created a structure of patronage, power and privilege that was inherently corrupt'. Networks of state capture allegedly entrenched themselves during apartheid, thrived and spilt over into the young democracy after 1994 (Lodge, 2019; Van Vuuren, 2018; Van Vuuren and Marchant, 2023; Van Wyk, 2018).

The Zondo Commission was burdened with exposing the scope and nature of corruption during the Zuma administration (Buthelezi and Vale, 2023; Gordon and Pienaar, 2025). It scrutinised the role of public servants, revealing that most officials lacked the expert knowledge, technical autonomy and public service orientation required of professionals (Thacker and Pillay, 2023). The Commission found that in many instances, appointment processes were tampered with, and undeserving individuals were recruited into lucrative positions; and this became the hallmark of state capture and patronage (Thacker and Pillay, 2023). The Commission published six detailed reports on corruption that took place in several state departments and SOEs (Pillay, 2022). The final volume (Part VI, Vol. 4) of the report provides detailed recommendations for each entity implicated in the state capture project (Zondo, 2023).

There have always been powerful business interests working closely with the South African state (Legassick and Wolpe, 1976; Marais, 2011), which have been instrumental in supporting White business and the minority White population in general, which have both been beneficiaries of the exploitation of African labour and job reservation, among their various benefits from colonial and apartheid capital accumulation (Fine and Rustomjee, 1996; Terreblanche, 1994). In the 'Gold Maize Alliance', sectors such as mining and agriculture were buttressed by the colonial and apartheid governments which provided rafts of legislation creating monopolies and value chains for White capital to benefit the White minority (Terreblanche, 1994). However, the establishment of the colonial state should not be confused with the concept of state capture as it is understood today. The British colonies of the Cape and Natal, the Boer republics of the Orange Free State and the Transvaal, the Union of South Africa, and the apartheid state were all established to benefit White people. The reductionist misconception of capture within the modern state arises, partly, from misconceptions about classic Marxist arguments relating to the capitalist state.

According to Marxists, the state is positioned for capital accumulation, the defence of private property, and certain class interests (Vincent, 2002). The state sustains capitalism and primarily serves as an oppressive or coercive instrument of the dominant bourgeoisie (Vincent, 2002). In the words of Marx and Engels, 'The executive of the modern state is but a committee for managing the common affairs of the whole bourgeoisie' (Marx and Engels, 1888). Thus the classical Marxist view is that class divisions in a capitalist society produce the state as their by-product (Albo and Jenson, 1989). So, the ruling classes control the state and use it to realise their common political and economic interests (Albo and Jenson, 1989). The concept of state capture in a democracy, denoting a state operating under the undue influence, and for the sole benefit, of external interests, such as business, should not be confused with a racialised state that was overtly and unapologetically designed to serve the White minority. Thus, arguments that South Africa as a polity has always been captured since the arrival of European settlers in 1652 should be dismissed as they fail to appreciate the complexity and nuance of the concept of capture as conceived in political science today. This is because, theoretically, 'state capture' is understood in the context of a democratic state; in a racialised state like South Africa, the state was not 'captured' by certain group interests; it was designed specifically to serve those interests.

It would deepen the analysis of state capture to reflect on how the advent of state capture tampered with the state's autonomy to formulate public policy. It is important to address these issues of concept formation and classification to avoid collapsing all forms of malfeasance and corruption into a single category. State autonomy refers to bureaucratic cohesiveness as a component of the state's capacity to act independently of and against the demands of non-state interests as it pursues collective goals (Evans, 1995; Polidano, 1998). I emphasise the state's capacity to formulate its own policy goals away from pressures of societal interests such as capital, organised labour or even political formations (Shangase, 2018). Accordingly, the narrative of state capture has dominated the South African public discourse for at least the past decade without indicating how state autonomy has been compromised.

Bussell (2015) argues that the literature is rich in typologies of corruption. One framework distinguishes between petty and grand corruption; another between 'retail' and 'wholesale' corruption, where the former refers to a multiplicity of small transactions while the latter is about macro-scale actions of corruption. Morris (2011) uses an 'Institutional Location Framework' which distinguishes between 'upper-level' (senior politicians) and 'lower-level' (public servants) corruption. Vargas-Hernández (2009) notes that there is no universally valid typology of corruption and thus researchers utilise multiple classifications. If one were to attempt to apply some typology or spectrum of corruption that moves from petty to grand corruption, and ultimately 'state capture', it is unlikely that most of the reported cases in South Africa would qualify for the last category. At best, most incidents of corruption at state level in South Africa arguably fall within the category of grand corruption. Gumede (2017) describes 'grand corruption' as instances in which public officials, elected representatives and leaders plunder public resources on a large scale. Individuals close to power essentially treat state resources like their personal assets (Gumede, 2017). There should be a systematic way of distinguishing between petty and grand corruption, and the capture of laws and regulations. Common and materialistic forms of corruption should be separated from ideational ones that involve the manipulation of laws, regulations or public policy.

In their pioneering work, Hellman et al. (2000) argue that state capture, influence and administrative corruption are shown to have distinct causes and consequences. Petty corruption and administrative corruption – unlike both state capture and influence – are not associated with specific benefits for the beneficiaries in a direct material sense (Hellman et al., 2000). Hellman et al.'s definitions are useful, narrow and conceptually discriminating, but a problem may arise with narratives that refer to corruption and state capture interchangeably without paying attention to nuance and distinctiveness. For example, Hosken (2017, cited in Van Niekerk et al., 2022) defines state capture generically as the seizing of 'national resources and the appropriation of funds through money laundering, looting of state-owned enterprises and bribing of executives and top functionaries in key positions, in order to prevent investigations'. Such a definition creates more conceptual confusion.

Admittedly, corruption among politicians, as regular news, auditing and law-enforcement reports highlight, is quite widespread. Von Holdt (2019) argues that a 'system is shaped by the intersection of patronage and factionalism, as patronage networks form political factions in order to gain power in the state'. This pervasive informal political-economic system existed before Zuma's tenure, and will not be extinguished by the prosecution and incarceration of those involved; rather it will persist and outlive those interests (Von Holdt, 2019). Corruption generally manifests itself as bribery, and/or dishonest, unauthorised or fraudulent activities (Budhram and Geldenhuys, 2018). It characteristically involves misconduct by politicians, public officials and private persons aimed at improper and unlawful self-enrichment or at profiting those approximal to politicians and authority through the misuse of power (Budhram and Geldenhuys, 2018). As the Zondo Commission reports show, at the heart of this spectacle of corruption have been some individual members of the ANC, who were found to be the drivers and beneficiaries of the looting of public resources.

The ANC policy of cadre deployment is well documented. Chipkin (2013) says it has been justified by the liberation movement's historic mission to overthrow oppression and redress past injustices, and its resulting need to strengthen transformative control over the bureaucracy intended to realise its vision of a National Democratic Revolution. He argues that this legacy and the need to compensate for it have rendered the post-apartheid state more permeable to corruption. Certainly, the evidence presented before the Zondo Commission pointed to a symbiotic relationship between 'state capture' and factions within the ANC (Kotze, 2022). Moreover, Zuma, who was eventually identified as the main protagonist of 'capture', justified his role in it as the pursuit of 'radical economic transformation' (Kotze, 2022). State capture has thus become synonymous with all forms of vulgar corruption involving party members and their networks within business and the public sector. This chapter argues that state capture should be regarded as an antithesis to state autonomy because capture should be viewed as the compromising of the state's capacity to act autonomously and formulate public policy goals away from non-state interests. In this framework, the conflation of common corruption and ideational forms of influencing policy processes creates a trivial, possibly misguided classification.

DECONSTRUCTING STATE CAPTURE IN SOUTH AFRICA

The notion of state capture gained currency largely in discourse around institutional changes in post-socialist Eastern Europe. However, it is acknowledged by objective analysts that it is a phenomenon prevalent in many other regions, including established democracies such as the United States of America. If powerful external or internal actors venture to influence a country's policies, laws and economy, or to obtain state regulatory authority undemocratically to benefit their private interests through corrupt means, that constitutes state capture (Bracking, 2018; De Klerk and Solomon, 2018). Thus, state capture has been defined by Hellman and Kaufmann (2001) as:

> …the efforts of firms to shape the laws, policies, and regulations of the state to their own advantage by providing illicit private gains to public officials… firms seek to shape decisions taken by the state to gain specific advantages, often through the imposition

of anticompetitive barriers that generate highly concentrated gains to selected powerful firms at a significant social cost. Because such firms use their influence to block any policy reforms that might eliminate these advantages, state capture has become not merely a symptom but also a fundamental cause of poor governance. In this view, the capture economy is trapped in a vicious circle in which the policy and institutional reforms necessary to improve governance are undermined by collusion between powerful firms and state officials who reap substantial private gains from the continuation of weak governance.

The World Bank (2000: xv) contends that state capture refers to the actions of individuals, groups or firms, both in the public and private sectors, to influence the formation of laws, regulations, decrees and other government policies to their own advantage through the illicit and non-transparent provision of private benefits to public officials. The World Bank's formulation allows for agents that infiltrate public policy processes to be from the public as well as the private sector. This assertion shifts the focus from agents to the architecture of public policy itself, i.e. laws, rules and regulations. The race to capture the state by both internal and external agents culminates in the usurping of this public policy architecture.

A critical, defining feature of the concept of state capture is that it is characterised by the actions of principal agents and corporations external to the state (Bester and Dobovsek, 2021). Pesic (2007, cited in Sitorus, 2011) asserts that any external group or social stratum that exercises decisive influence over state institutions and policies for their own interests, and against the public good, engages in state capture.

Bester and Dobovsek (2021) go further, arguing that 'state capture' implies that the state has lost its social autonomy and is rendered unable to function as an efficient and credible polity. The mention of autonomy is significant because it links directly with Hellman et al.'s (2000) definition of state capture as firms shaping the rules of the game through private payments to public officials and politicians. Some new entrants, such as businesses that had previously been excluded, resort to capture to take advantage of weaknesses in the legal and regulatory framework (Hellman et al., 2000). On the other hand, administrative corruption, such as 'petty' bribery, takes place on the implementation side of laws, rules and regulations (Hellman et al., 2000). Therefore, it is clear that state capture is not simply widespread corruption (Fazekas and Toth, 2014); in other words, widespread petty corruption does not necessarily constitute state capture.

The Gupta-Zuma family networks formed the nexus of a set of interconnected individuals and companies (Bhorat et al., 2017) in a web of relationships that was termed a 'shadow state'. Dealings within the state had been usurped by well-placed individuals in the most significant centres of state power (in government, SOEs and the bureaucracy) (Bhorat et al., 2017). In this 'shadow state' structure, the highly organised Zuma-centred elite established several informal structures to produce profit, power and protection (Madonsela, 2019), similar to the approach in a war economy. The 'capture' networks avoided formalising or documenting their project, in order to prevent traceability, save for the case of Mosebenzi Zwane, which is discussed later. A rhetorical commitment to radical economic transformation was the motif and justification for the political project initiated by the Zuma-centred power elite (Bhorat et al., 2017).

Report No. 6 of 2016/17 of the Public Protector, Advocate Thuli Madonsela, was given an elaborate title delineating the parameters of the investigation (Madonsela, 2016):

> State of Capture: Report on an investigation into alleged improper and unethical conduct by the President and other state functionaries relating to alleged improper relationships and involvement of the Gupta family in the removal and appointment of Ministers and Directors of State-Owned Enterprises resulting in improper and possibly corrupt award of state contracts and benefits to the Gupta family's businesses.

One recommendation of the report was the establishment of a commission of inquiry to be headed by a sitting judge. Subsequently, Zuma appointed Deputy Chief Justice Raymond Zondo in 2017 to head the Commission of Inquiry into State Capture. The Commission's terms of reference were extensive: it aimed 'to investigate matters of public and national interest concerning allegations of state capture, corruption and fraud' (Pillay, 2022).

The Public Protector's report (Madonsela, 2016) mentions the term 'state capture' twice without providing a working definition. Thus, while the concept of 'state capture' is arguably central to the investigation of alleged corruption and the document itself, it is not afforded the requisite importance. The Public Protector (2016: 30) underscores:

> The media reports alleged that the relationship between the President and the Gupta family had evolved into 'state capture' underpinned by the Gupta family having power to influence the appointment of Cabinet Ministers and Directors in Boards of SOEs and leveraging those relationships to get preferential treatment in state contracts, access to state provided business finance and in the award of business licences.

Subsequent media and academic narratives enthusiastically snatched the term 'state capture' from the report without interrogating its intricacies, save for a few mentions of the World Bank and Hellman and Kaufmann's works. The term subsequently became ubiquitous and is now a staple of South Africa's political lexicon and public discourse. In what has come to be regarded as the classical definition of state capture, commentators point at the way formal procedures (such as laws and social norms) and government bureaucracy were manipulated by government officials, state-backed companies, private companies or private individuals in their own favour (Hellman et al., 2000). The way the state capture concept was originally conceived internationally lost its conceptual clarity in South Africa. Thus, the South African popular application of the term is incongruent with the international norm and original definition by Hellman et al. (Chipkin, 2020b). The Zondo Commission defined state capture in the South African context as a project in which a relatively small group of actors, together with their network of collaborators inside and outside the state, conspired systematically to redirect resources from the state for their own gain (Zondo, 2023).

Gryzmala-Busse (2008) identifies clientelism – the exchange of political support for material benefits – as a key tool of state capture. However, in South Africa, it remains unclear whether political elites directly use state resources to reward their supporters, particularly the poor Black majority that relies on state-provided social services such as grants, public housing and free basic utilities. While some argue that the ANC's welfare programmes secure voter loyalty, these social democratic policies do not necessarily constitute clientelism. Moreover, as Lemstra (2020) suggests, the entrenched clientelist networks typical of state capture appear absent in South Africa's politik. The understanding of state capture as a group phenomenon in which members of the business and/or political elite appropriate functions of the state, and use its resources for their own benefit while harming the public good, is inadequate without cognisance of lawmaking and related processes (Fazekas and Toth, 2014).

From this ideational viewpoint, if state capture has taken place there should be clues to it in state processes for formulating public policy – clues such as the manipulation of laws, rules and regulations to benefit particular groups. State capture should be demonstrable in a compromised policy process and, importantly, through the erosion of state autonomy.

ZEROING IN ON STATE AUTONOMY

In South Africa, what is regarded as the state capture project was assisted heavily by officials and professionals within reach of the levers of power in the targeted state institutions. For violation of state autonomy to occur, these officials and individuals would have needed to have demonstrably colluded with some lawmakers and other technocrats to manipulate the drafting or implementation of laws and regulations in a manner distinguishable from grand corruption. What is notable instead is that the corrupt networks managed to gain control of governance and procurement in SOEs and government agencies (Pillay, 2022). These acts left a trail of evidence of fraud, money laundering, racketeering and various other illegal activities in public entities and government at all levels (Pillay, 2022).

It has been argued that state autonomy is centred on the notion that the state has interests and policy goals that have developed independently of the needs of pluralist groups or classes, and the state is structured and acts to further these interests and achieve these goals (Klyza, 1992). The state bureaucracy, as a sector that draws people from all social backgrounds and not a social class in a Marxist sense, acts autonomously in the pursuit of the public interest. Therefore, public officials or state managers possess the ability to execute power independently of non-state forces such as capital, organised labour and political parties, even in the event of resistance from such external interests (Jessop, 2001). State autonomy thus becomes necessary not only to formulate collective goals for the fulfilment of public interest, but also to implement those goals (Rueschemeyer and Evans, 1985, cited in DeCanio, 2010). Neo-Marxist scholars such as Nicos Poulantzas have, however, pointed out that within the capitalist state the infrastructural power of the state is circumscribed (Ianoni, 2013). Poulantzas introduced the concept of 'relative state autonomy', signalling that within democracies, the autonomy of the state is not absolute but restricted by the separation of powers doctrine, and other checks and balances. This relative autonomy enables the state to act authoritatively as arbitrator of local conflict, thus fulfilling a genuine need in society (Hallenberg et al., 2008). Thus, the state is viewed as 'relatively autonomous' while its exercise of power remains influenced by class-based determinants, such as economic elites and the needs of capitalism (Amenta, 2005). Relative autonomy of the state in Poulantzas' conception is considered specific to the capitalist state and indivisible from it (Ianoni, 2013).

Nevertheless, the crux of state autonomy is well explained by the very etymological roots of the word 'autonomy'. The term has its origin in ancient Greek, and breaks down into autos (self) and nomos (rule, law, or custom), with the latter also referring to governance (Agich, 1994; Dworkin, 2015; Swaine, 2016). A city (polis) had *autonomia* when its citizens made their own laws, as opposed to being under the control of a conquering power, and the term was originally applied to Greek city-states (Dworkin, 2015), within which the term involved the notion of and reference to self-rule or self-governance (Agich, 1994).

Extended to the modern state, autonomy came to refer to a sovereign state that could write and pass its own laws without meddling by an external authority. The importance of state actors in upholding state autonomy and capacity has come to mean that state agents are more likely to prevail in any given political decision (Alford and Friedland, 1985, cited in Amenta, 2005). The question that then arises is whether the clientelist networks (Gryzmala-Busse, 2008; Lemstra, 2020) of the Zuma-Gupta relationship, and other relationships deemed to have been indicative of state capture, indeed eroded the state's capacity to formulate its own rules, laws and regulations.

The extent to which internal and non-state networks of corruption succeeded in infiltrating public policy and lawmaking processes in South Africa needs further interrogation. There is, however, at least one stark instance: former Minister of Mineral Resources, Mosebenzi Zwane, who has been accused of corruption, allegedly attempted to amend policy in order to accommodate and benefit the Gupta family. The 'Broad-Based Black Socio-Economic Empowerment Charter for the South African Mining and Minerals Industry' (Department of Mineral Resources, 2017: 2) was allegedly doctored as follows:

'Black Person' is a generic term which means Africans, Coloureds, and Indians-

(a) Who are citizens of the Republic of South Africa by birth or descent; or

(b) Who became citizens of the Republic of South Africa by naturalisation:

  (i) *before 27 April 1994; or*

  (ii) *on or after 27 April 1994 and who would have been entitled to acquire citizenship by naturalisation prior to that date* (italics, added for emphasis).

The Gupta family arrived in South Africa after 1994 and had in no way suffered under colonialism or apartheid in South Africa. The amendment to the policy shoehorned the Guptas, Indian nationals, into the South African Indian community by stealth and fraudulent drafting. This specific amendment, labelled 'The Gupta clause' by some media reports (Nkwashu, 2018; Peyper, 2017), was the closest development to the appropriation of lawmaking in South Africa. In this sense, it was the one, textbook foray into violating state autonomy. Using the typology of corruption suggested earlier, the infiltration of lawmaking and policy processes would constitute an important element of violation of state autonomy and capture of the state; however, it did not have to succeed as other centres of state power could be used to effect state capture.

CONCLUSION

This chapter attempted to delineate conceptual parameters around the concept of state capture. Admittedly, administrative corruption, grand corruption and state capture all fall on the same spectrum in ascending order. Nonetheless boundaries should be drawn around each to denote the modalities and scales that separate the categories from each other. It is highly unlikely that corruption will disappear from South Africa's political economy – as it would be well-nigh impossible to eliminate altogether in any part of the world – and scholars must remain vigilant in studying it.

The World Bank (2000) attempted to unbundle the phenomenon of corruption by placing primary emphasis on the distinction between state capture and administrative corruption. Bribes to parliamentarians to 'buy' their votes for important pieces of legislation, bribes to government officials to enact favourable regulations or decrees, and bribes to judges to influence court decisions are the classic examples of grand corruption through which firms can encode advantages for themselves into the basic legal and regulatory structure of an economy (Sitorus, 2011). Since the Zondo Commission submitted its reports in 2021, prosecutions have been few and far between; perhaps the minefield of systemic corruption which also penetrated deep into the workings of law enforcement agencies also contributes to the poor performance in this regard. Hellman and Kaufmann (2001) assert that in transition economies, corruption has taken on a new image – that of so-called oligarchs manipulating policy formulation and even shaping the emerging rules of the game to their own very substantial advantage. They referred to this behaviour as *state capture*.

State capture should be regarded as the antithesis of state autonomy. Once state autonomy is compromised, state programmes insidiously benefit certain interests without being immediately identifiable.

REFERENCES

Agich, G.J. 1994. 'Key concepts: Autonomy'. *Philosophy, Psychiatry & Psychology*, 1(4), 267–269.

Albo, G. and Jenson, J. 1989. 'A contested concept: The relative autonomy of the state', in Clement, W. and Williams, G. (eds), *The New Canadian Political Economy*. Kingston: McGill University Press.

Amenta, E. 2005. 'Institutionalist and state-centric theories of political sociology', in Alford, R., Hicks, A., Janoski, T. and Schwart, M.A. (eds), *The Handbook of Political Sociology*. Cambridge: Cambridge University Press.

Bester, D. and Dobovsek, B. 2021. 'State capture: Case of South Africa'. *NBP. Nauka, bezbednost, policija*, 26(1), 73–87, doi:10.5937/nabepo 26-3234

Bhorat, H., Buthelezi, M., Chipkin, I., Duma, S., Mondi, L., Peter, C., Qobo, M., Swilling, M. and Friedenstein, H. 2017. 'Betrayal of the promise: How South Africa is being stolen'. State Capacity Research Project, Public Affairs Research Institute (PARI), Johannesburg, pp. 1–72.

Bond, P. 2024. 'Corporate corruption of South African politics and economics: Accumulation by dispossession as a structural process, beyond state capture'. *New Agenda: South African Journal of Social and Economic Policy*, 93, 33–46.

Bracking, S. 2018. *Corruption & State Capture: What Can Citizens Do?* American Academy of Arts & Sciences.

Budhram, T. and Geldenhuys, N. 2018. 'Combating corruption in South Africa: Assessing the performance of investigating and prosecuting agencies'. *Acta Criminologica: African Journal of Criminology & Victimology*, 31(2), 23–46.

Bussell, J. 2015. 'Typologies of corruption: A pragmatic approach', in Rose-Ackerman, S. and Lagunes, P. (eds), *Greed, Corruption, and the Modern State*. Edward Elgar Publishing, pp. 21–45.

Buthelezi, M. and Vale, P. (eds). 2023. *State Capture in South Africa: How and Why it Happened*. Johannesburg: Wits University Press, https://doi.rg/10.18772/22023068318

Callaghan, N., Foley, R. and Swilling, M. (eds). 2021. *Anatomy of State Capture*. Stellenbosch: African Sun Media.

Camerer, L. 2000. 'Corruption in South Africa, Results of An Expert Panel Survey'. European Union.

Centre for Development and Enterprise. 2024. 'NPA falling short on State Capture prosecutions', https://cde.org.za/npa-falling-short-on-statecapture-prosecutions/

Chipkin, I. 2013. 'Whither the state? Corruption, institutions, and state-building in South Africa'. *Politikon*, 40(2), 211–231.

Chipkin, I. 2020a. 'Why challenge by Zuma's advocate could checkmate Zondo inquiry'. *Business Live*, https://www.businesslive.co.za/bd/opinion/2020-11-18-why-challenge-by-zumas-advocate-could-checkmate-zondo-inquiry/#google_vignette, accessed 16 June 2025.

Chipkin, I. 2020b. 'Defining "State Capture" in South Africa: Democracy, Bureaucratic Autonomy and Elite Populism'. GAPP Working Paper, Vol. 1, No. 1, pp. 1–19.

Chipkin, I., Swilling, M., Bhorat, H., Qobo, M., Duma, S., Mondi, L., Peter, C., Buthelezi, M., Friedenstein, H. and Prins, N. 2018. *Shadow State: The Politics of State Capture*. New York: NYU Press.

Corruption Watch. 2022. 'Analysis of Corruption Trends'. Johannesburg, https://www.corruptionwatch.org.za/wp-content/uploads/2022/09/corruption-watch-ACT-2022-digital-combined-agent-orange-design-20220907.pdf, accessed 16 June 2025.

Corruption Watch. 2025. *State Capture Cases to Look Out for in 2025*, https://www.corruptionwatch.org.za/state-capture-cases-to-look-out-for-in-2025/, accessed 16 June 2025.

Cruywagen, V. 2024. 'Lack of state capture prosecutions ignites fiery debate'. *Daily Maverick*, http://www.dailymaverick.co.za/article/2024-03-14-lack-of-state-capture-prosecutions-ignites-fiery-debate/, accessed 16 June 2025.

Dávid-Barrett, E. 2023. 'State capture and development: A conceptual framework'. *Journal of International Relations and Development*, 26(1).

DeCanio, S. 2010. 'Bringing the state back in ... again'. *Critical Review: A Journal of Politics and Society*, 14(2/3), 139–146.

De Klerk, R. and Solomon, H. 2018. 'The Institutionalisation of endemic corruption: State capture in South Africa'. University of the Free State.

Democratic Alliance. 2025. 'Track the consequences of Zondo's State Capture reports', https://www.da.org.za/statecaptureconsequences

Department of Mineral Resources. 2017. 'Reviewed Broad Based Black-Economic Empowerment Charter for the South African Mining and Minerals Industry, 2016', https://www.gov.za/sites/default/files/gcis_document/201706/40923gon581.pdf, accessed 31 August 2025.

Dworkin, G. 2015. 'The nature of autonomy'. *Nordic Journal of Studies in Educational Policy*, 22, 28479, DOI: 10.3402/nstep. v1.28479

Evans, B. 1995. *Embedded Autonomy: States and Industrial Transformation*. Princeton, New Jersey: Princeton University Press.

Fazekas, M. and Toth, I.J. 2014. 'From corruption to state capture: A new analytical framework with empirical applications from Hungary'. Working Paper Series: CRC-WP/2014:01.

February, J. 2024. 'Commissions, Corruption and State Capture: Charting the Way Forward for South Africa'. South African Institute of International Affairs.

Fine, B. and Rustomjee, Z. 1996. *The Political Economy of South Africa: From Minerals-Energy Complex to Industrialisation*. United Kingdom: C. Hurst and Co.

Gordon, S. and Pienaar, G.D. 2025. *Corruption and Behaviour Change Tracking Social Norms and Values in South Africa.* Human Sciences Research Council (HSRC), Commissioned by the German Agency for International Cooperation (GIZ).

Grzymala-Busse, A. 2008. 'Beyond clientelism incumbent state capture and state formation'. *Comparative Political Studies,* 41(4/5), 638–673.

Gumede, W. 2017. 'Combating Corruption in South Africa'. Policy Brief No. 14, Monitoring Policy Briefs, 3 March.

Gustafsson, H. 1998. 'The conglomerate state: A perspective on state formation in early modern Europe'. *Scandinavian Journal of History*, 23(3/4), 189–213.

Hallenberg, M., Holm, J. and Johansson, D. 2008. 'Organization, legitimation, participation'. *Scandinavian Journal of History*, 33(3), 247–268.

Hellman, J.S., Jones, G. and Kaufmann, D. 2000. 'Seize the state, seize the day: State capture, corruption, and influence in transition'. September.

Hellman, J. and Kaufmann, D. 2001. 'Confronting the challenges of state capture in transition economies'. *Finance & Development: A quarterly magazine of the IMF*, 38(3).

Heydenrych, H. 2017. *Skermutselings en Skandale: Paul Kruger deur ander oë 1890–1895*. Pretoria: Impravatur.

Holden, P. 2023. *Zondo at your Fingertips*. Johannesburg: Jacana Media.

Ianoni, M. 2013. 'Autonomy of the state and development in democratic capitalism'. *Brazilian Journal of Political Economy,* 33(4), 577–598.

Innes, A. 2016. 'Corporate state capture in open societies, The emergence of corporate brokerage party systems'. *East European Politics and Societies and Cultures,* 30(3), 594–620.

Jonas, M. 2019. *After Dawn: Hope After State Capture*. Pan Macmillan South Africa.

Jessop, B. 2001. 'Bringing the state back in (yet again): Reviews, revisions, rejections, and redirections'. *International Review of Sociology*, 11(2), 149–173.

Judicial Commission of Inquiry into State Capture. 2023a. *State Capture Report* (Johannesburg: Judicial Commission of Inquiry into State Capture), Part 6, Vol. 4, 1.

Judicial Commission of Inquiry into State Capture. 2023b. *State Capture Report* (Johannesburg: Judicial Commission of Inquiry into State Capture), Part 1, Vol. 2, 298.

Klaaren, J. 2023. 'Legal mobilisation against state capture', in Buthelezi,

M. and Vale, P. (eds), *State Capture in South Africa: How and Why It Happened*. Johannesburg: Wits University Press, https://doi. org/10.18772/22023068318

Klyza, C.M. 1992. 'A window of autonomy: State autonomy and the forest service in the early 1990s'. *Polity,* 25(2), 173–196.

Kotze, D. 2022. 'South Africa's State Capture Commission nears its end after four years. Was it worth it?' *The Conversation*, https://theconversation. com/south-africas-state-capture-commission-nears-its-end-after-four- years-was-it-worth-it-182898, accessed 16 June 2025.

Krasner, S.D. 1995. 'Compromising Westphalia'. *International Security*, 20(3), 115–151.

Legassick, M. and Wolpe, H. 1976. 'The Bantustans and capital accumulation in South Africa'. *Review of African Political Economy*, 3(7), 87–107.

Lemstra, M. 2020. 'The destructive effects of state capture in the Western Balkans'. Netherlands Institute of International Relations Policy Brief, https://www.clingendael.org/sites/default/files/2020-10/Policy_Brief_ Undermining_EU_enlargement_2020.pdf, accessed 18 June 2025.

Lodge, T. 1998. 'Political corruption in South Africa'. *African Affairs*, 97(387), 157–187.

Lodge, T. 2019. 'Apartheid, guns and money: A tale of profit'. *Small Wars & Insurgencies*, 30(3), 716–718, DOI: 10.1080/09592318.2019.1601875

Madonsela, T. 2016. 'State of Capture: Report', Report No. 6 of 2016/17. Public Protector of The Republic of South Africa.

Madonsela, S. 2019. 'Critical reflections on state capture in South Africa'. *Insight on Africa*, 11(1), 113–130.

Mail & Guardian. 2018. 'Editorial: Definition of State Capture', https:// mg.co.za/article/2018-09-14-00-definition-of-state-capture/, accessed 18 June 2025.

Marais, H. 2011. *South Africa Pushed to the Limit: The Political Economy of Change*. London: Zed Books.

Martin, M.E. and Solomon, H. 2016. 'Understanding the phenomenon of "state capture" in South Africa'. *Southern African Peace and Security Studies*, 5(1), 21–35.

Marx, K. and Engels, F. 1888. *Manifesto of the Communist Party*. Chicago: Charles H. Kerr & Company.

Mathebula, N.E and Munzhedzi, P.H. 2017. 'Trias Politica for Ethical Leadership and Good Governance: Praxis of Checks and Balances in the South African Context'. *Bangladesh e-Journal of Sociology,* 14(2).

Morris, S. 2011. 'Forms of corruption'. *CESifo DICE Report*, 9(2), 10–14.

Motloba, P.D. 2018. 'Understanding of the principle of autonomy (Part 1)'. *South African Dental Journal*, 73(6), 418–420.

Myburgh, P.L. 2017. *The Republic of Gupta: A Story of State Capture*. Johannesburg: Penguin Random House.

Newham, G. 2002. 'Tackling Police Corruption in South Africa'. Centre for the Study of Violence and Reconciliation, Johannesburg.

Nkwashu, N. 2018. 'The genesis of the "Gupta clause" within the financial regulatory framework of South Africa', https://www.derebus.org.za, accessed 17 June 2025.

Nordlinger, E.A., Lowi, T.J. and Fabbrini, S. 1988. 'The return to the state: Critiques'. *The American Political Science Review,* 82(3), 875–901.

Olver, C, 2020. 'Shadow state: The politics of state capture'. *South African Historical Journal,* 72(2), 345–349, DOI: 10.1080/02582473.2020.1774640

Olver, C. 2021. 'State capture at a local level', in Callaghan, N., Foley, R. and Swilling, M. (eds), *Anatomy of State Capture.* Stellenbosch: African Sun Media, pp. 173–187.

Parliament Research Unit, 2022. Special Bulletin: 'State Capture (Updated). Key recommendations and findings: Judicial Commission of Inquiry into State Capture Report'.

Peyper, L. 2017. '"Gupta clause" in Financial Bill worries DA', https://www. news24.com

Pienaar, G. and Bohler-Muller, N. 2023. 'Implementation of the State Capture Commission Recommendations. An institutional perspective on ethics and accountability'. *New Agenda: South African Journal of Social and Economic Policy,* 90(1).

Pillay, D. 2022. 'The Zondo Commission: A bite-sized summary'. Public Affairs Research Institute, https://pari.org.za/summary-the-state-capture-commission/, accessed 17 June 2025.

Polidano, C. 1998. 'Don't discard State Autonomy: Revisiting the East Asian experience of development'. Institute for Development Policy and Management, University of Manchester.

Public Protector South Africa. 2016. 'State of Capture', https:// www.gov.za/sites/default/files/gcis_document/201611/ stateofcapturereport14october2016_0.pdf, accessed 31 August 2025.

Renwick, R. 2018. *How to Steal a Country: State Capture and Hopes for the Future in South Africa.* London, United Kingdom: Biteback Publishing.

Republic of South Africa. 2016. Broad-Based Black Socio-Economic Empowerment Charter for the South African Mining and Minerals Industry, Government Gazette, Vol. 610, No. 39933.

Republic of South Africa. 2020. *National Anti-Corruption Strategy 2020-2030,* ISBN: 978-0-620-92434-4, https://www.dpme.gov.za

Seale, W. 2017. 'In defence of the academic – State capture and the failure to deconstruct Apartheid's Shadow State: A response to the State Capacity Research Project – "Betrayal of the Promise – How South Africa is Being Stolen"', https://blackopinion.co.za/wp-content/uploads/2017/10/Wesley-FINAL.pdf, accessed 30 June 2025.

Shai, K.B. 2017. 'South African state capture: A symbiotic affair between business and state going bad(?)'. African Studies Association of India.

Shangase, M. 2018. 'Stability and change in South African public policy 1994–2014'. Doctoral thesis, University of Edinburgh.

Sitorus, L.E. 2011. 'State capture: Is it a crime? How the world perceived it'. *Indonesia Law Review,* 2(1).

Skocpol, T. 1985. 'Bringing the state back in: Strategies of analysis in current research', in Evans, P.B., Rueschemeyer, D. and Skocpol, T. (eds), *Bringing the State Back.* Cambridge: Cambridge University Press.

Swaine, L. 2016. 'The origins of autonomy'. *History of Political Thought,* 37(2), 216–237.

Terreblanche, S.J. 1994. 'From white supremacy and racial capitalism towards a sustainable system of democratic capitalism: A structural analysis'. *Transit,* SJT 33.

Thacker, C. and Pillay, D. 2023. 'How professionals enabled state capture', in Buthelezi, M. and Vale, P. (eds), *State Capture in South Africa.* Johannesburg: Wits Press, pp. 109–129.

Van Niekerk, T., L'Heureux, A.V. and Holtzhausen, N. 2022. 'State capture in South Africa and Canada: A comparative analysis'. *Public Integrity,* 25(4), 1–13.

Van Vuuren, H. 2018. *Apartheid, Guns and Money: A Tale of Profit.* London: Hurst & Company.

Van Vuuren, H. and Marchant, M. 2023. 'Cycles of state capture: Bringing profiteers and enablers to account', in Buthelezi, M. and Vale, P. (eds), *State Capture in South Africa: How and Why It Happened.* Johannesburg: Wits University Press, pp. 197–216.

Van Wyk, E. 2018. 'The unfinished business of apartheid'. 10 January, https://www.wits.ac.za/curiosity/stories/the-unfinished-business-of-apartheid.html, accessed 30 June 2025.

Vargas-Hernández, J.G. 2009. 'The multiple faces of corruption: Typology, forms and levels', https://ssrn.com/abstract=1413976 or http://dx.doi.org/10.2139/ssrn.1413976, accessed 18 June 2025.

Vincent, A. 2002. 'Conceptions of the state', in Hawkesworth, M. and Kogan, M. (eds), *Encyclopaedia of Government and Politics.* New York: Routledge.

Von Holdt, K. 2019. 'The political economy of corruption: Elite-formation, factions and violence'. Society, Work and Politics Institute Working Paper No. 10.

World Bank, 2000. *Anticorruption in Transition A Contribution to the Policy Debate.* Washington D.C.: The World Bank.

Zondo, R.M.M. 2023. 'Judicial Commission of Inquiry into State Capture Report: Part VI, Vol 4: All the Recommendations', https://www.statecapture.org.za/site/files/announcements/672/OCR_version_-_State_Capture_Commission_Report_Part_VI_Vol_IV_-_Recommendations.pdf, accessed 31 August 2025.

EIGHT

Politics and power: The contested state and the just energy transition in South Africa

Laurence Caromba

INTRODUCTION

Since 2007, South Africa has experienced an energy supply crisis, which forced the national power utility, Eskom, to implement increasingly frequent planned electricity loadshedding. After two years with minimal power cuts in 2016 and 2017, loadshedding resumed in 2018, and in 2023 there were a record 335 days with electricity cuts (Jordaan, quoted in BusinessTech, 2023). The situation significantly improved in 2024, resulting in cautious optimism and relief that the crisis might have finally ended. Nevertheless, the years in which the state was unable to ensure a reliable supply of energy remain one of the most visible public policy failures of the country's democratic era.

The energy crisis inflicted enormous economic costs on South Africans from 2007 to 2022 (Akpeji et al., 2020; Erero, 2023; Walsh et al., 2021). The overall cost to the economy is estimated to range from

R35 billion for the 2007–2019 period, when the energy shortfall was lower (Walsh et al., 2021: 16), to as high as R560 billion in 2022 alone (Erero, 2023: 90). In 2022, the South African Reserve Bank estimated that loadshedding had reduced South Africa's economic growth rate by 2 percentage points (Naidoo, 2023). According to South Africa's energy minister, Kgosientsho Ramokgopa, the country suffered 650,000 job losses due to loadshedding in 2022 (Ramokgopa, quoted in Fraser, 2023).

In addition to these economic impacts, electricity supply interruptions also had important political consequences. In a 2023 poll of voters who supported South Africa's governing African National Congress (ANC), 24 per cent said they would stop voting for the party if the loadshedding problem was not resolved before the 2024 national election (Social Research Foundation, 2023). Indeed, the ANC lost approximately 35 per cent of its voters between the 2019 and 2024 elections, suggesting that many of those polled followed through on this threat. This, in turn, raises the puzzle of why the South African state was slow to respond to the crisis, given the powerful political incentives for the government to resolve it.

South Africa's energy supply crisis intersects with a broader, longer-term environmental crisis: global climate change. Both during and after the apartheid era, South Africa practised a model of economic development in which cheap and abundant access to coal was used to subsidise energy-intensive mining and minerals beneficiation (Baker et al., 2014: 792). While South Africa is far from being the world's largest carbon emitter, its economy is unusually carbon-intensive, making it the fifteenth-largest emitter of greenhouse gases in the world in 2020 (World Resources Institute, 2023). South Africa therefore serves as an important test case for whether developing states can reduce their carbon emissions without compromising economic development or reducing citizens' access to energy.

This chapter explores the history of South Africa's shift towards renewable energy, highlighting how politics and institutional factors have shaped the process. It suggests that the self-interested actions of competing groups within the state and society, in combination with the country's path-dependent institutional development, created a system with powerful 'veto players' who could block changes to the status quo (Tsebelis, 2002: 19), and argues that these dynamics slowed down the implementation of renewable energy policies that would have benefited both the economy and the environment.

BACKGROUND: THREATS AND OPPORTUNITIES FROM DECARBONISATION

From South Africa's perspective, the intersection of the energy supply crisis and the broader global climate crisis presents both threats and opportunities. South Africa is highly vulnerable to the adverse effects of climate change, due to a combination of geographic, social and political factors (World Bank, 2021: 3). Furthermore, even if policymakers choose to discount the direct costs of climate change, it is possible that South Africa's long-term growth will be adversely affected by the carbon intensity of its economy.

Scholars of economics and international relations have theorised that states which are highly committed to climate change mitigation may form 'climate clubs' (Keohane and Victor, 2016; Nordhaus, 2015) that will engage in preferential trading arrangements among themselves while sanctioning polluters outside the club. The European Union's (EU) Carbon Border Adjustment Mechanism (CBAM), introduced in 2023, arguably represents the first real effort to establish such a climate club. This EU policy could significantly adversely affect South African companies exporting to the European Union, especially in energy-intensive sectors such as steel (Presidential Climate Commission, 2023: 2). This risk will be amplified if similar climate clubs are formed in other regions.

The chief proximate cause of loadshedding in South Africa has been the declining energy availability factor (EAF) of its coal-fired power stations, most of which were constructed during the 1970s and 1980s. Eskom has a nominal generation capacity of 44,000 MW, which should be enough to supply South Africa's energy requirements. However, many of Eskom's coal plants are reaching the end of their life cycles and suffer from high failure rates. This problem stems from a combination of political directives by previous administrations to 'keep the lights on' at the expense of planned maintenance, overspending due to corruption and malfeasance, and deliberate sabotage (Comrie, 2022). Consequently, Eskom's EAF trended downward since 2017, reaching a low point of 50 per cent by the end of 2022 (Eskom, 2024).

In the past, the simultaneous collapse of so much of South Africa's coal fleet might have been an insurmountable challenge. However, with the declining cost of renewable energy and the increasing availability of financing for renewable energy, South Africa has an unusual opportunity to simultaneously increase its energy supply while also mitigating the threat of climate change (Xaba, 2023: 34). Renewable energy production can be quickly scaled up, is inexpensive to produce (Hörsch and Calitz, 2017: 8), and would lead to a reduction in both air pollution and South Africa's vulnerability to fluctuations in the global market for fossil fuels. Various modelling studies have found that the most cost-effective way for South Africa to increase its generation capacity would be to invest in renewable energy generation, rather than in competing technologies such as nuclear or coal (Hörsch and Calitz, 2017; Knorr et al., 2016; Solomon et al., 2019; Steyn et al., 2022). However, it has also been argued that baseload generation, including nuclear and gas, is critical for the stability of the system (Ramokgopa, 2024).

Recognising the advantages of renewable energy generation, the South African government has embraced the concept of a 'just energy transition' as a central pillar of its energy policy (Department of Mineral Resources and Energy, 2019: 44–45; Presidential Climate Commission, 2022; The Presidency, 2022b). Important gains have been made; however, the overall pace of investment into renewable energy has been slow and, at times, appears to have been actively hindered by factions within the state. This raises a puzzling question: why has South Africa struggled to increase its production of renewable energy despite economic and environmental benefits, and in the face of an ongoing energy supply crisis?

THE PUZZLE: SOUTH AFRICA'S STALLED
RENEWABLE ENERGY TRANSITION

In 2017, Vietnam introduced a 'feed-in tariff' designed to promote private investment in solar energy, guaranteeing a purchase price of US$93.5 per MWh for 20 years for projects started before June 2019 (Do et al., 2021). This spurred a massive increase in solar capacity, adding 16,600 MW to the grid by 2020. So much energy was added to Vietnam's grid that it exceeded the country's demand, indicating that the tariff was probably too generous (Le, 2022). Still, this rapid and extensive expansion stands in sharp contrast to South Africa's Medupi power station, which not only took longer to build and offered less capacity but also incurred significantly higher costs (Yelland, quoted in Illidge, 2022).

South Africa has not followed Vietnam's trajectory by embracing renewable energy, despite the existence of powerful political and economic incentives to do so. This apparent puzzle might be explained by examining South Africa's energy transition through the lens of historical institutionalism (Lockwood et al., 2017). Institutions shape the interactions of state and societal actors by setting formal and informal rules. Historical institutionalism focuses on the role of history, path dependence, and unexpected outcomes in institutional development (Lockwood et al., 2017: 3; North, 1991: 97). Actors aim to promote their interests within and through institutions, often trying to reform the rules to strengthen their bargaining power both in the present and in the future. Institutions may not reflect the interests of their designers, however, due to the limited time horizons and information available at the time of their creation (Pierson, 2004: 115–119).

A useful starting point is to conceptualise South Africa's institutional structure as an arena in which a conflict between a pro-transition coalition and a pro-status quo coalition plays out. These coalitions are far from monolithic. For instance, pro-transition actors might include private sector producers of renewable energy, workers in the renewable sector and anti-capitalist environmental NGOs. Similarly, a pro-status quo coalition might include fossil fuel energy producers, mining firms and workers within each sector. The specific policy preferences of these groups are likely to differ considerably. Nevertheless, actors tend to form alliances with each other and to lobby sympathetic actors within the state, with the cumulative effect of pushing policy towards either a transition or the maintenance of the status quo.

The state is not monolithic and includes various actors with competing (and sometimes contradictory) priorities. In South Africa, the most important state actor in the energy sector is the Department of Electricity and Energy which is responsible for setting overall energy policy and the procurement of generation capacity.[1] Other important actors include Eskom; (until recently) the Department of Public Enterprises, Eskom's sole shareholder; the National Energy Regulator of South Africa (NERSA), which regulates energy prices; the Department of Forestry, Fisheries and the Environment, which formulates policy on climate change; and the National Treasury, which is responsible for funding (Baker et al., 2015: 19–21). This complex system creates numerous entry points into the state at which societal actors can try to influence policy towards their preferred direction.

DEMOCRACY AND TIME HORIZONS

From an institutionalist perspective, the central fact about post-1994 South Africa is that it is a constitutional democracy characterised by regular and free elections and vigorous political competition. In comparative scholarship on political economy, countries with inclusive and democratic political institutions are generally seen as being more responsive to the needs of their citizens (Acemoglu and Robinson, 2013; De Mesquita et al., 2005).

In terms of electricity distribution, the South African case is consistent with these expectations. In 1990, towards the end of apartheid, only about 35 per cent of South African households were

---

1   This department was known as the Department of Minerals and Energy (DME) prior to 2009. It was split from the minerals portfolio and renamed the Department of Energy (DoE) in 2009; it was then re-combined with the minerals portfolio and renamed the Department of Mineral Resources and Energy (DMRE) in 2019. After the 2024 election it was again split from the minerals portfolio and given its current name.

connected to the electricity grid. After South Africa's democratic transition in 1994, the new government embarked on an ambitious programme of electrification, and, by 2021, this had risen to 89.3 per cent (Statistics South Africa, 2022). Analysis drawn from satellite data demonstrates that the expansion of electricity access in the post-1994 period was closely correlated with the extension of the voting franchise (Kroth et al., 2016).

Despite this progress in extending electricity provision, South Africa has been less successful in increasing total energy supply. This can partly be explained by 'short-termism', planning only for short periods in order to attain successes in the short term, a common problem in democracies. Factors contributing to short-termism include voter bias towards immediate benefits, pressure from interest groups, politicians' focus on the next elections, and the challenge of accounting for future generations' interests (MacKenzie, 2016). This results in prioritising 'quick wins' over long-term investments in infrastructure. During the early 2000s, South Africa attempted to address its energy supply issues by shifting most investment responsibility to the private sector (Eberhard, 2005: 5309). However, due to unattractive, low energy prices and union opposition, the initiative was abandoned. Meanwhile, Eskom was restricted from expanding generation capacity, despite predictions of an impending energy shortfall by 2007 (Department of Minerals and Energy, 1998: 41).

In 2007, when the energy supply crunch arrived on schedule, the South African government responded by authorising the construction of the Medupi and Kusile coal-fired plants. These were conceived as new-generation 'clean coal' plants which would run at supercritical temperatures and make use of flue gas desulphurisation technology to reduce their carbon emissions. On this basis, the government was able to fund the construction of these plants with a US$3.75 billion loan from the World Bank (National Treasury, 2010).

Unfortunately, these projects became mired in cost overruns, delays and quality control problems. Medupi was initially budgeted at R79 billion and Kusile at R69.1 billion, and both power stations were expected to be in operation by 2014 (Tshidavhu and Khatleli, 2020: 128–129). By 2024, Kusile was still not fully completed, and the combined cost of both projects was officially listed as R300 billion. Yelland (quoted in MyBroadband, 2019) argues that the true cost of the projects is higher, and is likely to reach a combined total of R460 billion when accounting for newer expenditure. Despite this enormous capital investment, both plants have been beset with operational problems, including a catastrophic explosion that destroyed one of Medupi's generation units only one week after it began commercial operations in 2021.

INSTITUTIONAL PATH DEPENDENCY AND UNINTENDED CONSEQUENCES

The Medupi and Kusile plants were one part of the South African state's response to the 2007 loadshedding shock. Simultaneously, another policy response, which initially attracted far less attention, was underway: the development of a renewable energy programme aimed at mobilising private sector investment.

In the immediate post-apartheid period, faced with extreme levels of poverty and inequality, South African policymakers understandably chose not to prioritise environmental issues (Hochstetler, 2020: 37–38). However, from the early 2000s, the country became active within the United Nations Framework Convention on Climate Change (UNFCCC) and began to consider policy options for decarbonising its energy system. In 2003, the South African government published a white paper stating its intention to allow independent power producers to generate renewable energy and sell it to Eskom (Department of Minerals and Energy, 2003: 33). However, the policy's implementation was left to Eskom, and there was little progress over the next five years.

When South Africa did introduce a renewable energy programme, the impetus came from NERSA rather than Eskom. With its mandate to protect consumers, NERSA disregarded Eskom's resistance to renewable energy and launched the Renewable Energy Feed-in Tariff (REFIT) programme in 2009 (Baker, 2014: 800). Inspired by similar initiatives in Europe, REFIT allowed independent power producers to sell energy via the Eskom grid at fixed prices for five years, after which the pricing would adjust to market rates (NERSA, 2009: 2,

17). The National Treasury, however, raised concerns about the fiscal implications of REFIT, fearing it could impose an unsustainable burden on state finances. In 2011, after legal consultations suggested that a feed-in tariff might contravene legislation against non-competitive procurement, the government transitioned from REFIT to a competitive bidding system, the Renewable Energy Independent Power Producer Procurement Programme (REIPPPP) (Eberhard and Naude, 2017: 69–70).

Unlike a feed-in tariff, a competitive bidding system makes use of periodic, government-run reverse auctions, or 'bid windows', in which power producers compete to supply energy to the national grid. In most of the countries that use this system, projects are awarded to the lowest bidder; in contrast, the South African programme also requires bidders to satisfy additional socioeconomic criteria related to job creation, localisation of supply chains, and community ownership (Baker et al., 2014: 800). Despite these criteria, many successful REIPPPP winners were large South African corporations, some bidding alone and others in combination with international partners (Eberhard and Naude, 2017: 69–70).

NERSA's original policy document on REFIT considered the option of a competitive bidding system but worried that it would favour large incumbent producers (NERSA, 2009: 27). Eberhard and Kåberger (2016: 190) point out that, in contrast, there are significant advantages to a competitive bidding system. The main problem with a feed-in tariff is that regulators must set the price without access to market signals, which creates a high risk that they will get the price wrong. If the tariff is set too high, it causes overproduction of energy and leads to unaffordable prices for consumers; if the tariff is set too low, however, the policy is ineffective. In contrast, a competitive bidding system ensures that prices will adjust automatically over successive rounds in response to technological advancements and changes in market conditions. In theory, this should result in a steady decrease in prices while still encouraging investment.

The competitive bidding model proved to be successful in South Africa. In its first four years, the REIPPPP added 4,322 MW to South Africa's grid, almost as much as the Medupi power station (Joemat-

Pettersson, quoted in Barbee, 2015). One comparative study contrasts the REIPPPP with similar programmes in Europe and finds that South Africa's programme has the highest project realisation rate: 100 per cent of the share of winning projects that are commissioned, compared to only 23–87 per cent of projects in its European counterparts (Kitzing et al., 2022: 5). The South African programme also resulted in the sharpest decline in bid prices, with a 75 per cent decrease in the prices of photovoltaic solar bids and 54 per cent decrease in those of onshore wind bids during the first three REIPPPP bid windows (Kitzing et al., 2022: 13).

From a political economy perspective, the effects of the REIPPPP were mixed. On the one hand, it altered the balance of forces between the pro-transition and the pro-status quo coalitions by creating new classes of actors: independent power producers and their industry associations, as well as large energy consumers who benefited from the increasing energy supply. However, the process that created the REIPPPP also introduced institutional bottlenecks that could be used to obstruct the transition to renewable energy.

With the switch from a feed-in tariff to a competitive bidding system, key control points reverted from NERSA to the Department of Energy and Eskom. In combination with section 34 of the Electricity Regulation Act of 2006, the new system meant that the Minister of Energy would be solely responsible for determining when new energy capacity should be built, and whether it should be built by Eskom or another actor (Baker et al., 2015: 20). Furthermore, the Department of Energy and Eskom would be responsible for signing power purchase agreements with successful REIPPPP bidders. These two veto points became key issues of political contention during the mid-2010s.

STATE CAPTURE AND VETO PLAYERS

Earlier in that decade, there were good reasons to assume that South Africa's transition to renewable energy was well underway. In 2009, the South African government promised at the Copenhagen Summit that South Africa's emissions would peak by 2025, plateau for a decade, and then decline (The Presidency, 2009). In 2011, South

Africa's first Integrated Resource Plan called for the country to adopt a mix of energy sources, including renewables and nuclear. After the REIPPPP's introduction in 2011, South Africa quickly began adding renewable capacity to its grid.

Behind the scenes, however, South Africa had become afflicted by an extreme form of rent-seeking and corruption that has come to be known as 'state capture' (see Chapter 7 in this volume for a discussion of this) in which public institutions were repurposed to facilitate private wealth extraction and weaken democratic oversight. The extent of this phenomenon was later documented by the Zondo Commission, which ran for three and a half years, questioned 300 witnesses, and considered more than 1.7 million pages of documentary evidence (Public Affairs Research Institute, 2022). The Zondo Report found that state capture had distorted almost every aspect of South Africa's public policy, including its energy policy.

During this period, South Africa's energy policy increasingly focused on nuclear energy, with the government planning to commission nuclear power plants from Russia's state energy corporation, Rosatom. According to Weiss and Rumer (2019), the groundwork for this plan was laid in 2010, with the acquisition of an unprofitable uranium mine by the politically influential Gupta family and Duduzane Zuma, President Zuma's son. This was followed by a secret nuclear cooperation agreement signed in Vienna in 2014, shortly after President Zuma visited Russia. The agreement was leaked, and critics estimated the project would cost US$76 billion, equivalent to R1 trillion at the time (Weiss and Rumer, 2019). That was clearly unaffordable; by way of comparison, South Africa's entire state budget during the 2014/15 financial year was R1.25 trillion (National Treasury, 2014: v).

The state capture era also saw a renewed emphasis on coal power, especially after the Gupta family acquired the Optimum Coal Mine (OCM) from Glencore. This acquisition was facilitated by collusion involving Eskom officials and the Department of Mineral Resources, including the appointment of a minister who would support the OCM acquisition (Zondo, 2022b: 837). The Gupta family then received favourable contracts and financial arrangements from Eskom, creating powerful incentives to further invest in renewable energy (Zondo, 2022b: 842–843).

Within this context, it is likely that officials linked to the state capture project began to view the REIPPPP as a threat. As such, they sought to sabotage it. The key figures in carrying out this agenda were two Eskom CEOs: Brian Molefe (2015–2016) and Matshela Koko (2016–2018), both implicated in the Zondo Report (Zondo, 2022b: 805–810, 813–818). After his appointment in 2015, Molefe refused to sign power purchase agreements with the successful bidders of the REIPPPP bid windows 3.5 and 4; this refusal continued under Koko, despite contravening the government's Integrated Resource Plan (Bloom, 2022; De Ruyter, 2023).

The pro-transition coalition attempted to push back. In 2016, the South African Wind Energy Association (SAWEA) filed a complaint with NERSA, alleging that Eskom was abusing its position and contravening government policy (Creamer, 2016). In 2017, the Organisation Undoing Tax Abuse (OUTA), a civil society group, filed a complaint with the Competition Commission alleging that Eskom's refusal to sign power purchase agreements was a form of illegal anti-competitive behaviour (Yelland, 2017b). That year, President Zuma promised in his State of the Nation Address that the government would soon sign the outstanding agreements; however, before the Minister of Energy, Tina Joemat-Pettersson, could do so, she was removed from the Cabinet (Yelland, 2017a). South Africa's renewable energy programme remained stalled for the remainder of the Zuma presidency.

Ultimately, Zuma's push for nuclear energy set in motion a chain of events that resulted in his political downfall. In December 2015, after Finance Minister Nhlanhla Nene refused to sign off on the nuclear programme, Zuma removed him from the Cabinet (Zondo, 2022a: 81–87). This triggered a rapid depreciation in the value of South Africa's currency and stock market. Mcebisi Jonas, Nene's deputy, was allegedly offered R600 million by the Gupta family if he agreed to replace Nene as Finance Minister and advance the Guptas' interests (Jonas, 2016). He refused and made these events public, setting off a firestorm of controversy that resulted in a formal investigation into state capture by Public Protector Thuli Madonsela. This, in turn, led to the establishment of the Zondo Commission in 2018, which further exposed the phenomenon of state capture. In February 2018, the ANC instructed Zuma to resign.

Unfortunately, the state capture period created path-dependent outcomes that outlasted Zuma's administration. In the medium term, the suspension of the REIPPPP contributed significantly to the loadshedding crisis from 2021 onwards. Modelling by Meridian Economics found that if the REIPPPP had not been suspended, this would have eliminated 96 per cent of the loadshedding that took place in South Africa during 2022 (Roff et al., 2022: 8–19). Furthermore, by refusing to sign power purchase agreements, the government inflicted lasting damage on South Africa's credibility as a safe destination for renewable energy investment. While the subsequent administration of President Cyril Ramaphosa tried to resuscitate the REIPPPP, subsequent bid windows struggled to generate a large enough pipeline of projects to solve the loadshedding crisis or to replace coal plants that were approaching the end of their lifecycles (Hopkins, 2023).

From the perspective of historical institutionalism, the key flaw in the REIPPPP was that it vested power in two veto points that could be used to obstruct the programme: Eskom and the Department of Energy. Under Ramaphosa, these veto points persisted as key sites in the ongoing struggle over renewable energy.

THE 'JUST TRANSITION' AND
THE CONTESTED STATE

In February 2018, Ramaphosa became the new president of South Africa and his government began working on a new Integrated Resource Plan that sought to resume the REIPPPP, reform Eskom and resolve the nuclear procurement issue (Department of Mineral Resources and Energy, 2019). Unfortunately, this did not resolve the underlying tension over South Africa's energy transition. On the contrary, contestation between pro-transition and pro-status quo actors intensified.

During this period, the South African government increasingly framed its energy policy as a 'just transition'. This term was previously used in the 2012 National Development Plan (National Planning

Commission, 2012: 211–213) and the 2019 Integrated Resource Plan (Department of Mineral Resources and Energy, 2019: 44–45). However, use of this concept dramatically expanded during Ramaphosa's first term, especially after the establishment of a multi-stakeholder Presidential Climate Change Commission in 2020 and the subsequent development of a Just Transition Framework to guide the process (Presidential Climate Commission, 2022: 3).

There are many ways of conceptualising a just transition (McCauley and Heffron, 2018; Newell and Mulvaney, 2013; Wang and Lo, 2021). In the South African context, the term is most frequently used from a labour-centric perspective, describing a process in which the economy decarbonises while the economic welfare of workers in carbon-intensive sectors is protected. As of 2019, there were approximately 200,000 workers employed in the coal energy sector in activities such as mining, working in power plants, and coal transportation (World Resources Institute, 2021). With South Africa's official unemployment rate at 32.9 per cent as of Q1 2025 (Statistics South Africa, 2025: 1), it is unlikely that workers displaced from this sector could easily find new jobs. Furthermore, the coal sector is heavily concentrated in certain regions of the country – in particular, in the province of Mpumalanga – where a sudden loss of coal mining income could lead to a collapse of entire regional economies.

The just transition framework can be seen as an attempt to solve this dilemma by redistributing some of the gains from the 'winners' of the transition to those who stand to lose, but workers understandably tend to view promises of future redistribution sceptically. The problem is essentially one of credibility. As Rodrik (2018: 6) points out, with respect to the debate over free trade: 'governments always have the incentive to promise compensation, but rarely to carry it out. The winners need the losers' assent for the agreement. But once the agreement is passed, there is little reason for the winners to follow through.' This observation would seem familiar to workers at the Komati power station, decommissioned in 2022, where the promise of a 'just' transition was followed by job losses and community upheaval (Patel, 2024).

One of Ramaphosa's first actions as president was to direct his

185

Energy Minister, Jeff Radebe, to sign the long-delayed power purchase agreements with the successful bidders of REIPPPP bid windows 3.5 and 4. Before these agreements were signed, however, they were interdicted by an emergency court order brought by the National Union of Metalworkers of South Africa (NUMSA) in conjunction with Transform RSA, a pro-Zuma NGO (Le Roux, 2018). NUMSA argued that the agreement would violate the workers' rights by causing 30,000 job losses in Mpumalanga (NUMSA, 2018). The NUMSA/Transform RSA case was dismissed, and Radebe signed the agreements, but the legal action sent a clear signal that labour unions in the coal mining sector would oppose a revival of the REIPPPP.

In 2019, Ramaphosa merged the departments of Mineral Resources and Energy, which had the effect of strengthening a key veto point in the energy system. Gwede Mantashe – a former coal mineworker, former general secretary of the National Union of Mineworkers (NUM), and an ardent supporter of coal energy – was appointed minister of the combined department. Under Mantashe's leadership, the procurement of new renewable generation did not progress much. Instead of opening up new REIPPPP bid windows, the department seemed to focus on various other policies to add capacity to the grid: a nuclear programme; the creation of a second state-owned power utility to compete with Eskom; and, faced with increased loadshedding, an urgent plan to lease power ships from Turkey (BusinessTech, 2022). These plans proved to be impractical; the powerships deal in particular faced significant legal challenges. With this impasse over energy generation, no new capacity was added, and by 2021 the country faced an energy deficit of 6,000 MW (Creamer, 2022).

CRITICAL JUNCTURES AND PATHWAYS TO REFORM

In 2021, faced with the prospect of an energy-induced economic disaster, President Ramaphosa began a series of emergency reforms. Many of these reforms originated from a new initiative in South Africa's institutional environment: Operation Vulindlela (OV), a joint initiative of the Presidency and National Treasury, which had quietly been established in 2020 and given a mandate to unblock obstacles to economic growth (Operation Vulindlela, 2024: 3). The first package of reforms was introduced in the 2021 State of the Nation Address, and included a fifth REIPPPP bid window which promised to add 2,600 MW to the power grid (Ramaphosa, 2021). That bid window opened as scheduled, but the finalisation of the agreements was delayed, pushing the expected operational date of the new capacity to 2025. Perhaps more significantly, Ramaphosa also raised the limit for 'embedded generation' projects from 1 MW to 100 MW. This allowed individuals and businesses to produce renewable energy without the need for government approval or participation in the REIPPPP. This policy change led directly to a massive expansion in rooftop solar capacity, from 983 MW in March 2022 to 4,412 MW in June 2023 (Eberhard, quoted in Ferris, 2023).

In July 2022, faced with the continuation of Stage 6 loadshedding, Ramaphosa announced a second package of reforms known as the Energy Action Plan (The Presidency, 2022a). The plan included the procurement of 5,200 MW of renewable energy through a sixth REIPPPP bidding window and the relaxation of local content requirements for new generation projects. Ramaphosa also proposed reviving the long-dormant idea of a feed-in tariff, which would allow Eskom to buy excess power from embedded generation projects and resell it elsewhere on the grid. By April 2024, the reform process had resulted in a pipeline of over 130 confirmed private sector projects producing a staggering 22,500 MW (Operation Vulindlela, 2024: 4).

To drive the implementation of these reforms, Ramaphosa sought to alter South Africa's institutional landscape. The government created a National Energy Crisis Committee, which brought together multiple government departments and Eskom under the oversight of the Presidency (Operation Vulindlela, 2024: 13). Ramaphosa also introduced a new Cabinet-level Minister of Electricity housed within the Presidency.

After the May 2024 election, in which the ANC lost its parliamentary majority and was forced to form a coalition government referred to as a Government of National Unity (GNU), Ramaphosa made this change permanent. He split the Department of Mineral Resources and Energy back into two separate departments, thereby reversing the 2019 merger that had strengthened a key veto point in the energy system. Kgosientsho Ramokgopa, who had previously served as the Minister of Electricity and was generally perceived as being more supportive of renewables, was appointed Minister in the new Department of Electricity and Energy. Analysed through the lens of historical institutionalism, this restructuring suggests that Ramaphosa may have viewed the formation of the GNU as a critical juncture, and taken the opportunity to lock in institutional changes that would reduce the possibility of his reforms being undone by future administrations.

CONCLUSION

This chapter argued that South Africa's energy transition has been shaped by the interplay between interest group politics and the country's institutional framework. Currently, the pro-transition coalition seems ascendant, while the strength of the status quo coalition is waning. But shifts in energy policy can be unpredictable. In the early 2010s, with the burgeoning success of the REIPPPP, it would have been easy to imagine that South Africa was on the cusp of a rapid transition to renewable energy. Instead, progress was stalled for a decade.

It is unlikely that political contestation over energy in South Africa has ended; many important questions still need to be resolved. Although the country's coal plants have experienced significant improvements in their EAF after 2022, they will continue to age and, at some point, will need to be replaced. Some form of large-scale energy transition is therefore inevitable; the question is what form will this transition take?

One possible scenario would be a reversal of fortune for the anti-renewables coalition. In policy terms, this might entail the replacement of South Africa's legacy system with a new set of centralised and large-scale plants that will continue to be powered largely by the country's abundant local coal reserves, perhaps in combination with secondary sources such as natural gas and nuclear energy. Such a scenario now appears unlikely, however. One of the core insights of the historical institutionalist perspective is that while policies and personnel can shift easily, institutions tend to create path dependencies that are more difficult to reverse. In the South African case, recent institutional reforms have not merely altered policy direction; they have also changed the balance of power between the two coalitions. The removal of the limit on embedded generation is particularly significant, since it has incentivised the installation of enormous, privately owned generation capacity which would be difficult to remove. A shift towards renewable energy is effectively 'locked in' by a combination of institutional changes and private investment.

A more likely scenario is a continuation of the current reform path, with an uneven transition driven mostly by the private sector. In such a scenario, we can expect that renewables will continue to grow as a percentage of South Africa's energy mix. This will increase South Africa's total stock of energy, prevent a return of the loadshedding crisis of the early 2020s, and allow the country to benefit from positive global trends such as decreasing prices and increasing efficiency of photovoltaic solar panels and wind generators. It is also likely that new challenges might emerge: greater intermittency of supply, increased pressure on the distribution network, job displacement in coal-producing regions, and perhaps rising energy prices for consumers. While loadshedding would likely be resolved in this scenario, questions might arise about the 'justness' of the transition.

It is also possible to imagine the outlines of a third scenario, in which South Africa develops an energy system that is inclusive, beneficial for the environment, and advances the country's economic development – while at the same time ensuring stable baseload generation underpinned by gas, nuclear and remaining coal-fired power stations. The state would also facilitate the transition through investments in public infrastructure, such as high-quality transmission networks and energy storage, which would allow renewable energy to be efficiently transmitted and used across the country. Surplus gains resulting from increasing energy availability could be redistributed to provide new opportunities for affected workers in the coal sector, ensuring that such a transition would be 'just' in fact as well as in name. In essence, this approach would help resolve the underlying grievances that sustain popular opposition to the transition.

REFERENCES

Acemoglu, D. and Robinson, J.A. 2013. *Why Nations Fail: The Origins of Power, Prosperity, and Poverty*. Reprint edition. New York, NY: Crown Currency.

Akpeji, K.O., Olasoji, A.O., Gaunt, C.T., Oyedokun, D.T., Awodele, K.O. and Folly, K.A. 2020. 'Economic impact of electricity supply interruptions in South Africa'. *SAIEE Africa Research Journal*, 111(2), 73–87.

Baker, L., Burton, J., Godinho, C. and Trollip, M. 2015. *The Political Economy of Decarbonisation: Exploring The Dynamics of South Africa's Electricity Sector*. Cape Town: Energy Research Centre, University of Cape Town.

Baker, L., Newell, P. and Phillips, J. 2014. 'The political economy of energy transitions: The case of South Africa'. *New Political Economy*, 19(6), 791–818.

Barbee, J. 2015. 'How renewable energy in South Africa is quietly stealing a march on coal'. *The Guardian*, 1 June, https://www.theguardian.com/environment/2015/jun/01/how-renewable-energy-in-south-africa-is-quietly-stealing-a-march-on-coal, accessed 4 September 2023.

Bloom, K. 2022. 'Grim Reippp(er): Undoing the choke-hold on SA's renewable energy programme'. *Daily Maverick*, https://www.dailymaverick.co.za/article/2022-09-26-grim-reippper-undoing-the-choke-hold-on-sas-renewable-energy-programme/, accessed 5 September 2023.

BusinessTech. 2022. 'Mantashe says a "second Eskom" would be established in his department – report'. *BusinessTech*, https://businesstech.co.za/news/energy/607426/mantashe-says-a-second-eskom-would-be-established-in-his-department-report/, accessed 4 October 2024.

BusinessTech 2023. 'From bad to worse: Load shedding vs blackout hours in South Africa'. *BusinessTech*, https://businesstech.co.za/news/business-opinion/681001/from-bad-to-worse-load-shedding-vs-blackout-hours-in-south-africa/, accessed 31 August 2023.

Comrie, S. 2022. 'The collapse of old king coal (part 1)'. *AmaBhungane*, https://amabhungane.org/stories/220928-the-collapse-of-old-king-coal-part-1/, accessed 31 August 2023.

Creamer, T. 2016. 'Wind body wants NERSA to fine Eskom for failing to comply with IPP policy'. *Engineering News*, https://www.engineeringnews.co.za/article/wind-body-wants-nersa-to-fine-eskom-for-failing-to-comply-with-ipp-policy-2016-10-17, accessed 5 September 2023.

Creamer, T. 2022. '2021 confirmed as most intensive load-shedding year yet as Eskom's EAF continues to fall'. *Engineering News*, https://www.engineeringnews.co.za/article/2021-confirmed-as-most-intensive-load-shedding-year-yet-as-eskoms-eaf-continues-to-fall-2022-06-07, accessed 6 September 2023.

De Mesquita, B.B., Smith, A., Siverson, R.M. and Morrow, J.C. 2005. *The*

Logic of Political Survival. Cambridge: MIT Press.

De Ruyter, A.M. 2023. 'Case Number: 2023/005779 in the Matter Between: United Democratic Movement and 18 Others and Eskom Holdings SOC Limited and 7 Others', https://bosa.co.za/wp-content/uploads/2023/03/Answering-affidavit-signed-part-1.pdf

Department of Mineral Resources and Energy. 2019. 'Integrated Resource Plan (IRP2019)', https://www.energy.gov.za/irp/2019/IRP-2019.pdf, accessed 5 September 2023.

Department of Minerals and Energy. 1998. 'White Paper on the Energy Policy of the Republic of South Africa', https://www.energy.gov.za/files/policies/whitepaper_energypolicy_1998.pdf, accessed 1 September 2023.

Department of Minerals and Energy. 2003. 'White Paper on Renewable Energy'. United Nations Framework Convention on Climate Change, https://unfccc.int/files/meetings/seminar/application/pdf/sem_sup1_south_africa.pdf, accessed 4 September 2023.

Do, T.N., Burke, P.J., Nguyen, H.N., Overland, I., Suryadi, B., Swandaru, A. and Yurnaidi, Z. 2021. 'Vietnam's solar and wind power success: Policy implications for the other ASEAN countries'. *Energy for Sustainable Development*, 65, 1–11, https://www.sciencedirect.com/science/article/pii/S097308262100096X

Eberhard, A. 2005. 'From state to market and back again: South Africa's power sector reforms'. *Economic and Political Weekly*, 40(50), 5309–5317.

Eberhard, A. and Kåberger, T. 2016. 'Renewable energy auctions in South Africa outshine feed-in tariffs'. *Energy Science & Engineering*, 4(3), 190–193.

Eberhard, A. and Naude, R. 2017. 'The South African Renewable Energy Independent Power Producer Procurement Programme: Review, Lessons Learned & Proposals to Reduce Transaction Costs'. University of Cape Town Graduate School of Business, https://www.gsb.uct.ac.za/files/EberhardNaude_REIPPPPReview_2017_1_1.pdf, accessed 20 June 2025.

Erero, J.L. 2023. 'Impact of loadshedding in South Africa: A CGE analysis'. *Journal of Economics and Political Economy*, 10(2), 78–94.

Eskom. 2024. 'Eskom Generation performance takes a positive turn', https://www.eskom.co.za/eskom-generation-performance-takes-a-positive-turn/, accessed 17 September 2024.

Ferris, N. 2023. 'Weekly data: South Africa's unprecedented rooftop solar boom'. *Energy Monitor*, https://www.energymonitor.ai/tech/renewables/weekly-data-south-africas-unprecedented-rooftop-solar-boom/, accessed 6 September 2023.

Fraser, L. 2023. 'Jobs bloodbath in South Africa'. *BusinessTech*, https://businesstech.co.za/news/energy/687597/jobs-bloodbath-in-south-africa/, accessed 23 August 2023.

Hochstetler, K. 2020. *Political Economies of Energy Transition: Wind and Solar Power in Brazil and South Africa.* Cambridge: Cambridge University Press.

Hopkins, T. 2023. 'Proximo Weekly: Bid Window 5 – cracked and not what it was cracked up to be'. *Proximo*, https://www.proximoinfra.com/articles/8283/proximo-weekly-bid-window-5-cracked-and-not-what-it-was-cracked-up-to-be, accessed 5 September 2023.

Hörsch, J. and Calitz, J. 2017. 'PyPSA-ZA: Investment and operation co-optimization of integrating wind and solar in South Africa at high spatial and temporal detail', http://arxiv.org/abs/1710.11199, accessed 21 July 2023.

Illidge, M. 2022. 'Medupi and Kusile — eight years late and R300 billion over budget'. *MyBroadband*, https://mybroadband.co.za/news/energy/443784-medupi-and-kusile-eight-years-late-and-r300-billion-over-budget.html, accessed 31 August 2023.

Jonas, M. 2016. 'Media Statement: Statement by Deputy Minister of Finance Mr. Mcebisi Jonas (MP)'. National Treasury of the Republic of South Africa, https://www.treasury.gov.za/comm_media/press/2016/2016031601%20-%20Statement%20by%20Deputy%20Minister%20Jonas.pdf, accessed 5 September 2023.

Keohane, R.O. and Victor, D.G. 2016. 'Cooperation and discord in global climate policy'. *Nature Climate Change*, 6(6), 570–575.

Kitzing, L., Siddique, M.B., Nygaard, I. and Kruger, W. 2022. 'Worth the wait: How South Africa's renewable energy auctions perform compared to Europe's leading countries'. *Energy Policy*, 166, 112999, https://www.sciencedirect.com/science/article/pii/S0301421522002245

Knorr, K., Zimmermann, B., Bofinger, S., Fraunhofer, A.G., Bischof-Niemz, T. and Mushwana, C. 2016. 'Wind and Solar PV Resource Aggregation Study for South Africa. Council for Scientific and Industrial Research', https://www.csir.co.za/sites/default/files/Documents/Wind%20and%20Solar%20PV%20Resource%20Aggregation%20Study%20for%20South%20Africa_Final%20report.pdf, accessed 7 September 2023.

Kroth, V., Larcinese, V. and Wehner, J. 2016. 'A better life for all?: Democratization and electrification in post-apartheid South Africa'. *The Journal of Politics*, 78(3), 774–791.

Le, L. 2022. 'After renewables frenzy, Vietnam's solar energy goes to waste'. *Al Jazeera*, https://www.aljazeera.com/economy/2022/5/18/after-renewables-push-vietnam-has-too-much-energy-to-handle, accessed 31 August 2023.

Le Roux, J. 2018. 'The IPP interdict: Transform RSA's murky management'. *News24*, https://www.news24.com/news24/the-ipp-interdict-transform-rsas-murky-management-20180313, accessed 6 September 2023.

Lockwood, M., Kuzemko, C., Mitchell, C. and Hoggett, R. 2017. 'Historical institutionalism and the politics of sustainable energy transitions: A research agenda'. *Environment and Planning C: Politics and Space*, 35(2), 312–333, https://sci-hub.st/10.1177/0263774x16660561

MacKenzie, M.K. 2016. 'Institutional design and sources of short-termism', in González-Ricoy, I. and Gosseries, A. (eds), *Institutions for Future Generations*. Oxford: Oxford University Press, pp. 24–48.

McCauley, D. and Heffron, R. 2018. 'Just transition: Integrating climate, energy and environmental justice'. *Energy Policy*, 119, 1–7.

MyBroadband. 2019. 'Here is the true cost of Eskom's Medupi and Kusile power stations', https://mybroadband.co.za/news/energy/318251-here-is-the-true-cost-of-eskoms-medupi-and-kusile-power-stations.html, accessed 1 September 2023.

Naidoo, P. 2023. 'Blackouts may cost South Africa $51 million a day, Central Bank says'. *Bloomberg*, https://www.bloomberg.com/news/articles/2023-02-06/blackouts-may-cost-s-africa-51-million-day-central-bank-says, accessed 23 August 2023.

National Energy Regulator of South Africa (NERSA). 2009. 'South Africa Renewable Energy Feed-in Tariff (REFIT) Regulatory Guidelines', https://www.gov.za/sites/default/files/gcis_document/201409/32122382.pdf, accessed 4 September 2023.

National Planning Commission (NPC). 2012. 'National Development Plan 2030: Our Future - Make it Work', https://www.gov.za/sites/default/files/gcis_document/201409/ndp-2030-our-future-make-it-workr.pdf

National Treasury. 2010. 'South Africa welcomes the decision by the World Bank', https://www.treasury.gov.za/comm_media/press/2010/2010040901.pdf, accessed 1 September 2023.

National Treasury. 2014. 'Budget Review 2014', https://www.treasury.gov.za/documents/national%20budget/2014/review/fullreview.pdf, accessed 2 September 2025.

National Union of Metalworkers of South Africa (NUMSA). 2018. 'NUMSA and Transform RSA Granted an interdict to prevent Eskom IPP contracts!', https://numsa.org.za/2018/03/numsa-and-transform-rsa-granted-an-interdict-to-prevent-eskom-ipp-contracts/, accessed 6 September 2023.

Newell, P. and Mulvaney, D. 2013. 'The political economy of the "just transition"'. *The Geographical Journal*, 179(2), 132–140.

Nordhaus, W. 2015. 'Climate clubs: Overcoming free-riding in international climate policy'. *American Economic Review*, 105(4), 1339–1370.

North, D.C. 1991. 'Institutions'. *The Journal of Economic Perspectives*, 5(1), 97–112.

Operation Vulindlela. 2024. 'Phase 1 Review: Progress in Driving Economic Reform 2020-2024'. The Presidency and National Treasury, Republic of South Africa, https://www.stateofthenation.gov.za/assets/downloads/Operation_Vulindlela_Phase_1_Review.pdf, accessed 19 September 2024.

Patel, O. 10 February 2024. 'Tour of Komati power station reveals dilemmas'. *Mail & Guardian*, https://mg.co.za/thought-leader/opinion/2024-02-10-tour-of-komati-power-station-reveals-dilemmas/, accessed 19 September 2024.

Pierson, P. 2004. *Politics in Time: History, Institutions, and Social Analysis.* Princeton: Princeton University Press.

Presidential Climate Commission. 2022a. 'Just Transition Framework', https://pccommissionflo.imgix.net/uploads/images/A-Just-Transition-Framework-for-South-Africa-2022.pdf, accessed 31 August 2023.

Presidential Climate Commission. 2022b. *A Framework for a Just Transition in South Africa.* Johannesburg: Presidential Climate Commission.

Presidential Climate Commission. 2023. 'Carbon Border Adjustment Mechanisms and Implications for South Africa'. Presidential Climate Commission Working Paper, https://pccommissionflo.imgix.net/uploads/images/PCC-Working-Paper-CBAM.pdf, accessed 31 August 2023.

Public Affairs Research Institute. 2022. 'The Zondo Commission: A bite-sized summary', https://pari.org.za/wp-content/uploads/2022/09/PARI-Summary-The-Zondo-Commission-A-bite-sized-summary-v360.pdf, accessed 5 September 2023.

Ramaphosa, C. 11 February 2021. 'State of the Nation Address by President Cyril Ramaphosa'. South African Government, https://www.stateofthenation.gov.za/assets/2021/SONA%202021.pdf, accessed 19 September 2024.

Ramokgopa, K. 2024. 'Minister Kgosientsho Ramokgopa provides an update on the finalisation of the Integrated Resource Plan 2023 and Eskom's Key Revision Number Programme'. Department of Mineral Resources and Energy, https://www.dmre.gov.za/news-room/post/2748, accessed 1 July 2025.

Rodrik, D. 2018. 'Populism and the Economics of Globalization'. *Journal of International Business Policy*, 1, 12–33.

Roff, A., Klein, P., Brand, R., Renaud, C., Mgoduso, L. and Steyn, G. 2022. 'Resolving the Power Crisis Part A: Insights From 2021, SA's Worst Load Shedding Year So Far'. Meridian Economics, https://meridianeconomics.co.za/wp-content/uploads/2022/06/Resolving-Load-Shedding-Part-A-2021-analysis-01.pdf

Social Research Foundation. 2023. 'The Effect of Loadshedding on Support for the ANC. 21/2023'. Social Research Foundation, https://srfreports.co.za/wp-content/uploads/2023/05/SRF-Report-21-Loadshedding-and-ANC-support.pdf, accessed 31 August 2023.

Solomon, O.A., Aghahosseni, A., Ram, M., Lohrmann, A. and Breyer, C. 2019. 'Pathway towards achieving 100% renewable electricity by 2050 for South Africa'. *Solar Energy*, 191, 549–565.

Statistics South Africa. 2022. 'General Household Survey, 2021', https://www.statssa.gov.za/?p=15482, accessed 1 September 2023.

Statistics South Africa. 2025. 'Quarterly Labour Force Survey: Quarter 1: 2025', https://www.statssa.gov.za/publications/P0211/P02111stQuarter2025.pdf, accessed 23 May 2025.

Steyn, G., Klein, P., Roff, A., Renaud, C., Mgoduso, L. and Brand, R. 2022. 'Resolving the Power Crisis Part B: An Achievable Game Plan to End Load Shedding'. Meridian Economics, https://meridianeconomics.co.za/wp-content/uploads/2022/06/Resolving-Load-Shedding-Part-B-The-Game-Plan-01.pdf

The Presidency. 2009. 'President JG Zuma to attend Climate Change talks in Copenhagen', https://www.gov.za/president-jg-zuma-attend-climate-change-talks-copenhagen, accessed 5 September 2023.

The Presidency. 2022a. 'Confronting the Energy Crisis: An Action Plan to End Load Shedding'. https://www.gov.za/documents/other/confronting-energy-crisis-action-plan-end-load-shedding-25-jul-2022, accessed 19 September 2024.

The Presidency. 2022b. 'South Africa's Just Energy Transition Investment Plan for the initial period 2023–2027'. Presidential Climate Commission, https://www.thepresidency.gov.za/download/file/fid/2649, accessed 31 August 2023.

Tsebelis, G. 2002. *Veto Players: How Political Institutions Work*. Princeton: Princeton University Press.

Tshidavhu, F. and Khatleli, N. 2020. 'An assessment of the causes of schedule and cost overruns in South African megaprojects: A case of the critical energy sector projects of Medupi and Kusile'. *Acta Structilia*, 27(1), 119–143.

Walsh, K., Theron, R. and Reeders, C. 2021. 'Estimating the economic cost of load shedding in South Africa'. Paper submission to Biennial Conference of the Economic Society of South Africa (ESSA).

Wang, X. and Lo, K. 2021. 'Just transition: A conceptual review'. *Energy Research & Social Science*, 82, 102291.

Weiss, A.S. and Rumer, E. 2019. 'Nuclear Enrichment: Russia's Ill-Fated Influence Campaign in South Africa', https://carnegieendowment.org/2019/12/16/nuclear-enrichment-russia-s-ill-fated-influence-campaign-in-south-africa-pub-80597, accessed 5 September 2023.

World Bank. 2021. 'Climate Risk Country Profile: South Africa'. Climate Change Knowledge Portal, https://climateknowledgeportal.worldbank.org/sites/default/files/country-profiles/15932-WB_South%20Africa%20Country%20Profile-WEB.pdf, accessed 31 August 2023.

World Resources Institute. 2021. 'South Africa: Strong Foundations for a Just Transition', https://www.wri.org/update/south-africa-strong-foundations-just-transition, accessed 5 September 2023.

World Resources Institute. 2023. 'Historical GHG Emissions'. Climate Watch, https://www.climatewatchdata.org/ghg-emissions, accessed 31 August 2023.

Xaba, N. 2023. 'Whose just energy transition? A South African perspective'. *WIREs Energy and Environment*, e478.

Yelland, C. 2017a. 'No end in sight to Eskom delays in signing renewable energy PPAs'. *Daily Maverick*, https://www.dailymaverick.co.za/

article/2017-08-07-op-ed-no-end-in-sight-to-eskom-delays-in-signing-renewable-energy-ppas/, accessed 5 September 2023.

Yelland, C. 2017b. 'Outa files complaint against Eskom with CompCom'. *Moneyweb*, https://www.moneyweb.co.za/news/south-africa/outa-files-complaint-against-eskom-with-competition-commission/, accessed 5 September 2023.

Zondo, R.M.M. 2022a. 'Report: Part IV, Vol. 1: The Attempted Capture of National Treasury EOH Holdings and the City of JHB Alexkor. Judicial Commission of Inquiry into Allegations of State Capture, Corruption and Fraud in the Public Sector Including Organs of State', https://www.statecapture.org.za/site/files/announcements/680/OCR_version_-_State_Capture_Commission_Report_Part_IV_Vol_I_-_NT,EOH,COJ,Alexkor.pdf, accessed 7 September 2023.

Zondo, R.M.M. 2022b. 'Report: Part IV, Vol. 3: The Capture of Eskom. Judicial Commission of Inquiry into Allegations of State Capture, Corruption and Fraud in the Public Sector Including Organs of State', https://www.statecapture.org.za/site/files/announcements/682/OCR_version_-_State_Capture_Commission_Report_Part_IV_Vol_III_-_Eskom.pdf, accessed 7 September 2023.

NINE

The South African state's ability to govern water: Leviathan or Gulliver?

RICHARD MEISSNER

INTRODUCTION

The politics and governance of South Africa's water services have come under intense scrutiny by scholars since democracy in the country. The state's involvement in the water sector applies formal rule making, monitoring, and enforcement in deploying and privileging water regulations (Levi-Faur, 2013). South Africa implemented widespread reforms in the water sector after the first democratic elections in 1994 (Backeberg, 2007: 2). The institutionalisation of the regulatory reforms commenced in 1996 with the adoption of the Constitution. Section 27 of the Bill of Rights states, 'Everyone has the right to have access to sufficient food and water' (RSA, 1996). The Water Services Act (No. 108 of 1997) (RSA, 1997) was the subsequent legislation directly mandating municipalities as water service providers. A water services authority is a local government body responsible for ensuring access to water services (RSA, 1997). Since provinces do not have a water service authority mandate, they are not discussed in this chapter.

The National Water Act (No. 36 of 1998) (RSA, 1998) introduced a complete overhaul of the earlier Water Act (No. 54 of 1956) (Union of South Africa, 1956). As a regulatory instrument, the 1998 Act affords authority over managing (bulk) water resources to the Department of Water and Sanitation (DWS). Equity for everyone and the need for the government to serve as the custodian of water for all were the guiding principles of restructuring efforts. In effect, through the new laws, the government appointed itself as the water management warden charged with promoting inclusion, fairness and water distribution to all without favour, and safeguarding and preserving the country's vital water resources. The state was also a central actor in earlier water management regimes but it distributed water based on race – rather than on a principle of inclusion – and economic growth goals. This changed role transformed all water resources – including those previously regarded as private property – to a national resource governed by the state, which took responsibility for ensuring that essential water services are accessible to all citizens.

Over the years, the state has come under scrutiny for failing to deliver on its water services delivery mandates. There has been tension between political rhetoric and the practicalities of enhancing citizens' living conditions. This is not to say that the ANC-in-government failed in all instances to uphold its end of the social contract for the mandatory provision of water. Since 1994, more people have access to water than before. As the political entities responsible for water services, municipalities are required to fulfil their mandatory role as water service authorities. Many municipalities, however, are affected by adverse water quantity and quality conditions. This can be observed through the decline in the number of municipalities with Blue Drop and Green Drop statuses, which are indicators introduced by the DWS in 2009 (Ntombela et al., 2016; Steyn et al., 2019). According to the 2023 Blue Drop Report, Minister Senzo Mchunu admitted, 'As with the Green Drop released in 2022, there has been a decline in the status of our water supply services…' (DWS, 2023).

In this chapter, I use the hydro-social contract theory and Pierre and Peters' (2005) governance models to evaluate the state's capability in water governance. South African and international literature point not towards a water *scarcity* crisis, but a water *governance* crisis, particularly in the local government sphere (Tempelhoff et al., 2019: v) when organisations fail to become resilient and adaptable to shifting circumstances (Enqvist and Ziervogel, 2019: 2). It should also be noted that South Africa is a water-scarce country, which aggravates the impact of poor governance.

This chapter addresses this research gap by examining whether South Africa is experiencing a water scarcity *and* governance crisis. I explain the hydro-social contract theory before briefly discussing the various governance models that Pierre and Peters (2005) have outlined and debating the conceptualisation of the state as a Leviathan or Gulliver in the politics of water governance. The chapter then uses several recent cases to reflect on the South African state's capacity and capability to supply water services, and evaluates which governance models best explain how South Africa is attempting to fulfil its hydro-social contract.

THE HYDRO-SOCIAL CONTRACT

The philosophical writings of Thomas Hobbes (1651) and John Locke (1690) inform hydro-social contract theory. Their perspectives explain society's water utilisation through engineered solutions and political arrangements. The notion of a social contract between the state and the water-consuming public assumes several (political) transitions in water management (Warner, 2000: 1). It is when water security is threatened, as in the case of droughts, floods and compromised water quality, that the relevance and role of infrastructure projects, like large dams and extensive irrigation schemes, may be viewed through the lens of hydro-social contract theory (Meissner and Turton, 2003: 115). The first Hobbesian-like transition appears when society experiences water scarcity. A bipolar arrangement develops between the government and society as the state and engineers supply the country with water through the hydraulic mission[1] (Warner, 2000: 5, 8). Responses to water scarcity challenges – caused by biophysical and societal changes

---

1   The 'hydraulic mission' refers to the entirety of the state's efforts to create large-scale hydraulic infrastructures, including both its discourse and practice.

(Martin-Carrasco et al., 2013: 1694) – may include engineering solutions and adaptive behaviours such as water restrictions and water policy reforms. There are several possible ways in which a state may respond to water crises. It could ignore society's calls for water provisioning – whether because of capacity constraints, corruption or other reasons. Alternately, it could cater only to specific sections of the population that legitimise the government (Warner, 2000), as in the case of the South African state during apartheid. However, social instability could follow if the state does not deliver on its side of the contract. In a democracy, the state is the foundation for developing institutional arrangements and for establishing their mandates and functions. These arrangements could include government departments (such as DWS). The mandatory functions indicate to the public what is regarded as fair and legitimate practices, such as sustainable water use, and also indicate which issues or challenges politicians should react to, in order to uphold the social contract (Warner, 2000: 17).

A second transition occurs when water deficits surface, even after engineering solutions have been implemented. This transition results from a Lockean type of hydro-social contract (Warner, 2000: 6), characterised by a triangular configuration between the government, engineers, the public, interest groups or other elements in civil society.

Two conditions are essential to consider within this transition and the context of adaptive behaviour. Firstly, there is the cost of implementing engineering solutions. Government and local authorities are finding it increasingly hard to be facing the options of either financing water infrastructure programmes or having no water sources. Public demands around a social contract start to surface, and the public becomes a prominent actor. If the state is unable to address water scarcity issues, or allows the system to fall into disrepair, this could lead to social instability through public protest.

The public asserts its position through lobbying activities and interest groups (Meissner, 2005); these actions are reminiscent of Jonathan Swift's (1667–1745) Lilliputians tying down Gulliver and restricting his movement, as captured in *Gulliver's Travels* (1726). This metaphor is apt, considering that individuals in the polity not only play a role in politics, but can also hamper the implementation of the hydraulic mission through, for instance, criminal activity, like the theft and vandalism of water infrastructure and the unlawful pollution of water resources (Meissner, 2023).

The metaphors of the state as an unbridled Leviathan or restrained Gulliver in the hydro-social contract are applicable when discussing the state's and society's governance roles.

In the next section, I define and discuss politics and governance, explain their relationship, and outline Pierre and Peters' (2005) five governance models: the *étatiste* model, the liberal democracy model, the state-centric model, the Dutch governance model and the governance-without-government model.

GOVERNANCE MODELS

Two perspectives on governance exist. The first is a network perspective, in which the state's involvement is minimal, if not unimportant, and the second is that the state dominates governance by controlling essential resources. According to Pierre and Peters (2005: 1), this is a 'false dichotomy' since social networks and a vital state are both necessary for the most efficient governance systems. Even though the government's ability to govern may have waned, the state can still participate in governance, although not in a command-and-control manner. Pierre and Peters (2005: 3) argue that networks may steer some policy aspects if all members agree. Yet, networks need help with disagreements among members or across policy sectors. It is up to the government to address the more complex problems of conflict resolution and total authoritative resource allocation through politics and political processes, as described by Easton (1965: 50) and Rosenau (2006: 183).

Politics is a crucial factor in governance arrangements, whether networked or state-centric or a combination of the two options. These arrangements consist of authoritative persons such as municipal representatives, politicians, traditional leaders and interest groups (Rosenau, 2006: 183). Politics determines the governing methods and interventions within the state's policy processes, the various problematisations, theories and moral principles guiding these strategies and interventions, as well as the conflicts that develop around them.

Within and outside the state apparatus, methods and interventions are set and have an impact (Sørensen and Triantafillou, 2009: 5). The procedural and contextual character of politics is evident, indicating the various roles of networks and the state in governance models.

Pierre and Peters (2005) describe five governance models. In the first, the *étatiste* model, the state is the principal actor in all governance aspects, and it controls how societal actors are allowed to be involved in governance, if at all. This model is often associated with Westminster-type governments and their constitutional doctrine. In this model, the state can more conveniently make decisions and address issues through policy processes, in contrast to systems in which social players have independent powers (Pierre and Peters, 2005: 11).

In the second model, the liberal democracy model, the state acts as the principal actor in governance, with other actors competing to influence it. The state thus has a less dominant role, but the government chooses the interest groups and social actors it will allow to influence it. The state prefers to be influenced by those it perceives as crucial since it does not accept the legitimate right of the whole spectrum of interest groups to participate. Yet, the state remains committed to representative democracy (Pierre and Peters, 2005: 11), as reflected in South Africa's electoral system.

The third model, the state-centric paradigm, is compatible with various forms of corporatism and formalised state-society partnerships. The state institutionalises its relationship with societal actors and is central to governmental activities. Given the state's central position, it can turn down partners when setting up governance arrangements. Compared to the *étatiste* and liberal democracy models, in this model the state is more dependent on its partners (Pierre and Peters, 2005: 11).

The fourth model, the Dutch governance one, is distinct from the earlier three models since it reflects Dutch researchers' development of a strategy within a particular polity, the Netherlands. The concept depends on how social networks are used in governance structures since networks play a significant role in governance. The state is one of the many actors in the process. The ability of society to organise and subvert the authority of the state may make it the most potent actor (Pierre and Peters, 2005: 12).

Proponents of the fifth model, the governance-without-government model, contend that the state has lost its ability to rule. They argue that the state is at a stage where private actors pursue the establishment of self-directing governing structures. This model has a dichotomous system; when the state's legitimacy declines, society actors acquire legitimacy at the state's expense. According to Pierre and Peters (2005: 12), this suggests that public sector actors may be less significant than society actors.

The rest of this section uses selected case studies to determine which of these models reflects contemporary water politics and governance in South Africa.

Water boards

Water boards play a critical role in South Africa through their operation of dams, bulk water supply infrastructure, retail infrastructure, and, in some cases, wastewater treatment systems. Since they are central actors in water management, they report to the DWS (DWA, 2012). The Water Services Act mandates the establishment of water boards, which support municipalities by providing, managing and operating the regional infrastructure for bulk water services (RSA, 2023).

The report on the 2020–21 audit of South Africa's nine water boards showed that the institutions achieved some successes in financial management, but only four of the water boards achieved higher than 80 per cent of their planned targets. The Auditor-General, Tsakani Maluleke, also noted a lack of proper coordination between the DWS and the water boards concerning formulating and reporting performance objectives in the National Water and Sanitation Master Plan. Additionally, the annual performance plans only sometimes reflected the achievement of the important goals outlined in this plan, such as providing quality water, minimising water losses, boosting investment and upgrading and maintaining infrastructure (AGSA, 2022: 4).

Since water boards play a crucial role in water management, the lack of coordination between these statutory bodies and the DWS indicates limited governance processes across policy sectors. This could have political costs, including a decline in trust in the ability of the water boards to act responsibly, making governance more challenging. Authority and legitimacy enable coordination and the exchange of information, which are low-cost ways of facilitating effective governance (Pierre and Peters, 2005: 4).

Information exchange between the water boards and the public is essential. If the water boards' performance plans show underachievement of crucial goals, the public could lose confidence in the boards' abilities to supply potable water and treat wastewater. Consumers' water security is dependent on sufficient quantities of water being available to meet their needs. Treated wastewater is released back into aquatic and marine ecosystems. What could be more problematic about the Auditor-General's report is the water boards' limited success in boosting investment and upgrading and maintaining infrastructure, thus making efficient water management harder, and so directly affecting consumers and their rights to access potable water.

Water management is not only a governance, managerial and operational function; it is a political matter that finds expression at national and local government levels in efforts to enhance people's water security. As the custodian of water resources, the state, together with its governing apparatuses, is the water security warden. If the state compromises this role by displaying a lack of coherent policy, as was the case with the uncoordinated governance between the DWS and some of the water boards, then non-state actors, such as interest groups and NGOs, could step in to take over the role of water security warden. In so doing, they would show that there is an alternative to the state playing this role.

CONTEMPORARY WATER POLITICS AND GOVERNANCE IN SOUTH AFRICA

Several instances highlight South African society's often complicated water politics and governance, with many political actors involved in both processes. The examples discussed here include the 2023 cholera outbreak in Hammanskraal and parts of the Free State, coupled with deteriorating water infrastructure; the impact of loadshedding on water infrastructure; the Auditor-General's 2020–21 report on water boards; and the management of water services in the Kgetlengrivier Local Municipality.

Cholera outbreak and dilapidated water infrastructure

The cholera outbreak in Hammanskraal, north of Pretoria, and parts of the Free State province in May 2023 highlighted the importance of functioning water infrastructure and safe water sources for human consumption and agricultural production. In the aftermath of the outbreak, the source of the disease remained unclear; infected travellers to the area cannot be excluded since some of the victims travelled to Malawi in January of that year (Mitchley, 2023). The situation garnered much media attention because of the high death toll of 47 people. Even so, this was not the first sign that the country's water infrastructure was in dire need of proper maintenance and upgrading (Du Plessis, 2023a; Meissner and Du Plessis, 2022).

President Cyril Ramaphosa later said that poor governance was a crucial reason for the water crisis in Hammanskraal. He also noted that a failure to maintain infrastructure had worsened the cholera outbreak (eNCA, 2023), indicating that public perception of a water governance crisis had the executive's attention.

For over two decades, the National Green Drop Certification Programme indicated inadequate infrastructure in a significant number of South African municipalities for delivering potable water, treating wastewater and protecting the country's aquatic ecosystems. As these services are a local government responsibility, it indicates a failure on the part of local authorities to properly manage their infrastructure. Between 2009 and 2016, there was a slight improvement in the Green Drop performance of some municipalities, but much more remained to be done (Ntombela et al., 2016: 707). The situation is particularly acute in rural areas (Meissner, 2015: 79), where greater financial resources and trained personnel are required for the management of water purification and wastewater treatment. Theft, the vandalism of water infrastructure and illegal water connections befuddle the maintenance of the vital infrastructure responsible for urban and rural communities' water security (Meissner et al., 2018: 112). What is odd about the Green and Blue Drop reports is that, although there was a slight improvement in the municipalities' Green Drop performances in 2013, the DWS suspended the reports in 2014. Research conducted by the author as part of a Council for Scientific and Industrial Research (CSIR) team discovered that the DWS and municipalities were, in that period, not permitted to disclose Green Drop performance scores, presumably in an effort by the governing party not to cast ANC-governed municipalities and the DWS in a bad light (Ntombela et al., 2016: 708).

The suppression of the reports coincided with allegations of state capture and with increasing political pressure from civil society to establish a commission of inquiry. The first Green Drop report in 2009 indicated that most municipalities' wastewater works were not well maintained. Opposition parties criticised the government for this, which resulted in government becoming more resistant to publishing the reports. The department cancelled publication of the 2013 Green Drop report, 'pending submission to Cabinet'. The last set of abbreviated reports was published in 2014, and reporting was thereafter suspended due to an alleged funding shortage. No further reports were published (Muller, 2020: 28) until 2023. In his 2021 State of the Nation Address (SONA), President Ramaphosa revitalised the reporting programme 'to strengthen water quality monitoring' (Ramaphosa, 2021), which is essential for assessing the state of water infrastructure conditions and the ability of local governments to supply critical water services. The head of government thus emphasised the importance of the local government mandate to deliver wastewater treatment services.

Loadshedding

The loadshedding implemented in 2008 to manage South Africa's shrinking energy supply further added to the country's water woes over the coming decades. In 2023, loadshedding was still present, especially in Gauteng's large metropolitan areas. It was suspended in the first half of 2024. An inextricable relationship exists between water, energy and food production, exemplified by the water-energy-food (WEF) nexus perspective (Bruns et al., 2022: 79). Bulk water and municipal water reticulation systems need a reliable electricity supply. Without electricity, water cannot be purified, pumped and treated (Du Plessis, 2023b). Loadshedding has an immediate impact on consumers' water security; without electricity, water availability rapidly decreases (Meissner et al., 2018: 105). Biophysical factors add to deteriorating water security. For example, South Africa experienced a heat wave in October 2022 and January 2023, and municipal water utilities warned consumers to use water sparingly (Johannesburg Water, 2023).

Human Rights Commission inquiries

Investigations undertaken by the South African Human Rights Commission (SAHRC) highlight failures in the state's fulfilment of its water security mandate as it relates to governance and water politics.

Since 2016, microbiologists at the CSIR have been studying groundwater at Stinkwater, near Hammanskraal. They found that it was unfit for human consumption, with the risk of people contracting waterborne diseases. The SAHRC launched an investigation in July 2018 after it received complaints from residents that the water was unsafe, and that the municipality had violated citizens' rights to human dignity (Pretoria Record, 2018). The SAHRC further found that the city council violated the rights of the Temba community in Hammanskraal (Afro Worldview Reporter, 2018).

In June 2019, the SAHRC again found unsafe drinking water in Hammanskraal (Mbeki, 2023) after CSIR microbiologists found E. coli bacteria in more than 80 per cent of the 144 samples tested. It issued a warning about the water quality (TimesLive, 2019). Again in 2021, the Commission found that the wastewater treatment plants operated and maintained by the City of Tshwane were not working or were being inadequately maintained, thus polluting nearby rivers (Mbeki, 2023).

The Commission also conducted an inquiry in KwaZulu-Natal in 2022 after the public complained about a lack of access to water in various parts of the province. According to the Commission, the media reported on the problems experienced by individuals, communities, schools and businesses and most municipalities' responses to these failures were inadequate. The Commission stated that the complaints highlighted a *prima facie* violation of the fundamental human right to access sufficient clean water (SAHRC, 2022a). It added that a theme running clearly through the issues under investigation was corruption and its impact on the fulfilment of human rights, particularly when public monies are misused. In 2022, the Commission held hearings in Mpumalanga and North West province on service delivery related to water and sanitation in communities and schools (SAHRC, 2022b).

The SAHRC's work on water-related human rights violations is critical in articulating a standard set of principles for the polity and, by extension, water governance. Its inquiries emphasise that the principle of access to good quality water by municipalities is a priority. Where such services are lacking, local governments must focus on rectifying the problem to prevent further human rights violations and the spread of waterborne diseases. Furthermore, the emphasis on the right to water in the Constitution's Bill of Rights indicates the political mandate of the state to ensure water security.

The curious case of the Kgetlengrivier Municipality

There are several instances in the past decade in which non-state actors have challenged the government's role as the water warden. For example, in 2018, the residents of Reagile township in North West province protested against poor service delivery and corruption in the Kgetlengrivier Municipality. The municipality rented water tanks at a significant cost to distribute water in the township, but protestors burned the water tankers. Subsequently, no water was supplied for a week, and raw sewage flowed into the streets. Reagile and Koster residents approached the high court in Mahikeng, asking that residents be allowed to take over the water services. The court granted the request. The municipality promised to fix the water problems and resumed management of the services. In 2019, the court again handed the water services to the residents when municipal workers cut off the water supply to the town due to a salary dispute (Eybers, 2021).

Judge F.S. Gura, of the high court in Mahikeng, sentenced the municipal manager of Kgetlengrivier Municipality to 90 days in prison on 18 December 2020, which the court suspended on the condition that the municipality would treat the raw sewage flowing into the Elands and Koster rivers within 10 days. With assistance from the Democratic Alliance and AfriForum, residents had gathered evidence that the infrastructure had been neglected for years (Cilliers, 2023; Eybers, 2021). They also said that the municipal manager had deliberately diverted sewage into the town's water reservoir, sabotaged the pumping station and turned off supply taps in Reagile township. They alleged that the rationale for his actions was that the municipality would be forced to hire private contractors to deliver water with water tankers (Eybers, 2021).

Judge Gura ordered the municipality to temporarily allow the applicants, the Kgetleng River Concerned Citizens, to take over the sewerage works at the municipality's expense. The residents repaired infrastructure that pumped water from the Koster Dam to a substation, a water treatment plant, and the Koster and Swartruggens sewerage works. They also renovated a storage pond to provide sufficient water for the community. On 12 January 2021, the applicants and the city council reached an agreement with an order of the court stipulating that the council would appoint a service provider before the end of that month. The municipality approached Magalies Water (Eybers, 2021) to manage the services. There was a gradual improvement in the water and sewerage services from January to May 2021, while the residents managed these with the help of a private company. In May 2021, the municipality took back management of the water and sewerage services following a court order (Cilliers, 2023).

Although a back-and-forth situation developed between the interest groups and the municipality over the responsibility for maintaining the infrastructure, the Kgetlengrivier case shows how non-state actors and the public can reach a desperate stage at which they step in to manage water infrastructure. It illustrates how a local municipality's actions can diminish its legitimacy and public faith that it will act in the interests of citizens' water security. In other words, the municipality's actions contributed to a situation of distrust, which added to citizens' sense of water insecurity. The interest groups did not take over the governance of the service but by exercising their agency – in this case, using the courts – they took over the operational activities which the municipality had failed to carry out.

CONCLUSION

As climate variability influences weather patterns, South Africa experiences variable water supply availability across time and space.

Oscillations between drought, water scarcity and flooding, as well as water (over-)abundance, are realities that can have disastrous consequences. In 2023, South Africa, on average, experienced water abundance. Despite this, water quality and the maintenance of water infrastructure were worrying. While South Africa is not necessarily water-scarce (some parts, like the eastern regions, experience water abundance at times), poorly maintained and operated water infrastructure negatively affects water availability at the level of local government.

The state, particularly at municipal level, needs to improve its ability to effectively manage water purification, supply and waste treatment. Its inability raises serious questions about its involvement in and responsibility to manage its side of the hydro-social contact. But it is not only the state that is to blame; private individuals and organised crime are also responsible through the theft and vandalism of critical water infrastructure (Meissner, 2015). Even so, with its *étatiste* governance model, the state should be able to manage such criminal activity. This ability is, however, hampered by several factors. The first is the lack of the necessary resources, such as personnel, money and intelligence, to combat criminal behaviour. Further, in many municipalities, political will seems to be sorely lacking. However, there are also more deep-seated factors negatively affecting the state's ability to manage water services. In the party-executive management interface, some officials believe their superiors tolerate their misbehaviour even when they engage in illegal activity (Booysen, 2015: 6, 31). South Africa's governance and political culture lend themselves to wayward political actors, exercising control for their own benefit. A political paradox exists between exercising authority and diminishing such authority by pushback from the administrative apparatus and civil society. While the state has, over decades, changed society through involvement in all spheres of the polity and through dictating how the polity should function, Lilliputians from inside government's ranks undermine the regulatory Leviathan.

At the time of writing, South Africa was experiencing water abundance over large parts of the country. But if we view the state and its governing apparatus as the main actors in water politics and governance, then we must conclude that South Africa is experiencing a water governance and management crisis, particularly at local government level. Using the state as the Leviathan in water politics and the *étatiste* governance model, we are forced to conclude that there are severe shortcomings in government fulfilling its mandate as a water security warden. It is, however, not only the state that plays a role in the water sector. Checks and balances in the form of the SAHRC, Auditor-General and civil society have proven essential in highlighting the shortcomings in state-led water management, and even in the allocation of the resources needed for the functioning of water infrastructure, often through the courts. Looking at water governance and politics in South Africa from the perspective of democratic accountability and civil society actions reveals a picture wherein a clear answer to the water governance crisis would need further investigation to flesh out the nuances of water politics and governance opportunities and problems. This view shows that water politics and governance are a hybrid of two models: Dutch governance and governance-without-government, with the state being more of a Gulliver than a Leviathan.

REFERENCES

Afro Worldview Reporter. 2018. 'Makhura visits Hammanskraal after protests over water quality'. South African Human Rights Commission, 25 July, https://www.sahrc.org.za/index.php/sahrc-media/news/item/1471-makhura-visits-hammanskraal-after-protests-over-water-quality, accessed 3 July 2023.

Auditor-General South Africa (AGSA). 2022. 'Water boards: Consolidated report on 2020–21 audit outcomes. September 2022'. Office of the Auditor-General, Pretoria.

Backeberg, G.R. 2007. 'Allocation of water use rights in irrigated agriculture: Experience with designing institutions and facilitating market processes in South Africa'. Paper presented at USCID 4th International Conference on Irrigation and Drainage, 5 October 2007, Sacramento, California, USA.

Boelens, R., Hoogesteger, J. and Baud, M. 2015. 'Water reform governmentality in Ecuador: Neoliberalism, centralisation, and the restraining of polycentric authority and community rule-making'. *Geoforum*, 64, 281–291.

Booysen, S. 2015. *Dominance and Decline: The ANC in the Time of Zuma*. Johannesburg: Wits University Press.

Bruns, A., Meisch, S., Ahmed, A. and Meissner, R. 2022. 'Nexus disrupted: Lived realities and the water-energy-food nexus from an infrastructure perspective'. *Geoforum*, 133, 79–88.

Cilliers, S. 2023. 'Mense wat "vreemde voorwerpe" wegspoel, laat Koster-rioolvuil oorloop'. *Netwerk24*, 23 June, https://www.netwerk24.com/netwerk24/nuus/munisipaliteite/kyk-mense-wat-vreemde-voorwerpe-wegspoel-laat-koster-rioolvuil-oorloop-20230623

Delaney, J.A. 2005. *The March of Unreason: Science, Democracy, and the New Fundamentalism*. New York: Oxford University Press.

Department of Water Affairs (DWA). 2012. 'National Water Resource Strategy 2012: Department of Water Affairs briefing'. Briefing to the Parliamentary Portfolio Committee on Water and Sanitation, 19 September, https://pmg.org.za/committee-meeting/14915, accessed 31 August 2025.

Department of Water and Sanitation (DWS). 2018. 'National Water and Sanitation Master Plan. Volume 1: Call to Action, Ready for the Future and Ahead of the Curve'. Department of Water and Sanitation, Pretoria.

Department of Water and Sanitation (DWS). 2023. 'Blue Drop Watch Report 2023'. Department of Water and Sanitation, Pretoria.

Du Plessis, A. 2023a. 'Cholera in South Africa: A symptom of two decades of continued sewage pollution and neglect'. *The Conversation*, 23 May, https://theconversation.com/cholera-in-south-africa-a-symptom-of-two-decades-of-continued-sewage-pollution-and-neglect-206141, accessed 11 July 2023.

Du Plessis, A. 2023b. 'Power cuts in South Africa are playing havoc with the country's water system'. *The Conversation*, 23 January, https://theconversation.com/power-cuts-in-south-africa-are-playing-havoc-with-the-countrys-water-system-197952, accessed 11 July 2023.

Easton, D. 1965. *A Framework for Political Analysis*. Englewood Cliffs, New Jersey: Prentice Hall.

eNCA. 30 May 2023. 'Poor governance behind Hammanskraal cholera crisis: Ramaphosa', https://www.enca.com/news/poor-governance-behind-hammanskraal-cholera-crisis-ramaphosa, accessed 28 June 2023.

Enqvist, J.P. and Ziervogel, G. 2019. 'Water governance and justice in Cape Town: An overview'. *WIREs Water*, 6(4), e1354.

Eybers, J. 2021. 'Koebaai stadraad, nou loop ons water weer'. *Rapport*, 14 February.

Johannesburg Water. 2023. 'Infrastructure update: Monitoring of severely strained systems'. Urgent Customer Notice issued on 23 January 2023, https://twitter.com/JHBWater/status/1619357417267146754?lang=en, accessed 21 July 2023.

Levi-Faur, D. 2013. 'The odyssey of the regulatory state: From a "thin" monomorphic concept to a "thick" and polymorphic concept'. *Law & Policy*, 35(1/2), 29–50.

Martin-Carasco, F., Garrote, L., Iglesias, A. and Medeiro, L. 2013. 'Diagnosing causes of water scarcity in complex water resources systems and identifying risk management actions'. *Water Resource Management*, 27, 1693–1705.

Mbeki, Z. 2023. 'Cholera crisis'. *eNCA*, https://www.youtube.com/watch?v=-T5UEr4-9LM, accessed 28 June 2023.

Meissner, R. 2005. 'Interest groups and the proposed Epupa Dam: Towards a theory of water politics'. *Politeia*, 24(3), 354–370.

Meissner, R. 2015. 'The governance of urban wastewater treatment infrastructure in the Greater Sekhukhune District Municipality and the application of analytic eclecticism'. *International Journal of Water Governance*, 2, 79–110.

Meissner, R. 2022. 'Why "political will" isn't the magic bullet that can fix South Africa's energy crisis'. *The Conversation*, 4 August, https://theconversation. com/why-political-will-isnt-the-magic-bullet-that-can-fix-south-africas-energy-crisis-188168, accessed 11 July 2023.

Meissner, R. 2023. 'Eerbiedig dié waterkontrak'. *Beeld*, 23 June.

Meissner, R. and Du Plessis, A. 2022. 'South Africa's increasing water stress requires urgent informed actions'. *The Conversation*, 13 September, https:// theconversation.com/south-africas-increasing-water-stress-requires-urgent-informed-actions-189659, accessed 11 July 2023.

Meissner, R., Steyn, M., Moyo, E., Shadung, J., Masangane, W. et al. 2018. 'South African Local Government Perceptions of the State of Water Security'. *Environmental Science and Policy*, 87, 112–127.

Meissner, R. and Turton, A.R. 2003. 'The hydrosocial contract theory and the Lesotho Highlands Water Project'. *Water Policy*, 5(2), 115–126, https:// www.researchgate.net/profile/Richard-Meissner/publication/278965669_ The_Hydrosocial_Contract_Theory_and_the_Lesotho_Highlands_Water_ Project/links/58c0faf192851c2adfed02d4/The-Hydrosocial-Contract-Theory-and-the-Lesotho-Highlands-Water-Project.pdf

Mitchley, A. 2023. 'Source of Hammanskraal cholera outbreak remains unclear, but probe finds high levels of E. coli'. *News24*, 26 July.

Muller, M. 2020. 'Money down the drain – Corruption in South Africa's water sector'. Corruption Watch and the Water Integrity Network, Johannesburg and Berlin.

Ntombela, C., Funke, N., Meissner, R., Steyn, M. and Masangane, W. 2016. 'A critical look at South Africa's Green Drop Programme'. *Water SA*, 42(4), 703–710.

Oakeshott, M. 2017. 'Introduction to Leviathan', in *Thomas Hobbes*. London: Routledge, pp. 3–76.

Pahl-Wostl, C. and Knieper, C. 2023. 'Pathways towards improved water governance: The role of polycentric governance systems and vertical and horizontal coordination'. *Environmental Science & Policy*, 44, 151–161.

Pierre, J. and Peters, B.G. 2005. *Governing Complex Societies: Trajectories and Scenarios*. London: Palgrave Macmillan.

Pretoria Record. 2018. 'HRC to investigate Hammanskraal water "crisis"'. South African Human Rights Commission, https://www.sahrc.org.za/index. php/sahrc-media/news/item/1439-hrc-to-investigate-hammanskraal-water-crisis, accessed 3 July 2023.

Ramaphosa, C. 2021. 'State of the Nation Address'. Cape Town: Parliament.

Republic of South Africa (RSA). 1996. *Constitution of the Republic of South Africa (No. 108 of 1996)*. Pretoria: Government Printer.

Republic of South Africa (RSA). 1997. *Water Services Act (No. 108 of 1997)*. Pretoria: Government Printer.

Republic of South Africa (RSA). 1998. *National Water Act (No. 36 of 1998)*. Pretoria: Government Printer.

Republic of South Africa (RSA). 2023. 'Water and sanitation', https://www.gov.za/about-sa/water-affairs, accessed 18 July 2023.

Rosenau, J.N. 2006. *The Study of World Politics: Theoretical and Methodological Challenges*. Volume 1. London: Routledge.

Sørensen, E. and Triantafillou, P. 2009. 'The politics of self-governance: An introduction', in Sørensen, E. and Triantafillou, P. (eds), *The Politics of Self-Governance*. London: Routledge, pp. 1–22.

South African Human Rights Commission (SAHRC). 2022a. 'The SAHRC's Kwazulu-Natal inquiry on access to water has been rescheduled to commence from Monday, 15-19 August 2022'. Media Advisory, South African Human Rights Commission, https://www.sahrc.org.za/index.php/sahrc-media/news-2/item/3173-media-advisory-the-sahrc-s-kwazulu-natal-inquiry-on-access-to-water-has-been-rescheduled-to-commence-from-monday-15-19-august-2022, accessed 18 July 2023.

South African Human Rights Commission (SAHRC). 2022b. 'Annual report for the year ended 31 March 2022'. South African Human Rights Commission, Braamfontein, Johannesburg.

Steyn, M., Meissner, R., Nortje, K., Funke, N. and Petersen, C. 2019. 'Water security and South Africa', in Meissner, R., Funke, N., Nortje, K. and Steyn, M. (eds), *Understanding Water Security at Local Government Level in South Africa*. London: Palgrave Macmillan.

Swift, J. 1726. *Gulliver's Travels*. London: Benjamin Motte.

Tempelhoff, J. 2017. 'The Water Act, No. 54 of 1956 and the first phase of apartheid in South Africa (1948–1960)'. *Water History*, 9, 189–213.

Tempelhoff, J., Jaka, H., Mahabir, S., Ginster, M., Kruger, A., Mthembu, N. and Nkomo, L. 2019. 'The Anthropocene and the Hydrosphere: A case study of sanitation governance in Emfuleni Local Municipality (2018–19)'. Cultural Dynamics of Water, North West University, Vanderbiljpark.

TimesLive. 27 September 2019. 'CSIR confirms groundwater at Stinkwater is contaminated', https://www.timeslive.co.za/news/south-africa/2019-09-27-csir-confirms-groundwater-at-stinkwater-is-contaminated/, accessed 3 July 2023.

Union of South Africa. 1956. *Water Act (No. 54 of 1956)*. Parow, Cape Town: Cape Times Limited under the supervision of the Government Printer.

Vaughn, K.I. 1978. 'John Locke and the Labor Theory of Value'. *Journal of Libertarian Studies*, 2(4), 331–326.

Warner, J. 2000. 'Integrated management requires an integrated society: Towards a new hydrosocial contract for the 21st century'. Occasional paper, the African Water Issues Research Unit (AWIRU), Pretoria.

TEN

Traditional leadership in the era of multi-party democracy: A focus on South Africa

Lungisile Ntsebeza

INTRODUCTION

The role of traditional authorities in a democracy remains unresolved in South Africa. This issue attained prominence in Africa in the early 1990s, when multi-party democracy and decentralisation became the vogue in many African countries, partly egged on by the Bretton Woods institutions (Ntsebeza, 2006). Politicians who were engaged in electoral politics saw traditional authorities as important actors, and surmised that the support of these authorities would help win the support of the 'subjects'. Complicating matters, colonial governments – and in South Africa, apartheid-era governments – often attempted, successfully in most cases, to co-opt traditional authorities to enforce repressive policies. While many individual traditional leaders resisted this co-option, sometimes taking up arms against the colonial governments, the institutions of traditional authority often became instruments of these governments, making them unpopular with the broad anti-colonial/apartheid movement.

In South Africa, the democratic post-1994 regime inherited a system of 'bantustans': rural areas mostly administered by traditional authorities who had been appointed and paid by the apartheid government, making them accountable to their paymasters; disobedient traditional leaders who opposed the colonial authorities were subjected to state repression or replaced by compliant ones. Democratic South Africa adopted a constitution whose Bill of Rights enshrined principles of accountable leadership based on the will of its citizens. However, the Constitution also recognised institutions of appointed traditional leadership. It does not elaborate, except to say, in section 211(1), that traditional leadership is recognised 'subject to the Constitution', and stipulating that national and provincial legislatures 'may' pass relevant legislation clarifying the role of traditional authorities.

This chapter situates South Africa's post-apartheid democracy against the background of the colonialism and apartheid that African countries share, and in a political context arising from the introduction of multi-party democracy in African countries. Its key argument is that recognising an institution of unelected traditional leadership in a democracy whose central principle is elected representation, and giving such an institution political and executive powers over land and natural resources, undermines the democratic project. This chapter also highlights the complexities and intricacies associated with the role of traditional authorities in a multi-party democracy, explores the relationship of traditional authorities to the state and the democratically elected government, and interrogates how the reality of often-influential traditional leaders might be dealt with in a way that does not compromise democratic principles.

This argument attains new relevance in a context in which the South African debate about land has come to be discussed internationally (Friedman, 2025), and where numerous proposals are being considered for improving South Africa's democracy through electoral and other reforms (Thorne, 2024). Its relevance is further enhanced by the fact that traditional authorities 'continue to manifest themselves in a vibrant array of forms across the continent, co-existing in various ways – sometimes in collaboration, sometimes in contestation, sometimes in creative confusion, always in reciprocally transforming interplay – with dominant regimes of power, governance, knowledge, and capital accumulation' (Comaroff and Comaroff, 2019).

The role of traditional authorities will be situated in post-1994 South Africa within the country's historical context, and continental and global contexts. This chapter begins with a brief discussion about the relationship between the African National Congress (ANC) – as a liberation movement – and traditional authorities in South Africa from a historical perspective. Analysis of the ANC is privileged because it was the dominant party in South African politics, especially since the 1980s, dominated parliamentary decision-making and was the governing party from 1994 until 2024. It ends with raising critical questions that are yet to be resolved regarding the role of South Africa's traditional leadership in the democratic milieu.

TRADITIONAL LEADERSHIP AND THE ANC

In 1912, the ANC's founders included traditional leaders opposed to the Union of South Africa. Nevertheless, several chiefs and headmen had already been co-opted into colonial structures, a colonial strategy to rule the indigenous majority (Mamdani, 1996; see also Tabata, 1950). That some chiefs helped found or supported the ANC led to a belief in the liberation movement that chiefs could be divided between compliant and progressive. This distinction, and the characteristics of a 'progressive chief', lie at the heart of the ANC's longstanding ambiguity on traditional authorities, both during the liberation struggle and in South Africa's democracy (Ntsebeza, 2006).

Internal ANC debates on the role of traditional authorities became public in the 1940s, when the ANC Youth League was formed to give direction to a moribund ANC (Ntsebeza, 2006). Two groups emerged: ANC members who supported traditional authorities who were critical of apartheid government policies; and those who, influenced by communists, argued that the institution belonged to a previous feudal era and must be replaced by democratic structures. The ANC continued wooing 'progressive' traditional authorities, rather than relying solely on democratic structures to replace traditional authorities in rural areas (Ntsebeza, 2006). One reason for this strategy was that the ANC was weak in rural areas, and had no coherent programme for building alternative democratic structures there (Ntsebeza, 2006); another was a seeming revival, from the mid-1990s into the 2000s, of the notions of custom and traditional leadership (Oomen, 2005).

The role of traditional authorities received renewed attention within the ANC after political organisations were banned in 1960 (Ntsebeza, 2006). It debated cooperating with people such as Prince Mangosuthu Buthelezi, who worked within the apartheid system. The debate 'raged', according to Govan Mbeki (1996: 92), 'for years … especially on Robben Island'.[1] Mbeki cautioned against working with traditional authorities operating within the system (Ntsebeza, 2006), but Nelson Mandela maintained good relations with Buthelezi (Mandela, 1995).[2] According to Mbeki, exiled ANC members 'encouraged Buthelezi to establish a political party in the homeland' (Mbeki, 1996: 92). This position 'met with strong opposition from the ANC's internal membership in Natal' (Mbeki, 1996: 92), who were in the thick of the struggle (Ntsebeza, 2006).

The issue received renewed attention in the 1980s, when internal struggles in South Africa started shifting to rural areas. The dominant internal organisation in this period was the United Democratic Front (UDF), formed in 1983 and regarded as the internal, above-ground wing of the banned ANC. Like the ANC, the UDF was urban orientated, and poorly organised in rural areas (Ntsebeza, 2006). Van Kessel (1993; 1995; 2000) argues that rural mobilisation in these areas owed more to local youth initiatives than to planning or co-ordination by the UDF leadership.

The formation of the Congress of Traditional Leaders of South Africa (CONTRALESA) on 20 September 1987 had a major

---

1 I assume that Mbeki's reference to the ANC includes members of the SACP.

2 At a personal level, Buthelezi and Mandela corresponded with each other, and Buthelezi ostensibly refused 'independence' because of the continued incarceration of Mandela.

influence on the ANC's position, leading the party to recognise traditional authorities in South Africa's interim (1993) and final (1996) Constitutions. CONTRALESA was launched by a group of traditional authorities who opposed the declaration of apartheid-style independence by KwaNdebele, as well as some disgruntled traditional leaders – such as the Southern and Northern Ndebele leaders – whose chieftaincies were threatened because they initially did not have their own homelands. Harassed by the apartheid state, they looked to the UDF for protection and help to organise other traditional authorities (Oomen, 1996: 49).

The ANC urged a CONTRALESA delegation that visited it in Lusaka on 24 February 1988 'to spread itself into the whole of South Africa, organising all patriotic chiefs who are longing for a political home' (Zuma, 1990: 70). In its 1992 policy guidelines, the ANC said the powers of traditional authorities 'shall always be exercised subject to the provisions of the constitution and other laws' (quoted in Oomen, 1996: 103).

After CONTRALESA's establishment, traditional authorities were divided into two categories: members of CONTRALESA, who supported the ANC, and members of what became the Inkatha Freedom Party (IFP).[3] The IFP violently opposed the UDF and, after its unbanning in 1990, the ANC. Mbeki (1996) says relations between the ANC and Buthelezi soured in 1979 when the latter broke a secrecy pact in which the ANC had recommended in a meeting that Buthelezi use his leadership of the KwaZulu bantustan to mobilise rural people for a united and non-racial South Africa. Buthelezi used the meeting to raise his own profile and gain legitimacy, claiming to have the ear of the ANC leadership (Mbeki, 1996: 96). When the UDF was established in 1983, tensions arose between it and Buthelezi, leading to bloody conflict through most of the 1980s and the early 1990s.

Buthelezi's supporters displayed intense hostility towards CONTRALESA, and he was angered when Chief Maphumulo of KwaZulu was elected CONTRALESA's president in 1989 (Ntsebeza,

---

3 The IFP transformed itself from a 'cultural' movement into a political party in July 1990.

2006). CONTRALESA was attempting to 'thrust the spear into the very heart of Zulu unity' (Zuma 1990: 72), Buthelezi said. A few months later, he summoned KwaZulu's traditional leaders, including King Goodwill Zwelithini, to Ulundi (Ntsebeza, 2006) and told them, 'We have come to close ranks and to rejoice in our unity and to tell Inkosi Maphumulo to go to hell'. Zwelithini agreed and also verbally attacked Maphumulo (Zuma, 1990: 72; Oomen; 1996).

Relations between CONTRALESA and the ANC changed after Maphumulo's murder on 25 February 1991.[4] Chief Phathekile Holomisa took over as CONTRALESA president and relations with the ANC shifted. First, CONTRALESA rejected the ANC's position that the institution of chieftainship should be ceremonial and advisory. Instead, it demanded that traditional authorities be recognised as the primary level of government in rural areas, rejecting the notion that municipalities and elected councillors would fulfil this function in the rural areas of the former bantustans[5] (Ntsebeza, 2006). Unlike the IFP, which opposed the ANC from outside of the party, CONTRALESA raised its issues from within (Ntsebeza, 2006).

Traditional authorities did not participate in the 1990s political negotiations as part of a distinct institution. Rather, individual traditional leaders formed part of delegations from the former bantustans, and CONTRALESA members as part of the ANC (Ntsebeza, 2006). Buthelezi attached conditions to his participation, including demanding separate delegations for his KwaZulu government and for King Zwelithini. When this was not granted, he and the king withdrew.

Ultimately, CONTRALESA was party to Resolution 34 of the National Negotiating Council (National Negotiating Council, 1993), which was unanimously adopted on 11 November 1993. It stipulated that:

- Traditional authorities would continue to exercise their functions in terms of indigenous law as prescribed and regulated by enabling legislation;

---

4   After prior attempts on his life, Chief Maphumulo was shot and killed at his home in Pietermaritzburg by assassins. No one was apprehended.
5   I shared numerous platforms with Chief Holomisa in the late 1990s and early 2000s, debating the role of traditional authorities in a modern democracy.

- Elected local governments would take political responsibility for the provision of services within their areas of jurisdiction;
- Traditional leaders within the area of jurisdiction of a local authority would be ex officio members of the local government; and
- The chairperson of any local government would be elected from among the local government members.

Thus, traditional authorities managed to secure guarantees in the interim Constitution, albeit in a subordinate position to elected bodies. However, the IFP rejected the interim Constitution.

TRADITIONAL AUTHORITIES IN THE FIRST DECADE OF SOUTH AFRICA'S DEMOCRACY

Established in 1994, the ANC-led Government of National Unity took almost 10 years to meet its constitutional obligation of promulgating legislation to clarify the role of traditional leadership. These laws were passed in 2003 (Traditional Leadership and Governance Framework Act, No. 41 of 2003) and 2004 (Communal Land Rights Act, No. 11 of 2004). In the intervening years, the ANC tried to reconcile the interests of traditional authorities with those of rural residents who, mainly led by the South African National Civic Organisation (SANCO), were battling these traditional authorities. The ANC enjoyed support from both traditional authorities and civic activists, and did not want to alienate either.

While the role of traditional authorities in a democracy was not directly addressed in the first decade after South Africa's first free elections, strides were made to promulgate legislation in local government. The government took a significant step in its attempts to democratise rural local governance. It separated the functions of local government and land administration, thus undoing a major legacy of apartheid: to concentrate and fuse power in traditional authorities. Furthermore, the division between the rural and the urban was abolished in the sense that municipalities with elected councillors were extended to all parts of the country, including rural areas under traditional authorities where municipalities had not previously existed.

This was in line with the 1993 interim Constitution and the final Constitution of 1996 (Ntsebeza, 2006).

Regarding the land question in the rural areas of the former bantustans, the 1997 White Paper on South African Land Policy announced that the 'key area of concern' of the national Tenure Reform Programme was 'the rights in land of the people living in' rural areas. It provided a guide for the legislative process that would define land tenure rights of rural people, and a system of land administration. It also distinguished between 'ownership' and 'governance', and implied that tenure reform in these areas would entail transferring 'ownership' of land 'from the state to the communities and individuals on the land' (1997: 93). By the beginning of 1998, the then Department of Land Affairs (DLA) had developed principles to guide its legislative and implementation framework. The principles emphasised that where land rights '... exist on a group basis, the rights holders must have a choice about the system of land administration, which will manage their land rights on a day-to-day basis'. In addition, 'the basic human rights of all members must be protected, including the right to democratic decision-making processes and equality. Government must have access to members of group-held systems in order to ascertain their views and wishes in respect of proposed development projects and other matters pertaining to their land rights' (Ntsebeza, 2006; Thomas et al., 1998: 528).

It seems clear from this that both the then Department of Provincial and Local Government and the DLA intended to subject traditional authorities to a system that would make them more representative of, and accountable to, their communities (Ntsebeza, 2006).

Unsurprisingly, the moves by the ANC-led government towards democratising rural local governance drew fierce criticism and resistance from traditional authorities, including those in CONTRALESA. This resulted in a narrowing of the ideological gap between members of CONTRALESA and traditional authorities sympathetic to the IFP (Ntsebeza, 2002; 2004; 2006). Already, in the run-up to the first democratic local government elections in South Africa in 1995/1996, the two organisations had been working together. They challenged the government in the Constitutional Court over the issue of establishing municipalities throughout the country, including in rural areas under their jurisdiction. The then president of CONTRALESA, Chief Phathekile Holomisa, who had become an ANC Member of Parliament, took an increasingly defiant stand towards the ANC, and called for a boycott of the 1995/1996 local government elections (Ntsebeza, 2006).

While the initial collaboration between the IFP and CONTRALESA was around local government, it became clear that the main issue that brought them together was their opposition to the introduction of new democratic structures. They wanted traditional authorities to be the primary structures in rural areas, and insisted on preserving the functions they had enjoyed under apartheid, particularly regarding land administration. Not only did they oppose the separation of powers, but they also opposed any attempt to introduce alternative structures that would compete with them.

Traditional authorities adopted a similar stand on land tenure reform. While they agreed with government that land in the rural areas of the former bantustans should not be the property of the state, they rejected the notion that where land was held on a group basis, its administration should be transferred to democratically constituted and accountable structures. They demanded that the land be transferred to undemocratic and unaccountable tribal authorities. Such a move would legally exclude ordinary rural residents from vital decision-making processes, including those regarding land allocation (Ntsebeza, 2006).

GOVERNMENT SUCCUMBS TO PRESSURE FROM TRADITIONAL AUTHORITIES

Things came to a head in the run-up to the second democratic local government elections in December 2000. Traditional authorities pressured the government, threatening to boycott the elections, resulting in a delay in the announcement of the election date. After a series of meetings between government and traditional authorities, government made some concessions. The first significant concession was the amendment of the Municipal Structures Act (No. 117 of 1998) which had successfully been rushed through Parliament just before the elections. The amendment increased traditional authorities' representation in local government from 10 to 20 per cent of the total number of councillors. Furthermore, it granted traditional authorities representation not only at local government level, but also at district and, in the case of KwaZulu-Natal, metropolitan level. Traditional authorities, though, would not have the right to vote. This concession encouraged traditional authorities to reject the 20 per cent increase and demand more. They insisted on amendments to the Constitution and legislation regarding municipalities in rural areas in the former bantustans, and demanded municipalities be scrapped in these areas and be replaced by apartheid-era tribal authorities (Ntsebeza, 2006).

The government response was, for the second time in two months, to present a Bill to Parliament to amend the Municipal Structures Act. The Bill did not address the traditional authorities' central demand: scrapping municipalities in rural areas in favour of tribal authorities. It merely sought to give local government the authority to delegate certain powers and functions to traditional authorities. Additionally, several peripheral duties would be assigned to traditional authorities. Predictably, traditional authorities rejected the Bill, threatened to boycott the 2000 local government election, and threatened violence in their areas if their demands were not met. The Bill was subsequently withdrawn on a technicality. The president, it seems, gave some undertakings, given that traditional authorities eventually participated in the election (Ntsebeza, 2006).

At the same time as these discussions occurred, shifts were underway in the DLA. First, Thoko Didiza replaced Derek Hanekom as Minister of Land Affairs. One of her first moves was to disband the drafting team of the Land Rights Bill that she had inherited from Hanekom and unveil, in February 2000, her 'strategic objectives' regarding land tenure and administration in rural areas. On land administration, she committed herself to building on 'the existing local institutions and structures, both to reduce costs to the government and to ensure local commitment and popular support' (Lahiff, 2000: 63).

It was only in 2003 and 2004 that a degree of clarity about the role of traditional authorities in South Africa's democracy emerged. In 2003, Parliament passed the Traditional Leadership and Governance Framework Act (the Framework Act). One objective of this law was the establishment and recognition of 'traditional councils', which, according to section 3(1), would be established in an area recognised by the province's premier as a traditional community. The Act's preamble says that this would occur within the context of transforming 'the institution of traditional leadership ... in line with constitutional imperatives ... so that democratic governance and the values of an open and democratic society may be promoted'. The Act provided for a role for traditional leadership in all three spheres of government, but did not specify a role for traditional authorities in land administration. This would be dealt with in the Communal Land Rights Act (CLaRA), which was promulgated in 2004. The 2003 Act recognised apartheid-era tribal authorities as the basis on which traditional councils would be established.

Traditional councils were constituted in a manner that resembled the tribal authorities they were meant to replace. Although there was provision for a minimum of 30 per cent representation of women in the councils, most members would not be popularly elected. Initially, there was a recommendation that a mere 25 per cent of members should be elected. After strong protests from various civil society organisations, this number was increased to 40 per cent, still giving unelected traditional authorities and their appointees a majority.

Following the Framework Act of 2003, CLaRA was passed in 2004. It granted traditional councils established under the Framework Act powers over land allocation and administration, and functions in areas they had controlled under apartheid. Section 21(2) reads: 'If a community has a recognised traditional council, the powers and duties of the land administration committee of such community may be exercised and performed by such council.' This gave enormous and unprecedented powers to a structure with mostly unelected members. Under the colonial and apartheid systems, the final authority in land allocation and the issuing of permits to occupy land resided with magistrates and, later, district commissioners; CLaRA made traditional councils the supreme structures in land allocation.

The draft Communal Land Rights Bill, gazetted on 14 August 2002, proposed to transfer registrable land rights to individuals, families and communities. It proposed to divest traditional authorities of their land administration functions, including land allocation, in favour of democratically elected administrative structures. Where applicable, 'legitimate' traditional authorities were to be accorded *ex officio* representation in land administration committees not exceeding 25 per cent. The draft Bill clearly attempted to strike a balance between the constitutional obligation to extend democracy to all parts of the country, including rural areas, and constitutional accommodation of traditional leadership (Ntsebeza, 2006).

However, traditional authorities rejected the Bill. CONTRALESA's president, Chief Holomisa, and the National House of Traditional Leaders' Chief Mzimela, indicated their opposition and their intention to raise the issue, as previously, with the president (Sunday Times and City Press, 25 August 2020).

An amended Communal Land Rights Bill drew criticism from a range of civil society organisations, and gender and land rights activists, organised by the University of the Western Cape's Programme for Land and Agrarian Studies (PLAAS) and the National Land Committee (NLC), and from some ANC MPs.[6] The uproar was based on the view that traditional councils were 'a retreat from democracy' and an attempt to revive a defunct apartheid institution which deeply discriminated against women, among others. Cousins and Claassens (2003) argue that under 'customary law', women would be dependent on men and vulnerable to losing their land and other property upon divorce or the death of their husbands. Despite the protest, the controversial Bill was bulldozed through and was passed unanimously by Parliament on 27 January 2004 (Ntsebeza, 2006).

For the first time in over ten years, traditional authorities gave their overwhelming support for CLaRA.[7] In a December 2003 article, the then chairperson of the National House of Traditional Leaders, Chief Mpiyezintombi Mzimela, supported the second draft of the Bill, writing: 'The Communal Land Rights Bill aims to restore to rural communities ownership of the remnants that they occupy of land that the colonial and apartheid government took from them by force –

---

6   Based on my own observation of and participation in some of the meetings.
7   Disagreements between traditional authorities and government about their respective roles in a democracy go back to the political negotiation period in the early 1990s.

giving the communities registered title, so that it cannot happen again' (Business Day, 2003).

CLaRA was, however, legally challenged by some rural residents (Claassens, 2013) concerned about their right to land tenure, given that control over their land was in the hands of traditional councils with mostly unelected members. The applicants contested the process followed in making a last-minute amendment to the Bill. The matter proceeded to the Constitutional Court which, in 2010, declared CLaRA invalid in its entirety. Then Chief Justice Sandile Ngcobo said the judgment was based on administrative grounds. The court found that the provinces were never properly consulted when the Bill, which had the impact of customary law, was enacted. This could be interpreted to mean that not only traditional authorities but rural residents too should be consulted (Ntsebeza, 2006).

THREE DECADES LATER

Despite promises to introduce a Green Paper to kickstart the process of promulgating legislation on tenure reform in the former bantustans, nothing of substance has been done to pass the necessary legislation. The land rights of rural residents in areas controlled by traditional authorities continue to be precarious. In KwaZulu-Natal, land that was once under the KwaZulu bantustan is held by the Ingonyama Trust, rendering rural residents in that province tenants on their own land.

The same applies, by and large, with respect to governance. The only difference is that the Framework Act has been replaced by a new law, the Traditional and Khoi-San Leadership Act (TKLA), which President Cyril Ramaphosa signed into law on 20 November 2019. Some provisions of the Act are:

- To provide for the recognition of traditional and Khoi and San communities and leadership positions within them, and the conditions for the withdrawal of such recognition; and
- To provide for the functions and roles of traditional and Khoi and San leaders.

This Act extends apartheid-era structures to new territories, notably the Western Cape and Northern Cape, with new actors who identify themselves as Khoi and San.

Notably, this Act was declared unconstitutional in a Constitutional Court judgment handed down on 30 May 2024. The grounds for the decision were technical rather than substantive; the court ruled that there had been insufficient public participation, especially by those who would be directly affected by the law. This is similar to the judgment in the CLaRA case. However, unlike CLaRA, the TKLA is still operational. Parliament was given 24 months to address the issue of public participation (*Mogale and Others v Speaker of the National Assembly and Others – CCT 73/22 (2023) ZACC 14*).

Thus, insofar as the rural areas of the former bantustans are concerned, little has changed from the apartheid past. In these areas, the same system is perpetuated both in land tenure and governance, raising pertinent questions about the meaning of democracy for those living in these areas.

CRITICAL ISSUES THAT NEED TO BE ADDRESSED

The key issue relating to the debate and status of traditional leaders in South Africa is the extension of executive authority to unelected traditional authorities. As discussed earlier, this creeping extension of powers has a long history, going back to decades-old debates within the ANC. Traditional leaders' roles in a democracy need to be defined more carefully to ensure that they do not impinge on the constitutional powers and roles of elected representatives.

In the past two decades there has been a tendency towards the assertion of executive powers for traditional leaders. This was usually accompanied by legal battles by civil society on behalf of communities, challenging the impact of laws such as CLaRA. However, in 2013, after the legal battle against CLaRA was won, the Department of Rural Development and Land Reform (DRDLR) introduced the Communal Land Tenure Policy (CLTP), pushing a similar position as the invalidated law.

Before CLaRA, Chapter 5(20:1) of the Traditional Leadership and Governance Framework Act (TLGFA) conferred what might be regarded as executive authority on traditional institutions. Chapter 5 of the Act states that national or provincial governments may, through legislation or other measures, provide a role for traditional leaders in respect of, *inter alia*, arts and culture, land administration, agriculture, health, administration of justice, safety and security, economic development, disaster management and the management of natural resources. Giving traditional authorities the powers to make decisions on such critical issues is akin to giving the institution the right to make executive decisions, at least at local level. The key problem with this approach is the recognition, in a democracy, of institutions based on unelected leaders, and, further, granting these institutions executive powers over such critical functions as the use of land and other natural resources or the administration of justice. Such powers granted to unelected leaders undermine the democratic project, particularly in the case of one still transitioning from authoritarianism. It remains unclear whether the symbiotic relationship between the post-1994 government and traditional leaders has compromised how the government has responded to the dictates of democracy, according to which elected leadership is prioritised and is responsible for oversight over all governance, and in which a constitution espousing democratic values and practices reigns supreme.

It must be acknowledged that the persistence of traditional leadership is due to its ability to adapt and institutionally renew itself in changing – and sometimes challenging – circumstances. The challenges to democracy occur when this reality infringes on or compromises people's rights of choice and affiliation, and when they are unable to opt out of the authority of traditional leaders or traditional courts. This has partly been the basis of the numerous contestations of the Traditional Courts Bill (Pikoli, 2020), which was tabled in 2008 and, because of legal and other protests, was amended several times before it was passed as the Traditional Courts Act of 2022 (Republic of South Africa, 2023).

Traditional leaders' powers are defined in legislation and range from power over cultural and traditional issues to certain judicial functions and the management of land and resources. To ensure consistency with basic human rights and administrative justice, various laws provide for properly constituted traditional councils in which issues such as gender representation are considered. However, many of these provisions are observed mostly in the breach. For example, matters such as traditional courts, provisions for voluntary affiliation and for individuals to opt out of these courts' processes, which were included in earlier versions of the Bill, were narrowed in successive versions. This was partly the basis of contestations against the Bill: that it infringes on people's rights of choice and affiliation. The contestation has also been that the proposed legislation will enable the concentration of power in one individual, the traditional leader.

While traditional leaders' powers are minimal and mostly ceremonial at national and provincial levels, through the National House of Traditional Leaders and informal arrangements, the matter is more complicated at local level. No locality in South Africa is excluded from being part of a municipality constituted on democratic principles. In communal areas, traditional leaders are accorded a mix of powers – by the legislation referred to earlier – that might be considered ceremonial, executive and those possessed by absolute monarchies.

To make progress on this question in a way that accords with South Africa's democratic principles, a conceptual question must be addressed: how should traditional leaders relate to local government, and how should constitutional rights find full expression in communal areas, while simultaneously accommodating some form of traditional 'governance'?

This critical question raises several other issues related to the powers and authority of traditional authorities. It questions whether the kind of powers envisaged in the TKLA and the Traditional Courts Bill are constitutional, and whether traditional leaders should have power over land administration and arrangements with commercial entities such as mining companies, as is currently the case. Should they, instead, be merely ceremonial figureheads, or should their powers be increased? If their powers are to be increased, what additional powers would be appropriate, from which authorities would those be transferred, and would such transfers accord with democratic principles? It is also unclear where in history the precedent for such powers would be traced to. Would it be in colonial and apartheid laws and politics, or in pre-colonial political systems, and, whatever the source, would it be consistent with current constitutional rights?

In whatever direction the responses to these questions take us, it is also crucial to understand what the citizen responses to these might be – both among those supporting more powers for traditional authorities and those opposing these. Can citizens voluntarily surrender basic constitutional rights? And what recourse exists for those people who refuse to surrender these rights?

CONCLUSION

Throughout the apartheid era, traditional authorities in South Africa were unelected, and most of them collaborated with the regime through the tribal authorities that it created. The regime gave traditional authorities and their appointees executive powers, the most powerful being land administration and influence over the management and use of natural resources within areas of their jurisdiction. Although they did not own the land, no decision on land carried weight if it was not endorsed by the tribal authority concerned. In many instances, traditional authorities took decisions without consulting residents, even when the decision directly affected them.

Mamdani (1996: 23) characterises such concentration of power in one authority as a 'clenched fist', i.e. the fusion of various powers – judicial, legislative, executive and administrative – within one office. Such a situation leaves no room for the classic liberal democratic notion of separation of powers that undergirds South Africa's Constitution. Mamdani further reminds us that 'Native Authorities', to use his term for what, in South Africa, were tribal authorities, were protected by colonial governments from any form of external threat. Tribal authorities' officials were appointed from above, had an indefinite term of office, and remained in power for as long as they enjoyed their superiors' confidence (1996: 53). For Mamdani (1996), native (tribal) authorities in a postcolonial/post-apartheid situation should be dismantled so as 'to link the urban and the rural – and thereby a series of related binary opposites such as rights and custom, representation and participation, centralisation and decentralisation, civil society and community – in ways that have yet to be done' (1996: 34).

In many ways, Mamdani's proposals echo the spirit of the South African Constitution. The same sentiment is expressed in the Traditional Leadership and Governance Framework Act of 2003. In its preamble, the Act categorically states its purpose is to 'define the place and role of traditional leadership within a system of democratic governance', and 'to transform the institution in line with constitutional imperatives'. The preamble to the Constitution points out that it lays 'the foundations for a democratic and open society in which government is based on the will of the people and every citizen is equally protected by law'. Section 1(d) asserts one value of the Republic of South Africa as 'universal adult suffrage, a national common voters' roll, regular elections, and a multi-party system of democratic government, to ensure accountability, responsiveness and openness', while section 19(2) guarantees every adult citizen 'the right to free, fair and regular elections for any legislative body established in terms of the Constitution'.

The principles and values of democracy in the Constitution were upheld in a landmark Bisho High Court (Full Bench) judgment, *The Premier of the Eastern Cape* v *Penrose Ntamo (2015)*, involving the appointment of headmen in terms of the Framework Act. The Eastern Cape premier had appealed a lower court decision that upheld an application by villagers from Cala Reserve in the Eastern Cape that their longstanding practice of electing their headmen be maintained. They opposed the appointment of a headman without their participation. Justice Plasket wrote the judgment, which was endorsed by his two colleagues. In paragraph 49, he said (Bisho High Court Judgment, 2015):

> The facts set out in Professor Ntsebeza's affidavit establish a practice (of electing their headman) of long duration... It is a reasonable practice in that it is not in conflict with legislation or the Constitution. Indeed, it is a practice that is consonant with the value of democratic governance, aimed at the achievement of accountability, responsiveness and openness that is one of the Constitution's founding values. It is also consistent with various fundamental rights, such as the right to dignity, the right to freedom of opinion, the right to freedom of association and the right to make political choices.

The judge returned to this point when interpreting section 18 of the Eastern Cape version of the Framework Act. According to him, this section should be understood to mean that the 'royal family', when appointing a headman, should consider the custom in the area. In this respect, the judge argued (paragraph 82) that section 18 'advances, rather than retards the promotion of democratic governance and the values of an open and democratic society by recognising the customary law of local communities in the identification of those who will govern them on the local, and most intimate, level'. This paragraph ended with a remark that identifying 'those who will govern ... is a recipe for the legitimacy of local government' (Bisho High Court Judgment, 2015).

Regarding customary law, Plasket insightfully observed in paragraph 85 that the nature of this law meant that it not only differed from place to place, but, crucially, 'may also change over time' (Bisho High Court Judgment, 2015).

The demands made by traditional authorities for a return to apartheid-era rule in areas under their jurisdiction must be situated within the context of the Constitution, the supreme law of the land and the legislation flowing from it. As this chapter has demonstrated, traditional authorities are fighting vehemently for the restoration of apartheid-era tribal authorities, euphemistically referred to as traditional councils, and are demanding that what is effectively a fourth sphere of government be established for them. Policy formulators, politicians and scholars focusing on policy issues must not only respect the country's statutes but must also be sensitive to historical and current empirical evidence when defining a role for traditional authorities. While the institutions of traditional leadership are a reality that cannot be wished away, political posturing that grants them – or any other authority – powers beyond those envisaged by the Constitution must be resisted. These include governance powers and powers over natural resources such as land and minerals. Inserting role players into the state in ways not countenanced by the Constitution poses a serious challenge to South Africa's democracy and is unlikely, in any case, to pass legal muster.

REFERENCES

African National Congress (ANC). 1992. 'Ready to Govern: ANC policy guidelines for a democratic South Africa'. Adopted at the National Conference, 28–31 May, Policy Unit of the African National Congress.

Bisho High Court Judgment. 2015. *Premier of the Eastern Cape et al. v Penrose Ntamo et al. Case no. 169/14.* Date heard: 7 August 2015; Date delivered: 18 August 2015 (Reportable). Eastern Cape Local Division, Bisho. Full Bench.

Bowen, M.L. 2000. *The State Against the Peasants: Rural Struggles in Colonial and Postcolonial Mozambique.* Charlottesville: University Press of Virginia.

Claassens, A. 2000. 'South African proposals for tenure reform: The draft Land Rights Bill', in Toulmin, C. and Quan, J. (eds), *Evolving Land Rights, Policy and Tenure in Africa.* London: DFID/IIED/NRI, pp. 247–266.

Claassens, A. 2001. '"It is hard to challenge a chief": Transfer of title to tribes – the Rakgwadi case'. Research Report No. 9, Programme for Land and Agrarian Studies, Cape Town.

Claassens, A. 2013. 'Recent changes in women's land rights and contested customary law in South Africa'. *Journal of Agrarian Change*, 13(1), 71–92.

Comarrof, J.L. and Comaroff, J. 2019. *The Politics of Custom: Chiefship, Capital, and the State in Contemporary Africa.* Chicago: University of Chicago Press.

Cousins, B. and Claassens, A. 2003. 'Looming land disaster'. *Mail & Guardian*, 31 October – 6 November.

Department of Land Affairs. 1997. 'White Paper on South African Land Policy', http://www.ruraldevelopment.gov.za/phocadownload/White-Papers/ whitepaperlandreform.pdf, accessed 22 September 2020.

Department of Provincial Affairs and Constitutional Development. 1998. 'The White Paper on Local Government', http://www.cogta.gov.za/cgta_2016/ wp-content/uploads/2016/06/whitepaper_on_Local-Gov_1998.pdf, accessed 22 September 2020.

Dinerman, A. 2001. 'From "Abaixo" to "chiefs of production": Agrarian change in Nampula province, Mozambique, 1975–87'. *The Journal of Peasant Studies*, 28(2), 1–82.

Friedman, I.B. 2025. 'Explainer: Understanding the South Africa land reform law that provoked Trump's ire'. *Jurist News*, 11 February, https://www.jurist. org/features/2025/02/11/explainer-understanding-the-south-africa-land-reform-law-that-provoked-trumps-ire

Henrard, K. 1999. 'The Interrelation between Individual Human Rights, Minority Rights and the Right to Self-determination for an adequate Minority Protection'. Doctor of Law degree thesis, Leuven University.

Houston, G.F. 1997. 'Traditional leadership and the restructuring of rural local government'. Paper presented to the Internal Conference on Traditional Leaders in Southern Africa, Umtata, 16–18 April.

Lahiff, E. 2000. 'Land tenure in South Africa's communal areas: A case study of the Arabie-Olifant's Scheme'. *African Studies*, 59(1), 45–69.

Libombo, A. 2000. 'Mozambique's bitter war between chiefs and liberation government'. *Land and Rural Digest*, 5(2), 120–145.

Maloka, T. 1995. 'Traditional leaders and the current transition'. *The African Communist*, 2nd Quarter, 25–43.

Mamdani, M. 1996. *Citizen and Subject: Contemporary Africa and the legacy of late colonialism*. Cape Town: David Phillip Publishers.

Mandela, N. 1995. *Long Walk to Freedom: The Autobiography of Nelson Mandela*. London: Abacus.

Marais, H. 1998. *South Africa, Limits to Change: The Political Economy of Transformation*. London: Zed Books.

Mbeki, G. 1984. *South Africa: The Peasants' Revolt*. London: International Defence and Aid Fund.

Mbeki, G. 1996. *Sunset at Midday: Latshon' ilang' emini!*. Braamfontein: Nolwazi Educational Publishers.

National Negotiating Council. 1993. 'Resolution 34: The Role of Traditional Leaders at all Levels of Government', 11 November, https://archive. wethepeoplesa.org/uploads/r/constitution-hill-trust-2/3/b/9/3b9fcab8df9 fc9dfc2f5eae5e2a43c8a5f765929fd675fff7137aed1652c2a85/ITEM_NEG-0055-0006-_-034.pdf

Ntsebeza, L. 2002. 'Structures and struggles of rural local government in South Africa: The case study of traditional authorities in the Eastern Cape'. PhD thesis, Rhodes University.

Ntsebeza, L. 2004. 'Democratic decentralisation and traditional authority: Dilemmas of land administration in rural South Africa'. *European Journal of Development Research*, 16(1), 71–89.

Ntsebeza, L. 2006. *Democracy Compromised: Chiefs and the Politics of Land in South Africa*. Cape Town: HSRC Press.

Ntsebeza, L. 2013. 'The more things change, the more they remain the same', in Hendricks, F., Ntsebeza, L. and Helliker, K. (eds), *The Promise of Land: Undoing Centuries of Dispossession in South Africa*. Johannesburg: Jacana Media, pp. 54–75.

Oomen, B. 1996. 'Talking Tradition: The position and portrayal of traditional leaders in present-day South Africa'. MA thesis, Leiden University.

Oomen, B. 2005. *Chiefs in South Africa: Law, Power and Culture in the Post-Apartheid Era*. Oxford: James Currey.

Pikoli, Z. 2020. 'Activists implore President Ramaphosa not to sign the controversial Traditional Courts Bill into law'. *Daily Maverick*, 3 December, https://www.dailymaverick.co.za/article/2020-12-03-activists-implore-president-ramaphosa-not-to-sign-controversial-traditional-courts-bill-into-law/, accessed 23 July 2024.

Pitcher, M.A. 1996. 'The politics of the countryside: Democracy and economic liberalisation in Northern Mozambique'. Paper presented to the annual meeting of the African Studies Association, 23–26 November.

Republic of South Africa. 1996. The Constitution of the Republic of South Africa, 1996. Pretoria.

Republic of South Africa. 2023. 'The Traditional Courts Act, 2022', https://www.gov.za/sites/default/files/gcis_document/202310/49373 traditionalcourtsact92022.pdf, accessed 23 July 2024.

Sachs, A. 1992. *Advancing Human Rights in South Africa: Contemporary South African Debates*. Cape Town: Oxford University Press.

Tabata, I.B. 1950. *The All African Convention: The Awakening of a People*. Johannesburg: People Press.

Thomas, G., Sibanda, S. and Claassens, A. 1998. 'Current developments in South Africa's land tenure policy'. Proceedings of the International Conference on Land Tenure in the Developing World with a focus on Southern Africa, University of Cape Town, 27–29 January.

Thorne, S. 2024. 'Election changes on the cards for South Africa'. *BusinessTech*, 29 October, https://businesstech.co.za/news/government/797255/election-changes-on-the-cards-for-south-africa, accessed 21 June 2025.

Traditional Leadership and Governance Framework Act, 41 of 2003. 11 December 2003, http://www.cogta.gov.za/cgta_2016/wp-content/uploads/2016/06/TLGFA-Traditional-Leadership-and-Governance-Framework-Act-2003-Act-No-41-of-2003.pdf, accessed 10 September 2020.

Van Kessel, I. 1993. 'From confusion to Lusaka: The youth revolt in Sekhukhuneland'. *Journal of Southern African Studies*, 19(4), 593–614.

Van Kessel, I. 1995. '"Beyond our Wildest Dreams": The United Democratic Front and the transformation of South Africa'. PhD thesis, Leiden University.

Van Kessel, I. 2000. *'Beyond our Wildest Dreams: The United Democratic Front and the Transformation of South Africa*. Charlottesville, VA: University Press of Virginia.

Zuma, T. 1990. 'The role of chiefs in the struggle for liberation'. *The African Communist*, 121, 65–76.

Newspaper articles[8]

Business Day, 2 December 2003.
City Press, 25 August 2002.
Daily Dispatch, 2 November 2002.
Mail & Guardian, 31 October to 6 November 2003.
Sunday Times, 25 August 2002.

---

8   The newspaper articles used to write this chapter are not available online and are listed only by their dates of publication.

ELEVEN

The state of the post-apartheid security sector in South Africa: An overview

Sandy Africa

INTRODUCTION

In *The Rise of the Securocrats in South Africa*, Jane Duncan argues that there was a systematic reduction in the country's democratic space since 2009, and that the security services were instrumentalised by political elites to reverse gains from the earlier years of democracy. She highlights increasing levels of state repression in response to legitimate dissent by impoverished and marginalised communities demanding improvements in public services. Duncan also points to the growing abuse of surveillance powers by the security establishment and a tightening of legislation restricting access to information in the name of national security (Duncan, 2014: 3–34). This is a far cry from the principle contained in South Africa's Constitution: 'National security must reflect the resolve of South

237

Africans, as individuals and as a nation, to live in peace and harmony, to be free from fear and want and to seek a better life' (RSA, 1996b, s 198(a)). The Constitution further says: 'The security services must act, and must teach and require their members to act, in accordance with the Constitution and the law, including customary international law and international agreements binding on the Republic' (RSA, 1996, s 199(5)) and: 'No member of any security service may obey a manifestly illegal order' (RSA, 1996b, s 199(6)).

Several norms and standards regarding good practice in security governance in a democracy have gained recognition in policy, practitioner and academic circles in many countries. These include effective executive control over security services to prevent them from acting extra-judicially or advancing narrow political agendas and interests, and the question of whether a state has robust parliamentary oversight for holding the executive and security services accountable. Also critical is whether there is oversight by independent complaints bodies, and how society interfaces with the security services. An implied question is whether ordinary citizens understand the role of security institutions and are able to influence policy about how these institutions should operate. The latter point presupposes that the security services perform a legitimate and lawful role in society, have clearly articulated mandates, and are subject to the Constitution and the rule of law (see for example, Ball and Fayemi, 2004; Born and Leigh, 2005; Bryden et al., 2008; Bucur-Marcur et al., 2009).

This chapter assesses the state of governance of the security sector in post-apartheid South Africa through these lenses, mindful that contextual realities – historical, political, economic and social – will always be factors when weighing up the efficacy, relevance and applicability of norms and standards. The reflections in this chapter occur against an appraisal of the contextual realities facing the South African state, including its external and internal challenges.

The term 'security sector' is used to denote the major actors involved in governance of the security services, including the executive, which is responsible for exercising civil control; multi-party parliamentary oversight committees exercising legislative control; independent oversight institutions and complaints bodies; and the security services as defined in the Constitution, namely, the defence force, the police service and intelligence services (RSA, 1996b, Chapter 11).[1]

RE-IMAGINING SOUTH AFRICA'S 'SECURITY DILEMMA' IN THE TRANSITION TO DEMOCRACY

Traditional international relations theory regards the international state system as anarchic; states therefore prepare militarily to defend their sovereignty. However, this leads rival states to strengthen their own military capabilities to feel more secure, initiating a cycle of ever-growing militarisation (Sorenson, 2001: 93). This 'security dilemma' – rooted in an epistemology of fear – results in a further dilemma that plagues modern democracies: how to ensure that the military and the security sector more generally are strong enough to protect a state from domestic and international threats, while ensuring that they do not dominate the state or become instruments of internal repression (Alagappa, 2001: xv). The presumption that the modern state must protect its citizens against internal and external threats is so prominent in the realist approach because of the arbitrariness of violence in the era preceding the founding of modern states. Earlier, according to Sorenson (2001: 96), 'In the absence of a monopoly of violence, security was provided by knights, nobles and other local rulers who had sufficient power to protect their towns, castles or fiefs.' Typically, it was their subjects who bore the brunt of the wars and conflicts. By contrast, the rise of the modern state has created conditions and safeguards under which centralised systems of rule, policing and military organisations are sanctioned by law, and the state's monopoly over the use of force is regarded as a necessary and legitimate exercise of power. In many modern states, the development of capitalism has resulted in strong economic bases, and the population has been invested in the notion of

---

1   The security services established by law to give effect to the constitutional requirement were the South African National Defence Force, the South African Police Service, the National Intelligence Agency and the South African Secret Service.

sovereignty. 'Sovereignty created a territorial space within which rulers could shape and regulate national economic systems. Competition with other rulers was not limited to the military sphere, of course, it took place in the economic field as well' (Sorenson, 2001: 80).

The security dilemmas of African states have differed from those of the modern Western states that followed a capitalist growth trajectory. Colonialism and imperialism left newly independent African states weak, with limited capacity and underdeveloped economies, and, in some cases, only a fragile sense of nationhood – often due to the divide-and-rule tactics used on subjugated populations during the colonial period (Markowitz, 1977). One challenge facing new African leaders was to build and develop cohesive, capable security forces responsive to the needs of their nations. In some cases, the relatively weak states became sites of contestation (McGowan, 2003). Whoever controlled the armed forces could wield power over the population. Moreover, the absence of strong democratic institutions created conditions in which the armed forces could themselves usurp power through military coups.

Ongoing instability during the Cold War period resulted in armed forces' impunity against local communities in most African states. This was mostly tolerated by the international community, especially where many African states were proxies in geopolitical rivalries. Several authors have described the security establishment's firm hold over domestic and foreign policymaking in apartheid South Africa as central to the survival of the apartheid regime (Cawthra, 1986; Frankel, 1984; Grundy, 1986). In the negotiations leading up to the democratic dispensation in the early 1990s, it was a significant political achievement to include on the agenda the future of defence, intelligence and policing structures, even though some members of the apartheid security establishment were hostile to the idea of liberation movements' combatants being integrated into the security structures of the democratic state (Cawthra, 2013: 36). The negotiators ultimately agreed that apartheid security forces would be integrated into the post-apartheid security services, along with combatants of the ANC's armed wing, Umkhonto weSizwe (popularly called 'MK'), and the armed wing of the Pan Africanist Congress (PAC), the Azanian People's Liberation

Army (APLA) (Africa, 2011: 17).[2] Apartheid security forces included the police, military and intelligence services of the central apartheid state as well as those in the jurisdictions of the ethnically defined, so-called 'homelands' and 'self-governing territories'.

During the negotiations, significant attention was paid to reframing the security dilemmas facing South Africa in the post-Cold War world as it was coming out of its own armed, political conflict. Mindful of the atrocities committed during the apartheid era, there was discussion about how to ensure transparency and accountability of the security organs and to promote ethical conduct. The discussion was influenced by the view that with the end of superpower rivalry, the traditional approach to security, which saw interstate rivalry as the main potential source of instability, would be overtaken by a host of non-military threats, including economic, social, political and environmental sources of insecurity (Duncan, 2014). Also influential in the discussion was the belief that there could be no development without peace and security, and there could be no peace and security without development. This approach was reflected in policy discourses in multilateral organisations such as the United Nations, and influenced the ways in which governments sought to redefine their approaches to security in the post-Cold War world. These debates filtered into thinking about national security for a post-apartheid South Africa in the 1990s.

FRAMING NEW MISSIONS FOR THE SECURITY SERVICES

The country's first democratic elections, in 1994, resulted in the establishment of a representative parliament that could create new security services through legislation. Parliament, with the former liberation movement in the majority, tackled this role with vigour, determined to avoid a repeat of the dark history of apartheid repression. The widened view of security, which had influenced the thinking about security during the negotiations, also influenced post-apartheid

---

2   See Motumi (1994) for an analysis of the liberation movement forces at the time of the transfer of power.

policy debates. The first five years of freedom were important for consolidating notions about the philosophical tenets that should guide the creation of a post-apartheid security dispensation, and for framing how the state should respond to its unique security dilemmas. The policy framework for the legislation that established the country's post-apartheid intelligence services, for example, was contained in a 1994 White Paper on Intelligence. The White Paper's assessment was that the end of the Cold War had ushered in a new security landscape in which threats would be defined less by interstate rivalry and increasingly by conditions brought about by non-traditional risks. In a sub-section titled 'Principles of Intelligence', it acknowledged that the apartheid security policy had been formulated by a minority government, and that there had been virtually no institutional checks and balances on the state's security apparatus. Going forward, it asserted, the philosophical outlook on intelligence should align with new thinking, which encompassed the following features (RSA, 1994):

• Security was a holistic phenomenon incorporating political, social, economic and environmental issues.
• The objectives of security policy went beyond achieving an absence of war to pursuing democracy, sustainable economic development and social justice.
• Regional security policy should advance the principles of collective security, non-aggression and the peaceful settlement of disputes.

The White Paper on Defence (1996), which set out the new policy framework regarding the role of the defence force, stated:

The Government of National Unity recognises that the greatest threats to the South African people are socio-economic problems like poverty, unemployment, poor education, the lack of housing and the absence of adequate social services, as well as the high level of crime and violence.

In 1998, completing the trio of security-related white papers, the White Paper on Safety and Security (RSA, 1998), in assessing the state of law enforcement, identified the following causes of crime in South Africa:

gender inequality; proliferation of arms; social-psychological factors; vigilantism; inadequate support to victims of crime; youth marginalisation; economic underdevelopment and inequality; poverty and unemployment; institutionalised violence in the society; and the encroachment of international criminal groups.

The negotiations between 1990 and 1994 provided a window of opportunity for creating a common set of principles for management of the security sector, and, therefore, a common and consistent resetting of the relationship that should exist between the security apparatus of the state and the people. In short, what was intended was that where the organs of state were previously used to suppress the people, they would instead be in service of protecting, physically if need be, their democratic rights.

CHALLENGES OF INTEGRATING APARTHEID AND LIBERATION FORCES

The composition and structure of the South African security apparatus under apartheid reflected the racially fragmented nature of the apartheid design. There was a proliferation of security entities at the height of apartheid that had to be integrated into the new security organs of the post-apartheid state (Africa, 2011: 16):

- Five defence forces (one for the central South African state; and four separate defence forces of the nominally independent republics of Transkei, Bophuthatswana, Venda and Ciskei);
- Eleven police forces (one for the central South African state; and ten separate police services for the republics of Transkei, Bophuthatswana, Venda and Ciskei; and the self-governing territories of KwaZulu, KwaNdebele, QwaQwa, Lebowa, KaNgwane and GaZankulu; and
- Four intelligence services (one for the central South African state and three separate intelligence services for the Transkei, Bophuthatswana and Venda).

In addition, liberation movement combatants had to be integrated into the security apparatus of the newly democratic South Africa. Numerically much smaller than the apartheid security apparatus, the liberation movement had to use political persuasion during the negotiations, and its decisive electoral victory in the first democratic elections, to create the legal framework for a security dispensation that reflected its values. Getting political agreement between all parties on the policy and legal frameworks for the creation of the unified services was only one part of the challenge. Creating single entities for defence, intelligence and police out of disparate and fragmented apartheid-era entities came with numerous complexities, some of whose consequences are still being felt.

On the one hand, bringing former enemies together under a disciplined command contributed to a sense of national identity among the security forces, notwithstanding the difficulties of building trust and a sense of common purpose. The absorption of different components into the new South African National Defence Force (SANDF) was a massive exercise involving tens of thousands of armed personnel from various components of former apartheid and anti-apartheid armies. Prior to integration, the South African Defence Force (SADF) numbered 100,000 permanent force members; by the time of integration, this number had been reduced to 70,000 (Crawford and Winkates, 1995: 101). In the first years of democracy, much time and effort were spent on the verification of personnel; the disarmament, demobilisation and reintegration process; settling newly integrated combatants into their new roles; facilitating the movement of personnel; training; and creating and implementing new corporate policies and procedures.

The establishment of a single police service under the banner of the South African Police Service (SAPS) was another massive exercise. Eleven police forces (one for the central apartheid state, and ten separate forces for the Transkei, Bophuthatswana, Venda and Ciskei 'independent states', as well as one for each of the self-governing territories of KwaZulu, KwaNdebele, QwaQwa, Lebowa, KaNgwane and GaZankulu) were absorbed into a single national police service. A relatively small number of former combatants from the ANC and PAC were absorbed into the police, in line with agreements reached during the negotiations. These included about 200 protectors integrated into the VIP Protection Service; several ANC intelligence personnel posted to the Crime Intelligence Division of the SAPS – formerly the notorious Security Branch; and a small number of young people who had been part of ANC 'self-defence units' and Inkatha 'self-protection units' were integrated as constables (Rauch, 2000). In the case of the civilian intelligence services, the amalgamation process involved bringing together underground intelligence operatives from the ANC and PAC with the apartheid government's National Intelligence Service (NIS), and the services that had existed in Transkei, Bophuthatswana and Venda.

The democratic state inherited security infrastructures that had been established by the apartheid government. This was a double-edged sword as it created the impression that the ex-guerillas were newcomers to already-existing institutions, even though all members were entering institutions under a new political dispensation. Barry Gilder, a former senior ANC intelligence operative who was appointed a general manager in the South African Secret Service (SASS), the foreign service of the Department of Intelligence Services, points out the irony: 'Although we were creating a new service, we had no choice but to do so on the foundation of the apartheid statutory service – its infrastructure, its systems, its processes and procedures, its presence abroad and – to large measure – its personnel' (Gilder, 2012: 249). This was the case for all the security services. The ANC may have been successful in having human rights-centred policies adopted in the negotiations, but it was still dependent on all who ended up in the security services to cooperate in implementing them.

EARLY OVERSIGHT OF THE SECURITY SECTOR IN THE NEW DISPENSATION

Multi-party parliamentary oversight, a new experience for the security services, was implemented for the first time in South Africa after 1994, satisfying a constitutional requirement: 'To give effect to the principles of transparency and accountability, multi-party parliamentary committees must have oversight of all security services in a manner determined by national legislation or the rules and orders of Parliament' (RSA, 1996b, s199 (8)). Two parliamentary committees provided oversight of the SANDF: the Joint Standing Committee on Defence (JSCD), which consisted of members of both Houses of Parliament – National Assembly and the National Council of Provinces (the erstwhile Senate), and a Portfolio Committee on Defence, a committee of the National Assembly. Modise (2004: 50) notes that it took some time for Members of Parliament to adapt to their roles and to see the need to develop a culture of robust debate about defence. This was the case in broader society too. Oversight of the police was provided by the National Assembly Portfolio Committee on Police, and its scrutiny covered an extensive range of structures, including the SAPS, the Civilian Secretariat for Police, the Independent Police Investigative Directorate (IPID) and the Private Security Industry Regulatory Authority (Van Wyk, 2014). The Joint Standing Committee on Intelligence (JSCI) exercised multi-party parliamentary oversight of the civilian intelligence services – the National Intelligence Agency (NIA) and SASS, along with the intelligence divisions in the SAPS (Crime Intelligence) and the SANDF (Defence Intelligence) (Dlomo, 2004). Additionally, legislation mandated an inspector general to provide a layer of civilian oversight to ensure that the intelligence services always acted lawfully and to investigate intelligence failures (Fazel, 2009: 31). To ensure the security services were subject to civilian control and supervision, the president, under the terms of the Constitution, appointed members of the National Assembly as political heads of the security services. They were in the Cabinet Committee for Security and Intelligence, where they were jointly responsible for security policy and the implementation of executive decisions.[3]

The development of policy, under the new administration, was under civil control. A civilian Secretariat for Defence was established, which went on to champion the White Paper on Defence (1996). This

---

3   Under the GNU, this was initially headed by Deputy President F.W. de Klerk. O'Brien (2011) contends that this concession was probably intended to give assurances to the former apartheid-era leaders of the security forces that the new government would accommodate their reservations.

set out a new policy direction for a defence force at peace with its own people – a departure from the past. For the police, a civilian Secretariat for Safety and Security was established to drive policy formulation for the post-apartheid police service. The secretariats were important in that they provided civilian oversight of the security services and assisted the respective ministers to meet their national and international obligations.

On the whole, in the first five years of democracy, changes in the security sector focused on implementing agreements that had been negotiated before 1994. The necessary legal frameworks, policy reviews and the establishment of oversight structures constituted important work carried out in this period. This work was critical to ensuring that the security services would be subject to the rule of law and would be mindful of human security and human rights – in contrast to the repressive ethos and culture that had existed under apartheid. Government framed its security priorities as being to fight poverty and to eliminate the social and economic inequalities that had characterised apartheid. The security dilemma, however, was that these tasks did not require the security services' intervention. Rather, they required policy measures to create opportunities to meet the population's expectations of the post-apartheid dispensation, including the effective redistribution of wealth. Criminals found an ideal breeding ground in the conditions in which the new government was finding its feet and having to decide where to deploy its resources. Rising crime levels were the consequence of the wide disparities in wealth, and a reflection of the choices made by marginalised, disgruntled and often desperate citizens, and equally desperate illegal migrants entering through South Africa's porous borders (Maharaj and Rajkumar, 1997). Added to this was the challenge of dealing with the elements responsible for violence directed against communities especially in the last decade of apartheid who were resistant to democratic change.

In the first five years of democracy, the major achievement of the security sector was achieving a hitherto unknown degree of legitimacy. But while this period saw many positive developments – including laws that were underpinned by values promoting human rights, inclusion and accountability, and the prioritisation of socioeconomic development for the country's previously marginalised majority – the state struggled to meet all the people's expectations. Domestically, the security forces increasingly found themselves having to maintain law and order during protests in communities demanding basic services, sparking resentment among the people. Community protests over poor public services became a persistent feature of life in peri-urban settlements, and in overcrowded and under-serviced local communities frustrated by the failure of the local state to afford them decent living conditions. Communities often used the language of violence to signal their desperation to the state (Von Holdt et al., 2011). Ironically, this was the state's security dilemma of the post-1994 era: because it was unable to create the conditions necessary for human security, the security services were given the role of containing this failure of the state, and responding with force to the very people it was meant to protect.

THE EXTERNAL DIMENSIONS OF SOUTH AFRICA'S SECURITY DILEMMA

After South Africa's first democratic elections, the country made rapid progress in normalising its role in the international community. It was readmitted to the United Nations (UN) and joined the Southern African Development Community (SADC) in 1994. One of the earliest decisions that had to be made about South Africa's use of force externally arose when, as chair of SADC, South Africa was approached by Lesotho's prime minister to intervene in his country to quell a mutiny by the armed forces. This led to South African and Botswana armed forces mounting a military operation to restore order in Lesotho. The operation was mired in controversy because, contrary to claims that it was a peacekeeping mission, it had not been authorised by the UN or the African Union (AU), and had never been ratified by SADC (Likoti, 2007: 260). Critics said it undermined South Africa's stated commitment to resolving disputes by peaceful means. Others felt the intervention was justified, given Lesotho's geographical position, within South Africa's belly, and the fact that South Africa's vital interests in the Katse Dam could come under threat (Likoti, 2007).

South Africa claims that when its armed forces are deployed externally, it is only to serve its national interests – to intervene in intra-state conflicts requiring political solutions rather than dominance by military means. Later deployments of SANDF troops in AU and UN missions in Burundi, the Democratic Republic of the Congo (DRC) and Sudan followed this logic: to support a peace process rather than to use force for its own sake. South Africa has had objective reasons for playing peacemaker in Africa: a stable Africa is essential for the continent to position itself more competitively on the global stage. But it is also important to ensure that instability in the region does not negatively impact South Africa's domestic developmental agenda.

During Thabo Mbeki's presidency (1999–2008), there was a maturing of both South Africa's domestic priorities and its foreign policy ambitions. Emboldened by the international stature South Africa had gained in the Mandela years, and the prestige attached to its own internal democratic transition, Mbeki was assertive about South Africa's role on the African continent. Among his principal ideas, shared with prominent African leaders including Meles Zenawi of Ethiopia and Olusegun Obasanjo of Nigeria, was the establishment of the New Partnership for Africa's Development (NEPAD), and, in 2002, the creation of the African Union as the successor to the Organisation of African Unity (Lopes, 2013). Mbeki's diplomatic engagement with the West revolved around setting up equal terms of engagement, a significant manoeuvre in establishing the soft power of the African continent.

One challenge of democratic governance is ensuring that the internal politics of the governing party do not disrupt the running of the state. During Mbeki's tenure, the civilian intelligence services found themselves increasingly embroiled in party-political disputes. In 2006, following an investigation into abuses of power by the intelligence services, Mbeki fired Billy Masetlha, the Director General of the NIA, the domestic intelligence service (Nathan, 2010). An interesting factor facing the post-apartheid professionals in the security services was that members of the executive often had independent views about global and domestic developments. Gilder (2012: 274) observes:

[T]his was the reality of providing intelligence support to policymakers who were not, and are still not, career politicians who entered the political arena and government through universities and local communities. They were seasoned revolutionaries who were steeped in struggle, in international politics, in the deep histories of the South African resistance, who had lived and travelled throughout the world, who had schooled and shared platforms with many of the world's leaders, who were steeped in the ANC traditions of deep analysis of domestic and global dynamics.

There was considerable continuity in South Africa's continental aspirations under Jacob Zuma, who became president of the Republic in 2009, amid fractious politics leading to his political ascent. After his election, South Africa continued its prominent role in peacekeeping and mediation efforts on the continent. In 2014, the government deployed over 1,300 troops in the DRC as part of the UN Force Intervention Brigade of MONUSCO. Earlier, in 2012, it had renewed an agreement to provide training and capacity building to the DRC's military. However, the fragile peace did not hold, and when the 200 SANDF troops deployed to protect the trainers were caught in crossfire, leading to the death of 13 soldiers (Thompson et al., 2021), there was a public outcry. This led to the withdrawal of the contingent and a termination of the bilateral arrangement.

These developments – combining a security strategy with development goals – align with the South African approach to post-conflict reconstruction and development, one in which the military and civilian components in a mission play complementary roles. In 1999, the White Paper on South African Participation in International Peace Missions presented the government's concept of 'developmental peace missions' as a philosophical approach to peace missions for the SANDF. However, some analysts argue that this approach was never fully operationalised, primarily because of budget constraints (Olivier, 2013). Others argue that the SANDF's chronic underfunding compromised its effectiveness in peace missions. A key finding of the 2012 Defence Review (Department of Defence, 2012) was that South

Africa would be unable to retain its influence on the continent if it were unable to maintain and adapt its defence capabilities to changing requirements.

The firmness of executive control over the security services was not always matched by consistent and rigorous parliamentary oversight of the security sector. A notable exception was Parliament's Standing Committee on Public Accounts (SCOPA), the parliamentary financial oversight committee, which mounted a principled effort to hold the executive to account when allegations of corruption in the Strategic Arms Procurement Programme (which later came to be known as 'the Arms Deal') were brought to its attention around 1998. In 2001, the committee chairperson, ANC member Andrew Feinstein, resigned from Parliament in protest over what he saw as executive-led efforts to obstruct a meaningful probe by SCOPA (Feinstein, 2007).

Ill-disciplined elements in the security sector either became emboldened to act in increasingly self-serving ways, or to further partisan political objectives. Many were abused by the executive for political ends. In 2006, Intelligence Minister Ronnie Kasrils established the Matthews Commission to investigate the intelligence services after reports revealed that the NIA was illegally spying on senior ANC members and other politicians. The Commission's mandate was to review the operations of the civilian intelligence structures with the aim of strengthening mechanisms of control over them, and to ensure compliance and alignment with constitutional principles and the rule of law. The intention was to minimise the potential for illegal conduct and the abuse of power. The Commission found that the NIA had veered into the sphere of politics because of a culture of 'intelligence exceptionalism' in which bending the rules and not adhering to the Constitution were regarded as acceptable under certain conditions (Nathan, 2010: 207). Apart from the firing of the Director-General, the Commission's recommendations were not implemented and were lost in the political contestations within the ANC that led to Mbeki being replaced by Jacob Zuma.

As president, Zuma reintroduced military-type ranks in the South African Police Service, rejecting an ethos of civilianising the police, as laid out in the 1998 White Paper on Safety and Security.

The civilian secretariat responsible for setting policing policy, the Secretariat for Safety and Security, was renamed the Secretariat for Police. Various organs of the state, including the NIA, the SASS, the Intelligence Academy and the National Communications Branch, were incorporated into a single State Security Agency by a proclamation by the president (RSA, 2009), and without consulting Parliament. Another development in this period was the increasingly significant role of the Department of Home Affairs (DHA) in dealing with security matters. The ANC's 2012 policy discussion document on Peace and Stability (ANC, 2012) began with the section 'Positioning Home Affairs to be the backbone of security, service delivery and the developmental state'. It argued that a well-managed immigration system was crucial to achieving South Africa's national objectives, and that weaknesses in the law and systems had been exploited.

The context for the DHA's increased engagement had been a pattern of anti-migrant sentiment in South Africa, particularly among poor, marginalised communities who were resentful about what they saw as already scarce opportunities and resources for South Africans being accessed by undocumented migrants (Ukwanda, 2017). Public discourse, in some instances informed by communities' lived experience, linked undocumented migrants with crime, including illicit drugs, contraband, human trafficking, the hijacking of buildings, paying bribes to occupy RDP houses, running unlicensed businesses, and trafficking in weapons, exacerbated existing prejudices and resentment among local communities. The absence of a comprehensive policy framework on migration was a weak link both in South Africa's domestic policy and in its regional security strategy. The country had become a hub for migrants in this period, but the state lacked a long-term vision of how to deal with this reality.

THE 'GUNS OR BUTTER' DILEMMA

For all South Africa's efforts to contribute to peace on the African continent, failure to resolve the domestic challenges of poverty, inequality and unemployment led to people venting their anger in the streets. From 2004, the country saw a spike in protests directed against local authorities over frustration at the insufficient municipal services in informal settlements and townships where the poorest citizens live. In some cases, protests became violent, resulting in the destruction of public infrastructure. Some analysts referred to this violence by marginalised communities as a 'language' of last resort, after peaceful protest had failed (Von Holdt, 2014). There is no indication, however, that such protests posed a significant threat to the state. Often, collective acts of violence were localised, aimed at expressing dissatisfaction around local grievances of marginalised groups. They were not welded together into a coherent popular uprising that challenged the legitimacy and authority of the state. Further, in some cases, the violence was more from the police than the protestors.

Protests for basic services were taking place during a period when levels of corruption were escalating, and crime in general could be regarded as out of control. For wealthier South Africans and business owners, the utilisation of private security companies is commonplace.[4] Such solutions are not realistic or affordable options for the millions of poor South Africans who bear the burden of crime. Providing proper, accountable and effective policing for poor communities is indispensable. But for the poor, the social contract that statehood is meant to confer, according to which the state protects its people in return for their allegiance, had evaporated, resulting in disillusionment with the ANC whose electoral majority at the national level had begun to decline. Parliamentary oversight of the security services remained lacklustre, and the legislature was slow to respond to the crises besetting the security services.

During then President Zuma's term, the SSA became deeply implicated in efforts to suppress investigations about malfeasance related to Zuma and those close to him (Chipkin et al., 2018: 126). His term as president was mired in controversy and allegations of 'state capture'. After pressure from his party, and to avoid a no-confidence vote in Parliament, he resigned, paving the way for Cyril Ramaphosa, the

---

4   According to the Private Security Industry Regulatory Authority, which is overseen by the Ministry of Police, there are four times as many registered private security guards as police in South Africa (Staff Writer, 2023).

newly elected ANC leader, to become president.[5] In 2018, Ramaphosa appointed a high-level panel to look into the SSA; it found that there had been growing politicisation of the agency, linked to factionalism within the ANC. Moreover, it found that from 2009 there had been 'a marked doctrinal shift in the intelligence community away from the prescripts of the Constitution, the White Paper on Intelligence, and the human security philosophy towards a much narrower, state security orientation' (RSA, 2018). In addition, excessive secrecy in the SSA had created a cover for the abuse of resources. 'The SSA had become a "cash cow" for many inside and outside the Agency' (RSA, 2018).

From the outset, the democratic South African state has been embroiled in a 'guns or butter' dilemma – how much of its resources to spend on security to deal with the insecurity instilled by rising levels of crime, porous borders and the breakdown of the rule of law, versus how much to devote to social spending and creating the necessary conditions to foster a thriving society. Reeling from the devastating effects of the Covid-19 pandemic, what little sense of security the South African population had was shaken by the devastating civil unrest and violence that overwhelmed KwaZulu-Natal and parts of Gauteng in 2021, leaving over 400 people dead and causing billions of rand worth of damage. Ramaphosa described the violence as an 'attempted insurrection' (SAnews, 2021), a calculated, orchestrated effort to destabilise the country, sabotage the economy and undermine South Africa's constitutional democracy. The security services were surprised by the rapid escalation of the violence, and they struggled to contain it for over a week. An external panel appointed by the president discovered that there had been various complex factors at play, including organised agitation by Zuma's supporters against his imprisonment, as well as the poverty, lack of access to opportunity and socioeconomic conditions of deprivation that many rioters endured daily.[6] The police lacked the capacity to employ appropriate tactics to quell the violence, and the panel concluded that there was a serious

---

5 For a detailed account of the internal party dynamics leading up to Ramaphosa becoming president, see Booysens (2021).
6 I served as the chairperson of this panel, working alongside Prof. Maxi Schoeman and Mr Silumko Sikupa.

intelligence failure that had prevented them from anticipating the scale of the violence. The unrest raised questions about the state's ability to protect its citizens and critical infrastructure. Vital transport corridors, necessary for the movement of goods and people, were affected, and the army had to be called in to protect these routes.

CONCLUSION

In 1994, South Africans had a unique opportunity to define the security challenges confronting the state and its people. The creation of a democratic constitutional state in which the roles and functions of the security services were redefined to support the democratic agenda was a major achievement. The security services inherited infrastructure, systems, processes and personnel from the apartheid era, but strong policy input forged in the transition period provided fundamental departure points to build accountable, legitimate security services. However, the security services' performance has at times been disappointing, sometimes reaching crisis points, as a result of lapses in the execution of their duties, a lack of effective oversight, inadequate resourcing and some political manipulation. It would be fair to say that the security services' levels of capability, relative to their tasks, have been degraded over the past 30 years. There is an urgent need for an invigorated debate about what security means for South Africans. This is an opportune time to embark on a wide-ranging process to explore what national security means for South Africa at a time when geopolitical shifts are signalling the need for new capabilities to confront 21st-century threats (Emerson and Solomon, 2018). Moreover, the current period has seen a rise in instability on the African continent, and other parts of the world. South Africa should not fall into the classical security dilemma, but should consider carefully what the strategic requirements are for its security services to best serve their constitutional role.

A clearly defined focus and proper equipping of the defence force, better training and resourcing of the police, and a retooling of the intelligence services are certainly needed. With other state actors increasingly playing a role in promoting national security, it may also be time to articulate more clearly the roles of other government agencies in matters of security, and to determine the checks and balances to which these agencies should be subjected. The private sector too, seems set to be an indelible player, even if security is a public good, and this must be considered.

The failure of the state to more decisively address the socioeconomic problems facing the country has resulted in increasing feelings of insecurity among its people. To retain the legitimacy of the South African security sector, the state must demonstrate that it can deliver prosperity for all. The alternative will be to have the majority of the South African population permanently vulnerable to crime, with the privileged living perpetually behind high walls in the hope that they will not become victims of crime. Addressing the systemic injustices in the economy and daily lives of the people must be at the top of the country's agenda. Until these are addressed, the security sector will spend its resources trying to keep the lid on the pent-up frustrations of the poor and disgruntled, and increasingly be perceived as enemies of the people.

REFERENCES

Africa, S. 2011. 'Transformation of the South African security sector: Lessons and challenges'. Occasional Paper Series, DCAF – Geneva Centre for Security Governance, Geneva.

African National Congress (ANC). 2012. 'Peace and Stability: Policy Discussion Document', https://www.anc1912.org.za/wp-content/uploads/2021/04/4th-National-Policy-Conference-Peace-and-Stability.pdf

Alagappa, M. (ed.). 2001. *Coercion and Governance: The Declining Political Role of the Military in Asia.* Stanford, California: Stanford University Press.

Ball, N. and Fayemi, K. (eds). 2004. *Security Sector Governance in Africa: A Handbook.* Centre for Democracy and Development.

BBC. 2013. 'Jacob Zuma: 13 soldiers killed in CAR'. *BBC*, 25 March, https://www.bbc.com/news/world-africa-21923624, accessed 18 February 2023.

Berg, J. and Scharff, W. 2004. 'Crime statistics in South Africa 1994–2004'. *South African Journal of Criminal Justice*, 17.

Booth, K. and Wheeler, N. 2007. *The Security Dilemma: Fear, Cooperation and Trust in World Politics.* Houndmills, Basingstoke, Hampshire and New York: Palgrave MacMillan.

Booysens, S. 2021. *Precarious Power. Compliance and Discontent under Ramaphosa's ANC*. Johannesburg: Wits University Press.

Born, H. and Leigh, I. 2005. *Making Intelligence Accountable: Legal Standards and Best Practice for Oversight of Intelligence Agencies*. Oslo: Publishing House of the Parliament of Norway.

Bryden, A., N'Diaye, B. and Olonisakin, F. (eds). 2008. *Challenges of Security Sector Governance in West Africa*. Zurich: LIT Verlag.

Bucur-Marcu, H., Fluri, P. and Tagarev, T. (eds). 2009. *Defence Management: An Introduction.* Geneva: DCAF.

Cawthra, G. 1986. *Brutal Force: The Apartheid War Machine*. London: International Defence and Aid Fund for Southern Africa.

Cawthra, G. 2013. 'Security transformation in post-apartheid South Africa', in Cawthra G. and Luckham R. (eds), *Governing Insecurity: Democratic Control of Military and Security Establishments in Transitional Societies.* London and New York: Zed Books.

Chipkin, I., Swilling, M., Bhorat, H., Buthelezi, M., Duma, S., Prins, N., Mondi, M., Peter, C., Qobo, M. and Friedenstein, H. 2018. *Shadow State: The Politics of State Capture*. Johannesburg: Wits University Press.

Crawford, N.C. and Winkates, J. 1995. 'South Africa's new foreign and military policy: Opportunities and constraints'. *Africa Today*, 42(1), 88–121, https://doi.org/4187033

Dlomo, D. 2004. 'An analysis of Parliamentary Intelligence Oversight in South Africa with specific reference to the Joint Standing Committee on Intelligence (JSCI)'. Master's dissertation, University of Pretoria.

Duncan J. 2014. *The Rise of the Securocrats: The Case of South Africa.* Johannesburg: Jacana Media.

Emerson, S. and Solomon, H. 2018. *African Security in the Twenty-First Century: Challenges and Opportunities.* Manchester: Manchester University Press.

Fazel, I. 2009. 'Civilian operational oversight and the Inspector-General of Intelligence', in Hutton, L. (ed.), *To Spy or Not to Spy: Intelligence and Democracy in South Africa.* Pretoria: Institute for Security Studies.

Feinstein, A. 2007. *After the Party: A Personal and Political Journey inside the ANC.* Johannesburg and Cape Town: Jonathan Ball Publishers.

Frankel, P.H. 1984. *Pretoria's Praetorians: Civil-military relations in South Africa.* Cambridge: Cambridge University Press.

Geldenhuys, D. 1998. *Engaging Political Engagement. Remaking States in the Post-Cold War World.* Houndmills, Basingstoke, Hampshire, and London: MacMillan Press Limited.

Gilder, B. 2013. *Songs and Secrets: South Africa from Liberation to Governance.* Johannesburg: Jacana Media.

Giliomee, H. 2003. *The Afrikaners: Biography of a People.* Cape Town: Tafelberg.

Gleijesis, P. 2005. 'Review: Scandinavia and the liberation of Southern Africa'. *The International History Review*, 27(2), 324–331.

Grundy, K.W. 1988. *The Militarisation of South African Politics*. Oxford: Oxford University Press.

Jordan, W. and Al Jazeera Investigative Unit. 2015. 'Inside the battle for intelligence in South Africa', https://www.aljazeera.com/features/2015/2/24/inside-the-battle-for-intelligence-in-south-africa, accessed 18 February 2024.

Kilander, M. 2016. 'Op-ed. Withdrawal from the ICC a Sad Day for South Africa', https://www.chr.up.ac.za/opinion-pieces/1047-op-ed-withdrawal-from-the-icc-a-sad-day-for-south-africa-and-africa, accessed 18 February 2024.

Krahman, E. 2008. 'Security: Collective good or commodity?'. *European Journal of International Relations*, 14(3), 379–404.

Likoti, F.J. 2007. 'The 1998 military intervention in Lesotho: SADC peace mission or resource war?'. *International Peacekeeping*, 14, 251–263.

Lodge, T. 1983. *Black Politics in South Africa since 1945*. Johannesburg: Ravan Press.

Lopes, C. 2013. 'The Pan-African ideal under new lens: Thabo Mbeki's contribution'. UN ECA, https://repository.uneca.org/bitstream/handle/10855/36462/b11557266.pdf, accessed 30 June 2025.

Maharaj, B. and Rajkumar, R. 1997. 'The "alien invasion" in South Africa: Illegal immigrants in Durban'. *Development Southern Africa*, 14(2), 255–273, DOI: 10.1080/03768359708439962

Makathini, S. 2023. 'Truth-seeking and sexual violence. South Africa Truth and Reconciliation Commission (1996–2002)', https://www.atjhub.csvr.org.za, accessed 13 February 2025.

Markowitz, I. 1977. *Power and Class in Africa. An Introduction to Change and Conflict in African Politics*. Englewood Cliffs, N.J.: Prentice-Hall Inc.

McGowan, P.J. 2003. 'African military coups d'état, 1956–2001: Frequency, trends and distribution'. *The Journal of Modern African Studies*, 41(3), 339–370, http://www.jstor.org/stable/3876235

Modise, T. 2004. 'Parliamentary oversight of the South Africa Department of Defence: 1994 to 2003', in Le Roux, L., Rupiya, M. and Ngoma, N. (eds), *Guarding the Guardians: Parliamentary Oversight and Civil-Military Relations: The Challenge for SADC*. Pretoria: Institute for Security Studies.

Motumi, T. 1994. 'Umkhonto we Sizwe – structure, training and force levels (1984–1994)'. *South African Defence Review,* 18(August).

Mpofu, W. 2013. 'African nationalism in the age of coloniality: Triumphs, tragedies and futures', in Ndlovu-Gatsheni, S. and Ndhlovu, F. (eds), *Nationalism and National Projects in Southern Africa. New Critical Reflections*. Pretoria: Africa Institute of South Africa.

Nathan, L. 2010. 'Intelligence bound: The South African constitution and intelligence services'. *International Affairs*, 86(1), 195–210, https://doi.org/10.1111/j.1468-2346.2010.00875.x

Neethling, T. and Hudson, H. (eds). 2013. *Post-Conflict Reconstruction and Development in Africa: Concepts, Role-Players, Policy and Practice*. Cape Town: UCT Press.

Nel, P. 1990. *A Soviet Embassy in Pretoria? The changing Soviet approach to South Africa*. Cape Town: Tafelberg Publishers.

O'Brien, K.A. 2011. *The South African Intelligence Services: From Apartheid to Democracy, 1948–2005*. London and New York: Routledge.

Olivier, L. 2013. 'Developmental peace missions: The South African conceptual approach', in Neethling, T. and Hudson, H. (eds), *Post-Conflict Reconstruction and Development in Africa: Concepts, Role-Players, Policy and Practice*. Cape Town: UCT Press.

Rauch, J. 2000. 'Police reform and South Africa's transition'. Unpublished paper presented at the South African Institute of International Affairs conference, https://www.csvr.org.za/docs/policing/policereformandsouth.pdf, accessed 25 June 2025.

Sorenson, G. 2001. *Changes in Statehood. The Transformation of International Relations*. Houndmills, Basingstoke, Hampshire, New York: Palgrave.

South African Government News Agency. 2021. 'President Ramaphosa: Attempted insurrection failed to gain popular support', https://www.sanews.gov.za/south-africa/president-ramaphosa-attempted-insurrection-failed-gain-popular-support, accessed 18 February 2024.

Staff Writer. 2023. 'Private security guards outnumber police 4 to 1 in South Africa'. *BusinessTech*, 9 May, https://businesstech.co.za/news/government/686425/private-security-guards-outnumber-police-4-to-1-in-south-africa/, accessed 23 February 2025.

Thompson, W., Hofstatter, S. and Oatway, J. 2021. *The Battle of Bangui: The Inside Story of South Africa's Worst Military Scandal since Apartheid*. Cape Town: Penguin Books.

Ukwanda, D.C. 2017. 'Reflections on xenophobic violence in South Africa: What happens to a dream deferred?' *African Journal of Public Affairs*, 9(9).

Van Wyk, A. 2014. 'Parliamentary oversight of the police in South Africa: Lessons and opportunities'. APCOF Policy Paper 10, November.

Von Holdt, K. 2014. 'On violent democracy'. *The Sociological Review*, 62(2), 129–151, https://doi.org/10.1111/1467-954X.12196

Von Holdt, K., Langa, M., Molapo, S., Mogapi, N., Ngubeni, K., Dlamini, J. and Kirsten, A. 2011. 'The smoke that calls: Insurgent citizenship, collective violence and the struggle for a place in the new South Africa'. CSVR and SWOP, https://www.csvr.org.za/docs/thesmokethatcalls.pdf, accessed 21 February 2025.

Zondi, S. 2015. 'Africanity, Pan-Africanism and the African Renaissance. South Africa's agenda under Mbeki and Zuma', in Masters, L., Zondi, S.,

Van Wyk, J. and Landsberg, C. (eds), *South African Foreign Policy Review. Volume 2*. Pretoria: Africa Institute of South Africa, pp. 97–118.

Government publications

Department of Defence. 2012. 'South African Defence Review 2012', https://static.pmg.org.za/docs/120515consultative.pdf, accessed 22 February 2025.

Republic of South Africa (RSA). 1994. 'White Paper on Intelligence'.

Republic of South Africa (RSA). 1996a. 'White Paper on Defence'.

Republic of South Africa (RSA). 1996b. 'Constitution of the Republic of South Africa, Act 108 of 1996'.

Republic of South Africa (RSA). 1998. 'White Paper on Safety and Security'.

Republic of South Africa (RSA). 2009. Government Notice No. 912, 913, 914, 915 regarding the Administration and Operations of the Government Components National Intelligence Agency, South African Secret Service, Intelligence Academy and COMSEC, in *Government Gazette* 17 September 2009.

Republic of South Africa (RSA). 2015. 'South African Defence Review 2015', dod.mil.za, accessed 19 February 2025.

Republic of South Africa (RSA). 2018. 'High-level Review Panel Report on the State Security Agency', https://www.gov.za/sites/default/files/gcis_document/201903/high-level-review-panel-state-security-agency.pdf, accessed 16 February 2025.

Republic of South Africa (RSA) Policy Communication and Advisory Services. 2004. 'Towards a Ten-Year Review'. Synthesis report on implementation of Government programmes - discussion document.

SAnews. 2021. 'President Ramaphosa: Attempted insurrection failed to gain popular support', 16 July, https://www.sanews.gov.za/south-africa/president-ramaphosa-attempted-insurrection-failed-gain-popular-support

TWELVE

Gender and the state: Assessing feminist institutionalism in South Africa

Amanda Gouws

INTRODUCTION

Many feminists are suspicious of the state, viewing it as an instrument of patriarchal domination of women and queer people, with limited opportunities for them to engage in policymaking. In South Africa, there was a concerted effort to include women in government and the state during the transition to democracy. The women's movement, the Women's National Coalition (WNC) – an umbrella movement that united many women's organisations, political parties, feminist scholars and activists (Hassim, 2006) – fought to get women into seats in Parliament through a quota system and for the creation of the National Gender Machinery (NGM) in the state to promote gender equality measures and policies. The women's movement knew the importance of getting women into the state and using the state to enable gender equality (changing unequal power relations between men and women and gendered minorities).

In this chapter, I will assess issues of women's representation and feminist institutionalism (getting women into the state) and the extent to which there has been success in promoting gender equality through the state in the past 30 years. I will discuss different feminist perspectives on the state, then look at women's representation in government and the creation of the National Gender Machinery as the vehicle for promoting feminist institutionalism in the state. Successes and failures will be illustrated with the state's engagement with a core issue of gender inequality – gender-based violence (GBV).

FEMINIST VIEWS OF THE STATE

In the 1980s, MacKinnon (1989) argued that 'feminism has no theory of the state', and that feminists should develop one. There has always been a general suspicion of and hostility to the state, specifically by second-wave feminists, who believe the state is a patriarchal instrument complicit in the oppression of women (Brown, 1992: 7; Hoffman, 1998: 161). Feminists have used different approaches to analyse the state, such as critiques of class exploitation in the capitalist state (Marxist/socialist feminists), male dominance in the patriarchal state (second-wave feminists) and structural inequalities in the liberal state (liberal feminists) (Rhode, 1994: 1181).

Liberal feminists, who support law reform as a solution to gender inequality, have been more willing to engage with the state and view it as a way to enlarge women's political possibilities. But as Brown (1992: 8) argues, liberalism encapsulates paternalism and the institutionalised protection of women. Therefore, one of the main ways of enforcing 'protection' is by keeping the public/private divide in place. Men/husbands, as proxies of the state, keep the state's 'protectionism' intact by preventing 'private' issues (e.g. gender-based violence) entering the political terrain. This split also depoliticises the family in relation to women's unpaid care work, and control over women's reproduction and labour. Rhode (1994) argues that the starting point of the liberal state is that women are already free and have agency, but the state manages women's needs/issues through legitimating, suppressing or redirecting them. For this reason, second-wave feminists criticise the state's neutrality and view it as an instrument of patriarchy, arguing that the claimed universality of the state and human rights mask men's interests.

From the Marxist/socialist feminist perspective, the liberal state is weak on the economic resource redistribution that would improve the material conditions of women. From a radical feminist perspective, the state is embedded in patriarchal relations and reproduces the relations of power used to oppress women. Many radical feminists therefore prefer not to engage with the state, arguing that this should be held in abeyance.

According to Brown (1992: 13), the state has four modalities of power that need to be understood in any analysis of it: (1) the juridical-legislative aspect which forms part of its formal and constitutional dimension; (2) the capitalist dimension which provides a framework for ownership, specifically of private property; (3) the prerogative dimension, which incorporates the legitimate use of power in policymaking and a monopoly on the use of violence and coercion; (4) the bureaucratic aspect which refers to institutional arrangements, activities and discourses (or disciplining power). Brown (1992: 16) argues that state power and male dominance are interwoven so that they create a hegemonic (patriarchal) effect. Through all these modalities, women's needs and interests are mediated and regulated.

According to Brown (1992: 26–27), it is not only that women are excluded from state power. Rather, even when women's inclusion is considered, women (and queer people) face the deeply gendered nature of the state, which has the ability to create feminine subjects through its regulatory and disciplining power, as well as its discursive frameworks.

Many feminists have therefore found a post-structuralist perspective more useful for analysing women's relationship to the state. Drawing on post-structuralist theorisation of the state, feminist activists and scholars view the state as a set of uneven relations of power that provide openings through which it can be engaged, and relations of power can be challenged. As Brown (1992: 14) argues, state power and male dominance are not unitary and do not act linearly, but rather have an intricate grid of conflicting strategies, technologies and discourses of power.

This view of the state has made it more possible for feminists to attempt to find opportunities for where and when women's interests can be inserted into the state and how to determine the most optimal space in the state for women to influence policy, make alliances and contribute to substantive representation. Earlier feminist theorisation of the state focused on functional liberal democratic states, but postcolonial states in the Global South present even bigger challenges for women and people from the lesbian, gay, bisexual, transgender, queer, intersex and asexual (LGBTQIA+) communities. Earlier Western feminist theories largely ignored the experience of women in developing and postcolonial countries.

Postcolonial states, specifically in Africa, can be considered weak states with limited ability to provide security for their citizens. Where conditions of weak states are present, state failure is highly possible, leading to internal violence preventing the state from delivering economic or political goods. This causes enduring political violence, high levels of criminal violence and corruption, deteriorating infrastructure, non-adherence to the rule of law, and a failure to deliver basic services (Lambrechts, 2017: 16).

The legacy of colonialism was material, cultural and political (Rai, 1996a: 8). Colonial interventions altered cultural practices and traditional systems captured in customary law and economic production, with the aim of extracting cheap labour from indigenous populations. The cooperation of traditional leaders with colonial forces reinforced gendered relations of power, facilitating the codification of oral traditions into static forms of customary law that were not women-friendly (see Gouws, 2014). For women, the distortion and reinterpretation of their sexuality which framed them as sexually insatiable and therefore not rape-able in law, and with limited control over their sexuality, in some countries on the African continent, had enduring effects in the high levels of gender-based violence (Gqola, 2015: 40).

It was the contribution of Black feminists and their theories on intersectionality that captured the intersections between markers of identity such as race, class, gender, sexuality and ability. These intersections exposed the limits of Western feminist theorisation of the state, and the inapplicable colonial impositions of certain categories of analysis (Mohanty, 1988). This also challenged nationalist freedom struggles against colonialism which reinvented women as the 'mothers of the nation' – their bodies the symbols of national reproduction and often the terrain on which struggles are fought violently. Women's movements, and specifically women's party auxiliaries or women's wings that developed during liberation struggles and decolonisation, had the effect of promoting the goals of modernising nationalist elites (Rai, 1996a: 10).

Being a postcolonial and post-apartheid state, South Africa's transition to democracy opened a window of opportunity for women and minorities to engage the state (Waylen, 2007). The promise of gender equality was inscribed in the Constitution with the assumption, among many, that state engagement would deliver on the promise of gender equality. After the 1994 election, women were included into the government with the help of a quota, and into the state through the creation of the National Gender Machinery that opened spaces for women to insert a gender agenda.

WOMEN'S DESCRIPTIVE AND SUBSTANTIVE REPRESENTATION IN SOUTH AFRICA

The Women's National Coalition (WNC), spearheaded by feminist activists and women's organisations during the early 1990s, understood the importance of increasing the number of women in Parliament to enhance descriptive and substantive representation. 'Descriptive representation' refers to the increase in the number of women in parliament, while 'substantive representation' relates to women representing women's interests through engaging with law- and policymaking. Through the endeavours of the ANC Women's League (ANCWL), the African National Congress (ANC) adopted a 30 per cent quota for women on its election lists prior to the 1994 election, against the resistance of men in the party (Hassim, 2006).

As Franceschet et al. (2012: 4) argue, quota policies and rates of implementation have diverse effects on the compositions of political elites and may therefore influence the capacity of quota women to pursue legislative change. The ANC increased its quota to 50 per cent of women on its election lists (and internal organisational structures) in 2007, and, consequently, there were 45 per cent women in Parliament until the 2024 election. This figure decreased to 35 per cent after the 2024 election, when the ANC only got 40 per cent support at national level.

Using a quota to increase women's numbers in legislatures is based on certain assumptions: (1) that women will eventually form a critical mass that will pursue women's policy concerns; (2) that women will form strategic coalitions that will promote legislative changes; and (3) that it will eventually change male behaviour in the legislative arena (Franceschet et al., 2012: 5–6).

In South Africa, the quota system improved women's descriptive representation greatly and bore fruit during the first Parliament (1994–1999), when 111 women were elected. During this period, a large number of women-friendly laws were passed by Parliament, spearheaded by the feminists who entered Parliament after the 1994 election. Many of them were the leaders of the WNC which initiated and monitored the making of these laws (Hassim, 2006).

During those first five years the following laws, among others, were passed, which sought to improve the lives of women: the Recognition of Customary Marriages Act (No. 120 of 1998); the Choice on Termination of Pregnancy Act (CTOP) (No. 38 of 2004, concluded in the second Parliament); the Maintenance Act (No. 99 of 1998); and the Domestic Violence Act (No. 116 of 1998). These laws showed that with committed feminists in the National Gender Machinery and as Members of Parliament, policies and laws could contribute to substantive representation.

The relationship between descriptive and substantive representation depends on opportunities in Parliament for women to develop a gender-equality agenda, and the building of coalitions and engagement with the women's movement. These conditions were present in the first Parliament (1994–1999) but seem to have been eroded over time.

While the ANC managed the increase of descriptive representation, it did not guarantee women's substantive representation. This was because of the alleged manipulation, discussed below, of the proportional representation (PR) system for participation in legislative bodies, as well as the shift away from the ANCWL's earlier support for a feminist agenda to loyalty towards men in the party and a conservative nationalist agenda, especially during the Zuma administration (2009–2017).

The PR closed-list system has the benefit of enabling women to enter the state, but its biggest drawback is its accountability deficit. Because political leaders draft the final lists, candidates may feel accountable to political leaders (mainly men) rather than to citizens. This enables party leaders to manipulate the process of compiling lists (Booysen, 2015: 107; Calland, 2013: 139). It also short-circuits policymaking that is not in line with the wishes of party leaders and therefore makes women beholden to party leaders.

Women are also disadvantaged by the highly criticised practice of 'slate politics' in the ANC. A slate is a list of candidates nominated as a group for election to party positions (Setati, 2012: 2). Often different factions within the party compile their own slates, thus reducing the chances of individuals outside these predetermined lists being nominated. Slates are hotly contested and entwined in self or factional interest. Butler (2015: 13) argues that the ANC exerts control through a mix of procedural manipulation, patronage, co-option, invented tradition and stepping stones for personal gain, and that this can significantly shrink spaces for women to be included on the PR lists for legislative bodies.

An investigation by the ANC's National Executive Committee (NEC) into widely disputed candidate processes for the 2010 local government elections found departures from the party's guidelines and manipulations of processes to achieve predetermined outcomes (Ntuli, 2022). According to Butler (2015: 24), public consultations in 419 wards had deeply concerning findings that showed that properly reached nominations were overturned to enable deeply engrained factionalism, tribalism, regionalism, gatekeeping and the bulk buying of membership. It also showed that provincial leaders did little to supervise registration and verification processes, ignored illegitimate participation from outside branches, and turned a blind eye to other forms of manipulation.

The presence of women in legislatures therefore does not guarantee substantive representation. Thus, feminist activists and scholars supported the idea of creating structures in the state, the National Gender Machinery, through which women's interests could be inserted into law- and policymaking to enhance substantive representation.

FEMINIST INSTITUTIONALISM IN THE STATE

Feminist institutionalism refers to a context where structures that promote gender equality are institutionalised. Also called state feminism, it combines the insights of post-structuralist feminists with liberal feminism which regards it as the mandate of the state to ensure equal opportunities and law reform. Feminist institutionalism also contributes to substantive representation through policy engagement and influence. The integration of a feminist or women's agenda into the state through state machineries can be viewed narrowly as the result of the advocacy of the women's movement inside the state (Kantola and Outshoorn, 2007: 2). The success of these machineries depends on their design, staffing, resources and political will.

National gender machineries create opportunities for women's agency in the state. Institutional structures consist of socially constructed norms and roles, and socially prescribed behaviours and expectations of role players, all of which may change over time (Goodin, 2009: 19–20). These norms and behaviours are embedded in power relations through '[the] stable, recurring, repetitive, patterned nature of the behaviour' (Goodin, 2009: 22). The configuration of these power relations can facilitate or constrain agency in the state (Chappell, 2014: 575). The exercise of agency is also determined by the intentional and unintentional outcomes of formal and informal rules, which take the form of norms, practices, arrangements and power relations that become naturalised and institutionalised and can only be changed through deliberate resistance (Chappell and Mackay, 2017: 16). The ways in which these rules are engaged with and enforced can entrench the status quo of male behaviour or open gaps for women to insert and defend feminist agendas. State institutions therefore constitute gendered interests, shape men's and women's political activities, and influence the character of social policies. The design of national gender machineries needs to engage the gendered nature of these institutions and rules in ways that make positive gender outcomes for women possible.

Feminist activists and scholars in South Africa used the opportunity afforded women by the democratic transition to insert a demand for a National Gender Machinery into the negotiations process, through the WNC (Hassim, 2006). South African women's demands for representation in the state led to the creation, globally, of one of the most integrated sets of structures tasked with mainstreaming gender through the state, and opening spaces in the state that benefit women (Gouws, 2022). With this 'package' design, feminists wanted to disperse access to power across different sites of government, such as the executive and the parliamentary committee system.

Women's issues were represented on the legislative and executive levels and in the autonomous Chapter 9 body created by the Constitution, the Commission for Gender Equality (CGE). As shown in Figure 12.1, there was an Office of the Status of Women in the Presidency, a Women's Empowerment Unit in the Office of the Speaker of Parliament, a multi-party women's caucus in Parliament as well as, in Parliament, the Joint Monitoring Committee on Improvement of Quality of Life and Status of Women (JMC) with oversight over all state departments, and gender desks in each state department.

The Office of the Status of Women in the Presidency produced the National Policy Framework for Women's Empowerment and Gender Equality (2000), providing detailed principles of gender equality to be incorporated into policies and programmes. It included long-term indicators to monitor changes in attitudes, beliefs and cultural practices, and a commitment to deal with GBV through educational programmes for police, prosecutors, magistrates and judges (Meyiwa et al., 2017: 8611).

Feminists attempted to steer clear of one-party structures such as Ministries of Women's Affairs that have a track record of failure in Africa (Gouws, 2022). These usually concentrate 'all things gender'

Figure 12.1: The South African National Gender Machinery

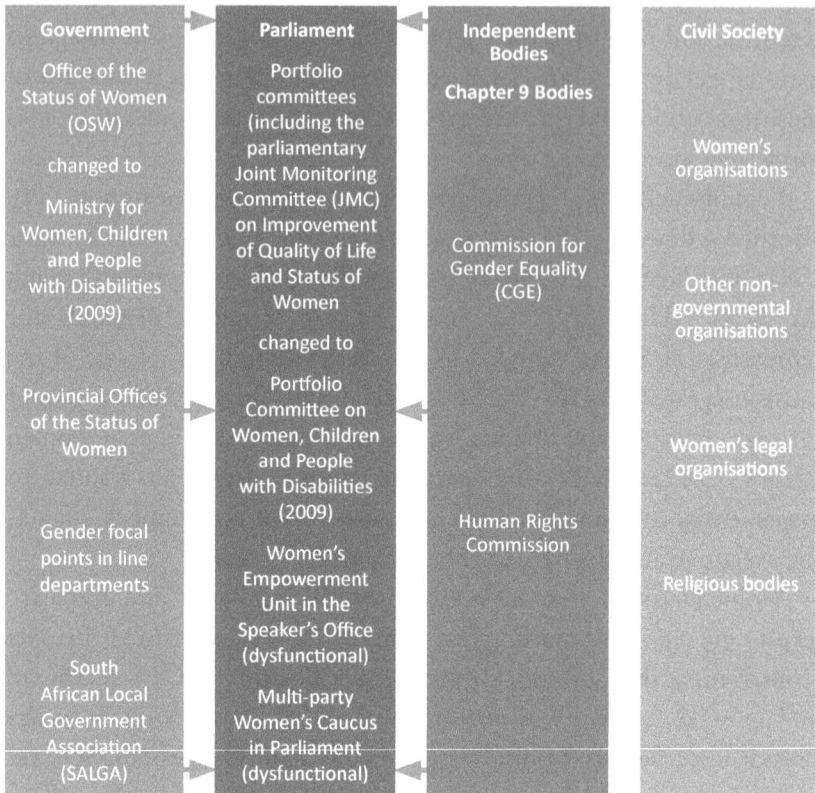

Government	Parliament	Independent Bodies	Civil Society
Office of the Status of Women (OSW)	Portfolio committees (including the parliamentary Joint Monitoring Committee (JMC) on Improvement of Quality of Life and Status of Women	Chapter 9 Bodies	Women's organisations
changed to			
Ministry for Women, Children and People with Disabilities (2009)		Commission for Gender Equality (CGE)	Other non-governmental organisations
	changed to		
Provincial Offices of the Status of Women	Portfolio Committee on Women, Children and People with Disabilities (2009)		Women's legal organisations
Gender focal points in line departments	Women's Empowerment Unit in the Speaker's Office (dysfunctional)	Human Rights Commission	Religious bodies
South African Local Government Association (SALGA)	Multi-party Women's Caucus in Parliament (dysfunctional)		

Source: Compiled by Author

in one place, with little policy output. The success of state structures or agencies often depends on their relationship with women's organisations and/or women's movements in civil society.

Several so-called 'femocrats' (former WNC activists) left state structures after the first five years, because they found the institutional space too constricting and they disagreed with government policy on several issues. For example, Pregs Govender, the chair of the JMC, resigned in 2002 because of President Mbeki's stance on HIV/Aids and the scandal around arms procurement in what came to be known as 'the Arms Deal' (Govender, 2007). The exit of committed feminists strengthened the voice for institutionalisation in the form of a ministry for women. The integrated and comprehensive set of structures negotiated before 1994 was replaced by a Ministry for Women,

Children and People with Disabilities in 2009, which was seen more as a reward for the ANCWL supporting Zuma during the 2007 ANC elective conference (Ntuli, 2022: 182). This spelt the weakening of the feminist vision of an NGM.

THE HOLLOWING OUT OF THE NATIONAL GENDER MACHINERY (NGM)

The key structure in the NGM is the Commission for Gender Equality (CGE), which was established under the Commission for Gender Equality Act (No. 39 of 1996). The Act gave the GCE a mandate for oversight over legislative activities, the power to subpoena people or organisations that undermine gender equality, and the power to have public hearings and to investigate complaints (Gouws, 2022).

As Albertyn (2022) shows, the CGE created a significant feminist footprint in law reform and in aligning gender equality legislation with the Constitution in its initial phase, and thus contributed to creating a gender-friendly legal regime. Hicks (2022) shows that when the CGE worked with excluded groups and trade unions, power could be leveraged to change conditions of gender inequality, as evidenced by her success in getting maternity leave for women in the informal sector as a CGE commissioner. The CGE also succeeded in having public hearings on poverty; on salary disparities between women and men soccer players with the South African Football Association (SAFA); and on the murders of lesbians in the Western Cape with the police. The Commission handles hundreds of complaints annually. Though some of these initiatives are more successful than others, the CGE delivers on its mandate.

But the CGE has never leveraged its powerful position as a Chapter 9 institution. It lacks visibility in the public eye, and its failure to communicate its successes and to prioritise serious issues such as GBV give it a public image as powerless and uninterested in tackling gender inequality.

The CGE Act requires that commissioners be non-partisan and independent to enable the Commission to function as an autonomous oversight body protected by Chapter 9 of the Constitution. Yet, many commissioners are perceived as partisan – either as members of or loyal to the ANCWL (Hassim, 2014: 124–125). This has affected the CGE in several ways, such as hampering oversight over government or resistance to criticising political leaders such as President Zuma, making the whole commission compliant with the Presidency.[1] This earned the Commission serious criticism from civil society, specifically women's organisations (Gouws, 2022). Consequently, the appointment of CGE commissioners has become politicised with party loyalty tending to trump skills in gender analysis and expertise (Vetten, 2022), and thus preventing the Commission from delivering on its mandate.

Since the components of the NGM are state institutions, any form of corruption that undermines them will also undermine the NGM. The large-scale repurposing of state institutions (state capture) under the Zuma administration also had far-reaching implications for NGM structures.

State capture aimed to change formal rules, legitimising informal ones and enabling some to become involved in corrupt actions. Chipkin and Swilling (2018: x) call this 'repurposing the institutions of state': institutions are structured, governed, managed and funded in a way that gives them purposes different from their formal mandates. This leads to a symbiotic relationship between the constitutional and the shadow state – the repurposed state of rent-seeking networks of corrupt politicians and state officials (Chipkin and Swilling, 2018: xi). These networks allow unelected people to engage in political decision-making.

The state department responsible for women has undergone a variety of shifts and name changes. Since its inception in 2009, as the Ministry for Women, Children and People with Disabilities, it has had five ministers, none of them able to elevate the department to an effective champion of gender equality. The unwieldiness of the department's three mandates is indicated by the fact that it has never reached more than 30 per cent of its targets (Ntuli, 2022). It lacks urgency to deal with even the most pressing issues of social justice challenging women, such as GBV, reproductive health and joblessness.

---

1 The author was a commissioner for the CGE during this time.

At the end of 2012, it was the second worst-performing national department, managing to meet only 14 per cent of its performance targets (Ntuli, 2022: 183). In 2014, it shed the portfolios of 'Children' and 'People with Disabilities' to become the Ministry of Women in the the Presidency. Again, it did not meet its targets. The annual report 2014/2015 of the Ministry shows that of 11 short-term goals/targets, only one was achieved. The bulk of its budget was spent on salaries and the procurement of goods and services. The constant reconfiguration of the department and changing targets frustrated the oversight role of the Portfolio Committee on Women, Youth and Persons with Disabilities to track performance. It also meant little policy output on long-term goals of achieving gender equality and empowering women (Ntuli, 2022: 187). After the 2019 election, the department was again reconfigured as the Department of Women, Youth and Persons with Disabilities (DWYPD).

Targets that were achieved relate to short-term, practical gender issues rather than longer-term strategic gender issues that aim to change gender power relations. The targets that were achieved were mainly those regarding the organising of events such as the celebration of National Women's Day or the 16 Days of Activism for No Violence Against Women and Children. These were just two of 24 core performance targets. In 2014/2015, the Department had a budget of R77,580,000 of which R48,504,000 was spent on salaries. From then onwards, more than 52 per cent of the budget was spent on salaries (Ntuli, 2022: 187). As Ntuli (2022: 194) points out:

> Because of the relationship of benevolence political appointees have with the appointing political structure, and culture of cadre deployment, they are constrained in their ability to raise critiques of the party. This has grave implications for women who may seek to challenge patriarchy within the political institutions that appoint them.

Another major problem with the way the DWYPD functions is that it duplicates the functions of the CGE, while also being responsible for allocating the Commission's budget. This complicates the CGE's oversight role over the department because it is difficult to criticise the institution that also provides its funding. This situation also allows for interference by the Portfolio Committee on Women, Youth and Persons with Disabilities in CGE matters, such as the appointment of its CEO (Vetten, 2022: 100). All this points to the co-optation of the NGM in a way that would result in anti-feminist outcomes.

FEMINIST INSTITUTIONALISM AND GENDER-BASED VIOLENCE

One of the most vexing problems to eradicate through policy, legislation and practical action is the high level of gender-based violence (GBV) and femicide in South Africa. One can consider GBV (which includes domestic violence, sexual assault and rape) as a contextual factor that influences many other policies. As long as women are not safe, many other policies essentially become meaningless. Statistics for sexual offences and rape of women in South Africa are among the highest in countries that monitor and report on this scourge. The South African Police Service (SAPS) reported that there were 52,694 cases of sexual offences in 2021/2022, of which 41,739 were rape. In 2023/2024, there were 53,285 cases, of which 42,569 were rapes (an increase of 2.5 per cent) (SAPS, 2023/2024; saps.gov.za). These figures must be considered within the context that rape is underreported in South Africa. The One-in-Nine Campaign shows that only one in nine rapes is reported. To make matters worse, South Africa's incidence of femicide is five times the global average (Brodie, 2020; Gouws, 2021).

Law-making and implementation

The protracted 30-year struggle for women and gendered minorities to use the state to alleviate the problems facing them is illustrated when using GBV as a lens through which to measure policymaking and implementation regarding gender justice.

In the first five years of the NGM, feminists and femocrats could point to the success of substantive representation, such as the Domestic Violence Act which was initiated as a legislative priority by the chair of the JMC (Vetten et al., 2012). In 1996, the ANC Parliamentary

Women's Caucus initiated the joint Campaign to End Violence Against Women and Children in collaboration with women and children's organisations in the Western Cape. This initiative involved weekly meetings and a range of activities, including working with organisations to draft submissions to the South African Law Reform Commission on domestic violence; intervening in rape cases involving schoolgirls in the Western Cape and Northern province (now Limpopo); drafting questions for MPs to raise during parliamentary meetings; and supporting ANC MPs in addressing violence against women within the ANC Parliamentary Caucus and their constituencies (Vetten, 2016).

The campaign proposed urgent tabling of the Domestic Violence Bill because Parliament had delayed after receiving the draft Bill from the Judicial Services Commission (JSC) (Hodes, 2011). In response, members of the ANC Women's Caucus met the then deputy president to advocate for women's legislative priorities. The JMC successfully prioritised the legislation and prevented the replacement of the feminist-influenced draft law with a more conservative version. These efforts culminated in the promulgation of the Domestic Violence Act in 1998 (Vetten, 2016). This Act was amended recently through, *inter alia*, the involvement of feminist legal scholars to enlarge the definition of domestic violence and make provision for online applications for court interdicts, and simultaneous issuance of a warrant of arrest and a protection order, among other reforms (Moolla, 2013). The Domestic Violence Act was successfully promulgated because of feminist initiatives, collaboration with femocrats in government, and the mobilisation of civil society to apply pressure for the Bill to be passed.

The process for the passing of the Criminal Law (Sexual Offences and Related Matters) Bill was more arduous and protracted, requiring feminist activist intervention. Its aim was to repeal the common law offence of rape and replace it with the expanded statutory offence of rape, applicable to all forms of sexual penetration without consent, and to all forms of sexual violation.

Despite constraints, including parliamentary schedules, women's legal organisations and non-governmental organisations developed the skills necessary to prepare legislative submissions. The passing of the Bill was delayed by parliamentary amendments that ignored feminist concerns. These changes included altering or removing crucial provisions, such as clauses mandating medical treatment and counselling, safeguarding adult and child victims from adversarial rape trial processes, reintroducing consent as a component of rape definition, and eliminating the concept of 'coercive circumstances' (Hodes, 2011; Vetten and Watson, 2009). The vigilance of feminist activists and legal scholars outside Parliament ensured substantive representation in this matter.

This legislative process prompted the Shukumisa Campaign, which involved a coalition of organisations. It started out as the National Working Group on Sexual Offences, formed in 2004 with organisations focused on violence (Gouws, 2016: 404). To promote understanding and engagement, the group developed 12 fact sheets about the proposed Bill and encouraged public submissions. They received support from several organisations: the Centre for Applied Legal Studies (CALS) at the University of the Witwatersrand; the Thohoyandou Victim Empowerment Programme (operating in rural areas); and the Tshwaranang Legal Advocacy Centre, which concentrates on violence against women. (Gouws, 2016: 405). Cape Town-based organisations closely monitored the deliberations by attending meetings of the Parliamentary Portfolio Committee on Justice and Constitutional Development. These examples show the importance of identifying openings in the state and utilising feminist allies within the state who are also able to draw on their relationships with civil society organisations. These organisations can help set the agenda and put pressure on the state to deliver.

Most research on GBV points to a failure to implement laws, a lack of inter-departmental cooperation within government, and a lack of engagement with civil society and consultation with communities (Connolly, 2017; Lewis, n.d.; Meyiwa et al., 2017; Vetten, 2014; 2016). Piecemeal and ad hoc implementations of progressive legislation are the order of the day. A major issue with GBV policy is that it does not include accountability mechanisms; for example, who holds the police or justice system accountable for failures? Where multi-sectoral processes exist, they are either not well developed, fragmented, overlap or are duplicated (Connolly, 2017: 27). The 2018 GBV Presidential Summit

Report (Department of Justice and Constitutional Development, 2018) acknowledges these weaknesses. It indicates that the core elements of an effective response to gender-based violence and femicide (GBVF) should be scaled to include, among others, rooting the response at a local level, optimising systems, policies and legislation, resourcing and calling for multi-sectoral responses.

In order to create the necessary mechanism to enforce GBV law and keep the criminal justice system accountable, structures in the state (now left to the DWYPD) must take responsibility for implementation. But as Bosilong and Mbecke (2019: 124) argue, there is no leadership forthcoming from the DWYPD, to the extent that the Deputy Minister of Justice and Constitutional Development, John Jeffery, had to acknowledge the insufficiency of specialised services for women victims of violence in 2017. He also indicated that existing services are underfunded and uncoordinated (Bosilong and Mbecke, 2019: 127). This would include the institutionalisation of Thuthuzela Care Centres (one-stop centres for rape victims) and Sexual Offences Courts. Those who have to enforce and implement the law, such as the police, lack the necessary training to deal with rape complainants.

As tackling GBV involves the services of more than one department, it requires cross-departmental collaboration, rather than ministries working in silos (Meyiwa et al., 2017: 8611). Departments must set priorities and allocate funding to implement laws and victim empowerment programmes. The CGE has an obligation to monitor and evaluate policies and the legislative agenda, but this is done in a very limited fashion, if at all.

Preventative policies are not developed, nor are the overlaps between GBV, poverty and HIV/AIDS considered in an intersectional way. This shortcoming is important, because GBV is not a single issue (Meyiwa et al., 2017: 8612). Lewis (n.d.) points out that there are many hidden forms of violence against women and minorities that cannot be solved only by law, such as harmful cultural practices (e.g. virginity testing). One ANC woman mayor wanted to create 'virgin scholarships' for young women to study and remain virgins. They would have had to undergo regular virginity testing (TMG Digital, 2016). The idea was prevented from gaining traction because of an outcry from civil society.

The relationship between government and civil society

Substantive representation requires a strong link between femocrats in government and women's organisations. As Connolly (2017) shows, this link is ephemeral and not sustained. It is often civil society organisations that approach the state, rather than the state having consultative processes with civil society organisations and communities.

In the case of both the Domestic Violence Act and the Sexual Offences Act, the involvement of women's organisations, feminist legal organisations and men's organisations was the determining factor in the passing of these laws. For GBV solutions to work optimally, it is important to involve men's organisations that specifically focus on masculinities. The work of Sonke Gender Justice, which has a 'men as partners' programme, has supported anti-GBV work for decades and helped to develop strategies around optimising its influence. Sonke, for example, joined the Shukumisa Campaign to work in a coalition that has a greater probability of influencing policy, rather than being only an NGO. Sonke also emphasises the importance of working across different levels, from communities to government. It drafts submissions for Parliament and carries out interventions with stakeholders (Connolly, 2017: 33). It also uses advocacy as a strategy to expose policy shortcomings.

The work of civil society organisations also involves follow-ups with government to see if their advocacy strategies have worked. It is often difficult to assess this, however, especially in the absence of interdepartmental cooperation. Where advocacy strategies fail, direct action becomes an option to engage the state.

It was #TotalShutDown and its march to the Union Buildings that forced government to draft a National Strategic Plan on Gender-Based Violence and Femicide in 2020 (Department of Justice and Constitutional Development, 2020). This comprehensive plan, with the potential to reduce violence, includes six pillars: (1) accountability, coordination and leadership; (2) prevention and rebuilding social cohesion; (3) justice, safety and protection; (4) response, care, support and healing; (5) economic power; and (6) research, information and management. What is, however, clear is that this plan can only be successfully implemented through interdepartmental cooperation, alliances with civil society and community-based organisations and researchers. Its ambitious nature has the potential to become its greatest obstacle to successful implementation. The plan was workshopped in all the provinces, enhancing substantive representation, but the roll-out and budgeting for it are not sufficiently coordinated.

Discursive shifts

Feminist responses to GBV have located violence in postcolonial and post-apartheid conditions of structural violence, dispossession, social exclusion and harmful attitudes. A multi-pronged approach is required to address these, in which both prevention and access to rights are crucial. Unfortunately, many decontextualised approaches are encountered. These reinforce the notion that rapists are exceptions to the norm, despite the fact that the number of GBV cases in South Africa show that GBV and rape are both normalised. The ANCWL, for example, invokes the carceral state as a solution to GBV; one of its mantras is 'rapists must rot in jail'. This approach is seen in some government articulations too. The Minister for Women, Youth and Persons with Disabilities in 2014, Lulu Xingwana, attended the bail hearing of the alleged rapists of a young woman, Anene Booysen, where she pleaded outside the court for the 'rapists to rot in jail' (author's notes from attending the hearing).

Another discursive shift is a move away from aligning an end to GBV with gender equality, to a more moralistic stance which equates violence with moral failure. Moreover, this approach centres the family as the primary moral bulwark against GBV. Vetten's (2014: 54) analysis of the White Paper on Families (2013) shows that it exhibits a complex blend of ideological approaches. It is primarily familialist, emphasising family-oriented policies. However, it also incorporates elements of moralism, traditionalism and what is termed 'innocuous constitutionalism'. It attaches significant importance to traditional leaders, viewing them as custodians of traditional values and, similarly, it designates faith-based and religious organisations as the guardians of morality.

The White Paper on Families should be read in tandem with the White Paper for Social Welfare (1997), which places the family at the centre of all kinds of services for those with social challenges. Examples include services for people with disabilities, ill family members and the aged. No consideration is given to whether the necessary infrastructure or finances exist for this work (Sevenhuijsen et al., 2003).

As Vetten (2014: 55) argues, the depoliticisation of the family and the framing of domestic violence as a symptom of moral failure (rather than of gender inequality) prevent the search for alternatives. Consequently, it prioritises a particular sort of family preservation as well as normalising interventions which leave women feeling blamed for domestic violence. It has the effect of obscuring men's central role in the violence.

With the creation of the Ministry of Women, Youth and Persons with Disabilities, there was a shift from emphasising women's agency to focusing on women (and children) as vulnerable groups. This casts women in the mould of permanent victimhood, framing women's difference as neediness and focusing on paternalistic and protectionist assumptions (Vetten, 2014). This discursive shift resulted, in 2011, in the Department of Social Development arguing that gender equality means equal treatment of men and women, and, therefore, that men should also be allowed into women's domestic violence shelters (Vetten, 2014).

By viewing state feminism through the lens of GBV, we see the importance of a post-structural analysis of the state, i.e. how the openings and closings of spaces make a difference to policy outcomes. Such a perspective also demonstrates the tensions and competing agendas in the state, and the importance of strong relationships with civil society, and of the timing of raising policy issues amid other competing imperatives.

CONCLUSION

This chapter assessed the state of feminism, and its relationship with the South African state, over South Africa's 30-year period of democracy.

The democratic transition in South Africa opened a window of opportunity for women. It enabled them to be elected to Parliament through a quota system and introduced state feminism through institutionalising, within the state, an integrated set of structures designed by feminist scholars, activists and women's organisations. The roll-back of the most important of these structures created opportunities for the strengthening of a nationalist discourse about women as mainly the reproducers of the nation. The establishment of the Department of Women, Youth and Persons with Disabilities (which is largely dysfunctional, especially on substantive issues), undermined the National Gender Machinery. This approach reduced women's access to the state, erased feminist spaces within the state and co-opted the remaining structures. Regarding women's representation, women's causes will be better served by a focus on critical actors who champion women's issues – who are prepared to speak out for gender justice, regardless of the consequences – than large numbers of women.

This chapter illustrated successes and failures of state feminism through the lens of gender-based violence in South Africa. The spaces to engage with the state need to be expanded, so as to create a virtuous circle in which the state and civil society work together to find solutions to GBV and to ensure more effective attention to broader issues of gender equality.

The approach to gender in the state in 2025 leaves a lot to be desired from a feminist perspective. Weaknesses in implementing progressive laws, and minimal cooperation with civil society organisations, as discussed earlier, underscore the reasons why feminists are wary of the state. At this point, the state protects a patriarchal bargain between the men in the state and women who are perceived as compliant. As a result, the argument that all women stand to lose rather than gain through women's access to the state finds resonance among many feminists.

The contraction of the National Gender Machinery after 2009 lends credence to post-structural theories of the state, namely that certain openings in the state are necessary to insert women's interests. As these spaces contracted, it became more difficult for women to engage with the state. The contradictory and, at times, competing agendas of women's interests in the state result in detrimental outcomes for women. An illustration of this is the feminist agendas – around law reform and well-resourced practical programmes, for example – versus narrow descriptive representation.

RECOMMENDATIONS

A revitalised National Gender Machinery (NGM) could help to advance gender equality in South Africa. However, there would need to be an important transformation in the staff structures of a recreated NGM. It must be staffed with people who have expertise in gender analysis and gender-responsive budgeting. Gender analysis is a specialised skill. The lack of skills in the state is evident in the undervalued capacity of gender analysis for policymaking, in contrast to the ability to organise events such as Women's Day and the 16 Days of Activism for No Violence Against Women and Children.

To resuscitate the National Gender Machinery, there should be an overhaul of Chapter 9 bodies (specifically the CGE) to strengthen their independence from interference by politicians. A women's ministry does not have to be dysfunctional, but it cannot be expected to include more than one mandate, such as 'women, youth and people with disabilities'. This list makes it impossible to do justice to any of the portfolios included. There have been suggestions that children, youth and people with disabilities be moved to the Department of Social Welfare, which seems a more appropriate home for them.

Since the institutionalisation of the Department of Women, Youth and Persons with Disabilities, many of the gains made in gender equality have been rolled back. These gains were made over the three decades of a democratic state, through feminist institutionalism and women's representation in the state. Feminist oversight and the vigilance of civil society are required to prevent further rollbacks.

REFERENCES

Albertyn, C. 2022. 'A feminist footprint?: The Commission for Gender Equality and the courts', in Gouws, A. (ed.), *Feminist Institutionalism in South Africa: Designing for Gender Equality.* Cape Town: UCT Press.

Booysen, S. 2015. *Dominance and Decline: The ANC in the Time of Zuma.* Johannesburg: Wits University Press.

Bosilong, K.P. and Mbecke, P. 2019. 'Violence against women: A snubbed tragedy in South Africa', in Kalunta-Crumpton, A. (ed.), *Violence against Women of African Descent.* New York/London: Lexington Books.

Brodie, N. 2020. *Femicide in South Africa.* Cape Town: Kwela Books.

Brown, W. 1992. 'Finding the man in the state'. *Feminist Studies*, 18(1), 7–34.

Butler, A. 2015. 'The politics of numbers: National membership growth and subnational power competition in the African National Congress'. *Transformation*, 87, 13–31.

Calland, R. 2013. *The Zuma Years*. Cape Town: Zebra Press.

Chappell, L. 2014. '"New", "old", and "nested" institutions and gender justice outcomes: A view from the International Criminal Court'. *Politics & Gender*, 10(4), 572–594.

Chappell, L. and Mackay, F. 2017. 'What's in a name?: Mapping the terrain of informal institutions and gender politics', in Waylen, G. (ed.), *Gender and Informal Institutions*. London: Rowman & Littlefield, pp. 23–44.

Chipkin, I. and Swilling, M. 2018. *Shadow State: The Politics of State Capture*. Johannesburg: Wits University Press.

Connolly, S. 2017. 'Assessing the successes of and challenges facing civil society organizations in South Africa, in influencing gender-based violence policy'. SIT Digital Collection, https://digitalcollections.sit.edu/cgi/viewcontent.cgi?article=3720&context=isp_collection, accessed 25 June 2025.

Department of Justice and Constitutional Development. 2018. 'The Report of the Presidential Summit against Gender-based Violence and Femicide, 2018', https://www.justice.gov.za/vg/gbv/GBV-Summit-Report-2018.pdf, accessed 30 June 2025.

Department of Justice and Constitutional Development. 2020. 'National Strategic Plan on gender-based violence & femicide: Human dignity and healing, safety, freedom & equality in our lifetime', https://www.justice.gov.za/vg/gbv/nsp-gbvf-final-doc-04-05.pdf, accessed 30 June 2025.

Franceschet, S., Krook, M.L. and Piscopo, J. 2012. 'Conceptualizing the impact of gender quotas', in Franceschet, S., Krook, M.L. and Piscopo, J. (eds), *The Impact of Gender Quotas*. Oxford: Oxford University Press.

Goodin, R.E. 2009. *Institutions and their Design*. Cambridge: Cambridge University Press.

Gouws, A. 2014. 'Multiculturalism in South Africa: Dislodging the binary between universal human rights and culture/tradition', in Gouws, A. and Stasiulis, D. (eds), *Gender and Multiculturalisms – North/South Perspectives*. London and New York: Routledge.

Gouws, A. 2015. 'The public discourse of rape in South Africa', in Verwoerd, M. (ed.), *Sexualized Violence in the National Debate*. Cape Town: Heinrich Bohl Foundation.

Gouws, A. 2016. 'Women's activism around gender-based violence in South Africa: Recognition, redistribution and representation'. *Review of African Political Economy*, 43(149), 400–415.

Gouws, A. 2021. 'Reducing women to bare life: Sexual violence in South Africa'. *Feminist Encounters: A Journal of Critical Studies in Culture and Politics*, 5(1), 1–12.

Gouws, A. 2022. 'In the belly of the Commission for Gender Equality: Of structural problems and straitjackets', in Gouws, A. (ed.), *Feminist Institutionalism in South Africa: Designing for Gender Equality.* Cape Town: UCT Press.

Govender, P. 2007. *Love and Courage: A Story of Insubordination.* Johannesburg: Jacana Media.

Gqola, P. 2015. *Rape: A South Africa Nightmare.* Johannesburg: MF Books.

Hassim, S. 2006. *Women's Organizations and Democracy in South Africa – Contesting Authority.* Scottsville: UKZN Press.

Hassim, S. 2014. *The ANC Women's League.* Johannesburg: Jacana Media.

Hicks, J. 2022. 'The Commission for Gender Equality: Leveraging rights to gender equality', in Gouws, A. (ed.), *Feminist Institutionalism in South Africa: Designing for Gender Equality.* Cape Town: UCT Press.

Hodes, R. 2011. 'The making of South Africa's Sexual Offences Act (2007): Structure and agency in a women's rights coalition'. CSSR Working Paper No. 298, University of Cape Town, https://humanities.uct.ac.za/cssr/making-south-africas-sexual-offences-act-2007-structure-and-agency-womens-rights-coalition, accessed 25 June 2025.

Hoffman, J. 1998. 'Is there a case for a feminist critique of the state?'. *Contemporary Politics*, 4(2), 161–176.

Kantola, J. and Outshoorn, J. 2007. 'Changing state feminism', in Outshoorn, J. and Kantola, J. (eds), *Changing State Feminism.* New York: Palgrave Macmillan.

Lambrechts, D. 2017. 'The state, state capabilities and non-state actors: A literature survey', in Lambrechts, D. and Fourie, P. (eds), *Modern State Development, Capacity, and Institutions.* Stellenbosch: SUN Media.

Lewis, D. n.d. 'Gender-based violence'. Unpublished paper, https://scholar.google.com/scholar?hl=en&as_sdt=0%2C5&q=Desiree+Lewis+GBV&btnG=, accessed 24 October 2024.

MacKinnon, C. 1989. *Towards a Feminist Theory of the State.* Cambridge: Harvard University Press.

Meyiwa, T., Williamson, C., Maseti, T. and Ntabanyane, G.M. 2017. 'A twenty-year review of policy landscape for gender-based violence in South Africa'. *Gender and Behaviour*, 15(2), 8607–8617.

Mohanty, C. 1988. 'Under Western eyes: Feminist scholarship and colonial discourses'. *Feminist Review*, 30, 61–88.

Moolla, M. 2013. 'Enhancing effectiveness: Strengthening protection for domestic violence victims through the Amendment Act'. *De Rebus*, https://www.derebus.org.za/enhancing-effectiveness-strengthening-protection-for-domestic-violence-victims-through-the-amendment-act/, accessed 14 October 2024.

Ntuli, P. 2022. 'A rapid undoing – from an integrated set of structures to a single ministry', in Gouws, A. (ed.), *Feminist Institutionalism in South*

Africa: Designing for Gender Equality. Cape Town: UCT Press.

Rai, S.M. 1996a. 'Women and the state in the Third World: Some issues for debate', in Rai, S.M. and Lievesley, G. (eds), *Women and the State.* London: Taylor & Francis.

Rai, S.M. 1996b. 'Women and the state in the Third World', in Afshar, H. (ed.), *Women and the Politics in the Third World.* London: Routledge.

Republic of South Africa. 2020. 'National Strategic Plan On Gender-Based Violence & Femicide Human Dignity And Healing, Safety, Freedom & Equality In Our Lifetime', https://www.justice.gov.za/vg/gbv/nsp-gbvf-final-doc-04-05.pdf, accessed 9 January 2024.

Rhode, D.L. 1994. 'Feminism and the state'. *Harvard Law Review*, 107(6), 1181–1208.

Setati, G. 2012. 'Through the eye of an ANC slate'. *Mail & Guardian Thought Leader,* 4 December, https://thoughtleader.co.za/garethsetati/2012/12/04/through-the-eye-of-an-anc-slate-2/, accessed 24 February 2019.

Sevenhuijsen, S., Bozalek, V., Gouws, A. and Minnaar-McDonald, M. 2003. 'South African social welfare policy: An analysis using the ethic of care'. *Critical Social Policy*, 23(3), 299–321.

South African Police Service (SAPS). 2023/2024. 'Crime Stats', https://www.saps.gov.za/about/stratframework/annual_report/2023_2024/SAPS_2023_24_Annual%20Crime%20Report_JG25.pdf, accessed 10 January 2024.

TMG Digital. 2016. 'Scholarships for virgins holds girls to a different sexual standard than boys – LHR'. *SowetanLive*, https://www.sowetanlive.co.za/news/2016-01-26-scholarships-for-virgins-holds-girls-to-a-different-sexual-standard-than-boys-lhr/, accessed 15 October 2024.

Vetten, L. 2014. 'The ghost of families past: Domestic violence legislation and policy in post-apartheid South Africa'. *Agenda*, 28(2), 48–57.

Vetten, L. 2016. 'Political representation makes women's voices heard? Lessons from South Africa'. *Feminist Dialogue Series*, 4, 1–5.

Vetten, L. 2022. 'The battle machine: Or how to undo a Commission for Gender Equality', in Gouws, A. (ed.), *Feminist Institutionalism in South Africa; Designing for Gender Equality.* Cape Town: UCT Press.

Vetten, L., Makhunga, L. and Leisegang, A. 2012. 'Making Women's Representation in Parliament Count'. Womenkind and the European Union.

Vetten, L. and Watson, J. 2009. 'Engendering the parliamentary agenda: Strategic opportunity or waste of feminist energy'. GAP Policy Brief 3.

Waylen, G. 2007. *Engendering Transitions: Women's Mobilization, Institutions and Gendered Outcomes.* Oxford: Oxford University Press.

THIRTEEN

South African foreign policy in the evolving global context

GARTH LE PERE AND NA'EEM JEENAH

INTRODUCTION

US president Harry Truman (1945–1952) once said: 'The President makes foreign policy' (Frankel, 1968: 21). This has certainly been the case in the evolution of South Africa's foreign policy. Its five post-1994 presidents – especially Nelson Mandela and Thabo Mbeki – played prominent roles in every major decision, challenge and issue concerning the country's international relations. While implicitly acknowledging that change and continuity in South Africa's foreign policy and international relations were profoundly shaped and influenced by the different presidents, this chapter is more concerned with the broad normative and conceptual thrusts and thematic emphases of that policy over the past three decades. It aims to interrogate the broad contours of South Africa's international relations as an integral part of the post-apartheid state's evolution.

To meet this objective, the evolution and conduct of the post-apartheid state's foreign policy will be located within a global context. South Africa's democratic transition was almost coterminous with the end of the Cold War's ideological tensions, symbolised by the collapse of the Berlin Wall in 1989 and the Soviet Union in 1991. This shift inaugurated tectonic shifts in international relations, characterised by greater interconnectedness and interdependence in a fast-globalising but turbulent and crisis-prone era.

The international and multilateral landscape became more volatile, uncertain and complex, mainly because of systemic imbalances of power and influence which exposed the weak foundations of global peace, security and stability. These weaknesses contained the symptoms of a fractured multi-polar system; the changed landscape also saw the proliferation of non-state actors and the growing weight of emerging powers in international relations (Ferguson and Mansbach, 2004). These factors challenged the foreign policy of the newly democratic South Africa, together with several 'crisis moments', such as the ruinous 'global war on terror'; the 2008–2009 global financial crisis; persistent African conflicts; climate change; the Covid-19 pandemic; the Russia-Ukraine war; and Israel's genocide in Gaza.

Against this background, this chapter briefly examines the transformation of the South African state from 1994. The first section examines the foreign policy dilemma facing government as it attempts to manage the tension between the national interest and its avowed internationalism. These tensions include South Africa's role – and contested leadership – in Africa, the wider diplomatic landscape, and the country's bilateral and multilateral relationships. The chapter then considers several themes relating to South Africa's foreign policy: institutional and diplomatic challenges, multilateral, trade and economic diplomacy, peace and security, and development aid.

Finally, it discusses critical considerations in the country's international relations. Examining the government's definition of the country's national interest, the last section considers the tension between government's proclaimed normative ambition and foreign policy, and its actual practice. It provides several examples: South Africa's interface with the African Union and the African continent more broadly; its military misadventure in the Central African

Republic; the impact of xenophobia on its continental relations; its ambivalent stance on the Russia-Ukraine war; and its principled approach to Israel's Gaza genocide.

STATE TRANSFORMATION

South Africa's global statecraft has been shaped by an amalgam of normative, substantive, circumstantial and managerial imperatives (Mbeki, 2021). South Africa's dramatic rehabilitation from international pariah to bastion of transitional democracy required that it address the critical challenges of redefining its roles on the African and global stages. Important considerations included representation and membership in regional and international organisations, establishing a global diplomatic presence, transforming the instruments of foreign policy, and introducing a new discourse about international relations (Chikane, 2001; DFA, 1996).

The policy dilemma

A persistent dilemma has been how to manage the dialectic between 'neo-mercantilist' financial, commercial, political and security interests and South Africa's 'internationalist' role as a moral champion for human rights, social justice and global redistributive fairness and equity (Cornelissen, 2021). The absence of conceptual and ethical coherence, and of an underlying strategic framework of rational choices, led to a critique that the country suffered from ambiguous and muddled internationalism which failed to distinguish cause and effect (Nel, 2006).

In global indices, such as the one offered by the United Nations Development Programme, South Africa has a medium human development ranking, but is scarred by high levels of racialised inequality, poverty and unemployment. This domestic context points to the capacity constraints inhibiting and circumscribing the state's ambitions on the African and global stages (Butler, 2011; Seidman Makgetla, 2011). These include:

- the need for financial resources and investment in the context of often weak and unstable macroeconomic fundamentals, compounded by

policy incoherence;
- limited institutional and diplomatic capacity due to difficulties with managing key foreign relations and the state's security institutions, exacerbated by a high proportion of ambassadors being political appointees;
- intellectual and conceptual deficits in understanding Africa's political and cultural complexities, and the intricacies and nuances of global politics; and
- persistent ambiguity about the country's identity in its international relations, highlighted by its transactional and equivocal response to the Russia-Ukraine war (Mathekga, 2023).

These constraints continue to shape South Africa's conduct, both in Africa and across the wider diplomatic landscape, in several strategic areas.

Contested leadership in Africa

South Africa's leadership has often been contested, especially in the southern African and continental milieus. Southern Africa — where South Africa could readily exercise its influence — has been more challenging for the country's leadership and diplomacy than expected (Alden and Le Pere, 2003). Since the adoption of the SADC Protocol on Trade in 1996 and the implementation of the SADC Free Trade Area in 2012, South Africa has made great strides in promoting positive trade and development agendas. However, this has been compromised by continuing authoritarian tendencies and weak governance in some countries; post-war and post-conflict reconstruction challenges; fragile peace and democratic transitions; widespread poverty and underdevelopment; sluggish economic growth; and the tragic effects of HIV/AIDS in the worst-affected region in Africa (Landsberg, 2015; Nkhonjera and Roberts, 2020).

Regarding its 'African Agenda', South Africa has focused on promoting peace, security and development on the continent, concerns emphasised by International Relations Minister Ronald Lamola as being at the core of the country's national interest (Lamola, 2024). Central to these concerns has been the quest to promote and reconstruct a new institutional architecture with the African Union (AU) as the custodian of peace and security. South Africa championed the New Partnership for Africa's Development (NEPAD) as the African socioeconomic blueprint; the African Peace and Security and Governance Architectures as stability templates; the African Peer Review Mechanism (APRM) as a domestic measurement index; Agenda 2063 as a 50-year growth and development vision; and the African Continental Free Trade Area (AfCFTA) as an instrument for expanding intra-regional trade (Hendricks, 2022; Mondi, 2020). African good governance is emphasised symbolically and practically by South Africa hosting the Pan-African Parliament.

The wider diplomatic landscape

Traditional bilateral diplomatic and trade relations with the US and the EU have been maintained (Firsing and Masters, 2015), and new relations nurtured with emerging markets and powers – China, India and Brazil, with whom high-level bi-national commissions were established. These were the incubators for the formation of the India, Brazil, South Africa (IBSA) dialogue forum in June 2003. A quintessential forum of 'southern multilateralism', its logic was elaborated in South Africa's aggressive pursuit of membership of the BRIC club of Brazil, Russia, India and China, which it joined in 2010 (Kornegay, 2015; Roy, 2022). This was auspicious for South Africa's political economy given China's growing influence as the country's largest trading partner. South Africa's and other industrialising countries' marginalisation and *de facto* 'second-class citizenship' in the global system have been particularly concerning. All democratic South Africa's presidents have been outspoken about the roles of the World Bank and the International Monetary Fund in perpetuating crises and instability in developing countries through onerous lending conditionalities and structural adjustment policies. Since the Doha Development Agenda was adopted in 2001, South Africa has been an integral part of an axis of developing countries in the WTO trying to introduce greater balance, equity and fairness in global trade. The restructuring of the UN Security Council and reform of the UN system continue to be critical multilateral themes which support the South African state's political legitimacy and reformist impulses (Rose-Innes, 2020).

Two important elements of South Africa's South–South focus have been the Non-Aligned Movement (NAM), which South Africa joined in 1994, and BRICS, the group formed in 2008 with Brazil, Russia, India and China, with South Africa joining in December 2010. While the NAM is a shadow of its former self, meeting just once every three years (most recently in January 2024) with no programme in between these meetings, South Africa and other countries of the Global South continue using the NAM discourse. This was the case, for example, when South Africa and several other Global South states suggested that the Ukraine war has, perhaps, again sparked the spirit of non-alignment (Lamola, 2024).

In the August 2023 BRICS Summit hosted by South Africa, invitations were issued to six additional states to join: Argentina, Egypt, Ethiopia, Iran, Saudi Arabia and the United Arab Emirates. Argentina withdrew its application after a change of government. Indonesia joined in 2025. South Africa took credit for the expansion initiative, promoted as a move towards constructing a multi-polar world, an objective South Africa had championed since the mid-1990s (Ismail, 2023). The concerns of Mandela and other presidents about the World Bank, the International Monetary Fund and the World Trade Organization also found expression in BRICS creating the New Development Bank in 2016.

South Africa also joined the G20 as its only African member. While that body's normative voice has been muted, especially when it comes to the Global North's continued dominance of economic affairs, it has evolved into an important steering mechanism for managing crises and changes in the global economy (Naidu, 2015; Rose-Innes, 2020). South Africa successfully lobbied for African Union membership. Crucially, South Africa is hosting the G20 summit in 2025.

SUBSTANTIVE THEMES

The Department of International Relations and Cooperation (DIRCO) released its first White Paper on foreign policy, *Building a Better World: The Diplomacy of Ubuntu*, in May 2011. Building on the 1996 discussion document of its precursor, the Department of Foreign Affairs (DFA), it attempted to provide a strategic roadmap for shaping the principles and practice of foreign policy, and represented a synthetic audit of the learning curve that the South African state had to navigate since 1994. Below are selected themes which have animated this journey.

Institutional and diplomatic challenges

The letter and spirit of active internationalism required intensive restructuring of the institutional architecture of statecraft and foreign policy (DFA, 1999). By 1995, South Africa had established 93 resident overseas missions, and, indicating its continental emphasis, full diplomatic relations with 46 African countries. Additionally, by end-1994, 136 countries had diplomatic representation in South Africa. In the following two years, South Africa was re-admitted to or joined 16 multilateral organisations, concluded 86 bilateral agreements, and acceded to 21 multilateral treaties (Muller, 1997).

However, transforming the institutional culture was difficult, especially regarding racial and gender balances in the DFA. The post-apartheid state also grappled with multiple actors with variable influence on shaping, determining and implementing policy. This resulted in serious coordination problems between the Presidency, Parliament, and departments such as Trade and Industry, Defence, Intelligence, Finance and Environment. Academics, research institutes and non-governmental organisations provided critical scrutiny and debate, often straining relations with government (Le Pere and Vickers, 2004).

Beyond internal transformation, DFA, and particularly its successor, DIRCO, also had to deal with allegations of corrupt or embarrassing behaviour by officials; alleged wrongdoers included ambassadors and even a director-general. In 2016, for example, R118 million was paid to purchase a non-existent piece of land in New York City. The land was supposedly meant to house South Africa's diplomatic mission. After the scandal was exposed, both the DIRCO Director-General, Kgabo Mahoai, and its Chief Financial Officer, Caiphus Ramashau, were forced to resign (AmaShabalala, 2021). The deal was also wrapped up in tender disputes that resulted in DIRCO being taken to court. Mahoai claimed the payment had been approved by his predecessor, Jerry Matjila, and that the minister at the time, Maite Nkoana-Mashabane, had supported the deal (Fabricius, 2021).

Other controversies involved a scandal around possible 'irregular expenditure' of more than R500 million by a director-general (Mail & Guardian, 2013), and allegations at the Zondo Commission that diplomatic posts were 'sold' and improper appointments were made to ambassadorial posts (Masondo, 2022).

Multilateral challenge

The state's multilateral credentials have been enhanced by its principled commitment to 'norm entrepreneurship' (Geldenhuys, 2006; Nagar, 2022). As such, since 1994, South Africa has carefully cultivated its soft power in Africa and globally. The following are relevant examples (Nel et al., 2001):

- leading roles in the 1995 indefinite extension of the Nuclear Non-Proliferation Treaty, the 1997 Ottawa Process for banning land mines, and the 1998 adoption of the Rome Statute to establish the International Criminal Court;
- assisting with finalising the Treaty of Pelindaba, which declared Africa a nuclear weapons-free zone;
- its leading role in the New Agenda Coalition on nuclear disarmament, and its election to the standing UN Conference on Disarmament; and
- its critical influence in the Kimberley Process for regulating 'conflict diamonds'.

South Africa's soft power brand also benefited from regional and global conference and summit circuits (Van der Westhuizen, 2006), including hosting the UN AIDS Conference in 2000; the UN World Conference Against Racism in 2001; the AU inaugural summit in 2002; the UN World Summit on Sustainable Development in 2002; the UN Climate Change Conference of the Parties in 2011; the 5th BRICS Summit in 2013; the 15th BRICS Summit in 2023; and the 20th AGOA Forum in 2023.

This record contrasted with controversial tenures on the UN Security Council from 2007 to 2008, when South Africa refused to take firm positions on human rights violations in Zimbabwe and Myanmar; and again, with its *volte-face* on Libya during its 2011–2012 stint (DIRCO, 2007; Graham, 2016). South Africa's UN General Assembly voting abstentions in 2022 and 2023 on the Russia-Ukraine war were also controversial, and widely interpreted as thinly veiled pro-Russian partisanship. Furthermore, as highlighted by examples below, South Africa's accumulated soft power capital – particularly in Africa – was substantially eroded during the Jacob Zuma presidency (Tella, 2018; 2021).

Trade and economic diplomacy challenge

South Africa adopted an outward-looking trade and economic policy to reverse apartheid's legacies and to address the country's high levels of poverty, inequality and unemployment (Vickers, 2012a).

South Africa's engagements in Africa are framed by three concentric circles: the Southern African Customs Union (SACU), the Southern African Development Community (SADC), and the broader African continent (Alden and Le Pere, 2009; Partridge, 2013). In SACU, South Africa led negotiations to restructure the treaty to benefit the smaller and more fragile economies of Botswana, Lesotho, Namibia and eSwatini through a revised revenue-sharing formula. In SADC, it was prominent in reforming the region's trade and market regimes. It thus made major asymmetric trade commitments, especially regarding the reduction of industrial tariffs and addressing supply-side constraints in logistics and investment to offset regional trade imbalances. These commitments attempted to partly redress skewed economic benefits and unequal infrastructural development, which had arisen due to the legacies of apartheid and colonialism, which left South Africa in a stronger condition than some of its neighbours.

However, South Africa's African trade and economic conduct has been controversial (Vandome, 2022). Often labelled 'neo-mercantilist', it reproduced the six most competitive sectors in its economy – mining, retail, manufacturing and construction, financial and banking services, telecommunications, and hotels and tourism – across the continent's economic landscape. The perception persists that South Africa enjoys an unfair economic edge, and its companies often behave arrogantly and disrespectfully (Soko, 2021).

Peace and security challenge

The state's 'African Agenda' has had to address some difficult and intractable wars, conflicts and coups. The attraction and power of its transition endowed South Africa with the moral authority and prestige to play critical roles in conflict resolution and mediation (Mabera, 2022; Van Nieuwkerk, 2012), convincing the government that 'it is quite possible for opposing forces to enter into political dialogue to deal with their differences and to transform the lives of their people for the better', according to former Deputy Minister of International Relations and Cooperation, Ebrahim Ebrahim (Ebrahim, 2012). For example, it helped shape a new ethical frontier in the African Union (AU) with the framing of Article 4(h) of the AU's Peace and Security Protocol, which empowers the organisation to intervene in African countries where there are war crimes, crimes against humanity, genocides or coups. More difficult for South Africa has been its failed attempts to mediate in crises as diverse as those of the Democratic Republic of the Congo (DRC), Nigeria, Lesotho, Zimbabwe, Sudan and Côte d'Ivoire (Lalbahadur and Van Nieuwkerk, 2020).

Major peacekeeping deployments started in 2002, with 650 troops sent to Burundi and 1,270 to the DRC in 2003. By the end 2003, 2,300 South African peacekeepers had been deployed across Africa. The number has since grown. By May 2008, there were 3,000 troops in AU and UN missions in Burundi, the DRC, Côte d'Ivoire, Darfur, Eritrea/Ethiopia and Uganda, making South Africa the 17th largest contributor to UN peacekeeping initiatives. More recently, there have been expanded but problematic peace support missions in Lesotho, Mozambique and the DRC.

These contributions to the continent's peace and security contend, however, with South Africa's controversial arms sales to conflict-affected states such as Rwanda and Sudan and those with questionable human rights records such as Algeria, Angola, Chad, Colombia, Syria and Indonesia (Shelton, 1998). By 1994, South Africa owned the 10th largest arms industry in the world; by 1997, it was selling weapons to 61 countries, reaping R1.2 billion in export earnings. Notwithstanding oversight by the National Conventional Arms Control Committee, arms sales to dubious clients continue, revealing loopholes in the system of approval (Landsberg, 2010).

Development aid challenge

As an emerging donor country, South Africa made major commitments, mainly in Africa. Its bilateral and multilateral aid programmes surpassed the UN target of 0.7 per cent of GDP. By one estimate, South Africa had contributed between R7.3 billion and R9.5 billion to its African assistance initiatives by 2010 (Vickers, 2012b). Most of these funds were for peacekeeping obligations.

The DFA set up the African Renaissance and International Cooperation Fund in 2000 to manage aspects of South Africa's development assistance programme. Its initial capital of R210 million was expanded to fund projects worth R1.1 billion by 2012/2013 (DIRCO, 2014), including support for Zimbabwean elections; the Burundian peace process; post-conflict reconstruction in the DRC and Comoros; humanitarian assistance in Western Sahara; public administration capacity in South Sudan; the AU Commission on Terrorism in Africa; preservation of ancient Timbuktu manuscripts in Mali; and financing of a conference on united cities and local government in Africa. While it is mainly African countries that enjoy the bulk of South Africa's development assistance, there are also other beneficiaries, such as Cuba to help offset the consequences of the US blockade, and Turkey for relief after the 2023 earthquake.

To improve DIRCO's assistance mechanisms, the South African Development Partnership Agency (SADPA) was established in 2009 to replace the Fund. Although its key objective is to improve the harmonisation, coordination and rationalisation of activities, SADPA's functional and operational effectiveness is questionable. Henceforth, emphasis will be shifted to promoting socioeconomic development and good governance, supporting peace and post-conflict reconstruction and strengthening SADC regional integration (Besharati, 2013).

CRITICAL CONSIDERATIONS

South Africa's post-1994 foreign policy has been challenged by attempts to act within both idealist and realist frameworks. Consequently, its foreign policy is often criticised as inconsistent. This is seen in the tension between normative ambition and realpolitik that characterises South Africa's international relations. President Mandela's statement that '(h)uman rights will be the light that guides our foreign policy' (Mandela, 1993: 86) initially established the character of South Africa's diplomacy. However, it soon confronted the cold realities of international relations, and the ANC government 'found that in practice, financial, commercial, and defence interests form stronger lobbies than the human rights community' (Manby, 2000: 372).

National interest framework

While South Africa has wrestled with understanding its core national interest since 1994 (Maimela, 2019), it was articulated in a single coherent text only in 2022, in the 'Framework Document on South Africa's National Interest and its advancement in a Global Environment' (DIRCO, 2022c). Since national interest concerns all aspects of a state's operations, it would be expected that a national interest position would be formulated at the most senior strategic level in government; in South Africa, that would be the Presidency. The Framework Document, however, was formulated by DIRCO, suggesting more of an international relations focus. Indications are that it therefore did not enjoy broad government support, especially from the security sector which is centrally involved in international relations but which felt excluded from contributing to the document (Masters and Landsberg, 2024).

The document says little that is new; it proposes to explicate the pursuit of South Africa's national interest 'in the domestic and global environment' (DIRCO, 2022c: 3) based on the country's needs, which 'include the eradication of the legacy of apartheid and overcoming the triple challenges of inequality, unemployment and poverty' (DIRCO, 2022c: 2). South Africa's national interest is: 'The protection and promotion of its national sovereignty and constitutional order, the well-being, safety and prosperity of its citizens, and a better Africa and world' (DIRCO, 2022c: 9). The definition suggests a blend of realist and domestic concerns, complicated by idealist and global underpinnings.

The Framework Document's idealism is prominent in the section 'A better Africa and world', which asserts that South Africa's 'normative posture' is derived from its constitutional values of human dignity, equality, human rights, non-racialism, non-sexism and democracy. These values, it states, are based on the anti-apartheid struggle and the democratic transition. The national interest, therefore, 'favours human rights, the peaceful settlement of disputes, transitional justice, respect for international law and norms and collective action through multilateral organs' (DIRCO, 2022c: 15).

Norm entrepreneurship: International law

Together with several other states, particularly Global South ones, South Africa has long championed a multi-polar and multilateral global system anchored to international law. The focus on international law was foregrounded in 2023 when South Africa instituted proceedings against Israel at the International Court of Justice (ICJ). On 29 December 2023, the ICJ announced (ICJ, 2023) that South Africa had requested it to rule on whether Israel was guilty of genocide under the Convention on the Prevention and Punishment of the Crime of Genocide (UNGA, 1948), and to indicate provisional measures against Israel. This followed strong condemnation from South Africa on Israel's actions in Gaza from October 2023, as indicated by numerous statements and speeches; the demarche of the Israeli ambassador; UN statements; the withdrawal of diplomats from Tel Aviv; and a parliamentary resolution calling on the government to shut down the South African embassy in Israel and to expel the Israeli ambassador from Pretoria (Jeenah, 2023).

The Court's ruling on 26 January 2024 upheld almost all of South Africa's assertions and granted almost all the provisional measures requested (ICJ, 2024). South Africa made three further requests to the Court for provisional measures, on 12 February 2024, 6 March 2024 and 10 May 2024. Each time, the Court accepted most of South Africa's arguments and indicated most of the provisional measures requested.

Although Israel has, to date, not abided by any of the Court's rulings or provisional measures, the South African case and the meticulousness of its presentation on all four occasions and in its memorial gained it enormous respect globally, from many governments as well as large sections of global civil society. The support was so overwhelming that when the Government of National Unity (GNU) was formed after the May 2024 elections, the Democratic Alliance, the second-largest party in Parliament, with established pro-Israeli credentials, announced that it would not seek the withdrawal of the ICJ case. The DA leader, John Steenhuisen, had already made this intention clear even before the election (Feinberg, 2024). As a result of the ICJ case, 'For much of the world, Pretoria has restored its reputation as a moral beacon' (Polakow-Suransky, 2024). The announcement of the case was also met with stinging criticism from many allies of Israel, and governments of the Global North, in general, either criticised the case or did not comment. That, however, changed over time as Israel's actions in Gaza became increasingly egregious so that, within less than 18 months, several governments had joined the case, including Spain and Ireland.

Normative ambition vs practice: Case studies
Despite its idealist 'normative posture', the realisation of the Framework Document on South Africa's National Interest has fallen short of the document's claims and the policies of all administrations since 1994. This has compromised South Africa's influence on the global stage, especially since early 2010. The Framework Document acknowledges this, saying that South Africa's foreign policy practitioners 'face the task of *restoring* and maintaining South Africa's image, stature, moral high ground and standing in the region, the continent and in global affairs' (DIRCO, 2022c: 8, emphasis added). The cases highlight how this resulted from missteps, failures and miscalculations over the past three decades.

Navigating the AU and Africa
South Africa graduated from being a pre-1994 pariah to becoming a leading country in Africa, particularly through President Mbeki's

leadership (Makgetlaneng, 2022). However, since 2010, its image in Africa has declined. This was despite several positions and actions that won the country plaudits, such as involvement in peacekeeping missions, its role in mediating peace in Darfur, and resolving the South Sudan question.

In 2011–2012, South Africa's reputation in Africa was severely compromised. An unwritten convention among the 'Big Five' African states – Algeria, Egypt, Nigeria, Libya, South Africa – committed them not to contest the position of AU Commission Chair. There was also an implicit understanding among member states that senior AU posts would not be occupied by persons from the same linguistic zone. Nevertheless, South Africa nominated former Foreign Minister, Nkosazana Dlamini-Zuma, for AU Commission Chair, to run against the incumbent, Gabon's Jean Ping (Amimo, 2016).

This caused resentment from most Francophone countries, which favoured Ping, among heavyweights such as Nigeria and Egypt, and even upset SADC member states. One southern African state representative said South Africa 'perpetuates the feeling that we [SADC] are not taken seriously. We are just there to rubberstamp South Africa's decisions rather than being part of the whole issue' (Lalbahadur, 2015: 10). South Africa thus alienated one of its closest concentric circles.

Central African Republic misadventure

In March 2013, 13 South African soldiers were killed in the Central African Republic (CAR) during a coup by Séléka rebels who overthrew President Francois Bozize. This was the highest number of South African National Defence Force (SANDF) soldiers killed in a single incident since 1994. Most South Africans were surprised that soldiers had been deployed to CAR, and there is still no clarity on their purpose. Opposition parties and the South African National Defence Union demanded answers (De Wet, 2013), unsuccessfully.

At a memorial service for the 13 soldiers, President Zuma repeatedly invoked the 'national interest' – both to justify the SANDF presence in CAR, and to obfuscate the purpose of their deployment. The Presidency and DIRCO provided contradictory reasons (Patel, 2013).

There seemed to be no United Nations or AU call for the deployment of fighting troops in the country. Later investigations suggested the soldiers' mission had been to protect private business interests linked to some ANC leaders (AmaBhungane, 2013; Lustig, 2013).

This episode led many to believe that President Zuma might have been 'using the South African military as a private security service to protect his and his cronies' international business interests' (Lustig, 2013). Despite DIRCO's denials, many on the continent accused South Africa of treating other African countries as targets for criminal extractivism as former colonial powers had done (Patel, 2013). The disquiet worsened after a South African soldier mentioned the horror of SANDF members killing children (Campbell, 2013) and questions were raised about the SANDF's capacity and ability to serve as peacekeepers (Lustig, 2013).

Xenophobia

Persistent attacks directed against nationals from other, especially African, countries resulted in a deterioration of South Africa's status and image across the continent, and in its relations with African states whose nationals have been the main victims. This was compounded by the government's desultory response to these attacks, even though as early as 2007, the APRM had warned of rising xenophobia in South Africa. Its forebodings were realised in May 2008, when the country erupted in xenophobic violence that left at least 60 people dead.

Almost every year since then, with spikes in 2011, 2013, 2015, 2017, 2019 and 2022, there have been attacks against those perceived as illegal foreigners – mostly Africans but also Pakistanis and Bangladeshis, many of whom are naturalised.

Government's 2008 response was a mixture of blaming criminals, referring to a 'third hand', and attributing the attacks to anti-ANC electioneering (Mhlana et al., 2008). The assaults raised concern in other African countries, especially since many had provided funding and support to the erstwhile South African liberation movement and hosted its exiles, often at great cost to their own countries and citizens (Hassim et al., 2008). Although the 2008 response from other African states was 'muted', criticism of subsequent violence, especially from

2015, was more strident (Saunders, 2021).

By the mid-2010s South Africa's gravitas, gained through its supposedly miraculous transition to democracy, had all but evaporated. It might proclaim that its foreign policy is based on the promotion of human rights and democracy, but other Africans seem no longer convinced. Notably, the Framework Document, released shortly after the 2022 xenophobic violence, acknowledges: 'It is [the] inherited psyche of racial prejudice, breakdown in values, inequality of opportunity and massive poverty, as well as competition for scarce resources, which help fuel racism and, more recently, xenophobia' (DIRCO, 2022c: 10).

Other cases

There are three other cases where South Africa struggled to sustain the claim that its foreign policy was guided by constitutional values of human rights and democracy: the Dalai Lama visa debacle, the 'Guptagate' scandal and the Russia-Ukraine war.

The Dalai Lama's failed attempts to visit South Africa resulted in global opprobrium. The Tibetan leader had visited the country in 1996 and 1999, but thrice thereafter – in 2009, 2011 and 2014 – South African authorities denied him a visa, with no cogent reasons provided.

In 2009 and 2014, the Dalai Lama was to participate in conferences of Nobel peace laureates; in 2011, he was to attend the 80th birthday celebrations of Archbishop Desmond Tutu. After the 2011 denial, Tutu railed against the government and the ANC, likening them to the apartheid government. Ela Gandhi, who was to present the Dalai Lama with a peace prize named after her grandfather, Mahatma Gandhi, expressed a commonly held view: 'Everybody thinks this is because of pressure from China. It's very sad that another country is allowed to dictate terms to our government. It's going back to apartheid times. I am ashamed of my own country' (Smith, 2011). The assertion about external duress is reinforced by the fact that when the Dalai Lama visited in 1999 and met Mandela, the South African president had stated that there had been Chinese pressure on him not to meet the Tibetan leader. The global perception was that South Africa had placed economic benefit over its claimed adherence to human rights.

The second case, which harmed South Africa's image globally, relates to revelations in 2013 that guests for a Gupta family wedding had flown in from India to the Waterkloof Air Base near Pretoria, a military installation not equipped to receive tourists. Several questions were raised about why permission had been granted for the irregular landing, which ignored established procedures (Masuabi, 2022).

The incident provoked numerous media investigations that uncovered 'state capture' and the Gupta family's role in corrupting and influencing government departments, state institutions and state-owned enterprises for financial gain. This is detailed in the report of the Judicial Commission of Inquiry into Allegations of State Capture, commonly referred to as the Zondo Commission.[1] The scandal that followed, the exposés on 'state capture', and the Commission's hearings over four years played out in the international media. This negatively affected investor confidence and placed South Africa close to the top of corruption indices, including Transparency International's Corruption Perceptions Index. South Africa's reputation abroad was dented, including its claims to adhere to high standards of human rights, democracy and ethical practice.

As the responsible department, DIRCO managed the incident poorly, viewed by many as a cover-up. Bruce Koloane, the Chief of State Protocol who had approved the landing, was 'demoted' and then promptly 'promoted' to become ambassador to the Netherlands.[2] His reassignment highlighted another way the country's international relations were abused for personal gain. In that period, several questionable ambassadorial appointments were made.

The third case concerns the Ramaphosa government's approach to the Russia-Ukraine war since February 2022, in particular, its tortuous attempts to explain its views on non-alignment and neutrality.

---

1   The role of the Gupta family in state capture is peppered throughout most of the six parts and 19 volumes of the Zondo Commission report. The full report is accessible at: Commission of Inquiry into State Capture, https://www.statecapture.org.za/site/information/reports

2   In that period, several questionable ambassadorial appointments were made, with suggestions that up to 80 per cent of ambassadors were political appointees rather than career diplomats, to accord with President Zuma's various personal agendas (Fabricius, 2020).

Although, over time, South Africa's position on Russia's invasion of Ukraine and the resultant war became more coherent, initial reactions reflected the tension between South Africa's normative aspirations and the demands of *realpolitik* that often drive its foreign policy. Immediately after the Russian invasion, both the ANC's International Relations Subcommittee and DIRCO issued statements calling for a diplomatic and peaceful resolution (DIRCO, 2022a), while many within civil society and the ANC expected a more assertive approach.

Soon thereafter, DIRCO issued a second, very contentious, statement – which has been removed from its website. Echoing South Africa's normative position on territorial sovereignty and the peaceful resolution of conflicts, it called on Russia to respect Ukrainian sovereignty and to withdraw its troops from Ukraine (Fabricius, 2022). However, the media reported that Ramaphosa was 'unhappy' about the statement. One report quoted an unnamed government official accusing individuals in DIRCO of wanting South Africa to 'be enemies with Russia' (Khoza and Madisa, 2022). A subsequent ANC leadership meeting tried to iron out the differences (Tandwa, 2022). DIRCO backtracked (Citizen Reporter, 2022), an unmistakable indication that realpolitik had won the day.

Between March 2022 and March 2023, South Africa abstained from voting on six resolutions tabled at Special Sessions of the UN General Assembly. These, together with South Africa's seemingly equivocal and ambivalent position on the war, highlighted the tension between its professed normative posture and realpolitik. Government defence of its position ranged from a professed non-alignment to calling for implementation of the Minsk Agreements of 2014 and 2015 (DIRCO, 2022b). Less generous commentary suggested Ramaphosa's disposition was based on his personal chemistry with Russia's President Vladimir Putin, complemented by the countries' BRICS membership (Mathekga, 2023).

CONCLUSION

South Africa's democratic transition highlights limitations in the state's ability to act in an international, and especially African, milieu where sovereignty remains sacred. South Africa may have the trappings of an emerging power, but it has struggled to translate this into long-term gains. Together with some successes, there have been a series of missteps, failures and miscalculations in dealing with critical realpolitik challenges in the country's attempted activist role as a global 'norm entrepreneur'. South Africa confronts serious deficits and shortcomings, which include weak diplomatic capacity to fulfil its foreign policy ambitions; the relative decline of its moral power and ethical influence in Africa and globally; and missed opportunities in trade and investment because of its troubled domestic situation.

The challenge for South Africa remains how to sustain a purposeful, coherent and cohesive foreign policy that balances its pragmatic and normative imperatives. This again raises questions about a clearer articulation of its inchoate definition of the country's national interest. South Africa's calculus is based on a tense dialectic of promoting a stable and prosperous domestic environment which, in turn, must confront the vicissitudes of an increasingly unstable, divisive and disenchanted world. It might, therefore, be appropriate to end with an injunction by Hans Morgenthau (1951: 241), the doyen of realism in world politics:

> Diplomacy without power is feeble, and power without diplomacy is destructive and blind… [N]o nation's power is without limits, and hence its policies must respect the power and interests of others.

REFERENCES

Alden, C. and Le Pere, G. 2003. 'South Africa's Post-Apartheid Foreign Policy: From Reconciliation to Revival'. Adelphi Paper No. 362, The International Institute for Strategic Studies, London.

Alden, C. and Le Pere, G. 2009. 'South Africa in Africa: Bound to lead?'. *Politikon*, 36(1), 145–169.

AmaBhungane. 2013. 'Central African Republic: Is this what our soldiers died for?'. *Mail & Guardian,* 28 March, https://mg.co.za/article/2013-03-28-00-central-african-republic-is-this-what-our-soldiers-died-for, accessed 8 November 2023.

AmaShabalala. 2021. 'DIRCO finance boss shown the door over R118m New

York land scandal'. *TimesLive,* 4 October, https://www.timeslive.co.za/
politics/2021-10-04-dirco-finance-boss-shown-the-door-over-r118m-
new-york-land-scandal, accessed 30 June 2024.

Amimo, U. 2016. 'Dlamini-Zuma: Reformer or remote leader'. *City Press,*
17 July, https://www.news24.com/citypress/News/dlamini-zuma-
reformer-or-remote-leader-20160717, accessed 8 November 2023.

Besharati, N.A. 2013. 'South African Development Partnership Agency
(SADPA): Strategic aid or development packages for Africa?'. Research
Report 12, South African Institute of International Affairs, Johannesburg.

Block, R. 1995. 'When Mandela went missing'. *The Independent,* 21
November, https://www.independent.co.uk/voices/when-mandela-went-
missing-1582997.html, accessed 8 November 2023.

Butler, A. 2011. 'State capacity and political accountability in post-apartheid
South Africa', in Plaatjies, D. (ed.), *Future Inheritance: Building State
Capacity in Democratic South Africa.* Johannesburg: Jacana Media,
pp. 25–57.

Campbell, J. 2013. 'Why were South African soldiers in the Central African
Republic?'. Council on Foreign Relations, 2 April, https://www.cfr.org/
blog/why-were-south-african-soldiers-central-african-republic, accessed
8 November 2023.

Chikane, F. 2001. 'Integrated Democratic Governance: A Restructured
Presidency at Work'. Office of the Presidency, https://www.goz.za/
reports/2001/presidency.doc/, accessed 13 May 2024.

Citizen Reporter. 2022. '"We don't take any side": Dirco denies backtracking
on Russia-Ukraine conflict'. *The Citizen,* https://www.citizen.co.za/
news/south-africa/dirco-russia-ukraine-invasion-5-march-2022, accessed
8 November 2023.

Cornelissen, S. 2021. 'The future of African multilateralism post COVID-19',
in Le Pere, G. and Van Nieuwkerk, A. (eds), *South Africa's Africa
Agenda: Prospects and challenges.* Johannesburg: Friedrich Ebert Stiftung,
pp. 51–58.

De Wet, P. 2013. 'DA wants SA's Central African Republic troops home'. *Mail
& Guardian,* 1 April, https://mg.co.za/article/2013-04-01-da-wants-sas-
central-african-republic-troops-home, accessed 10 May 2024.

Department of Foreign Affairs (DFA). 1996. *South African Foreign Policy
Discussion Document.* Pretoria: DFA.

Department of Foreign Affairs (DFA). 1999. *Thematic Reviews: Strategic
Planning.* Pretoria: DFA.

Department of International Relations and Cooperation (DIRCO). 2007.
'South Africa's vote on Myanmar: Frequently asked questions and
answers', http://www.dirco.gov.za/docs/2007/myan0206.htm, accessed 10
May 2024.

Department of International Relations and Cooperation (DIRCO). 2014.

'Annual Report of the African Renaissance and International Cooperation Fund — 2013/2014', https://static.pmg.org.za/141016dirco_aric_a-report.pdf, accessed 8 November 2023.

Department of International Relations and Cooperation (DIRCO). 2022a. 'South African Government calls for a peaceful resolution of the escalating conflict between the Russian Federation and Ukraine', https://www.dirco.gov.za/south-african-government-calls-for-a-peaceful-resolution-of-the-escalating-conflict-between-the-russian-federation-and-ukraine, accessed 1 December 2023.

Department of International Relations and Cooperation (DIRCO). 2022b. 'Government on Emergency United Nations General Assembly Special Session on Ukraine', https://www.gov.za/news/media-statements/government-emergency-united-nations-general-assembly-special-session-ukraine, accessed 26 July 2024.

Department of International Relations and Cooperation (DIRCO). 2022c. 'Framework Document on South Africa's National Interest and its advancement in the Global Environment', https://www.dirco.gov.za/national-interest-framework-doc, accessed 8 November 2023.

Ebrahim, E. 2012. 'Foreword', in Jeenah, N. (ed.). *Pretending Democracy: Israel, an Ethnocratic State,* Johannesburg: Afro-Middle East Centre, p. v.

Fabricius, P. 2020. 'Political appointees trump career diplomats in new postings'. *Daily Maverick*, 4 September, https://www.dailymaverick.co.za/article/2020-09-04-political-appointees-trump-career-diplomats-in-new-postings, accessed 15 June 2025.

Fabricius, P. 2021. 'DA says Naledi Pandor is scapegoating fired director-general over a property scandal'. *Daily Maverick,* 10 September, https://www.dailymaverick.co.za/article/2021-09-10-da-says-naledi-pandor-is-scapegoating-fired-director-general-over-a-property-scandal, accessed 30 June 2024.

Fabricius, P. 2022. 'Pretoria scrambles to repair relations with Russia after calling for invasion forces to leave Ukraine'. *Daily Maverick*, https://www.dailymaverick.co.za/article/2022-02-27-pretoria-scrambles-to-repair-relations-with-russia-after-calling-for-invasion-force-to-leave-ukraine, accessed 8 November 2023.

Feinberg, T. 2024. 'DA double speak: Steenhuisen trips over Gaza question'. *South African Jewish Report,* 28 March, https://www.sajr.co.za/da-double-speak-steenhuisen-trips-over-gaza-question.

Ferguson, Y.H. and Mansbach, R.W. 2004. *Remapping Global Politics: History's Revenge and Future Shock.* Cambridge, UK: Cambridge University Press.

Firsing, S. and Masters, L. 2015. 'South African foreign policy and the West: The art of foreign policy balancing', in Masters, L., Zondi, S., Van Wyk, J.A. and Landsberg, C. (eds), *South African Foreign Policy Review — Volume 2.* Pretoria: African Institute of South Africa, pp. 208–230.

Frankel, J. 1968. *The Making of Foreign Policy.* London: Oxford University Press.

Geldenhuys, D. 2006. 'South Africa's role as international norm entrepreneur', in Carlsnaes, W. and Nel, P. (eds), *In Full Flight: South African Foreign Policy after Apartheid.* Midrand: Institute for Global Dialogue, pp. 93–107.

Graham, S. 2016. *Democratic South Africa's Foreign Policy: Voting Behaviour in the United Nations.* London: Palgrave Macmillan.

Hassim S., Kupe, T. and Worby, E. (eds). 2008. *Go Home or Die Here: Violence, Xenophobia and the Reinvention of Difference in South Africa.* Johannesburg: Wits University Press.

Hendricks, C. 2022. 'South Africa's quest for continental peace and security', in Masters, L., Van Wyk, J. and Mthembu, P. (eds), *The South African Foreign Policy Review Volume 4: Ramaphosa and a New Dawn for South African Foreign Policy.* Pretoria: Africa Institute of South Africa Press, pp. 219–235.

International Court of Justice. 2023. 'The Republic of South Africa institutes proceedings against the State of Israel and requests the Court to indicate provisional measures'. 29 December, https://icj-cij.org/sites/default/files/case-related/192/192-20231229-pre-01-00-en.pdf

International Court of Justice. 2024. 'Order: Application of the Convention on the Prevention and Punishment of the Crime of Genocide in the Gaza Strip (South Africa v. Israel)'. 26 January, https://icj-cij.org/sites/default/files/case-related/192/192-20240126-ord-01-00-en.pdf

Ismail, S. 2023. 'Saudi Arabia, Iran among six nations invited to join BRICS'. *Al Jazeera,* 24 August, https://www.aljazeera.com/economy/2023/8/24/saudi-arabia-iran-to-join-brics-as-grouping-admits-six-new-members, accessed 25 June 2025.

Jeenah, N. 2023. 'Democratic South Africa's relations with Israel and Palestine'. Mapungubwe Institute for Strategic Reflection, MISTRA Briefing Paper, 20 March, https://mistra.org.za/wp-content/uploads/2024/03/BRIEIFING-PAPER-South-Africas-relations-with-Israel-and-Palestine-FINAL-March-2024.pdf, accessed 25 June 2025.

Khoza, A. and Madisa, K. 2022. 'Ramaphosa "unhappy" over SA's Russia invasion flip-flop'. *The Sunday Times,* https://www.timeslive.co.za/sunday-times/news/2022-02-27-ramaphosa-unhappy-over-sas-russia-invasion-flip-flop, accessed 8 November 2023.

Kornegay, F. 2015. 'South Africa and the global South in critical perspective: 1994–2014', in Masters, L., Zondi, S., Van Wyk, J. and Landsberg, C. (eds), *South African Foreign Policy Review: Volume 2.* Pretoria: Africa Institute of South Africa, pp. 231–251.

Lalbahadur, A. 2015. 'South Africa's foreign policy: Tempering dominance through integration'. South African Institute of International Affairs, Occasional Paper 213, https://www.jstor.org/stable/resrep25891, accessed

8 November 2023.

Lalbahadur, A. and Van Nieuwkerk, A. 2020. 'South Africa's security interests in Africa: Recommendations for the 2020s', in Bradlow, D.D. and Sidiropoulos, E. (eds), *Values, Interests and Power: South African Foreign Policy in Uncertain Times*. Pretoria: Pretoria University Law Press, pp. 93–116.

Lamola, R. 2024. 'Address by DIRCO Minister Ronald Lamola on SA Foreign Policy'. South African Institute of International Affairs, Cape Town, 11 July, https://saiia.org.za/research/address-by-dirco-minister-ronald-lamola-on-sas-foreign-policy, accessed 25 June 2025.

Landsberg, C. 2010. *The Diplomacy of Transformation: South African Foreign Policy and Statecraft*. Johannesburg: Macmillan.

Landsberg, C. 2015. 'Sub-continental entente: Twenty years of South Africa's SADC strategy', in Masters, L., Zondi, S., Van Wyk, J. and Landsberg, C. (eds), *South African Foreign Policy Review: Volume 2*. Pretoria: Africa Institute of South Africa, pp. 119–142.

Le Pere, G. and Vickers, B. 2004. 'Civil society and foreign policy', in Nel, P. and Van der Westhuizen, J. (eds), *Democratizing Foreign Policy? Lessons from South Africa*. Lanham, Maryland: Lexington Books, pp. 63–80.

Lustig, H. 2013. 'What was the South African military doing in the Central African Republic?'. *Vice,* 25 April, https://www.vice.com/en/article/dp4md7/what-were-the-south-african-military-up-to-in-central-african-republic, accessed 8 November 2023.

Mabera, F. 2022. 'South Africa's defence diplomacy: A viable instrument of foreign and security policy', in Masters, L., Van Wyk, J. and Mthembu, P. (eds), *The South African Foreign Policy Review – Volume 4: Ramaphosa and a New Dawn for South African Foreign Policy*. Pretoria: Africa Institute of South Africa Press, pp. 151–175.

Mail & Guardian. 2013. 'Matjila on special leave after half-a-billion rand corruption charge'. *Mail & Guardian,* 19 September, https://mg.co.za/article/2013-09-19-matjila-on-special-leave-after-half-a-billion-rand-corruption-charge, accessed 25 June 2025.

Maimela, D. 2019. 'South Africa's national interests in Africa during the Mbeki years, 1999–2008'. MA dissertation, ResearchGate, https://www.researchgate.net/publication/352545820_SOUTH_AFRICA'S_NATIONAL_INTERESTS_IN_AFRICA_DURING_THE_MBEKI_YEARS_1999-2008, accessed 8 November 2023.

Makgetlaneng, S. 2022. *The African Renaissance Project of Thabo Mbeki: Its South African Roots and Targets*. Pretoria: The Institute for Preservation and Development.

Manby, B. 2000. 'Human rights and South Africa's foreign policy: A guiding light or a flickering candle?'. *South African Journal on Human Rights,* 16(2), 372–401.

Mandela, N. 1993. 'South African Foreign Policy'. *Foreign Affairs*, 72(5), 86–97.

Masondo, S. 2022. 'Jobs-for-pals at Dirco? ANC sold posts for kickbacks, career diplomats tell Zondo'. *News24*, 23 April, https://www.news24.com/news24/investigations/jobs-for-pals-at-dirco-anc-sold-posts-for-kickbacks-career-diplomats-tell-zondo-20220423, accessed 25 June 2025.

Masters, L. and Landsberg, C. 2024. 'South Africa foreign policy and the national interest: Which interest?'. *Revista Brasileira de Política Internacional*, September, https://www.scielo.br/j/rbpi/a/CLqD355vmg8Jf7BK7NL3bpH, accessed 30 June 2025.

Masuabi, Q. 2022. 'The Guptas' Waterkloof landing symbolises their influence'. *City Press*, 2 May, https://www.news24.com/citypress/news/the-guptas-waterkloof-landing-symbolises-their-influence-20220502, accessed 8 November 2023.

Mathekga, R. 2023. 'South Africa's Russian ties come under scrutiny'. GIS Reports, 20 June, https://www.gisreportsonline.com/r/south-africa-russia-war/, accessed 10 May 2024.

Mbeki, T. 2021. 'South Africa's role in Africa: Looking back and forward', in Le Pere, G. and Van Nieuwkerk, A. (eds), *South Africa's Africa Agenda: Prospects and challenges*. Johannesburg: Friedrich Ebert Stiftung, pp. 14–20.

Mhlana, Z., Tolsi, N. and Alcock, S.S. 2008. '"Third force" allegations abound'. *Mail & Guardian*, https://mg.co.za/article/2008-05-23-third-force-allegations-abound, accessed 8 November 2023.

Mondi, L. 2020. 'South Africa and African continental economic integration in the 2020s', in Bradlow, D.D. and Sidiropoulos, E. (eds), *Values, Interests and Power: South African Foreign Policy In Uncertain Times*. Pretoria: Pretoria University Law Press, pp. 160–177.

Morgenthau, H. 1951, *In Defense of the National Interest: A Critical Examination of American Foreign Policy*. New York: Alfred A Knopf.

Muller, M. 1997. 'The institutional dimension: The Department of Foreign Affairs and Overseas Missions', in Carlsnaes, W. and Muller, M. (eds), *Change and South Africa's External Relations*. Johannesburg: International Thomson Publishing, pp. 51–72.

Nagar, M. 2022. 'The art of reconciling power and morality: South Africa's norm entrepreneurship under Cyril Ramaphosa', in Masters, L., Van Wyk, J. and Mthembu, P. (eds), *The South African Foreign Policy Review—Volume 4: Ramaphosa and a New Dawn for South African Foreign Policy*. Pretoria: Africa Institute of South Africa Press, pp. 61–86.

Naidu, S. 2015. 'Understanding South Africa's global governance identity', in Masters, L., Zondi, S., Van Wyk, J. and Landsberg, C. (eds), *South African Foreign Policy Review: Volume 2*. Pretoria: Africa Institute of South Africa, pp. 59–72.

Nel, P. 2006. 'The power of ideas: "Ambiguous globalism" and South Africa's foreign policy', in Carlsnaes, W. and Nel, P. (eds), *In Full Flight: South African Foreign Policy after Apartheid*. Midrand: Institute for Global Dialogue, pp. 108–121.

Nel, P., Taylor, I. and Van der Westhuizen, J. (eds). 2001. *South Africa's Multilateralism and Global Change: The Limits of Reformism*. Basingstoke: Ashgate Publishers.

Nkhonjera, M. and Roberts, S. 2020. 'Regional integration and industrial development in Southern Africa: Where does South Africa stand?', in Bradlow, D.D. and Sidiropoulos, E. (eds), *Values, Interests and Power: South African Foreign Policy in Uncertain Times*. Pretoria: Pretoria University Law Press, pp. 140–159.

Partridge, A. 2 October 2013. 'Africa-South Africa trading relationship'. Policy Brief, The Trade Law Centre, Cape Town.

Patel, K. 2013. 'SA troops killed in Central African Republic: Why, Mr President?'. *Daily Maverick,* https://www.dailymaverick.co.za/article/2013-03-25-sa-troops-killed-in-central-african-republic-why-mr-president, accessed 8 November 2023.

Polakow-Suransky, S. 2024. 'What South Africa really won at the ICJ'. *Foreign Policy,* 1 February, accessed 25 June 2025.

Rose-Innes, C. 2020. 'Reforming the institutions of global economic governance and South Africa', in Bradlow, D.D. and Sidiropoulos, E. (eds), *Values, Interests and Power: South African Foreign Policy in Uncertain Times*. Pretoria: Pretoria University Law Press, pp. 200–229.

Roy, I. 2022. 'Southern multilateralism: Complementary competition vis-à-vis the liberal international order'. *Global Perspectives,* 3(1), https://doi.org/10.1525/gp2022.39589, accessed 9 May 2024.

Saunders, C. 2021. 'African responses to xenophobic attacks in South Africa in the context of Pan-Africanism', in Abidde, S.O. and Matambo, E.K. (eds), *Xenophobia, Nativism and Pan-Africanism in 21st-Century Africa*. Cham, Switzerland: Springer, pp. 157–171.

Seidman Makgetla, N. 2011. 'Improving the capacity of the state', in Plaatjies, D. (ed.), *Future Inheritance: Building State Capacity in Democratic South Africa*. Johannesburg: Jacana Media, pp. 236–251.

Shelton, G. 1998. 'South African arm sales to Africa and the Middle East: Promoting peace or fuelling the arms race?'. Occasional Paper, 16 October, Foundation for Global Dialogue, Johannesburg.

Smith, D. 2011. 'Desmond Tutu attacks South African government over Dalai Lama ban'. *The Guardian,* 5 October, https://www.theguardian.com/world/2011/oct/04/tutu-attacks-anc-dalai-lama-visa, accessed 8 November 2023.

Soko, M. 2021. *South Africa and the World: A Political Economy Journey Through Time*. Bryanston, SA: Tracey McDonald Publishers.

Tandwa, L. 2022. 'Top ANC officials to discuss SA's stance on Russia-Ukraine war'. *Mail & Guardian,* 28 February, https://mg.co.za/article/2022-02-28-top-anc-officials-to-discuss-sas-stance-on-russia-ukraine-war, accessed 8 November 2023.

Tella, O. 2018. 'Currencies, constraints and contradictions of South Africa's soft power'. *Journal of Asian and African Studies*, 53(3), 420–436.

Tella, O. 2021. *Africa's Soft Power: Philosophies, Political Values, Foreign Policies and Cultural Exports*. Routledge.

United Nations General Assembly (UNGA). 1948. 'Convention on the Prevention and Punishment of the Crime of Genocide'. General Assembly resolution 260 A (III), 9 December, https://www.ohchr.org/en/instruments-mechanisms/instruments/convention-prevention-and-punishment-crime-genocide, accessed 27 July 2024.

Van der Westhuizen, J. 2006. 'Pretoria and the global conference circuit: Hot air or hot stuff', in Carlsnaes, W. and Nel, P. (eds), *In Full Flight: South African Foreign Policy after Apartheid*. Midrand: Institute for Global Dialogue, pp. 137–146.

Vandome, C. 2022. 'South Africa's economic diplomacy in Africa', in Masters, L., Van Wyk, J. and Mthembu, P. (eds), *The South African Foreign Policy Review—Volume 4: Ramaphosa and a New Dawn for South African Foreign Policy*. Pretoria: Africa Institute of South Africa Press, pp. 253–274.

Van Nieuwkerk, A. 2012. 'A review of South Africa's peace diplomacy since 1994', in Landsberg, C. and Van Wyk, J. (eds), *South African Foreign Policy Review: Volume 1*, Pretoria: Africa Institute of South Africa, pp. 84–111.

Vickers, B. 2012a. 'South Africa's economic diplomacy in a changing world order', in Landsberg, C. and Van Wyk, J. (eds), *South African Foreign Policy Review: Volume 1*. Pretoria: Africa Institute of South Africa, pp. 112–138.

Vickers, B. 2012b. 'Towards a new aid paradigm: South Africa as an African development partner'. *Cambridge Review of International Affairs*, 25, 535–556.

FOURTEEN

Court of the people?
The judiciary and democracy
in post-1994 South Africa

Steven Friedman

Studies of the South African state rarely devote sustained attention to the judiciary; the state is often assumed to consist purely of the executive and legislature. While the judiciary may be mentioned in passing, it is rarely the subject of the same scholarly attention as the other two branches. But the judiciary is an essential element in any functioning state. And in constitutional democracies – such as South Africa – it plays an active role in setting the boundaries within which the other branches must operate and, at times, in instructing them to take action to meet their constitutional obligations. Studies of the state which ignore or minimise the role of the judiciary are, therefore, unable to offer an accurate and rounded account.

This chapter seeks to fill that gap. It treats the judiciary not only as an important branch of the South African state but as the state's most valuable asset. It has played a vital role in enhancing the state's legitimacy and in resolving conflicts which might, without the courts' intervention, have severely damaged the state. The chapter examines the implications of the judiciary's status for the future of the state and of the democratic system. It argues that, although the judiciary enjoys high legitimacy among those whose voices are heard in public debate, this does not necessarily extend to most of the population. Building legitimacy among the majority is thus an urgent priority. It argues too that the state's legitimacy among political and social actors is a double-edged sword because it encourages them to see the courts as a substitute for, rather than an essential support to, democratic politics. It examines ways in which the judiciary can deepen and broaden the state's legitimacy and that of the democracy promised by South Africa's Constitution.

AN ENVIABLE ASSET

To a considerable extent, the judiciary is the arm of the South African state which enjoys most legitimacy and credibility, at least among the roughly one-third of the country that dominates public debate.[1]

To say that an institution is legitimate does not necessarily mean that it is popular. Legitimacy is 'commonly defined in political science and sociology as the belief that a rule, institution, or leader has the right to govern' (Hurd, n.d.). Arms of the state are legitimate if their right to impose laws and regulations on citizens is recognised. Courts are accepted as legitimate if politicians, organised interest groups, and a significant section of the citizenry believe that the courts are entitled to settle disputes and to impose binding decisions on parties. Using this criterion, South African courts are accorded far more legitimacy than other arms of the state.

Court judgments and the judges who hand them down are treated with a respect that is rarely, if ever, given to the politicians and officials in the executive and legislative arms of the state. This regard for the law is a core feature of the democratic order established in 1994. It has created a hierarchy of courts: at its base are Magistrates' Courts;

---

1   For the argument on which the claim that around one-third of the country participates in public debate, see Friedman (2021).

more serious offences and civil disputes are tried in the High Courts of the nine provinces; and judgments can be appealed to the Supreme Court of Appeal. At the apex is the Constitutional Court, which also adjudicates constitutionality. The judicial system also includes an array of specialist courts, which include the Equality Court, the Electoral Court, the Labour Court, a Tax Court, a Children's Court, as well as special courts which judge sexual offences and commercial crimes (Department of Justice, n.d.).

It is assumed across the political and social spectrums that courts have the right to issue judgments, which must be implemented. The courts are routinely used to settle disputes between and within political parties and interest groups. The losers routinely accept the rulings and comply with them (or do their best to appear to comply). When courts rule against the government, which they often do, they are hailed as vital checks on executive power. Perhaps the clearest sign of the courts' legitimacy is that on the rare occasions on which they are questioned – as it was, most noticeably, by former President Jacob Zuma – those who challenge the courts' rights to decide continue to use them to protect their interests.

The courts have maintained their legitimacy despite controversies which seemed likely to undermine it. One is the lengthy scandal surrounding former Western Cape Judge John Hlophe, who was impeached after trying to persuade two Constitutional Court judges to find in favour of former President Zuma (Dentlinger, 2023). The other is the controversy surrounding former Chief Justice Mogoeng Mogoeng, who was censured and ordered to apologise for publicly supporting the Israeli state despite its repeated abuses of human rights, which are guaranteed by the South African Constitution (Hawker, 2022). In both cases, the public debate appeared to conclude that the conduct of individual judges did not reflect on the judiciary's integrity as an institution, even if the individuals concerned occupied senior positions.

Despite an oft-quoted 2018 Afrobarometer survey in which 32 per cent of respondents claimed that judicial officers were corrupt, and a claim at the Zondo Commission of Inquiry into State Capture that some judges received money to find in favour of former President

Zuma, '(t)here has never been any definite evidence of corruption by judges to support these perceptions' (Judges Matter, n.d.). This suggests that the Afrobarometer perceptions, which were recorded at the tail end of a 'state capture' period in which government was widely seen as corrupt, were based not on evidence but reflected cynicism about the morals of people in public office. There appears to be no research on why levels of corruption in the judiciary appear to be so low, but one possibility is that judges are senior legal practitioners who are usually affluent from having been practising lawyers, and who therefore do not need to use judicial office to enrich themselves. Whatever the reason, the lack of hard evidence of corruption obviously enhances the courts' legitimacy.

This legitimacy is particularly remarkable given the low credibility of other arms of the state (IJR, 2024). In recent years, a considerable part of the courts' legitimacy has stemmed from the fact that they are not associated with the state in the public mind, even though they are one of the three arms of the state. It is not uncommon for South Africans, including those with specialist knowledge, to assume that courts are a counterweight to 'the state', not a part of it. One example is the debate over the rights of people living in areas under the control of traditional authorities. The government has repeatedly attempted to erode these rights and the courts have repeatedly defended them. It is common for scholars and activists to complain that 'the state' seeks to remove those rights but is prevented from doing so by the courts, thus ignoring the fact that one arm of the state was protecting them from another (Friedman, 2021: 80). Since this is a widespread view, it suggests that the courts' legitimacy does not enhance that of the state – rather, they are seen as an antidote to it, not the part of it which protects rights.

Nevertheless, the courts' legitimacy strengthens the democratic state. In a divided and fractious society, an institution which offers a widely accepted means of settling disputes is crucial to the legitimate public order the state is meant to maintain. The courts have also, at critical times, offered crucial support to groups whose interests are often ignored by the other two arms of the state, such as homeless people[2] and people living with HIV and AIDS.[3] The claim that South Africa is a 'failed state' (Moche, 2023) expresses a prejudice rather than an analytical judgement but it is rendered even flimsier by the existence of an arm of state whose authority is widely accepted and which plays a core role in settling disputes and dispensing justice. A functioning judicial system is also crucial to the country's economic order since trade and investment in a market economy depend on the existence of courts which can settle disputes (Marciano et al., 2019). The post-1994 South African discourse tends to take the state for granted when it performs its task competently; the judiciary is one example. The fact that judges are not in the pay of those who can afford bribes, and are not loyal servants of the governing party, is assumed to be normal and natural. It is anything but that – even in countries such as the United States which are often viewed as paragons (Pahis, 2009). The judiciary is thus an asset of the South African state and nation whose importance is, despite its widespread support, probably undervalued.

But the judiciary's legitimacy is also a source of concern. Firstly, while the courts enjoy high legitimacy in public debate, there is evidence that the two-thirds of the population who are excluded from that conversation are not as convinced of their usefulness. There are also occasional reminders that not everyone sees court judgments as sacrosanct; a conspicuous example was the violence which gripped KwaZulu-Natal in July 2021, after Zuma's imprisonment following his refusal to accept the authority of the Constitutional Court. Among the one-third engaged in public discourse, dissatisfaction with what is seen as limited progress in convicting people accused of corruption is focused chiefly on the National Prosecuting Authority rather than the courts – a sign of the courts' continued legitimacy. But this could change if the courts are seen to be a reason for the delays.

Secondly, the courts' legitimacy often places them beyond public debate. Democratic states need a legitimate judiciary, but not one which is above criticism. A core feature of a democratic order is that

---

2 *Government of the Republic of South Africa v Grootboom 2000(11) BCLR 1169 (CC)*
3 *Minister of Health v Treatment Action Campaign (No. 2) 2002 (5) SA 721 (CC)*

all institutions of the state must be accountable to society and so must be scrutinised by it. But both judgments and the ways in which courts function are usually accepted without demur by a public discourse, which is often loud in its criticisms of the state's other arms. The merits of a Constitutional Court judgment holding that independent candidates should be eligible to contest national and provincial elections[4] are not self-evident. Yet, there was no debate on the ruling – rather, argument has centred on how it should be implemented.

Public opinion, in its enthusiasm for the courts, often ignores what should be a truism but is not accepted as one – that when judges dress in robes and preside over hearings, they do not cease to be human beings with their own opinions. The law is rarely so clear that any trained judge, whatever their beliefs, will interpret it in the same way. Judges, like the rest of us, are not politically neutral, and many legal systems cater for this in their arrangements for appointing people to the bench. In this country, the Judicial Services Commission (JSC) plays this role; it includes Members of Parliament and judges so that political perspectives are aired in the process of making appointments. But when the JSC does play the political role which this requires, its own legitimacy suffers as it is accused of introducing politics into judicial selections (News24, 2023). The reaction is usually based, implicitly or explicitly, on the assumption that judicial selections should somehow 'ignore politics', which means, in effect, that they should share the political biases of the person decrying political influence.

The courts may be fair and independent, but they are also extremely slow and expensive. Cases may take years to be resolved (Ally and Boonzaaier, 2022) and the price of litigation is beyond the means of most citizens unless they are fortunate enough to attract the attention of donor-funded public interest lawyers. This is true of court systems in many other countries too, but this does not alter the reality that the system operates mainly for those who can afford to wait for justice and to pay for it, which makes the courts one of society's many institutions which produce and maintain inequality.

---

4   *New Nation Movement NPC and Others v President of the Republic of South Africa and Others (CCT110/19) [2020] ZACC 11; 2020 (8) BCLR 950 (CC); 2020 (6) SA 257 (CC) (11 June 2020)*

The courts' legitimacy among political parties and interest groups is a weakness as well as a strength because it risks undermining democracy. The role of courts in a functioning democracy is to enable democratic politics, not to substitute for it. Courts are meant to protect the rights required to participate and to prevent the citizenry from unconstitutional exercises of power. They are not meant to decide public policy issues, allowing parties which have failed to win support from the majority of voters to impose their policy preferences on a society which does not support them. The judiciary's legitimacy is thus both a strength in the democratic state and a weakness.

THE STATE'S ACCEPTABLE FACE?

Three decades after democracy's advent, South Africa remains a society of 'insiders' and 'outsiders'. The 'insiders' are people who derive income from the formal market economy and who monopolise politics and public debate. But people who earn wages, salaries or dividends, and their dependents, comprise only about one-third of South African society, relegating two-thirds to the margins of public debate (Friedman, 2021: 25ff).

The courts, despite their limitations, are the arm of the state which have most been able to serve the needs of both 'insiders' and 'outsiders'. But the judgments which have attracted attention in public discourse – and have strengthened the courts' legitimacy among 'insiders' – respond to the concerns of the minority on the inside.

These are cases in which courts have been seen to support the battle against corruption and 'state capture' (the use of public power for private ends) and those responsible for it. The example which most fits this description is the Constitutional Court's 2017 unanimous judgment ordering then President Zuma to pay back to the state the money the government had spent on refurbishing his Nkandla residence.[5] There are other cases which have strengthened insiders' views that the courts are bulwarks against the illegitimate use of

---

5 *Economic Freedom Fighters and Others v Speaker of the National Assembly and Another (CCT76/17) [2017] ZACC 47; 2018 (3) BCLR 259 (CC); 2018 (2) SA 571 (CC)*

government power, including a series of rulings overturning decisions of the former Public Protector, Busisiwe Mkhwebane (Ensor, 2021); the courts' rejection of Zuma's attempts to institute a private prosecution against Billy Downer, who is prosecuting him for alleged illegalities in government arms purchases;[6] and court findings against Zuma's ally, the former African National Congress Secretary-General, Ace Magashule (Sidimba, 2021).

The justice of the poor

These cases show that the courts are performing one of their core tasks – ensuring that citizens enjoy the protections which the Constitution affords them. As noted above, far from showing the failure of the state, this is one of its successes. This sort of court intervention does not show that 'democracy has failed' and that it therefore needs rescuing by the courts, a claim which is sometimes made about the Zuma years. It shows, rather, that democracy is succeeding. When courts protect citizens' rights, they are making one facet of democracy act as it should and so are contributing to its health.

But this is not the only role the courts have played in enforcing citizens' rights. They have also acted to safeguard social and economic rights and have thus made a material difference to the lives of most citizens, who remain outsiders. The area in which courts have been most active is access to shelter. The Constitutional Court's celebrated Grootboom case ruled that people could not be evicted from informal housing unless they were provided with an alternative place to live. It became the foundation of a range of cases, all prompted by attempts to remove people from accommodation which had not been allocated to them by the authorities. An important focus of these judgments is the rights of people in inner-city flat blocks (Wilson, 2011). Famously, the court ruled in 2002 that the government was compelled to provide medication to prevent mother-to-child transmission of HIV and AIDS. In 2013 it overruled a decision by the governing body of a suburban school to exclude a pupil on the grounds that the school

---

6 *Zuma v Downer and Another (788/2023) [2023] ZASCA 132 (13 October 2023)*

had reached capacity.[7] This seemingly technical decision addressed the power of (mostly White) suburban school governing bodies to exclude poor Black learners. In so doing, it tackled a core South African issue – the role of race and class in limiting access to education. It has also protected women's rights, handing down judgments which struck down discrimination against women in customary marriages[8] or customary inheritance laws.[9] And, as noted earlier, it has come to the aid of rural people in traditional authority areas whose landholdings have been threatened by alliances between traditional leaders and provincial governments (Evans, 2015). The courts have, therefore, played a pivotal role in ensuring that people enjoy their constitutional rights to land, even if they are subject to the authority of a traditional leader.

This is not an exhaustive list. The courts have repeatedly acted to enforce the social and economic rights of citizens, most of them 'outsiders', whose needs are ignored in national debate. Their impact is often unnoticed because the rules they set may be implemented routinely over many years. Inner-city flat residents who are able, through lawyers, to protect themselves against eviction now may retain a roof over their heads because courts ruled that they should have one over a decade ago.

The right to negotiate

A decade and a half ago, the Constitutional Court introduced a new and important element into its rulings on social and economic rights. Beginning with a celebrated case which dealt with evictions,[10] it refrained from settling disputes by ordering an outcome – instead, it instructed the local or other authority that was party to the dispute to negotiate with the people who believed their rights were infringed. A core example was the 2010 Mazibuko case in which the Constitutional

---

7   *MEC for Education in Gauteng Province and Other v Governing Body of Rivonia Primary School and Others (CCT 135/12) [2013] ZACC 34; 2013 (6) SA 582 (CC); 2013 (12) BCLR 1365 (CC) (3 October 2013)*
8   *Bhe v Magistrate, Khayelitsha 2005 1 SA 580 (CC)*
9   *Gumede v President of the Republic of South Africa 2009 3 SA 152 (CC)*
10 *Occupiers of 51 Olivia Road, Berea Township and 197 Main Street Johannesburg v City of Johannesburg and Others (24/07) [2008] ZACC 1; 2008 (3) SA 208 (CC); 2008 (5) BCLR 475 (CC) (19 February 2008)*

Court overturned a lower court ruling that people unable to afford municipal water should receive 12 kilolitres free every month. Instead, it instructed the local authority to negotiate an agreed amount of free water with the plaintiffs.[11]

This approach was criticised by human rights lawyers who argued that the courts should give concrete effect to social and economic rights by stipulating the minimum amount of a publicly provided service or public good, to which people are entitled by right. They accused the court of failing people living in poverty by refusing to instruct the authorities to address their needs. It did this, they suggested, because the court wanted to avoid a battle with the government that it might lose (Dugard, 2008; 2010; Roux, 2003: 97, 98). A counterargument to the position of these human rights lawyers was that they were asking the court to substitute for democratic politics by deciding for citizens what they should receive from the state. The court's preference for negotiation, according to this counterargument, offered an opportunity to deepen democracy by enabling citizens to enjoy a say over decisions which affect them. This reliance on negotiation, the argument continued, could 'democratise the rights-enforcement process' (Ray, 2011: 107). Such a process acknowledged that people on whose behalf social and economic rights cases were brought might lack the power to negotiate on equal terms with the authorities but argued that courts should concentrate on redressing the power imbalance, ensuring that people who struggled to make themselves heard, like those in the Mazibuko case, were not ignored again.

The claim that the court was shrinking at a confrontation also highlighted another aspect of the courts' role which is taken for granted in South Africa. The debate assumes that governments will always obey the courts in constitutional democracies. But, in reality, governments often resist the courts' rulings. In countries where obeying courts has been the norm for very long periods, governments may well have become used to this. But in new democracies, such as South Africa's, there is no guarantee that governments will do what

---

11 *Mazibuko v City of Johannesburg (2010) (Centre on Housing Rights and Evictions as amicus curiae) 4 SA1 (CC)*

the courts tell them to do. It is therefore significant that, in the first decade of democracy, this country gained a reputation as one, among new democracies, whose Constitutional Court had most succeeded in enforcing the Constitution and ensuring government compliance when it did (Roux, 2009: 107).

Why did the government accept that it ought to enforce court rulings (even if at times it implemented them grudgingly and partially)? The first answer has nothing to do with anything the court or the government did. One of the oddities of South African political culture is that respect for court judgments was, by 1994, ingrained in the attitudes of the country's elites – despite the fact that, until 1994, courts had been subject to the authority of an all-White Parliament whose decisions they usually could not challenge even if they wanted to, and many judges were appointed because they shared the White supremacist biases of the political authority.

For reasons which have been discussed in other published work (Friedman, 2021: 46), a curious feature of the apartheid system was that, while it denied even basic rights to most citizens, and used the law to suppress opposition and impose racial domination, it insisted on using legal process to do this. White domination was imposed through carefully crafted legislation, backed by written regulations and enforced by the courts. This reflected and maintained a view among the White minority that legal process was 'civilised', and that obeying court orders was a mark of racial and cultural supremacy. The fact that the courts had, despite their role under apartheid, sometimes been able to defend the rights of the majority may have aided their legitimacy among the post-apartheid governing elite. Additionally, there was a strong view among Black elites that the arrangements enjoyed by Whites under apartheid should be extended to all citizens (Friedman, 2021: 13ff).

A second reason is that the Constitutional Court was, from its inauguration in February 1995, staffed by judges who had played some role in the fight against apartheid or shared many of the values of the post-1994 governing elite. Most court decisions were broadly consistent with the government's stated values and so were unlikely to be rejected. It has been argued that, at times, being told to do something by the courts may have been helpful to the government because it provided an 'objective' legal basis for the reversal of policies it needed to reverse (Roux, 2009: 124, 125).

Thirdly, the court was careful to pick its battles. It knew that government had the power to ignore it or make its functioning difficult, and so it was careful not to push government further than it seemed willing to go. This does not, of course, mean that it refrained from holding government to account; we have seen that it has done just that repeatedly. But it has not sought to impose on government orders which it might find overly onerous. The Treatment Action Campaign (TAC) judgment, in which it ordered the government to make HIV medication available, was the only case in the judgments discussed here in which the court ordered the government to take a specific action. For the rest, courts would set out broad guidelines and leave it to the government to decide how to give them flesh – or they would order government to negotiate. Where it felt it might be seen to be unduly restricting the latitude of an elected government, it avoided doing this. Its 2002 refusal to outlaw floor crossing[12] is an oft-cited case in point. This is not a unique approach. India's Supreme Court has, for example, sought to insulate itself from government attack by negotiating the terms of rulings with the government (Friedman and Maiorano, 2017). The polite – and principled – way of describing this approach is that it respects the right of elected assemblies to do the people's bidding. Its concrete effect is that the court voids issuing instructions that government may resist.

Whatever the reasons, the courts have been able to make a significant contribution to building the democratic state. But this has brought with it some cost and risk.

LEGITIMATE DOUBTS

The voices of the 'outsiders' are not given prominence in public debate, including by the media or in government consultations. This

---

12 *United Democratic Movement v President of the Republic of South Africa and Others CCT23/02A);[2002] ZACC 33; 2003 (1) SA 488 (CC); 2002 (11) BCLR 1213 (CC) (4 October 2002)*

makes it difficult to find evidence of whether they accord courts the same legitimacy as the 'insiders' do. But there are indications that they may not.

The evidence comes not from overt resistance to court rulings but from citizens' reactions to crime – particularly in high crime areas. Vigilantism is common and sometimes lethal (Ngcobo, 2023); while this is partly a response to the real or perceived failings of the police, it also expresses frustration with the criminal justice system and thus with courts. Citizens also protest, sometimes violently, at the court appearances of people accused of crimes such as murder and rape (Chabalala, 2022). The protests assume that the accused is guilty and are aimed at pressing the courts to punish them swiftly and severely. Neither these protests nor the vigilantism explicitly attack courts or the justice system. But they signal citizens' view that due process of law obstructs their demand for what they see as justice.

These reactions are directed not at a particular judge or verdict but at the criminal justice system and due legal process. This makes it harder to address the problem since courts cannot meet the demands of citizens without abandoning judicial fairness. Precisely because the discontent is aimed at the entire legal process, there are no immediately apparent ways of achieving legitimacy. But this points to the dangers of assuming that the courts' legitimacy among 'insiders' means that the entire society agrees.

Another, more complicated challenge to the legitimacy of the courts was the violence of July 2021. On the surface, this was a straightforward case of a refusal to accept court rulings which were inconvenient to some in the political class. It followed Zuma's arrest and imprisonment for ignoring court rulings, after he repeatedly refused to participate in court proceedings. Zuma made it clear at the time that he did not accept the legitimacy of the courts (Maeko et al., 2021). The violence seemed to show, therefore, that a significant section of the citizenry shared the former president's view that the courts were the playthings of particular interests and that court rulings should be rejected. A closer look at the violence, however, challenges this view.

While many reports and analyses of the violence portrayed it as a popular uprising, there is no evidence to support this. The only aspect which attracted broad participation was the looting of stores. This did not indicate support for Zuma or rejection of his imprisonment – looting is common across the globe when public order breaks down. There is no evidence that participants were trying to send a message; they were merely taking advantage of an opportunity to acquire goods. The violence which created the opportunity for looting was not a citizens' rebellion. The weapons used and the targets chosen – electricity installations and ammunition stores, for example – suggested that this was the work of small groups with training in the use of violence. It seems highly likely, therefore, that it was caused by criminal networks inside national and local government who feared that Zuma's jailing might herald action against them. Actions which seek to protect the turf of criminal rings are not expressions of many citizens' belief that the justice system is illegitimate.

Blind loyalty?

Insiders' respect for the judicial system is a double-edged sword since it often has the effect of ensuring that court rulings are not subjected to public scrutiny.

The decision to allow independent candidates to contest elections is a case in point. The problem is not that the ruling was clearly faulty, since a strong case could be made that preventing independents from seeking elected office infringes political freedom. But there is an alternative view which holds that no freedoms were at stake because individuals could run for office by forming a political party of which they are the sole member. Some have done precisely that – the KISS party, which contested the 1994 elections, appeared to be the creation and vehicle of a single individual (Magubane, 2014). There were also other examples. This alternative view also argues that altering the electoral system distorts it, making it less able to achieve its prime aim of offering a voice to as many political perspectives as possible. But this view was not heard in public; it was whispered in corridors, partly because those who held it did not want to be seen to be challenging the legitimacy of the courts. Much the same point can be made about the earlier judgment on floor crossing, which seemed to ignore the fact that voters cast ballots for parties rather than individuals, and that members who cross the floor could therefore be seen to be betraying their mandate from the electorate.

Democratic principle insists that all the institutions in democracies must be subject to constant scrutiny because they are always accountable to the citizenry and so are never beyond criticism (Mouffe, 1993). The courts have acknowledged that citizens have a right to criticise them (they did insist that the criticism should be 'constructive' but this is obviously subjective and is therefore hard to define) (Oliphant, 2022). Certainly, attacks on the judiciary aimed at preventing it from holding senior government officers to account do threaten democracy. However, critical comment which recognises the legitimacy of the courts but insists that they are not infallible does not. A reluctance to criticise the courts obviously narrows debate and places important issues beyond the reach of democratic politics.

This refusal to criticise courts is not total. Legal scholars do criticise judgments (Modiri, 2012) but their work is generally read only by fellow scholars. Courts lower than the Constitutional Court are sometimes criticised when judges are seen by some in society to have erred on issues of importance to public policy; a well-publicised example was a 2021 ruling by two judges which overturned a rape conviction[13] and was roundly condemned by non-governmental organisations who believed it gave men licence to rape women (Soul City Institute, 2021). But these are exceptions; the vigorous debate that court rulings should provoke is largely absent and this weakens democracy.

One of the unspoken assumptions that underpins failure to criticise the courts is the already mentioned view – which is pervasive – that judges cease to hold political opinions when they are elevated to the bench. They should, it is claimed, be appointed purely on their legal ability, not their politics. But the idea that judges render rulings in which their political opinions play no role is not credible. Thus, a strong supporter of judicial independence argues that judges are expected to clothe their opinion in legal reasoning if they wish to retain the respect of their colleagues, but assumes that their opinions play an

---

13 *Coko v S (CA&R 219/2020) [2021] ZAECGHC 91; [2021] 4 All SA 768 (ECG); 2022 (1) SACR 24 (ECG) (8 October 2021)*

important role in shaping the ruling (Roux, 2009). This implies that the selection of judges will always be at least a partly political process and that this should be recognised in the procedures that choose judicial officers. The much-criticised Judicial Services Commission (JSC) is only partly composed of politicians – elsewhere (the United States and Germany are two examples), politics alone decides judicial selection. To insist that politics should not be recognised as a crucial factor is to insist that what are, in effect, political appointments, should be made not by representatives elected by citizens but by small groups of legal professionals.

The speed of justice

One aspect of the judicial process which needs much greater public comment is the speed at which the courts operate.

Judicial processes across the globe are often slow and South Africa's are no exception. This may harm the interests of citizens: a dismissed worker who loses their job unfairly may have to wait many months without income for the courts to come to their aid. But it can also threaten judicial legitimacy. As noted above, there is currently a great deal of public frustration at the slow pace of ensuring that people who engaged in 'state capture' are punished. While the prosecuting authority has taken much of the blame, at least part of the reason is the slowness of court processes. Faster justice may also go some way towards addressing the frustration of citizens who want to see alleged murderers and rapists face swift retribution.

Who and what is to blame for this problem is less than clear. But, since the judiciary is meant to be independent of politics, the responsibility for a remedy lies with judges themselves. One cause of delays, which has been the subject of much comment within and outside the legal profession, is lawyers' use of technical points to delay court proceedings. The best-known example is again Zuma and his 'Stalingrad strategy' in which he and his lawyers are accused of using spurious legal points to delay justice (Maughan, 2023). But there seems to be no way of preventing this in a democratic legal system. However much they may be misused at times, legal niceties are meant to protect the rights of parties to legal actions – citizens who rail against the

'Stalingrad strategy' may be grateful for 'technicalities' if these come to their rescue when their rights are infringed.

The speed of the judicial system or lack thereof affects citizens' rights and so requires much greater public scrutiny.

CONCLUSION: SUPPORTING DEMOCRACY

Courts are essential features of democratic states but they are not substitutes for democratic politics. A core democratic principle is that no person's opinion on what is good for society is better than anyone else's – the university professor is no better equipped to decide whether people who murder should be put to death than an illiterate person. This obviously applies also to people trained in the law – their legal schooling does not make their moral and political opinions better than others'. The purpose of constitutional democracy is not to replace the elected representatives of the citizenry with small groups of lawyers. It is, rather, to protect people's rights to engage in that free contest over what society needs, which we call democratic politics.

The debate over social and economic rights mentioned earlier illustrates the point. In principle, courts protect and deepen democracy when they enable citizens to decide the policy questions which affect their lives, not when they assume that legal training somehow miraculously enables a person to decide how much free water citizens should receive.

The problem is not, in the main, that judges overreach by insisting on their right to make policy – this rarely happens. It is that political parties and interest groups insist on using courts to settle policy questions. In one extreme case, a judge refused to intervene when he was asked, in effect, to decide Parliament's schedule for it (Mail & Guardian, 2012). So serious is the problem that former Deputy Chief Justice Dikgang Moseneke warned that the courts could be overwhelmed by constant requests to settle political disputes (Janse van Rensburg, 2016).

It is easy to see the source of this problem. Between 1994 and 2024, only one political party governed at the national level. Those who were forced into opposition enjoyed access to resources which make frequent litigation affordable. The courts, precisely because they are independent of the government, were seen as a way of undoing the governing party's electoral majority.

Courts have, in the main, resisted these invitations to become allies in overturning majority rule. With notable exceptions, they have recognised and respected the role of democratic politics. The legitimacy of the courts depends on their willingness to hold the line. The most legitimate arm of the state will not enjoy that status for long if it allows itself to become a bludgeon which minorities use to frustrate the majority.

The courts have also moved some way towards enabling democracy by creating the means for 'outsiders' to negotiate the terms of their entitlement to public goods and services. They could further aid democracy's development by insisting not only on negotiation of social and economic rights, but also on imposing conditions on these discussions which would empower citizens and ensure that they can bargain with authorities on something approaching equal terms. The courts' legitimacy with 'insiders' owes much to their role in protecting citizens from government actions; their legitimacy with 'outsiders' may depend on their ability to ensure that these outliers in the system become part of democratic discussion and become citizens in substance as well as form.

REFERENCES

Ally, N. and Boonzaaier, L. 2022. 'The Constitutional Court's efficiency: Statistics from the Mogoeng era, 2010–2021'. *Constitutional Court Review*, 12, 317–342.

Chabalala, J. 2022. 'Protesters break down court gate, smash glass as murder-accused traffic officers appear'. *News24*, 14 September, https://www.news24.com/news24/southafrica/news/protesters-break-down-court-gate-smash-glass-as-murder-accused-traffic-officers-appear-20220914, accessed 12 November 2023.

Dentlinger, L. 2023. 'Parliament looks to put John Hlophe impeachment matter back on table'. *Eye Witness News*, 7 September, https://ewn.co.za/2023/09/07/parliament-looks-to-put-john-hlophe-impeachment-matter-back-on-table, accessed 14 November 2023.

Department of Justice (DoJ). n.d. 'Courts in South Africa', https://www.justice.gov.za/about/sa-courts.html, accessed 25 June 2025.

Dugard, J. 2008. 'Courts and the poor in South Africa: A critique of systemic judicial failures to advance transformative justice'. *SA Journal of Human Rights*, 24, 214–239.

Dugard, J. 2010. 'Response to Peter Danchin "A Human Right to Water? The South African Constitutional Court's Decision in the Mazibuko Case"'. EJIL: *Talk! Blog of the European Journal of International Law*, http://www.ejiltalk.org/a-human-right-to-water-the-south-african-constitutional-court%E2%80%99s-decision-in-the-mazibuko-case/, accessed 12 March 2014.

Ensor, L. 2021. 'Another court blow for Busisiwe Mkhwebane as appeal bid is rejected'. *Business Day,* 7 April, https://www.businesslive.co.za/bd/national/2021-04-07-another-court-blow-for-busisiwe-mkhwebane-as-appeal-bid-is-rejected/, accessed 12 November 2023.

Evans, S. 2015. 'ConCourt hands land back to North West community'. *Mail & Guardian*, 20 August, https://mg.co.za/article/2015-08-20-concourt-hands-land-back-to-north-west-community/, accessed 25 June 2025.

Friedman, S. 2021. *Prisoners of the Past: South African Democracy and the Legacy of Minority Rule*. Johannesburg: Wits University Press.

Friedman, S. and Maiorano, D. 2017. 'The limits of prescription: Courts and social policy in India and South Africa'. *Commonwealth and Comparative Politics*, 55(3), 353–376.

Hawker, D. 2022. 'It's not about religion, it's about politics: Conduct committee orders Mogoeng to apologise'. *Times Live*, 21 January, https://www.timeslive.co.za/news/south-africa/2022-01-21-its-not-about-religion-its-about-politics-conduct-committee-orders-mogoeng-to-apologise/, accessed 14 November 2023.

Hurd, I. n.d. 'Legitimacy'. The Princeton Encyclopedia of Self-Determination, https://pesd.princeton.edu/node/516, accessed 28 March 2025.

Institute for Justice and Reconciliation (IJR). 2024. 'Trust in the government and its institutions. What support for a GNU governing coalition in South Africa?', https://www.ijr.org.za/2024/07/trust-in-the-government-and-its-institutions-what-support-for-a-gnu-governing-coalition-in-south-africa/, accessed 25 June 2025.

Janse van Rensburg, A. 2016. 'Judiciary can't be the highest form of accountability'. *News24*, 8 December, https://www.news24.com/news24/xarchive/poor-governance-is-preoccupying-the-courts-and-its-hurting-our-democracy-20161208, accessed 13 November 2023.

Judges Matter. n.d. 'Judicial bribery and corruption'. *Judges Matter*, https://www.judgesmatter.co.za/opinions/judicial-bribery-corruption/, accessed 25 June 2025.

Maeko, T., Bates, E. and Omarjee, H. 2021. 'Zuma launches blistering attack on the judiciary'. *Business Day*, 1 July, https://www.businesslive.co.za/bd/national/2021-07-01-zuma-launches-blistering-attack-on-the-judiciary/, accessed 14 November 2023.

Magubane, K. 2014. 'KISS party ready to call it a day after 2014 elections'. *Business Day*, 24 April, https://www.businesslive.co.za/bd/politics/2014-04-24-kiss-party-ready-to-call-it-a-day-after-2014-elections/, accessed 12 November 2023.

Mail & Guardian. 2012. 'Court rejects DA motion for no-confidence debate', 22 November, https://mg.co.za/article/2012-11-22-court-rejects-da-motion-debate/, accessed 14 November 2023.

Marciano, A., Melcarne, A. and Ramello, G. 2019. 'The economic importance of judicial institutions, their performance and the proper way to measure them'. *Journal of Institutional Economics*, 15(1), 81–98.

Maughan, K. 2023. 'SCA takes aim at Zuma over Stalingrad, strikes blow to upcoming bid to remove Downer'. *News24*, 14 October, https://www.news24.com/news24/southafrica/news/sca-takes-aim-at-zuma-over-stalingrad-strikes-blow-to-upcoming-bid-to-remove-downer-20231014, accessed 14 November 2023.

Moche, T. 2023. 'SA has entered the realm of a failed state: Vavi'. *SABC News*, 8 September, https://www.sabcnews.com/sabcnews/sa-has-entered-the-realm-of-a-failed-state-vavi/, accessed 14 November 2023.

Modiri, J.M. 2012. 'The colour of law, power and knowledge: Introducing critical race theory in (post-) apartheid South Africa'. *South African Journal of Human Rights*, 28, 405–436.

Mouffe, C. 1993. *The Return of the Political*. London/New York: Verso Books.

News24. 2023. 'Serjeant at the Bar: Political influence at JSC doesn't bode well for our constitutional democracy'. 7 October, https://www.news24.com/news24/opinions/columnists/serjeant_at_the_bar/serjeant-at-the-bar-political-influence-at-jsc-doesnt-bode-well-for-our-constitutional-democracy-20231007, accessed 12 November 2023.

Ngcobo, K. 2023. 'Residents urged not to take law into their own hands after seven die in mob attacks in Mpumalanga'. *News24*, 27 October, https://www.timeslive.co.za/news/south-africa/2023-10-27-residents-urged-not-to-take-law-into-their-own-hands-after-seven-die-in-mob-attacks-in-mpumalanga/, accessed 10 November 2023.

Oliphant, M. 2022. 'Criticism of the judiciary in a constitutional democracy'. *De Rebus*, 1 March, https://www.derebus.org.za/criticism-of-the-judiciary-in-a-constitutional-democracy, accessed 14 November 2023.

Pahis, S. 2009. 'Corruption in our courts: What it looks like and where it is hidden'. *The Yale Law Journal*, 118, 1900–1943.

Ray, B. 2011. 'Proceduralisation's triumph and engagement's promise in socio-economic rights litigation'. *SA Journal of Human Rights*, 27, 107–126.

Roux, T. 2003. 'Legitimating transformation: Political resource allocation in the South African Constitutional Court'. *Democratization*, 1(4), 92–111.

Roux, T. 2009. 'Principle and pragmatism on the Constitutional Court of South Africa'. *I.CON*, 7(1), 106–138.

Sidimba, L. 2021. 'Ace Magashule loses in court again'. *Independent Online*, 13 September, https://www.iol.co.za/news/politics/ace-magashule-loses-in-court-again, accessed 13 November 2023.

Soul City Institute. 2021. 'Press Release: Ngcukaitobi and Gqamana judgment shows the extent of South Africa's rape culture crisis', https://www.soulcity.org.za/news-events/news/press-release-ngcukaitobi-and-gqamana-judgements-shows-the-extent-of-south-africas-rape-culture-crisis, accessed 10 November 2023.

Wilson, S. 2011. 'Litigating housing rights in Johannesburg's inner city: 2004–2008'. *SA Journal of Human Rights*, 27, 127–151.

Section Three

Responses and Solutions

FIFTEEN

Reorganising the state delivery machinery: Towards a performing state

Eddie M. Rakabe

INTRODUCTION

The question of whether South Africa's public service is adequately capacitated, organised and resourced to fulfil its developmental state objectives is a subject of ongoing debate, with some observers (Hausmann et al., 2023; Mello and Louw, 2023) likening the developments of the recent past to an underperforming or failed state. Former President Thabo Mbeki raised this concern in 2004 as government was grappling with mounting institutional and service delivery failures (Muthien, 2014). Arguably one of the first reform leaders of post-apartheid South Africa, Mbeki was confronted with the task of organising a myriad pre- and post-apartheid government structures subscribing to different administrative paradigms and staffed by thousands of employees. Debates about government's capabilities to translate policy into action linger to this day. This chapter argues that state capacity to deliver depends on the design of its organisational configuration. It explores the possibilities of reorganising the South African state delivery machinery to improve inter- and intra-organisational interfaces for a sustainable, efficient, effective and accountable public service.

Conceptually, state capacity affects public and development policy from two perspectives. The first is a macroeconomic view, which posits that nations prosper if they can guarantee peace, administer a buoyant taxation system, and enforce contract and property rights. The second perspective is premised on the assumption that state capacity to perform depends on how well bureaucracies translate policies into outcomes (Khemani, 2019). The second aspect draws from the Weberian model of bureaucracy in which state capacity is defined in terms of specialised roles, meritocracy, formalism, hierarchy and impersonality (Gomide et al., 2018). In this framework, governing capacity would be associated with governments' ability to formulate and implement decisions and allocate and manage resources strategically, to efficiently achieve desired results and to mobilise the support and approval of society (Painter and Pierre, 2005).

An efficient and effective organisational structure provides a useful way of coordinating decisions and resources, achieving control within the state and influencing a gamut of inputs, outputs and outcomes. At one level, organisational structure is concerned with the broad structural features of the state around which state organs and agencies interact, such as the size of government and the number of employees by occupational responsibilities. Another level deals with the structuring of activities undertaken by managers to influence the behaviour of the organisation and its members, such as political administrative interface, managerial autonomy in decision-making, performance incentives and levels of specialisation, among others (Cingolani, 2018). In this way, the structure arranges the competency of the state along three dimensions, including political, operational and analytical, in managing three levels of resources, namely systemic, organisational and individual.

The organisational architecture of the public sector matters for its performance (Schick, 2003) and overall economic development

(Vincenzo and Di Mascio, 2021). Countries that place a premium on performance have introduced numerous bureaucratic reforms to transform the state into a lean, efficient and effective delivery machinery, able to translate policies and programmes into outcomes. Further, reforms seek to configure leadership and employee management practices to inspire ability, motivation and accountability in public sector workers (World Bank, 2023).

South Africa introduced far-reaching bureaucratic reforms following the democratic transition, with the aim of democratising and modernising the state, building new institutions, professionalising the public service, and instilling a performance culture. The transformation process took place within the global context of a shift in public administration paradigms, from one of centralised bureaucratic models to managerialism or New Public Management (NPM) ideals. Drawing from this, the Presidential Review Commission on the Reform and Transformation of the Public Sector in South Africa (1996) recommended a fundamental rethink of the roles and functions of public services through, among other things, clarifying the administrative/political interface with a professional protocol to uphold it and creating appropriate organisational structures suited to the new state functions. The Commission's work influenced legislation such as the Public Service Act (No. 103 of 1994) as amended and the Municipal Structures Act (No. 117 of 1998) and the right-sizing of numerous erstwhile departments. Several other public service reforms have been introduced throughout the post-democracy period as the country continued to search for an optimal administrative – performance nexus.

The legislative framework giving effect to South Africa's model of bureaucratic governance embraces conflicting elements of various public administration paradigms (i.e. hierarchy, devolution and coordination). These in turn give rise to numerous organisational deficiencies and culminate in arrangements that bypass or undermine the state (Schick, 2003).

Bypassing and undermining the state, exemplified by the switch from public to private provision of certain services, arguably result from the collapse of public administration and management and what the National Development Plan (NDP) describes as the weaknesses of a capable developmental state. The NDP attributes the weaknesses in the functioning of structures to the tensions at the political and administrative interface, high turnover and instability of administrative leadership, skills shortages, the erosion of accountability and authority and low staff morale (NPC, 2012).

These weaknesses lead to another type of organisational deficit called fragmentation, which involves the dispersal of authority or decision-making powers to multiple structures and business units across the political and administrative spectrum. Fragmentation manifests in several ways: duplicating or not specifying many roles across the system; multiple coordination structures with unclear mandates; little to no decision-making power and too many participants; and the shadowing of state organisational units and roles by contractors and consultants. As Bach (2017) argues, the overriding operational motto of fragmented organisations is 'decide and execute' at the top of the pyramid, while at the bottom it is 'duplicate and align'. In 2012, the former Director-General of the Department of Social Development, Vusi Madonsela, observed that the big gap between policy intent and impact was due to the involvement of an excessive number of role players and accountability moving in different directions. Heads of provincial departments do not report to their national directors-general nor do municipal managers report to provincial heads of departments (PMG, 2012).

As the country continues to navigate conflicting public administration regimes, this chapter explores alternative ways through which to reorganise the state and reconcile hierarchical or bureaucratic management, New Public Management (NPM) and New Public Governance (NPG) ideals. NPM regards the monopoly of public service provision as a key impediment to state performance and therefore advocates for disaggregation, devolution and competition in the provision of publicly funded services, whereas NPG sees complexity and fragmentation as an overriding challenge that requires collaborative governance across organisational and institutional boundaries (Gumede, 2022).

TYPOLOGIES AND INTERFACE OF POLITICAL
AND ADMINISTRATIVE ORGANISATIONS

Organisational structures within government develop differently across countries and epochs, responding to the nature of political organisation, the diversity of public administration functions and growth in the size of administrations. In some instances, the structure may be premised on geographic or territorial interests to promote autonomy, equity and specialisation, or functional imperatives to enhance strategic management and overall performance (OECD, 2007). Other organisational settings arise from the personal preferences of those wielding power in politics and public administration. Khemani (2019) argues that politics fundamentally shapes the nature of state organisation and the culture of bureaucracies.

The design and nature of organisational structures are the centre of the administrative fundamentals that bedevil the performance of the state. Reformers, policymakers and bureaucrats tend to view operational structure as technical operational charts or organograms that display employee hierarchy in an organisation. As an administrative practice, the organisational structure defines positions, the relationship between positions, and the decision-making capacity and authority of each position. Organisational structure determines how work is organised, allocated and standardised across different political or administrative levels. Lastly, an organisational structure creates a framework for order and for coordinating the myriad tasks undertaken in an organisation. For this chapter, an organisational structure comprises a combination of administrative paradigms, processes and systems, be they political or managerial, involved in the planning, organising and implementation of government policies and programmes.

Old public administration
In Europe, the concept of organising a functional central state began to take root towards the end of the 19th century as the United Kingdom and Prussia undertook bureaucratic reforms to overcome the entrenched patrimonial system of public administration of earlier periods. This marked the beginning of the Weberian model

of administration, drawing largely from the seminal analytical work of German scientist Max Weber in which the prevailing paradigm was hierarchy and meritocracy. The overriding organisational logic was a vertical (top-down) separation of powers between and within ministries – from a politician at the top to a rank-and-file official at the bottom. The functional tenets of the Weberian model, which remain influential today, are central control of the state, clear hierarchical lines of decision-making powers and accountability, the presence of disciplinary and incentive systems, and scrutiny of politicians' actions by Parliament (OECD, 2007).

While premised on military-like principles of command-and-control, the Weberian model promotes efficient and effective management of budgetary and human resources (Robinson, 2015). Some of the design imperatives set out by Minogue (2001), Mccourt (2013) and the OECD (2007) to ensure efficiency are as follows: the separation of political representatives on one side and of the administration on the other; availability of information to facilitate accountability for action from officials and the ministers; continuity, predictability and stability (based on rules) of the administration; appointment of administrators based on qualifications and training; anonymity of officials in charge at the bottom; functional and hierarchical division of labour; organisational, rather than individual, ownership of resources; and public servants who are driven by public rather than private interests (Minogue, 2001; Mccourt, 2013; OECD, 2007)

The Weberian model was developed alongside the Swedish model. It proposes a distinct organisational pattern that focuses on a horizontal separation of responsibilities between government and ministries. It emphasises the importance of a collective, responsible for setting policies, allocating budgets and monitoring implementation. This collective should be distinct from constitutionally protected, autonomous agencies in charge of the day-to-day execution of government policies. These agencies account directly to Parliament. The schema relies on the institutional guarantee of an ombudsman to act as an independent Member of Parliament with the power to hold both government and agencies accountable. Numerous variations, adaptations and combinations of the two models have evolved over time, including the French system of managerial autonomy, the century-old British system of delegation, and the German system of executive federalism (OECD, 2007). The point here is that different forms of political organisation have resulted in different types of administrative paradigms directing how state institutions function.

From new public administration to new public governance

The centralised, bureaucratic models of public administration that developed in Europe influenced public service reform efforts in most developing countries and post-independence Africa. However, the failure to adopt the fundamental principles of effective and efficient centralised bureaucracies and safeguard against neopatrimonial practices undermined good public governance, and laid the groundwork for subsequent waves of compulsory reforms, at the behest of external institutions, under the rubric of structural adjustment programmes. In the 1980s, limited success in implementing IMF- and World Bank-imposed public service reforms prompted the emergence of new paradigms of public administration, most notably the New Public Management (NPM) and New Public Governance (NPG) models (Klijn, 2012).

NPM integrates competition and private sector management practices in addressing the provision of public services. It was conceived as a bureaucratic model to accommodate the modern complexities of highly varied citizen demands that require specialisation and intra-organisational coordination. In embracing efficient management, NPM adopts a technocratic approach to decision-making by separating policy and implementation roles (Pereira and Ckagnazaroff, 2020). The accompanying specialisation, however, leads either to the proliferation of agencies or to a 'hollow state' that relies on private actors to provide public services. As the challenges of coordinating complex networks intensify, the government becomes trapped in a vicious cycle of initiating public service reforms to create order in the chaos (Klijn, 2012).

NPG is a more recent public administration paradigm, premised on the principle of shared public interest rather than the consolidation of individual interests. Under this model, citizens are treated as co-creators of policy and service delivery while government involves multiple, inter-dependent service delivery providers and uses multiple processes and inputs to shape policy. The NPG approach emphasises inter-organisational or horizontal relationships in which trust, social capital and contracts – rather than organisational form or function – serve as the core mechanisms of governance. This governance framework relies on effective management to facilitate complex coordination (Robinson, 2015).

As with the Weberian approach, the NPM and NPG models present numerous opportunities for public service reform but the two have yet to offer a holistic approach to the problems of organisational design and functioning in developing countries. Consequently, most countries experiment with hybrid models, borrowing elements of various public administration paradigms in response to global trends, donor requirements and ongoing state-performance failures. Hybridity entails a mixture of organisational models, inside and outside government, which encompass specialised agencies, state-owned enterprises, quasi-autonomous structures, and different levels of government. This too has not yielded the desired results because the technological and human resource requirements of hybrid systems exceed the capabilities of the developing countries concerned (Robinson, 2015).

Administration and performance nexus

The contemporary state exists to successfully perform its responsibilities to deliver a range of services to the public. As citizens' needs and state responsibilities become ever more complex, new models of the modern state are devising nimble forms of public administration that seek to enhance performance by granting public managers greater managerial and budgetary discretion in exchange for greater performance accountability (Wang and Yeung, 2018). Some states are deregulating public administration while others are seeking to improve performance within the framework of established administrative norms. In other words, while performance remains the overriding objective of the modern state, governments have chosen different paths towards that end. Some rely on administrative procedures such as strategic plans and performance contracts, others on political and professional commitments, while others are grounded in the traditional public administration ideals discussed above.

Regardless of the path chosen, Schick (2003) argues that to perform well, public organisations require adjustments to both their operational cultures and managerial capacities. Organisations must question their purposes and objectives, redefine what they are and how they operate, abandon embedded habits and routines, and distribute authority among managers and political heads. Undertaking these tasks is, however, easier said than done, even with influential new public administration approaches. The difficulty arises from the fact that an organisation can be both an enabler of and a hindrance to performance, depending on the rigidity of the prevailing culture (Schick, 2003).

Efforts to change the culture of non-performing public organisations have evolved to include countless recommendations from advisory firms, often presented as practical and distinct from the old and new public administration approaches. Some of these recommendations include proposals to use strategic planning tools to align organisational objectives, resources and outcomes. Others entail grandiose recommendations to re-organise state departments and agencies or create new ones.

The conceptual framework for facilitating an interface between state organisational architecture and state performance must be centred on three competencies (analytical, operational and political) and involve the application of these at three levels of resources (systemic, organisational and individual) (Wu et al., 2015). In this regard, analytical competency ensures that policies are technically sound. Operational competency ensures alignment between resources and actions, while political competency assists in ensuring political support for government actions. Similarly, systemic resources include the support the state receives from key stakeholders. Organisational resources are financial, human and managerial resources, as well as information systems and individual resources concerned with the technical know-how of public administrators. This framing enables the measurement of state capacity in terms of its results and functioning (Gomide et al., 2018).

THE POST-1994 PUBLIC SERVICE
TRANSFORMATION JOURNEY

Public service reforms in South Africa have come a long way since 1994. They have followed a somewhat unique journey which sought to integrate the goals of national reconciliation and reconstruction with those of rationalising and restructuring the civil service. This entailed building new institutions, democratising the state, professionalising the public service and instilling performance imperatives and incentives. The White Paper on the Transformation of the Public Service (Ministry for the Public Service and Administration, 1995) outlines a broad policy framework for transforming the public service, drawing from the different public administration paradigms discussed above. It sought 'the creation of a people centred and people driven public service which is characterised by equity, quality, timeousness and a strong code of ethics' (Ministry for the Public Service and Administration, 1995). This strategic framing was and is consistent with the doctrine of NPG in which the relationship between the state and its citizens is based on partnership rather than the antagonistic relations of the apartheid past. Further, the White Paper characterised its model of administration, intended to facilitate reform goals, as 'strategic change management' or NPM in which the focus is on new forms of leadership, devolution of decision-making powers, democratisation of internal work processes and integration of civil society in governance processes (Ministry for the Public Service and Administration, 1995; Muthien, 2014). A characterisation of this model is, arguably, hybridity and, as indicated earlier, this requires enormous and adept technological and human resource capabilities which are often unavailable in most developing countries.

The outcomes of public service reform have been codified into the legal framework in what may be construed as translating managerialism approaches into rule-based administrative procedures. Chapter 3 of the South African Constitution establishes three spheres of government (national, provincial and local), which are 'distinctive, interdependent and interrelated'. While the Constitution does not envisage hierarchy in inter-governmental relations, the national government wields considerable legislative and executive authority; importantly, provinces and local government are expected to implement policies in accordance with nationally determined frameworks. This creates room for ambiguities in the exercise of responsibilities, leading to high administration and coordination costs (Mabugu and Rakabe, 2023).

There have been misgivings about the functionality of the three-sphere system, not least from the African National Congress, largely the sole governing party until 2024. Some of the issues raised are that the three-sphere system is a complex system to operate, resulting in inefficiency, overlapping roles, as well as long decision-making processes, weak information flows, and the dispersal of public sector skills and experience within the state (ANC, 2007). Despite this, the intra- and inter-cooperative governance framework set out in Chapter 3 of the Constitution remains the governance model, and all spheres are expected to be effective, transparent, accountable and coherent. They are also expected to avoid encroaching on each other's responsibilities and to cooperate with each other (RSA, 1996). Over and above that, Chapter 10 of the Constitution sets out public administration principles according to which every sphere, agency or entity of government must promote and maintain high standards of professional ethics; utilise resources efficiently, economically, and effectively; and promote inclusivity (RSA, 1996).

Operationally, the reforms introduced since the 1995 White Paper have resulted in a gamut of legislation, regulations and guidelines to achieve the goals and overriding constitutional administrative order set out in the White Paper. Key among these laws are: the Public Service Act (PSA) No. 103 of 1994; the Public Finance Management Act (PFMA) No. 1 of 1999, applicable to national government and provinces; the Municipal Structures Act No. 117 of 1998; the Municipal Systems Act No. 32 of 2000; and the Municipal Finance Management Act (MFMA) 56 of 2003, applicable to local government. The PSA devolves the authority to make executive administrative appointments to line-function ministers (through delegation from the president),[1] and the authority to make executive administrative decisions to line-function heads of departments. Further, the PSA vests the responsibility of determining the number of departments, and for establishing organisational structures with the line ministries, in consultation with the Department of Public Service and Administration (DPSA). Both the ministers and provincial premiers enjoy the latitude to establish other independent agencies or specialised delivery units, subject to approval processes (RSA, 2013). It is also worth mentioning that the PSA and PFMA create accountability asymmetry between human resources and financial performance. The Act bestows accountability for delivery performance on ministers, while the PFMA confers accountability for financial performance on heads of departments (DPME, 2019).

The resulting rules-based administrative regime has resulted in several complex organisational deficiencies which impact on state performance (DPSA, 2007). These are outlined in the 2005 report by the Forum of South African Directors-General (FOSAD) as follows (Picard, 2005):

- organisational structures were designed to create posts rather than job functions and harmonious workflow;
- the span of administrative control was uneven across departments and agencies;
- there was poor understanding of policymaking responsibilities, resulting in encroachment on each other's responsibilities;
- insufficient attention was paid to service delivery models (i.e. mapping of the business process from inputs to outputs); roles and functions were duplicated within and across spheres, departments and agencies; and
- performance monitoring and evaluation was overlooked.

---

1 Concentration of the power to appoint heads of department (administrative executives) in the Presidency and ministries has historical roots. The leadership that came to power in 1994 viewed the public service it inherited with suspicion and scepticism. The new leaders wanted to appoint senior managers from within their loyal ranks to quell the potential threat of sabotage by stubborn incumbents from the apartheid era (RSA, 1998).

As a remedial measure, the DPSA developed performance guidelines and a toolkit on organisational design in 2007.

The guidelines and toolkit in question are only applicable to individual departmental operations (mainly in the national and provincial spheres), notwithstanding that the state workflow straddles all government spheres, and independent and quasi-autonomous agencies, as envisaged in the Constitution. An organisational structure is required to manage the vertical political and administrative interface across and within the three spheres, and the horizontal interface across and within the spheres. As Neilson and Wulf (2012) and Lafley et al. (2012) postulate, the ability to deliver public services requires the re-engineering of the business process to simplify the number and layers of authority, responsibilities, decisions, discretion and approval processes. This view is echoed in the 2013 submission by the former Director-General of the Department of Social Development, Vusi Madonsela, to a parliamentary Joint Portfolio Committee meeting focusing on government performance. Madonsela highlighted the risks to service delivery posed by fragmented decision-making, reporting and accountability arrangements. He suggested a need to reevaluate the system of integrating service delivery across the three spheres, and to ensure that the fragmentation causes minimal rifts between policy intent and impact (PMG, 2012).

ADMINISTRATIVE CAPACITY AND STATE PERFORMANCE

The modern state has legitimacy to the extent that it successfully performs according to its mandate. When the state fails to pass performance tests, its legitimacy and competence become questionable. Yet state performance remains an elusive and imprecise concept owing to its multiple dimensions, which straddle ethical, contractual, management and measurement issues. Debates continue to rage over what constitutes a performing state – how to measure it; whether a particular measure is an output, outcome or intermediate outcome; and if goals, objectives and targets mean the same thing. For an administration, a crucial factor is whether personnel incentives and budget allocations are linked to performance. Reforms that seek to link the incentive framework and budget to performance often fail, due to a combination of poor organisational structure and administrative capacity (Schick, 2003).

The prevailing policy and media discourse on state performance in South Africa, notwithstanding the complexity of the concept and poor data to support the assertions, is that public services are collapsing or have collapsed (Gumede, 2022; Hausmann et al., 2023). Various local and international media often lead with headlines such as 'Why South Africa is on the brink of chaos' (Bloomberg, 2023a); 'South Africa is on the road to becoming a failed state' (Bloomberg, 2023b); and 'CEO warns of state collapse in South Africa' (BusinessTech, 2023). The reports support their claims with a range of poor track records and evidence of maladministration in public service, such as high unemployment, rolling energy blackouts, protracted currency depreciation, high national debt, the collapse of state-owned enterprises (SOEs), corruption and local government service delivery failures.

The South African government has an elaborate system of performance measurement. This is carried out through a range of departmental statutory reports (annual performance plans and annual reports) and a broad swathe of function-specific performance reviews by independent organisations such as the Public Protector, Statistics South Africa, the Public Service Commission (PSC) and the Auditor-General (AG). Some of these reports highlight specific administrative lapses that contribute to poor public service performance and perceptions of state failure.

The PSC's 2022 State of the Public Service Report reflects on the administrative capacity and capability challenges of the state and observes that state capacity and capability in departments and key state institutions have weakened over time and vary markedly both within and between spheres of government, departments and functional units; deficiencies exist side by side with pockets of excellence. The report further notes that budget consolidation has aggravated state capacity challenges by reducing headcounts and the resources available for delivery of services; inefficient resource allocation and the inability to translate resources into outcomes are both a cause and manifestation of capacity and capability challenges; and the deteriorating capacity and capability situation has ignited judicial activism as courts are increasingly invited to adjudicate over service delivery failures, resulting in a blurry executive and judiciary interface (PSC, 2022).

Figure 15.1 illustrates the poor performance of selected national departments against predetermined objectives over a five-year period, as per PSC findings. However, knowledge of various performance metrics is pointless if not complemented by an organisation's wide reorientation of what it hopes to achieve and reflections on whether the broader goals are met. The 2022 AG report suggests that government departments not only fail to reflect on these goals but also fail to plan adequately for them. By way of example, the 2019 Medium-Term Strategic Framework (MTSF) set out to deliver 300,000 serviced housing sites over five years, but the human settlements sector's target over the first three years of the five-year plan was set at 141,000 instead of the proportional 180,000 sites.

Figure 15.1: Selected departments' performance against predetermined objectives, FY2017 – FY 2020

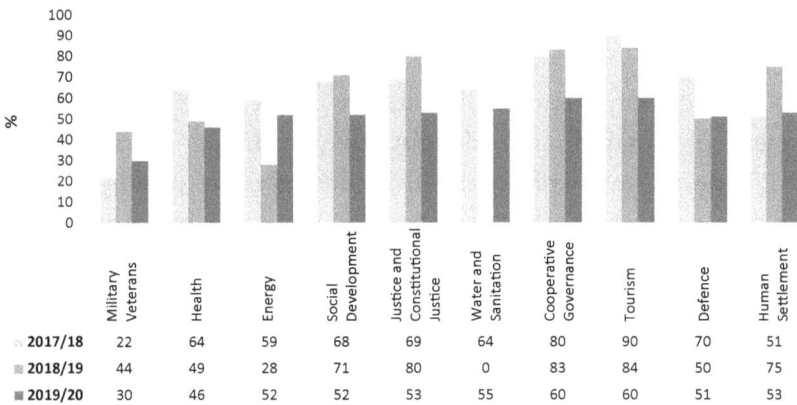

	Military Veterans	Health	Energy	Social Development	Justice and Constitutional Justice	Water and Sanitation	Cooperative Governance	Tourism	Defence	Human Settlement
2017/18	22	64	59	68	69	64	80	90	70	51
2018/19	44	49	28	71	80	0	83	84	50	75
2019/20	30	46	52	52	53	55	60	60	51	53

Source: Public Service Commission (2023)

For the AG, the crux of South Africa's public service performance challenges lies in aspects of the organisational structure and the effectiveness of the administrative regime. The 2022 report highlights some of these challenges by intuitively translating them into recommendations. The report suggests that vacancies in key positions must be filled by capable officials to ensure stability, consistency and continuity. This is consistent with a DPME (2019) report noting that the turnover rate of DGs and HoDs in South Africa is high and invariably impacts negatively on departmental performance and service delivery. It recommends that performance planning processes must be comprehensive and aligned to departmental mandates and the MTSF to ensure timely planning and reporting. It also calls for exemplary leadership to ensure compliance with legislation and address accountability failures to enable improved performance and service delivery (Auditor-General, 2022).

Increasingly, the AG has been calling for stricter accountability and financial controls in the wake of deteriorating audit and delivery results (measured through the auditing process). However, the earlier discussion alluded to the fact that the new performance movement requires government to dismantle established command-and-control systems in favour of managerial discretion to reduce compliance costs and encourage innovation.

ORGANISATIONAL STRUCTURE AND 'REFORM' IN SEARCH OF IDENTITY AND PERFORMANCE

No country's organisational structure is set in stone. South Africa's system of political and administrative organisation has evolved over time in search of an effective administrative paradigm and a performance focus.[2] Much of the journey towards a 'performing state' status relies on the legal and institutional framework setting out the politico-administrative structures and the nature of the vertical and horizontal relationships, as well as the public administration values set out in Chapter 10 of the Constitution. This utopian model of hybrid decentralisation and cooperative governance combines the old and new public administration approaches to reconcile historical and protracted aspirations for a centralised governance system and counter-arguments for a federal system. The difficulties in operationalising

---

2 Performance focus means paying attention to results, reflecting continuously about them, and using performance as a way of contemplating how well an organisation has done and how to go about future tasks.

the envisaged cooperative governance system have left a vacuum and room for interpreting dispersal of authority, the structures needed to fulfil government's responsibilities and the nature of the interfaces that should occur across the organisational chart. Consequently, the organisational chart is teeming with countless structures at various levels of government relating to each other formally and informally through different administrative approaches, as shown in Table 15.1.

Table 15.1 shows a chart comprising legislatively prescribed organisational settings across the three spheres of government and other enabling structures to facilitate coordination and execution of state responsibilities and enhance state performance. Every structure, whether the legislature, government department or agency, has an internal organisational structure according to which it operates and multiple lines of accountability. The National Assembly, with its various committees, is overseen by the Speaker, who in turn oversees the business of the National Assembly and various committees. The committees, individually and jointly, oversee the performance of Cabinet ministers and government departments on behalf of the National Assembly and public. The accountability system moves down the chain across the line departments, lower spheres of government, entities and departmental divisions. The reporting lines move in different directions before being aggregated and directed centrally towards Parliament through the offices of different ministers. This process repeats itself at every layer of political and administrative organisation within the three spheres. The prevalent administrative approach of this arrangement is hierarchical, with decision-making authority centralised in the offices of the ministers.

Another layer of hierarchical relationships occurs between the three spheres of government. The local government political leadership is accountable to the municipal councils as well as both the provincial and national legislatures, while the various administrative components of local government are accountable to municipal councils and the corresponding provincial executive authority and the premiers. Provinces account upwardly to the relevant national ministry or department, the president, and the National Assembly. The lines of reporting and accountability in this instance also move in different directions. A single municipality may account to different authorities in multiple areas of responsibility. For example, on water provision, the line of accountability includes a district municipality when factoring in the two-tier, local government system, the premiers' office, the national Minister of Water and Sanitation, and the national Finance Ministry.

Legal structures are supported by layers of administrative structures with varying and multiple roles and responsibilities across the three spheres, including policymaking and implementation, oversight and coordination. This medley of fragmented organisational structuring is very prominent in the national government sphere, including departmental internal operations, SOEs and parliamentary committees. Internally, the more than 30 national departments comprise countless divisions, subdivisions and units that require intra- and inter-horizontal coordination while reporting to DGs and HoDs or interdepartmental committees and workgroups. Inter-departmental structures do not always have clear roles and reporting lines. Similarly, the 714 SOEs have their separate, internal, hierarchical decision-making structures comprising boards and executives, but at the same time account to various ministries and to Parliament. The DPME's 25-Year Review Report (DPME, 2019) notes that public entities proliferated as the government sought to divert strict administrative bureaucracy of departments into flexible, specialised and efficient agencies. Creating a plethora of agencies, however, backfired. The report points out: 'The flexibilities and limited collective political accountability in these entities gradually became one of the sources of maladministration and corruption over the 25 years' (DPME, 2019).

DGs have a separate coordination structure – the Forum of South African Directors-General (FOSAD) – whose role is to foster dynamic relationships between political structures and administrative staff, coordinate government activities vertically and horizontally, provide technical services to national and provincial inter-governmental forums, and share best practices in public sector management and transformation. FOSAD operates alongside similar sector-specific coordination committees, such as the Technical Committee on Finance and HoD forums that oversee the activities of numerous functional areas or departments through an authority delegated by a single

Table 15.1: Complex political administrative interface in a three-sphere government system, 2023

Sphere	Vertical interface	Organisational structures	No of structures	No of staff	Political – administration interface
National government	Parliament	Committees	49		
	President	Presidential coordinating committee and advisory commissions/panel			
	Cabinet	Cluster & work groups			
	Ministers (clusters)	Councils or 10X10s			
	Directors-General	FOSAD	33		
	SOEs	Boards, Divisions & units	714	117,619	
	Organogram	Units, Divisions & IGR groups		395,267	
Provincial government	Provincial legislature	Committees	9		
	Premier	IGR forums	9		
	Provincial cabinet		10 per province		
	MECs		90		
	HoDs		90		
	Provincial SoEs	Board, divisions & units			
	Organogram	Divisions and units		912,856	
	District offices				
	Hospitals and schools				
Local government	Councils	Ward committees	4,468	4 297	
	Mayors		257	257	
	Mayoral committees	IGF forums			
	Municipal manager		257	257	
	SoEs				
	Staff		+-250,000	342,048	

Source: Author's compilation

minister. The lead department under which these technical committees are organised tends to set the agenda and dominate decision-making.

Administrative coordination structures take orders and report to a thick layer of political coordination and decision-making forums starting with the apex Presidential Coordinating Committee (PCC), the more powerful Budget Forum under the custodianship of the Finance Ministry and the various sectoral ministerial councils (MINMECs) comprising national ministers and the nine provincial Members of Executive Councils (MECs). Over and above this complexity, ministries are organised into a group of five clusters whose function is to ensure alignment of government-wide priorities, act as consultative forums for cross-cutting issues, monitor implementation of state priority programmes and decide on issues that require government attention. This model incorporates selected elements of the old public administration (in which a coordinating structure personifies the lead minister) as well as NPM and NPG where roles and responsibilities are dispersed across multiple structures but decision-making is centralised. Further, the authority of national departments and various coordination structures is increasingly being usurped and overshadowed by the growing introduction of arm's-length commissions and advisory panels under the Office of the President. These commissions take over selected responsibilities of existing departments on the pretext of presidential performance expediency, yet there is no established organisational framework on how these quasi-autonomous structures interface with other decision-making and coordinating authorities.

The system described above is prone to duplication, diffusion of roles and responsibilities, decision-making delays, intergovernmental and inter-departmental tensions, and high coordination costs.[3] This is exemplified by the roles and coordination clashes between the former departments of Energy and Mineral Resources and Public Enterprises, and the Presidential Climate Change Commission and the new Ministry of Electricity and Energy in dealing with the country's

---

3   The Presidential Review Commission on the Reform and Transformation of the Public Service noted in 1998 that poor information flow and communication between coordinating structures result in duplicate and contradictory decison-making.

energy crises and the failure of the state electricity utility, Eskom.

The 1996 Presidential Review Commission on the Reform and Transformation of the Public Service sought to define the public service reform agenda, circumvent organisational challenges described above and set a firm foundation for a performing state. The Commission recommended a fundamental rethink on the roles and functions of public services by, among other things, clarifying the administrative/political interface with a professional protocol to uphold it, and creating organisational structures appropriate to new functions. In addressing fragmentation and efficiency challenges, the Commission recommended the right-sizing of departments, informed by organisational audits and the redesign of departments and SOEs to determine appropriate staff complements and operational models. It also suggested an organisational review agency or unit to carry out ongoing evaluation and reconfiguration of structural organs of the state. With respect to coordination and the role of inter-governmental forums, the Commission found that many were weak and needed to be completely abolished. The state reconfiguration model of the Commission also proposed the rationalisation and phasing out of certain departments (such as the Department of Public Enterprises) and the transferring of SOE oversight to the relevant line departments (RSA, 1998). The overarching administrative regime reverberating in the Commission's report was that of hybridity as it cautioned against rapid decentralisation and outsourcing of certain functions to the private sector. These recommendations are still relevant today, especially in the context of slow progress in implementing the recommendations of the Presidential Review Committee on SOEs and the 2023 presidential instruction to rationalise government departments and SOEs.

CONCLUSION

Public sector administration in South Africa is becoming increasingly fragmented in ways reflected in the literature and the practice of public administration. Traditional public administration approaches were interrupted by political machinations, suboptimal arrangements of territorial governance, relentless reconfiguration of state administration, and the erosion of proven professional norms and practices. Service provision has become more diverse and disjointed, with responsibilities scattered across a complex mosaic of public, quasi-autonomous and private structures (De Wee and Jakoet-Salie, 2025).

This chapter reflected on the organisational reconfiguration of South Africa's public service delivery machinery amid growing concerns and perceptions of declining state capacity and performance. From this analysis, it can be seen that the country lacks an overarching and clear administrative paradigm and vision to manage complex state responsibilities and relations. Ongoing public service reforms depart from a historical legacy of fragmented political and administrative structures managed through a system of command and control. Post-1994 public service reform sought to amalgamate a myriad structures with different cultures and create a new constitutional order driven by values of people-centredness, professionalism, efficiency and effectiveness. The process has culminated in a legally constituted political structure to protect the integrity of the democratic project.

However, the system is battling to find vertical and horizontal harmony across the political and administrative stratosphere due to persistent organisational design failures and multiple structures. Not only are there too many points of decision-making, but there is also a disproportionate number of coordination structures. This results in duplication of roles and responsibilities, a lack of ownership for results, poor performance, and the blurring of lines of accountability. What is required is a reconfiguration of the state delivery machinery in line with the recommendations of the Presidential Review Commission on the Reform and Transformation of the Public Sector. South Africa needs to establish the basics of a functional public administration before it can experiment with hybrid models that draw selectively from public administration regimes. The actual shape and size of the new structure must be a subject of further research.

REFERENCES

African National Congress (ANC). 2007. '52nd National General Council, Legislature and Governance for a National Democratic Society'.

Auditor-General (AG). 2022. 'Consolidated General Report on National and Provincial Audit Outcomes'. Auditor-General, Pretoria.

Bach, O. 2017. 'How to address organizational fragmentation', https://managementkits.com/blog/2017/09/19/how-to-address-org-fragmentation, accessed 28 June 2025.

Bloomberg. 2023a. 'Why South Africa is on the brink of chaos'. *Bloomberg*, 16 June, https://www.bloomberg.com/news/features/2023-07-20/south-africa-s-private-sector-is-key-to-stopping-the-failed-state-cycle, accessed 30 June 2025.

Bloomberg. 2023b. 'South Africa is on the Road to Becoming A Failed State'. *Bloomberg*, 29 March, https://www.bloomberg.com/opinion/articles/2023-03-29/south-africa-is-on-the-road-to-becoming-a-failed-state, accessed 30 June 2025.

BusinessTech. 2023. 'CEO warns of state collapse in South Africa'. *BusinessTech*, 26 September, https://businesstech.co.za/news/business-opinion/720826/ceo-warns-of-state-collapse-in-south-africa, accessed 30 June 2025.

Cingolani, L. 2018. 'The role of state capacity in development studies'. *Journal of Development Perspectives* 2(1/2), 88–114.

Cooke, B. 2001. 'From colonial administration to development management'. IDPM Discussion Paper Series, Working Paper No. 63, Institute for Development Policy and Management, University of Manchester Precinct Centre, https://hummedia.manchester.ac.uk/institutes/gdi/publications/workingpapers/archive/gdp/dp_wp63.pdf, accessed 24 April 2024.

De Wee, G. and Jakoet-Salie, A. 2025. 'Policy Integration for Overcoming Fragmented Government Action in South Africa: The case of the national policy on food and nutrition security'. *Politics and Policy*, https://www.researchgate.net/publication/389427186_Policy_Integration_for_Overcoming_Fragmented_Government_Action_in_South_Africa_The_Case_of_the_National_Policy_on_Food_and_Nutrition_Security, accessed 30 June 2025.

Department of Planning, Monitoring and Evaluation (DPME). 2019. 'Stability at the political-administrative interface', https://www.dpme.gov.za/publications/research/STRATEGIC%20RESEARCH%20ASSIGNMENTS/2019_DPME_Synthesis%20Report_Stability%20at%20the%20Political-Administrative%20Interface.pdf, accessed 28 June 2025.

Department of Public Service and Administration (DPSA). 2007. *Guide and Toolkit on Organisational Design*. Pretoria: Government of South Africa.

Gomide, A., Pereira, A.K. and Machado, R. 2018. 'The challenges of state capacity and its operationalisation in empirical research'. International Public Policy Association (IPPA) 1st International Workshops on Public Policy, 26–28 June, University of Pittsburgh.

Gumede, W. 2022. 'SA's entire infrastructure is on the verge of total collapse', https://www.wits.ac.za/news/latest-news/opinion/2022/2022-07/sas-entire-infrastructure-is-on-the-verge-of-total-collapse.html, accessed 24 April 2024.

Hausmann, R., O'Brien, R., Fortunato, A., Lochmann, A., Shah, K., Venturi, L., Enciso-Valdivia, S., Vashkinskaya, E., Ahuja, K., Ahuja, K., Klinger, N., Sturzenegger, F. and Tokman, M. 2023. 'Growth through inclusion in South Africa'. CIP Working Paper No. 434, https://growthlab.hks.harvard.edu/publications/growth-through-inclusion-south-africa, accessed 24 April 2024.

Khemani. S. 2019. 'What is state capacity'. Policy Research Working Paper No. 8734, World Bank Group.

Klijn, E.H. 2012. 'Public management and governance: A comparison of two paradigms to deal with modern complex problems', in Levi Faur, D. (ed.), *The Handbook of Governance*. Oxford: Oxford University Press, pp. 201–214.

Lafley, A., Roger. L. and Martin, A.W. 2012. 'Bringing science to the art of strategy'. *Harvard Business Review*, https://hbr.org/2012/09/bringing-science-to-the-art-of-strategy, accessed 24 April 2024.

Mabugu, R. and Rakabe, E. 2023. 'Intergovernmental fiscal relations and public administration challenges in South Africa'. National Treasury, Republic of South Africa.

Mccourt, W. 2013. 'Models of public service reform: A problem-solving approach'. World Bank, https://documents1.worldbank.org/curated/en/823241468339619120/pdf/wps6428.pdf, accessed 30 June 2025.

Mello, D. and Louw, V. 2023. 'Usurping the role of an underperforming state: A case of South Africa'. *Politeia*, 42(1), https://doi.org/10.25159/2663-6689/15055

Ministry for the Public Service and Administration. 1995. 'White Paper on the Transformation of the Public Service'. Ministry for the Public Service and Administration, Pretoria, https://www.gov.za/sites/default/files/gcis_document/201409/168380.pdf, accessed 3 November 2024.

Minogue, M. 2001. 'The internationalization of new public management', in Mccourt, W. and Minogue, M. (eds), *The Internationalization of Public Management: Reinventing the Third World State*. Edward Elgar Publishing, pp. 1–19.

Muthien, Y. 2014. 'Public service reform in SA: Key challenges of execution'. *Strategic Review for Southern Africa*, 36(2).

Napier, C.J. 1997. 'Origins of centralised unitary states with special references to Botswana, Zimbabwe and Namibia'. PhD thesis, University of South Africa.

National Planning Commission (NPC). 2012. 'National Development Plan 2030: Our Future, make it work'. The Presidency, Pretoria, https://

www.nationalplanningcommission.org.za/National_Development_Plan, accessed 30 June 2025.

Neilson, G.L. and Wulf, J. 2012. 'How many direct reports?'. *Harvard Business Review*, https://hbr.org/2012/04/how-many-direct-reports, accessed 24 April 2024.

Organisation for Economic Co-operation and Development (OECD). 2007. 'Organising the Central State Administration: Policies and Instruments'. SIGMA Papers No. 43, OECD Publishing, Paris, https://doi.org/10.1787/5kml60q2n27c-en

Painter, M. and Pierre, J. 2005. 'Unpacking policy capacity: Issues and themes', in Painter, M. and Pierre, J. (eds), *Challenges to State Policy Capacity*. New York: Palgrave Macmillan.

Pereira, B.A.D. and Ckagnazaroff, I.V. 2012. 'Contributions to consolidate the new public governance: Identifying dimensions of analysis'. *Cad. EBAPE.BR*, 19(1).

Picard, L. 2005. 'State of the state: Institutional transformation, capacity and political change in SA'. *Review of African Political Economy*, 37(123), 109–110.

Parliamentary Monitoring Group (PMG). 2012. 'Public Service Commission and FOSAD on Performance Areas Requiring Attention by Executive Authorities and Heads of Departments', https://pmg.org.za/committee-meeting/14546/, accessed 28 June 2025.

Public Service Commission (PSC). 2022. 'State of the Public Service Report 2021: A reflection on Capacity and Capability of the Public Service'. Public Service Commission, Pretoria, South Africa.

Public Service Commission (PSC). 2023. 'Report on the performance of national departments: Adherence to the constitutional values and principles governing public administration'. 20 March, https://www.psc.gov.za/documents/reports/2023/Performance_of_National_Departments_on_Public_Administration_March_2023.pdf, accessed 30 June 2025.

Republic of South Africa (RSA). 1996. 'The Constitution of the Republic of South Africa', https://www.justice.gov.za/legislation/constitution/saconstitution-web-eng.pdf, accessed 30 June 2025.

Republic of South Africa (RSA). 1998. 'Report of the Presidential Review Commission on the Reform and Transformation of the Public Service in South Africa'. The Presidency, Pretoria.

Republic of South Africa (RSA). 2013. 'Service Charter: PSCBC Resolution 1 of 2013', https://www.gov.za/sites/default/files/gcis_document/201409/publicservicechartersept2013.pdf, accessed 30 June 2025.

Robinson, M. 2015. 'From Old Public Administration to the New Public Service, Implications for Public Sector'. UNDP Global Centre for Public Sector Excellence, https://www.undp.org/sites/g/files/zskgke326/files/publications/PS-Reform_Paper.pdf, accessed 28 June 2025.

Schick, A. 2003. 'A contemporary approach to public expenditure management'. World Bank Institute, Washington, DC.

United Nations Development Programme (UNDP). 2015. 'From Old Public Administration to the New Public Service: Implications for Public Sector Reform in Developing Countries', https://www.undp.org/sites/g/files/zskgke326/files/publications/PS-Reform_Paper.pdf, accessed 24 April 2024.

Vincenzo, A. and Di Mascio, F. 2021. 'Public sector organizational architecture and economic development: A comparative perspective'. *Journal of Comparative Policy Analysis: Research and Practice*, 23(5), 567–584.

Wang, W. and Yeung, R. 2018. 'Testing the effectiveness of "managing for results": Evidence from an education policy innovation in New York City'. *Journal of Public Administration Research and Theory*, 29(1), 84–100.

World Bank. 2023. 'Global Initiative for Public Administration Reforms', https://www.worldbank.org/en/topic/governance/brief/global-initiative-for-public-administration-reform-gipar, accessed 24 April 2024.

Wu, X., Ramesh, M. and Howlett, M. 2015. 'Policy capacity: A conceptual framework for understanding policy competences and capabilities'. *Policy and Society*, 34(3/4), 165–171.

SIXTEEN

Civil society and the South African state: Building a capable, ethical and responsive state

MARK HEYWOOD AND BRIAN LEVY

INTRODUCTION

Civil society played a key role in the struggle to end apartheid. In the first three decades of South Africa's democracy, civil society's continuing efforts to hold government to account have yielded some massive, vital victories. But times have changed and it is questionable whether changes in civil society's approach to activism have kept up with the challenges facing it. By exploring some aspects of the learning journey of reshaping the relationship between the state and civil society, this chapter addresses this question. As its authors, we have spent decades working as practitioners, researchers and writers at the state-society interface.[1] This chapter outlines what we hope is an

---

1   Heywood (2017) and Levy (2014) depict, in different ways, each author's 'lessons learned' from their decades-long journeys.

innovative approach to addressing some of the ongoing challenges at the interface of bureaucracy and civil society, using two case studies: South Africa's Treatment Action Campaign (TAC) and civil society efforts (in South Africa and elsewhere) to improve learning outcomes in basic education.

CIVIL SOCIETY AND ITS STRATEGIES

If by 'civil society' we mean organisations and individuals, independent of the state, who act voluntarily to advance the common good of a set of constituencies and social justice, then civil society organisations have been around for longer than democracy. In many countries, civil society was a precursor of democracy, organising for citizens' rights against the state. However, since the democratisation and human rights-centred constitutionalism that spread across most countries of the world in the 1990s, civil society has been given unprecedented recognition as a political stakeholder. It is often treated as a necessary – even if independent – partner to successful public governance and sustainable development.

Today, civil society takes numerous organisational shapes and forms and focuses on an endless and evolving list of social, political and economic issues. Legally, states have varying approaches to civil society. In China and Russia, for example, civil society is tightly controlled and there is extremely limited civic space.[2] Across Africa, although civil society is recognised by continental bodies such as the African Commission on Human and People's Rights (ACHPR), organisations such as the United Nations Office of the High Commissioner on Human Rights (OHCHR), Freedom House and Civicus show that 'civic space' is narrowing. OHCHR (n.d), for example, states that civil society is:

...increasingly under pressure from repressive laws and increased

---

2 'Civic space' is a term used by the United Nations and others to reflect on the degree of democratic space and freedom for organisations and individuals to organise voluntarily around social and political issues. Where that space is constrained by the state it is considered to be 'closed' or 'shrinking'.

restrictions on freedoms to express, participate, assemble and associate. Civil society actors, including human rights defenders and individuals who cooperate with the United Nations, are also facing a pushback, online and offline, across the world.

In contrast, since 1994, civil society in South Africa has been an indispensable pillar in the functioning of the new 'participatory democracy'. Its standing is entrenched in the 1996 Constitution and much jurisprudence that has flowed from it. People have the right 'to campaign for a political party or cause' and the Constitution, through its Bill of Rights (Chapter 2), unambiguously protects the civil and political rights that are considered the bedrock of an effective civil society (Constitution of the Republic of South Africa, 1996). Consequently, there has been a rapid growth of civil society organisations and activity since 1994. Some of it is organic to communities; some of it is a deliberate taking advantage of civic space permitted by the Constitution. Thus, by 2019, statistics from the Department of Social Development (DSD) recorded over 200,000 registered and 50,000 unregistered non-profit organisations (NPOs). In 2023, the DSD put the number of registered NGOs at 270,313, employing over a million people, making it not just a political sector but an economic one as well (DSD, 2023).

South Africa's civil society is hydra-headed and amorphous. However, since the late 1990s one of its most consistently visible and vociferous parts has been a relatively small subset of NGOs and social movements. These groups have sought to continue traditions started by the umbrella anti-apartheid organisation of the 1980s, the United Democratic Front (UDF) – to mobilise around rights in the new Constitution, and to demand social accountability and delivery from the state and, to a lesser extent, the private business sector (Raith Foundation, 2020). They mobilised successfully to protect and advance political rights, such as the rights of protest and assembly, as well as to demand social rights of access to adequate housing, healthcare services (particularly treatment for HIV/AIDS), basic education and children's rights (Brickhill, 2018).

Civil society, like South Africa's new democratic government, has been on a learning curve about how to operate effectively in a democratic state. The first 30 years of democratic civic activism and its relationship with the state have been diverse and evolutionary. However, it is possible to delineate two distinct approaches to the state that have been adopted by civil society organisations focused on social justice: an *adversarial approach*, oriented to holding government to account, and *a coalitional approach*, centred on building problem-focused developmental alliances among champions of reform, inside and outside of government. The preferred approach depends, to an important extent, on the agenda of the activists. It is important to emphasise that the two approaches are not necessarily mutually exclusive, and there are instances where they have been combined.

An adversarial approach

South African civil society has notched up many 'victories' using an adversarial approach to hold government to account. If the goal is to champion inclusion, then an adversarial approach that creates new 'facts' in the face of powerful, exclusionary status quo interests is almost certainly the preferred approach. This approach can also help civil society to act as a watchdog that helps deter the most egregious of laws, policies and actions. This is the dominant approach – focused on advocacy, social mobilisation and sometimes public impact litigation to *demand* the realisation of certain constitutional rights. The approach has led to demands for appropriate policy, sufficient resources and adequate budgets to bring about the actual realisation of constitutionally entrenched social and economic rights. A feature of this approach is that while it entails investment in research, policy development and direct service provision, legal services in particular, to marginalised communities, it is also confrontational and is therefore sometimes seen as divisive.

But even when an adversarial approach to improving public sector performance succeeds in bringing about the intended change, it operates on several assumptions: that the state *always* has the capability to implement demands; that it has the necessary financial resources and expertise to do so; and that it will abide by the will of the people or the order of the courts. This approach pays less attention to the capability of the state itself, or to the public servants employed within it, to be crucial instruments for implementing change. Indeed, a danger of social justice advocacy is that it may fuel polarisation and civic disillusion – because the method of engagement with the state may be on opposing sides in a courtroom or the street, and not always through negotiations and meetings.

Further, when the realities of the political environment in which public officials operate make it impossible for them to respond positively, they are likely to have the all-too-human response of retreating into a defensive crouch. Overall, it must therefore be debated as to what extent and in what contexts civil society adopting an adversarial approach to the state is capable of bringing about lasting and sustainable change in relation to social rights such as adequate housing, basic education and children's rights, or is able to tackle the social and economic determinants of exclusion and inequality.

An approach that builds cross-cutting coalitions

The coalitional approach seeks to realise social rights through formal and informal processes of problem-focused engagement. These processes include cross-cutting coalition-building, ongoing negotiation and social learning between civil society and the state. By 'cross-cutting coalitions' we mean civil society engagement that entails partnering with committed, developmental officials within the public sector. Underlying this phrase is a recognition that the South African state is not homogeneous. Some parts, and some staff within it, are deeply committed to a vision of public service; others pursue their private interests; yet others are 'captured' by one or other political, business or criminal faction.

A coalitional approach is less visible than its adversarial counterpart and does not generally get media coverage. After 1994, the government attempted to create fora for such processes through bodies at a national level such as the National Economic, Development and Labour Council (NEDLAC), which includes a community constituency alongside business and labour; and, at a local level, bodies such as school governing bodies and community policing forums. In 1999, it established the South African National AIDS Council (SANAC). More recently, similar bodies have been set up around anti-corruption efforts and early childhood development (ECD). Coalition-building can also take place through informal relationships with different departments and layers of government around the implementation of particular programmes.

Coalition-building has been the focus of sustained research in developing countries. Fox (2015) and Fox et al. (2023) detail the evolution of coalitional processes. These entail relationships between users of services, reform-oriented public officials, social movements and other developmental stakeholders. The research explores how the processes are set in motion, how coalitions consolidate, and how they (sometimes) lead to the establishment of sustainable, state-society bridging organisations.[3] As Fox et al.'s (2023) case studies show, reform-oriented public officials have leveraged these processes both to re-orient agency goals in more inclusive directions and to improve performance. As Fox et al. (2023: 12) put it, 'mutual empowerment between insiders and outsiders – a weapon of the weak'.

A coalitional approach to engaging with the public sector requires civil society actors to have different mindsets and skillsets from those required for the adversarial approach. Individuals or organisations that interface directly with government need to find ways to remain in contact with their constituencies and be seen as accountable to them, even as they engage collaboratively with reform-minded officials. They should not, in the language of the streets, be regarded as 'selling out'. For government, encouraging a coalitional approach requires political investment and systems that can demonstrate to civil society that cooperative engagement can actually make a difference. Collaboration must be viewed as capable of achieving beneficial outcomes.

The barriers to a coalitional approach do not lie only with civil society. Many government officials at national and provincial levels have an antipathy to civil society, and this sows distrust, including among public service employees and officials, and prevents effective collaboration. For example, painting civil society as a Trojan horse for 'imperialism' or 'White Monopoly Capital' – a common refrain of some government officials – does not assist attempts at cooperation.

---

3   For related contributions, see also Khan and Roy (2022), Mangla (2022), Tendler (1997) and Carpenter (2001).

CASE STUDY 1: ACCESS TO ANTIRETROVIRALS
– THE TREATMENT ACTION CAMPAIGN

The Treatment Action Campaign (TAC) is considered one of the most successful national civil society social movements since the end of apartheid and has been written about extensively (Forbath et al., 2011; Mbali, 2013). It was formed on 10 December 1998, International Human Rights Day and the anniversary of the signing of the South African Constitution two years earlier. Over 27 years later, it remains a vibrant and effective organisation.

Within a decade of its formation, TAC's activism contributed to a transformation of the landscapes of both policy and its implementation on the devastating HIV epidemic. Upon its formation in 1998, no person living with AIDS was receiving life-saving antiretroviral treatment (ARV) in the public health sector and almost all infected people died. HIV was widening inequalities and social exclusion. There followed almost a decade of intense conflict between TAC and the government over official policy, particularly government's refusal to include a treatment component to HIV prevention and care (Heywood, 2010a; 2010b). But ever since this was resolved in mid-2007, TAC has worked independently but collaboratively with the government to roll out the largest HIV treatment programme in the world, now covering over 5.8 million people and nearly 80 per cent of the eight million people living with HIV in South Africa (SANAC, n.d.). Perhaps the most dramatic evidence of this programme's results has been a rise in life expectancy of more than a decade for men and women and a massive drop in infant mortality due to HIV infection (SANAC, n.d.).

Viewed through the lens of the analytical framework outlined in this chapter, there are several distinct factors that help explain TAC's success:

- While TAC has been associated with confrontation, through adversarial activism, with the government of President Thabo Mbeki (1999–2008) and pharmaceutical companies, this approach was always combined with a coalitional approach; the balance/emphasis between these approaches depended on the response and capability of the state.

- Throughout its history, TAC attempted to engage with and strengthen the state bureaucracy in the public health service and the administration of health facilities. These relationships proved vital once policy obstacles were cleared, allowing the state and civil society to collaborate on the implementation of HIV treatment and prevention programmes.
- TAC always worked as the leader of a coalition of interests and organisations that it built patiently through advocacy; it managed to build sufficient power to catalyse change through the way it managed this coalition, making it more than the sum of its parts. TAC was created as a *campaign* (not a self-sufficient organisation) and its organisational architecture (of community branches and a national council of its different sectors) reflected this, bringing together trade unions, faith-based organisations, non-governmental organisation (NGOs), academics and clinicians, as well as influential international organisations such as Médecins Sans Frontières (MSF).

Understood within this framework, TAC's history can be divided into two parts: (i) the period of confrontation over government policy and President Mbeki's AIDS denialism (1998–2007); and (ii) the coalitional period (and when deemed necessary, confrontation and/or challenge), working with committed public officials over implementation of a policy that TAC eventually managed to co-create with the government (2007 to the present).

It is important to note that during the first period (1998–2007), TAC had simultaneously continued with its advocacy and political mobilisation to make demands, and worked to overcome obstacles that the government would encounter on the health service supply/delivery side should it come to implementation of a human rights-based programme. In particular:

- TAC addressed the excessive cost of medicines by continuing to campaign and litigate against multinational pharmaceutical companies to make them affordable. By 2007, the cost of ARVs and several other essential medicines, such as the anti-fungal Fluconazole (patented by Pfizer), had been reduced significantly.
- TAC tackled the very serious stigma that surrounds HIV infection

by building hundreds of branches for people living with HIV. Its branches were conduits for its pioneering programme of 'treatment literacy' carried out with the guidance and support of health professionals. It also worked with MSF to pilot treatment programmes in urban informal settlements such as Khayelitsha, and rural areas such as Lusikisiki in the Eastern Cape, to prove that a treatment programme was feasible. In this way, it empowered both patients and health providers with knowledge about AIDS treatment. This meant that when a government-led treatment programme was started in 2004 (albeit initially without the full political support of the then Minister of Health, Dr Manto Tshabalala-Msimang), there was high take-up and high adherence to the medicines; this has been sustained for two decades.

Although the first period was bitter and divisive, TAC worked behind the scenes to keep some channels of communication open with officials in the national Health Department and the Western Cape Health Department. This period ended in early 2007 when TAC reached agreement with then Deputy President Phumzile Mlambo-Ngcuka, on a new National Strategic Plan on HIV/AIDS and TB (2007–2011). Thereafter, TAC adapted its demand strategy to focus on working with the Health Department to encourage HIV testing and treatment, strengthening public health systems and financing, and closely monitoring implementation of the programme.

TAC worked from both inside and outside of the state. In late 2006/07, it delegated several of its leaders to work with the Office of the Deputy President to develop a new framework for a National Strategic Plan on HIV. The objective of this partnership was a plan that would encompass access to treatment (TAC's main demand) and an institutional framework that would be a coalition between government and civil society, capable of directing and overseeing implementation of the plan. This involved restructuring and thereby legitimising the South African National AIDS Council (SANAC), a body that had been set up by President Mbeki in 1999. Key TAC leaders were appointed to senior positions in SANAC, where they worked closely with the government and built the Council. For a period, SANAC became a forum for *de facto* co-governance of the AIDS response, although *de jure* power remained with government. SANAC created a forum for interactions between scientists, government departments, business and many sectors of civil society about policy and programmes. It also fostered greater transparency, a system of accountability and became a problem-solving institution.

At the same time, TAC's branches remained operational, treatment literacy and local advocacy campaigns continued, and TAC maintained an independent media profile. Through its branches, operating in all provinces except the Northern Cape, TAC assessed the actual state of delivery on the ground and frequently allied with local health workers. It was central to setting up organisations like the Stop Stockouts Project which monitors the availability of essential healthcare medicines and children's vaccines. More recently, TAC developed innovative new programmes that aim to improve the *quality* of service delivery, such as the Ritshidze programme of community-led clinic monitoring. TAC's general secretary is a board member of the Office of Health Standards Compliance, a statutory body, and it has allied itself with struggles over other health issues, particularly TB, mental health and cancer. This coalitional approach was aided in 2008 with the change of the Minister and the Director-General in the Department of Health; both were replaced with officials who were prepared to work with civil society. The new minister was first Barbara Hogan, followed by Dr Aaron Motsoaledi.

In the new coalitional context, there were rapid and demonstrable changes. Not only did the ARV-treatment programme expand rapidly, but important new interventions were introduced. For example, once the benefits of voluntary medical male circumcision (VMMC) for reducing HIV transmission were conclusively proven by research studies, a programme for it could rapidly be rolled out. SANAC's inclusion of traditional leaders and healers enhanced the likelihood of them accepting biomedical programmes like VMMC, and hence the high take-up of the programme. There was also a huge infusion of financial resources into the AIDS programme, mainly from international donors.

TAC offered public servants in the Health Department a vision of care and treatment that provided hope, encouraged innovation and inspired (rather than commanded) performance. However, TAC's coalitional approach has faced increasing strain in the last decade. Today, health systems are failing due to a combination of budget cuts, corruption and poor management. When coalitional approaches no longer appear to yield tangible progress, often due to macro factors that are beyond the control of the Health Department, there is pressure on civil society to return to a more aggressive 'them and us' adversarial approach – a 'populism' of social justice. In the face of this, there is a renewed risk of the AIDS programme failing (80 per cent of people on ARVs is still below the target of 90 per cent, and over one million people have been lost to care). This, perhaps, will be the real test of a coalitional approach: it remains to be seen whether civil society and government can work together on a programme aimed at finding a path through the current morass to continue to deliver quality healthcare services.

CASE STUDY 2: BASIC EDUCATION AND
CIVIL SOCIETY IN SOUTH AFRICA –
A COMPARATIVE PERSPECTIVE

Our second case study focuses on the role of civil society organisations in improving education outcomes for schoolgoers in South Africa. There are three desired outcomes. First, providing universal access to basic education, in which, relative to other middle-income countries, South Africa has done well. Second, providing the infrastructure and other inputs (textbooks, toilets and sanitation, qualified teachers) that are the 'scaffolding' of an education system. South Africa's performance has been uneven, demonstrated by some egregious failures in infrastructure provision which have been a high-profile focus of adversarial civil society activism. Third, fostering learning in teacher-student interactions; on this, South Africa has done poorly (Levy et al., 2018).

Three decades into democracy, an unconscionably large proportion of children leave South Africa's public school system without adequate literacy or numeracy skills. Civil society organisations have vocally challenged government to improve, including via a series of court victories. But the shortfalls persist. This case study explores the possible opportunities for civil society to aid in improving learning outcomes by complementing adversarial strategies with enhanced attention to cross-cutting coalitional initiatives.

In South Africa, the institutional arrangements established by the 1996 South African Schools Act opened up the possibility for coalitional approaches to improve learning across multiple tiers of the education sector: policymaking, regulation and financing are national responsibilities; implementation is delegated to provinces (and districts); school governing bodies play a significant role at school level. In practice, though, education sector governance has generally been legalistic, and civil society strategies adversarial. A contrast between South Africa's experience across the various tiers and those of other countries, such as Peru, India, Ghana and Kenya, is instructional.[4]

The national level – South Africa and Peru
Multiple stakeholders influence the education sector at the national level. They include political leaders, public officials, trade unions, professional organisations, academic specialists and NGOs, such as the learner-based movement, Equal Education. The contrasting experiences of Peru and South Africa illustrate the differences in sector performance that result from whether these national-level interactions are centred on coalitional or adversarial approaches.

As detailed by Balarin and Saavedra (2022), Peru has long had to navigate an extraordinarily turbulent political and institutional environment – including an education sector led by 20 ministers in 25 years. This has resulted in a form of 'protracted incrementalism': small incremental gains achieved by one administration are dismantled by the next, only to be partially reinstated at a later stage (Balarin and Saavedra, 2022: 15). Yet, contrary to expectations, Peru achieved

---

4 See Levy (2022) for a comparative analysis of the political economy of basic education across a dozen countries.

significant gains in learning outcomes between 2000 and 2018.[5]

Coalition-building accounts for Peru's impressive performance. As described by Balarin and Saavedra (2022), civil society entities such as NGOs, universities, think tanks and research centres also play a pivotal role in shaping policy agendas and driving education reforms. The country's messy, iterative process of policy formulation and adaptation helped build broad legitimacy among stakeholders. This legitimacy enhanced the ability of those technocrats within government orientated towards civil society and reform to push back effectively against idiosyncratic initiatives proposed by political appointees and their ministerial teams. This contributed to agenda continuity and incremental progress in reforms (Balarin and Saaveda, 2022: 16).

In contrast to Peru, South Africa's national-level education sector stakeholders (inside and outside of government) have failed to cooperate sufficiently to be able to bring about effective change. Part of the reason for this failure can be traced to more general societal preoccupations with adversarial civil society approaches and to bureaucratic insulation. However, there are also three sector-specific explanations:

• First, there has been a failure among experts to constructively work through their disagreements. Gustafsson and Taylor (2022) outline how an unusually strident conflict over how best to measure and monitor learning outcomes has been an important part of why the country has repeatedly failed to put in place any systematic assessments of learning before the end of twelfth grade.

• Second, perceptions within the sector about South Africa's leading teachers' union, South African Democratic Teachers Union (SADTU). As with teachers' unions everywhere, SADTU has to navigate inherent tensions between its role as an advocate of the material interests of teachers and its role as a professional organisation. Coalitional approaches to strengthening sector performance would include efforts to build common cause with teachers committed to the more professional parts of this dual

---

5 Between 2000 and 2018, Peru's Programme for International Student Assessment scores rose from 292 to 400 for mathematics, and from 327 to 401 for reading.

identity.[6] Instead, SADTU has almost uniformly been demonised by sector professionals, media and many politicians as disruptive and as a principal cause of the sector's failures.

- Third, fault-lines rooted in South Africa's racial history set the stage for adversarial modes of engagement between civil society and government over how to improve learning outcomes. The underlying issue was identified in the early 1990s by Blade Nzimande, who was later appointed Minister of Higher Education (Gustafsson and Taylor, 2022: 51):

> The National Education Policy Initiative classically represents the problem of this division of labour, in that the experts are academics, university-based people largely, who are predominantly white; whilst the mass-based structures … are predominantly black. That has got the potential of creating severe tensions.

Transcending these deeply rooted divisions and working instead to build a national-level, pro-learning developmental coalition will not happen easily. Yet, experience elsewhere suggests that this would be a more realistic way forward than either government efforts to insulate the education technocracy from external pressures, or adversarial strategies on the part of civil society.

Provincial and district levels – South Africa, India and Ghana
Subnational institutions play a central role in governance of the education sector in many countries. This section contrasts governance of provincial-level education in South Africa with that in India and district-level governance in South Africa with that in Ghana.

Mangla's (2022) pathbreaking analysis of education sector governance in two states in India, Uttar Pradesh and Himachal Pradesh, provides a useful point of reference for South Africa's provincial-level experience. Mangla's analysis centres on two distinctions: between logistical and

---

6   See Grindle's (2004) in-depth analysis of Mexico's education sector reforms for an example of a reform process, which placed working with the teachers' union at centre stage.

craft activities, and between legalistic and craft bureaucracies.

- Logistical activities (the provision of school infrastructure, for example) are engineering-oriented in nature; they combine up-front planning and tightly managed, top-down implementation by hierarchical organisations. By contrast, 'craft-oriented' activities (for example, classroom teaching and learning) are ones where ongoing iteration and adaptation to local-level circumstances produce the best results.

- A legalistic bureaucracy is insulated from political pressures and centred on a commitment to rational-legal norms. Mangla (2022: 52–55) writes: 'Bureaucrats are judged for following rules and not for the consequences that emanate from their actions.' Deliberative bureaucracy, on the other hand, '…promotes flexibility and problem-solving… it induces a participatory dynamic that urges officials to negotiate policy problems through discussion and adjust their outlooks to shifting circumstances.'

Table 16.1 summarises how Mangla's two distinctions align with each other, and how both align with the adversarial/coalitional distinction central to this chapter.

Table 16.1: Two contrasting patterns of sectoral governance

	Pattern I	Pattern II
Type of task	Logistical (e.g. school infrastructure)	Craft (e.g. teaching)
Approach to public administration	Legalistic	Deliberative
Civil society strategy	Adversarial	Coalitional

Source: Adapted from Mangla (2022)

Both the strengths and limits of legalistic bureaucracies are vividly evident in Mangla's in-depth case study of Uttar Pradesh (Mangla, 2022: 134, 168–170).

Legalistic bureaucracy in Uttar Pradesh has promoted gains in primary school enrolment and infrastructure … enabling officials to resist political interference when providing inputs to schools... [But] local administration's adherence to rules imposed administrative burdens... Cumulatively, these processes contributed to low-quality education.

In contrast (Mangla, 2022: 171–172, 217, 327, 332):

At independence, Himachal Pradesh was among India's least literate states... [Subsequently, it] began to record significant gains in primary schooling... HP is now among India's leading states with respect to literacy and primary education policy education indicators... Deliberative bureaucracy is found to have made a decisive impact ... enabling state officials to undertake complex tasks, co-ordinate with society and adapt policies to local needs, yielding higher quality education services.

As in India, national-level policymakers and civil society activists in South Africa pay close attention to implementation challenges at provincial level. However, rather than calibrating engagement to the varied realities of provincial-level governance, there has been something of a uniformity of approach. Bureaucracies generally are conceived to be legalistic; tasks generally are characterised as logistical and, as per the central theme of this chapter, civil society's default mode of engagement at provincial level often has been adversarial. Yet, as Levy et al. (2018) explored for South Africa's Western Cape and Eastern Cape provinces, adversarial approaches are not well calibrated to improve learning outcomes.

In politically and bureaucratically fragmented contexts such as the Eastern Cape (see Kota et al., 2018), judicial victories and resulting court-imposed obligations to improve infrastructure have limited potential for impact whereas bureaucracies lack the legalistic/logistical capacity for follow-through. In the Western Cape, though legalistic and logistical capacities are present, the legalistic norms that underpin the province's bureaucracy (Cameron and Levy, 2018) can all too readily stymie efforts to foster the motivation and flexibility that are key to improving learning outcomes.

Turning to the district level, it can be an intriguing intermediate locus for efforts to improve learning outcomes. For one thing, it is the most localised level of governance which encompasses the full range of services, capabilities and resources needed to improve learning outcomes.[7] For another, as Ghana illustrates, its locale between the hyper-local and the provincial makes it a potent strategic entry point for motivated local champions to come together to build coalitions to improve learning outcomes.

According to Ampratwum et al. (2019), Ghana's messy political realities created a stark disjuncture between the formal rules and the realities of education-sector governance. Even so, decentralisation of education service delivery enabled the emergence of islands of effectiveness. The drivers of performance and accountability did not simply trickle down from the national level; rather, they were shaped by district and school-level coalitional dynamics. In one district, intense intra- and inter-party competition among major political actors hindered efforts to promote teacher accountability and reduce absenteeism. Conversely, in another district, a developmental coalition among community, school and district-level actors, including political officials and teachers' unions, provided a valuable platform for improving learning outcomes (Ampratwum et al., 2019: 55–59).

South Africa's national Department of Basic Education is increasingly embracing localised districts as entry points for fostering improvement. Civil society could usefully follow suit. Following the lead of PILO, a not-for-profit organisation aimed at improving learning outcomes in South Africa, and a few other civil society organisations, heightened attention to coalitional approaches at district level could provide a valuable additional entry point for improving learning outcomes.

Community and school levels – South Africa and Kenya

Our concerns about civil society approaches to engagement at the school-level contrast with those about the national and provincial levels, where we fear an excess of adversarialism. At school level, our

---

7   We are grateful to Mary Metcalfe, Executive Director of PILO, for this insight.

concerns are more around whether there has been a (so far) under-realised opportunity to improve learning outcomes by fostering micro-level developmental coalitions.

The 1996 South African Schools Act (SASA) included reforms that gave far-reaching authority to school governing bodies (SGBs) in which parents were the majority. The reforms were motivated both by the concerns of apartheid-era elites about how schools would be governed, and by the liberatory impulses of the United Democratic Front and other grassroots movements. South African school-level case studies (Fleisch and Christie, 2004; Levy et al., 2018) document striking examples of how, within low-income communities, school-level coalitions incorporating school principals, motivated teachers, parents and community leaders have achieved successful learning outcomes. Yet, while a few exemplary civil society organisations work collaboratively at school and community levels, there has been little sustained effort to breathe life into the SASA/SGB architecture within low-income communities.[8] Kenya's experience illustrates what a more systematic commitment to micro-level coalition-building might achieve.

Kenya's public bureaucracy is notoriously uneven in its performance (Branch and Cheeseman, 2006). Yet, notwithstanding bureaucratic weaknesses, the country has long been a top performer among Eastern and Southern African countries; its learning outcomes are better than those achieved by South Africa's best-performing provinces.[9] Key to achieving these outcomes have been school-level coalitional strategies. Ben Piper, a senior adviser on education policy and practice in Kenya

---

8   A 2003 review of school governance commissioned by the Minister of Education, and led by Professor Crain Soudien, identified some key obstacles to horizontal governance in poor communities and put forward a series of proposals on how the obstacles might be overcome; the report was never released. Eberhard (2016), prepared as an input into Levy et al. (2018), provides an overview of South Africa's SGB support initiatives up to that date.

9   In the 2007 SACMEQ learning assessment (the most recent that provided directly comparable data), Kenya's median score was 548 and South Africa's 483. The median score for the Nairobi region was 535, as compared with the Western Cape's 496. See Levy et al. (2018): chapters 2, 7 and 10 for further details.

and head of the Gates Foundation's global education practice, offers further insights (quoted in Levy et al., 2018: 280):

> What one sees in rural Kenya is an expectation for kids to learn and be able to have basic skills… Exam results are far more readily available in Kenya than in other countries in the region. The 'mean scores' for the Kenya Certificate of Primary Education (KCPE) and equivalent KCSE at secondary school are posted in every school and over time so that trends can be seen. Head teachers are held accountable for those results to the extent of being paraded around the community if they did well, or literally banned from school and kicked out of the community if they did badly.

We recognise that, outside elite settings, it can be difficult for parents and communities to exercise their voices. Further, that inviting parents and other community stakeholders to participate in school governance can add to the risks of those with predatory interests capturing positions and resources. Nevertheless, it is not the practical challenges facing civil society that account for the lack of attention paid to the possibilities for inclusive governance created by SASA. Rather, it is the ideational lens through which South Africans approach the role of civil society in public service provision.

CONCLUSION

Has the time come to shift how South African civil society engages with government to emphasise more coalitional approaches? This question becomes even more pertinent considering the coalition Government of National Unity that followed the 2024 general election. Keeping in mind that adversarial approaches continue to have their place, our two case studies suggest that the answer is 'yes'. Here, stepping back from the details of the cases, are four conclusions from our analysis:

- First, since the late 1990s, South African civil society has mostly adopted adversarial approaches for reasons rooted in history. These adversarial approaches have yielded some massive, vital victories –

with gains more likely when the relevant tasks are logistical rather than craft.

- In cases where strategic coalitions between government and civil society have been forged, these have proven capable of yielding results that strengthen society's access to improved public services.
- Third, adversarial approaches are more likely to succeed when underlying state capability is strong than when it is weak – however, the administrative capability of the South African state has declined over the past 15 years.
- Fourth, going forward, there is a case for civil society also giving heightened attention to approaches to engagement that focus on building cross-cutting coalitions of stakeholders (inside and outside government) who are committed to addressing concrete problems.

A crucial, continuing challenge for the South African state is to renew a sense of hope and possibility. Mobilising around failures does not renew hope – on the contrary, it can risk deepening disillusionment. The times call not for deepening confrontation, but for a mode of social mobilisation on the part of civil society that fosters, rather than undercuts, a sense of solidarity and shared purpose. Our hope is that this chapter helps, in some small way, to add value to the call for a more hopeful path.

REFERENCES

Ampratwum, E., Awal, M. and Oduro, F. 2019. 'Decentralization and teacher accountability: The political settlement and sub-national governance in Ghana's education sector', in Hickey, S. and Hossain, N. (eds), *The Politics of Education in Developing Countries: From Schooling to Learning*. Oxford: Oxford University Press, pp. 44–63.

Balarin, M. and Saavedra, M. 2022. 'The political economy of education reforms in Peru, 1995–2020', https://riseprogramme.org/sites/default/files/inline-files/The%20Political%20Economy%20of%20Education%20Reforms%20in%20Peru%201995-2020.pdf, accessed 30 June 2025.

Branch, D. and Cheeseman, N. 2006. 'The politics of control in Kenya: Understanding the bureaucratic-executive state, 1952–1978'. *Review of African Political Economy*, 107, 11–31.

Brickhill, J. 2018. *Public Interest Litigation in South Africa*. Cape Town: Juta.

Cameron, R. and Levy, B. 2018. 'Provincial governance of education: The Western Cape experience', in Levy, B., Cameron, R., Hoadley, U. and Naidoo, V. (eds), *The Politics and Governance of Basic Education: A Tale of Two South African Provinces.* Oxford University Press, pp. 85–120.

Carpenter, D. 2001. *The Forging of Bureaucratic Autonomy: Reputations, Networks and Policy Innovation in Executive Agencies, 1862–1928.* Princeton: Princeton University Press.

Department of Social Development (DSD). 2023. 'Media Statement', https://www.dsd.gov.za/index.php/21-latest-news/463-minister-lindiwe-zulu-applauds-the-critical-role-played-by-non-governmental-organisations#, accessed December 2024.

Eberhard, F. 2016. 'A preliminary review of school governing body support initiatives in South Africa'. Mimeo.

Fleisch, B. and Christie, P. 2004. 'Structural change, leadership and school effectiveness/improvement: Perspectives from South Africa'. *Discourse,* 25(1), 95–111, https://www.researchgate.net/profile/Brahm-Fleisch/publication/43472808_Structural_Change_Leadership_and_School_EffectivenessImprovement_Perspectives_from_South_Africa/links/6422f32392cfd54f8435529d/Structural-Change-Leadership-and-School-Effectiveness-Improvement-Perspectives-from-South-Africa.pdf, accessed 30 June 2025.

Forbath, W. (with assistance from Zackie Achmat, Geoff Budlender, Mark Heywood). 2011. 'Cultural transformation, deep institutional reform and ESR practice: South Africa's Treatment Action Campaign', in White, L.E. and Perelman, J. (eds), *Stones of Hope: How African Activists Reclaim Human Rights to Challenge Global Poverty.* Stanford: Stanford University Press.

Fox, J.A. 2015. 'Social sccountability: What does the evidence really say?'. *World Development,* 72, 346–361, https://www.sciencedirect.com/science/article/pii/S0305750X15000704, accessed 30 June 2025.

Fox, J., Robinson, R.S. and Hossain, N. 2023. 'Pathways towards power shifts: State-society synergy'. *World Development*, 172, December, https://www.sciencedirect.com/science/article/pii/S0305750X2300164X, accessed 30 June 2025.

Fukuyama, F. 2004. *State-Building.* Ithaca NY: Cornell University Press.

González, P., Fernández-Vergar, A.E., Rojas, G. and Vilugrón, L. 2023. 'The political economy of regulation: Chile's education reforms since the return of democracy', https://riseprogramme.org/sites/default/files/2023-03/The_Political_Economy_of_Regulation_Chile%E2%80%99s_Educational_Reforms_since_the_Return_of_Democracy_2.pdf, accessed 30 June 2025.

Grindle, M.S. 2004. *Despite the Odds: The Contentious Politics of Education Reform.* Princeton, N.J.: Princeton University Press.

Gustafsson, M. and Taylor, N. 2022. 'The politics of improving learning outcomes in South Africa: Research on improving systems of education'. *PE03*, https://doi.org/10.35489/BSG-RISE-2022/PE03

Heywood, M. 2010a. 'Civil society and uncivil government: The Treatment Action Campaign vs Thabo Mbeki 1998–2008', in Glaser, D. (ed.), *After Mbeki*. Johannesburg: Wits University Press.

Heywood, M. 2010b. 'Picking-up the pieces: The end of AIDS denialism and its aftermath', in Abdool Karim, S. and Abdool Karim, Q. (eds), *HIV/AIDS in South Africa*. New York: Cambridge University Press.

Heywood, M. 2017. *Get up! Stand up!*. Cape Town: Tafelberg Publishers.

Hickey, S. and Hossain, N. (eds). 2019. *The Politics of Education in Developing Countries*. Oxford: Oxford University Press.

Honig, D. 2018. *Navigation by Judgment: Why and When Top-Down Management of Foreign Aid Doesn't Work*. Oxford: Oxford University Press.

Hossain, N., Hassan, M.M., Rahman, M.A., Ali, K.S. and Islam, M.S. 2019. 'The politics of learning in Bangladesh', in Hickey, S. and Hossain, N. (eds), *The Politics of Education in Developing Countries: From Schooling to Learning*. Oxford: Oxford University Press, pp. 64–85.

Kelsall, T., Schulz, N., Ferguson, W., Vom Hau, M., Hickey, S. and Levy, B. 2022. *Political Settlements and Development: Theory, Evidence, Implications*. Oxford: Oxford University Press.

Khan, M. and Roy, P. 2022. 'Making anti-corruption real: Using a "Power, capabilities and interest approach" to stop wasting money and start making progress'. ACE SOAS Consortium, Synthesis Paper 001.

Kota, Z., Hendricks, M., Matambo, E. and Naidoo, V. 2018. 'Provincial governance of education – the Eastern Cape experience', in Levy, B., Cameron, R., Hoadley, U. and Naidoo, V. (eds), *The Politics and Governance of Basic Education: A Tale of Two South African Provinces*. Oxford: Oxford University Press, pp. 121–148.

Levy, B. 2014. *Working with the Grain: Integrating Governance and Growth in Development Strategies*. New York: Oxford University Press.

Levy, B. 2022. 'How Political Contexts Influence Education Systems: Patterns, Constraints, Entry Points'. Research on Improving Systems of Education Working Paper Series No. 122.

Levy, B. 2025. 'Micro-foundations of socially embedded bureaucracies'. Thinking and Working Politically Community of Practice, University of Birmingham.

Levy, B., Cameron, R., Hoadley, U. and Naidoo, V. (eds). 2018. *The Politics and Governance of Basic Education: A Tale of Two South African Provinces*. Oxford: Oxford University Press.

Levy, B., Hirsch, A., Nxele, M. and Naidoo, V. 2021. 'South Africa: When strong institutions and massive inequalities collide'. Carnegie Endowment for International Peace.

Mangla, A. 2022. *Making Bureaucracy Work: Norms, Education and Public Service Delivery in India*. Cambridge: Cambridge University Press.

Mbali, M. 2013. *South African AIDS Activism and Global Health Politics*. London: Palgrave Macmillan.

Office of the High Commissioner on Human Rights (OHCHR). n.d. 'Civic space and human rights defenders', https://www.ohchr.org/en/topic/civic-space-and-human-rights-defenders, accessed 12 January 2025.

Pritchett, L., Woolcock, M. and Andrews, M. 2010. 'Capability traps? The mechanisms of persistent implementation failure'. Center for Global Development Working Paper No. 234.

Raith Foundation. 2020. 'Critical Reflections on the Social Justice sector in the post-apartheid era', https://www.wits.ac.za/media/wits-university/faculties-and-schools/commerce-law-and-management/research entities/cals/documents/Final%20SJS%20Review%20Report.pdf, accessed January 2025.

Scott, J. 1999. *Seeing Like a State: How Certain Schemes to Improve the Human Condition Have Failed*. New Haven: Yale University Press.

South African National AIDS Council (SANAC). n.d. 'The National Strategic Plan for HIV, TB and Sexually Transmitted Infections, 2023–2028', https://sanac.org.za/wp-content/uploads/2023/05/SANAC-NSP-2023-2028-Web-Version.pdf, accessed January 2025.

Tendler, J. 1997. *Good Government in the Tropics*. Baltimore: Johns Hopkins University Press.

SEVENTEEN

Conclusion: Building capacity, capability and deepening ethics

SANDY AFRICA, NA'EEM JEENAH
AND MUSA NXELE

INTRODUCTION

This edited collection reflects on and assesses the state of the South African state and its various institutions 30 years after the country's emergence as a constitutional democracy. The various chapters evaluate whether the state possesses the ethical foundations, institutional capacity and necessary capability to deliver on its promises to address the injustices associated with South Africa's past, become a vehicle for the social protection, well-being and prosperity of all its people, and, concordantly, assume a global role in improving the lot of humankind.

The views of this volume's authors about whether the state has lived up to expectations are mixed – even contradictory – on some issues. Achievements in policy formulation, implementation of certain objectives and improvements in the quality of life for some are acknowledged. However, the overall assessment is that the performance of the state in critical areas has been poor, and in others, a failure.

This book goes beyond an assessment of the state's capacity – understood as the resources and structures established for governance. It also explores how capability – the state's ability to effectively utilise these resources – shapes governance outcomes, and how ethics can define the trajectory of the state's agenda. It explores the character of the contemporary South African state and the historical global forces that have shaped it: colonialism and apartheid, on the one hand, and the struggles and resistance of the people of South Africa, on the other (Ngomane and Flanagan, 2003). It also deconstructs the regularly proclaimed ideal of South Africa as a developmental state. A key underpinning of the notion of the developmental state is it permitting – and even expecting – a significant degree of state intervention. This is at odds with the neoliberal idea that 'too much' state intervention in public life can stifle democracy and economic development because it disincentivises individual aspiration, competition and the race to get ahead (Barbara, 2008; Fine, 2014). The notion that less state involvement is good public policy has been the basis for some political battles in post-1994 South Africa. These different conceptions of the state are addressed by Abba Omar in Chapter 2.

HISTORY AND THE MAKING OF THE SOUTH AFRICAN STATE

For most of the three decades following apartheid, the ANC dominated the political landscape through its sweeping electoral majorities in national elections, until 2024 when its support plummeted (Southall, 2024). Consequently, it determined how state power was wielded in the first 30 years of democracy and dominated the policy landscape. Many South Africans, including the ANC's major allies – the South African Communist Party (SACP) and the Congress of South African Trade Unions (COSATU) – regarded the economic policies it introduced as neoliberal in orientation. In the interests of preserving the unity of the ANC-led Tripartite Alliance, however, these allies maintained rank with their political partner (Pillay, 2011).

Preceding these contestations within the Tripartite Alliance, and within society more broadly, is the legacy of struggles during the colonial and apartheid eras over how territory and people were to be integrated into a world system of trade and diplomatic relations. Over centuries, and especially in the 19th and 20th centuries, foreign powers used military force to subjugate the populations of Africa and other territories in what we now regard as the Global South (Falola, 2022).

The African experience of state-building that followed colonialism was, therefore, firstly concerned with political independence. The colonies, juridical extensions of the metropolitan authorities in Europe, were exploited for their abundant raw materials and cheap labour, in order to fuel the growth of industrialising European economies. In South Africa, where this pattern of state formation had its own peculiar trajectory, resistance by the Black majority was met with extreme repression. In 1910, the Afrikaner Republics merged with the British colonies to form the Union of South Africa, which became a British dominion. The Black majority was excluded from this arrangement, and the state represented the interests of whichever White minority elite was dominant (Terreblanche, 2010). When the National Party came to power in 1948, it expedited the political and economic exclusion of Black people through an intensified agenda of racial segregation. The apartheid state shrugged off its by-then nominal relationship with the British Crown and established the Republic of South Africa in 1961. Over the next three decades, the apartheid state was characterised by several pillars: the formal demarcation of the population into racial and ethnic groups; forcing the different designated groups to reside in different geographic areas; and the development of a system of racial capitalism. In spite of facing an extremely repressive security machinery, a combination of external and internal pressures, including resistance by the organised working class, finally saw apartheid fall in the early 1990s, with negotiations for a new political dispensation leading to a democratically elected government.

THEN AND NOW: LENSES TO UNDERSTAND THE CREATION OF THE POST-APARTHEID STATE

The immediate tasks of the post-apartheid government were to build state capacity by dismantling the apartheid state infrastructure and to strengthen state capability by ensuring new state institutions could respond effectively to the aspirations of the previously excluded majority. The negotiations of the late 1980s and early 1990s resulted in an agreement that South Africa would be a single, unitary state with nine provinces, and that apartheid state formations, including the 'homelands', would be dismantled. The first democratic parliament systematically repealed the laws that had propped up apartheid, and new legislation created state structures to entrench democracy. At the apex of this process of state-making-by-legislation was the adoption of the Constitution of the Republic of South Africa in 1996. Replacing the 1993 interim Constitution, which facilitated the creation of the country's first inclusive parliament, the Constitution outlined the broad aspirations of the South African nation and detailed the structures and functioning of the post-apartheid state (Ebrahim, 1998). While this sets the measure by which the effectiveness of the state may be judged and lays the basis for a constitutional state, it does not guarantee an effective state.

The chapters in this book seek to use the broad aspirations and parameters provided by the Constitution as measures against which to judge the performance and effectiveness of the post-apartheid state. It must be noted, however, that these contributions are made at a time when the constitution-making project of the 1990s is being interrogated by a younger generation of activists and politicians, different from those who ushered it in, as well as by intellectuals who reject liberal assumptions about the state-making project (Ansari, 2021; Mpofu-Walsh, 2021). In addition, certain disgruntled elements – some of whom are the beneficiaries of what has come to be termed state capture – see the Constitution both as a hindrance to their project of self-enrichment and impunity, and regard anti-constitutionalism as a useful lure to garner support. They view the constitution-making project with increasing suspicion, labelling it 'neoliberal' (and, sometimes, 'neo-colonial') and as designed to entrench White domination. This view is bolstered by the fact that the lives of the country's Black majority have remained overwhelmingly, and stubbornly wretched, while the lives of the minority White population (and those of a small, though growing, Black middle class) remain, in the main, comfortable.

For many wealthier White South Africans, the post-apartheid era has helped protect and grow their wealth. However, the argument that the Constitution is responsible for the slow pace of transformation has been cogently refuted, and many chapters in this volume identify the weaknesses in state capacity and coherence as fundamental to this state of affairs.

Some who dismiss the idea of South Africa as a 'developmental state' point to the failures of the country's major developmental plans. They are not swayed by the argument that South Africa has elements of a 'welfare state' – even though its social wage, relative to other developing countries', may be impressive. The exceptionally high levels of poverty and inequality, coupled with a chronically weak economy characterised by astronomically high unemployment and spluttering growth, mean that the state is unable to deliver many of the public goods required for citizens to live sustainably. The views of these critics are rooted in deep intellectual debates about the ongoing coloniality that pervades the international system, and in the notion that a decolonisation agenda is fundamental to achieving development (Anugwom, 2023). Several political parties mirror this discontent, with claims that the ANC has compromised too much and that more radical policies are needed for historical patterns of inequality to be reversed.

Apart from highlighting inter-generational and political tensions, the debate points to another interesting feature of the South African state: its hybridity, straddling multiple frameworks of governance and economic organisation. It is true that South Africa's macroeconomic framework exhibits elements of both neoliberalism and welfarism, reflecting tension between market-driven policies and a more interventionist state approach focused on redistribution and social justice. At the same time, the state itself blends different governance models, balancing aspects of a modern bureaucratic state with the recognition of traditional and customary systems. There is ongoing debate about whether these efforts to incorporate traditional governance are a necessary accommodation of South Africa's diverse political memory and lived realities (Gasa, 2011). Any attempt to rigidly categorise the state within a single framework will inevitably fail to capture its complexity. Thus, the chapters in this book, which may at times seem to be arguing against each other, ultimately complement and converse with each other to provide a fuller, more nuanced understanding of the South African state.

The 30th anniversary of democracy marks a critical juncture in South Africa's ongoing process of state- and nation-building. In the 29 May 2024 general election, the governing ANC lost its majority for the first time since 1994. The formation of a coalition government – the Government of National Unity (GNU) – which includes the ANC, the liberal Democratic Alliance and several smaller parties, would have been unthinkable were it not for the fact that similar scenarios had played out in local government across the country. Such political accommodation among the country's elites is becoming the norm, though they are not always effective in delivering the services they are mandated to provide and that citizens demand. Indeed, it remains unclear whether this national coalition government will improve on the state's record for fulfilling its constitutional mandate to deliver services to the population, especially the most vulnerable parts of it. Arguments have already erupted within the GNU over the Basic Education Laws Amendment (BELA) Act and the implementation of a National Health Insurance (NHI). The provision of education and health services is a critical function of the South African state, and such disagreements at national government level could have serious implications for the population as a whole. The truth is that state performance has already been negatively affected by these disputes. Cabinet was to sign off on the government's Medium-Term Development Plan, which would guide government departments' strategies and programmes, in October 2024, but disputes in the GNU on BELA and the NHI delayed its approval to the first quarter of 2025.

The GNU is not the only elite pact in South African politics; others, too, are unfolding. Several parties coalesced, for example, in opposition to the GNU, claiming to represent the interests of Black people, especially impoverished Black people. They promise a more radical and redistributive agenda, accusing what they call a 'neoliberal' alliance led by the ANC and DA of having no interest in undoing the injustices of apartheid and in uplifting the most marginalised sections of the South African population – mostly Black people. These parties challenge the GNU to prove that it has the political will and the authority to deliver on its mandate to ensure dignity, opportunity and a decent life for all citizens.

STATE CAPABILITY

It is important to assess, as this volume does, whether the various misgivings about the state are valid, if its legitimacy is accepted, and whether the state remains oriented towards serving the needs of all its people, as originally intended. The challenges that South Africa has faced in the three decades since democracy have become embedded in the very fabric of society, while new challenges have unfolded over time, testing the state's ability to adapt. Globalisation has tied the South African economy inextricably to a system dominated by highly industrialised nations and large multinational corporations, alongside an international finance system that has faced several crises. Rapid technological advances are transforming the ways in which key sectors of the economy function, with severe social and economic repercussions, not least in terms of employment.

Meanwhile, global inequality continues to rise, as the wealthy become alarmingly richer while the poor endure a steeply increasing cost of survival. Some argue that this trend signals a failure of capitalism and a need for alternative ways of organising society to produce and distribute wealth more equitably and sustainably. These unfolding pressures, both global and domestic, raise pressing questions about whether the state, in its current form, can still fulfil the mandate of meeting the needs of all its citizens.

The question is whether states – and, for our discussion, the South African state in particular – remain fit for purpose given the complex challenges they face, and what alternate paths might be taken. It is against this background that Netshitenzhe (Chapter 3) questions whether the centre is holding, and asks what model might help to deliver services more effectively – to live up to the aspiration of being a developmental state. He observes that even some neoliberal states recognise the need for a high degree of planning and coordination by the centre of government to ensure delivery. He advocates for the establishment of a 'pilot agency' at the centre of government, arguing that the Policy Coordination and Advisory Services (PCAS) in the Mbeki presidency had come close to such an idea. Central planning has, of course, not been absent in the work of government. The National Development Plan, published in 2012, as well government's Medium-Term Strategic Frameworks and, most recently, the 2024–2029 Medium-Term Development Plan are all part of efforts to plan centrally. This bolstering of centralised planning is aimed at ensuring that everything from macroeconomic policy to social cohesion can be addressed in efforts to build a more equal and democratic society. Netshitenzhe argues that failure is therefore less in the planning and more in the implementation of those plans, and the pilot agency he proposes is intended to bolster implementation capacity.

Sachs (Chapter 5) proffers a related contribution on how state capability could be reconceptualised. Traditionally, the literature assesses the capacity of the fiscal state by focusing on its ability to finance operations through taxation and borrowing. But Sachs argues that another aspect of the state derives from its ability to raise revenue to carry out its responsibilities vis-à-vis its citizens. He further argues that the traditional perspective is incomplete, as it overlooks the state's expenditure responsibilities and its role in regulating the public economy. He makes the case that the ability to manage and direct public expenditure in particular, as well as to regulate the commodification of infrastructure, is a crucial aspect of the state's capability to deliver on its developmental mandate.

Both Netshitenzhe's and Sachs's contributions are premised on the idea of a 'developmental state' and the need for concerted development planning if the South African state is to meet its oft-stated development goals. The lack of such planning, and a confusion about the meaning of a 'developmental state', have led, in some sectors, to a form of commercialisation and commodification of state services. Sachs refers to the provision of energy as one example of such commodification. Caromba (Chapter 8) takes up this theme, with an analysis of the contestations around South Africa's energy transition. The state, he argues, is an arena for competition between cabals of interest groups. Using the lens of historical institutionalism, he explores the interests of pro- and anti-transition forces, concluding that what is needed to drive a sustainable energy future is a just transition that considers the needs of all stakeholders. Similarly, in assessing water politics and governance in South Africa, Meissner (Chapter 9) argues that the state and society are in a hydro-social compact in which the state has not consistently lived up to its responsibilities nor delivered on its mandates. It is often poor governance, rather than an inadequate supply of water, which is the cause of state incapacity.

If state capability is a function of the means to deliver on the state's mandate, then a profound understanding of how the economy functions is an important and necessary part of any analysis. Nxele (Chapter 4) explores the political economy of the rounds of restructuring the South African economy has undergone since 1994, and concludes that not only has it failed to be inclusive, but it has also served the interests of predatory elites whose self-serving agendas have hindered nation-building. This analysis resonates with that of Shangase (Chapter 7), which observes that in the wake of the uncovering of 'state capture', South Africa still has not answered the question 'what will happen next?'. He asks us to interrogate to what extent the state is autonomous, and whether the state, by its nature, has historically always been 'captured' by whichever interest groups dominate it. This is a sobering insight, suggesting that 'state capture' might recur, and inviting us to engage with how best to ensure that the state acts as a vehicle for the aspirations and interests of the most vulnerable and needy.

Gouws (Chapter 12) uses another lens to evaluate whether the state has delivered on its promises: feminist institutionalism. She assesses state feminism in South Africa by examining whether the state's National Gender Machinery (NGM), which was set up to advance gender equality, has been effective. Her analysis, which coincides with that of many other contributors in respect of the state in general, is that the good intentions of the NGM – which includes the Commission for Gender Equality – have been undermined by political wrangling from within the ANC. A combination of slate politics, cadre deployment and a culture of compliance with party-political diktat has resulted in the gender agenda being displaced by political divisions and, earlier, the imperatives of state capture, to the detriment of the quest for gender equality.

Another fault-line in the state's alignment with societal aspirations arises from the challenges of situating traditional leadership and multi-party, representative democracy within a single framework. From 1994, these have co-existed uneasily, given the ambiguous role that traditional authorities had played during the colonial and apartheid periods, and the contradictions inherent in recognising unelected hereditary and patriarchal leadership – with its implications for resource ownership and gender relations – in a constitutional democracy. Colonialism and apartheid systematically ensured the co-option of traditional structures into the system. Ntsebeza (Chapter 10) points out that the ambivalence about the role of traditional authorities which preceded the end of apartheid rolled over into post-apartheid politics. Even within the ruling ANC, some saw traditional authorities as anti-democratic and anti-progressive, while others believed these leaders reflected the values of a significant portion of the population and should be accorded a greater role. As identity politics have become more present and more potent in South Africa, many parties have competed more openly for the support of traditional authorities. One misplaced argument around this – which ties in with other populist critiques of the Constitution – is that the Constitution is founded on Roman-Dutch Law, which is founded on premises alien to African traditional law, and, therefore, the precepts of the Constitution should be questioned, if not rejected – including the role of traditional authorities.

STATE CAPACITY AND ETHICS

The South African state is a vast edifice: it includes Parliament, the executive, the judiciary, various state departments, and independent bodies created by the Constitution to support democracy. While there is concern about the effectiveness of the state, the judiciary, according to Friedman (Chapter 14), has maintained a remarkable level of legitimacy and credibility, as it has protected its ability to function independently and without interference. But much as this is, in some respects, a success story of South Africa's democracy, the courts do not always deliver the kind of outcomes that reflect popular interests. This is mainly because access to the courts is slow and expensive, and is burdensome for those who most need it.

Another area in which the South African state has performed well, though not always consistently so, has been in the realm of international relations and foreign policy. From being the pariah of the world before 1990, South Africa used its soft power to push agendas that reflect a human rights-centred approach. It has been generally consistent in its foreign policy posture over the past three decades and pushed for the transformation of international institutions to advance African and Global South interests. However, as Le Pere and Jeenah (Chapter 13) point out, South Africa's idealism does not always match the realities of interest-driven politics (realpolitik) that shape policies and actions. This assessment can also be extended to the state's (in)ability to ensure peace and security for its people. Having been welcomed back into the international community after the end of apartheid, South Africa found itself at the centre of political initiatives to secure peace in several African conflicts. But not only was the protracted nature of some of these conflicts a strain on the country's defence budget, the government also increasingly had to contend with the spillover effect of instability in the region, as well as high levels of crime in the country. South Africa's most significant recent foreign policy initiative – its case at the International Court of Justice accusing Israel of genocide – highlights the tensions inherent in a foreign policy that seeks to be based on constitutional values and, simultaneously, to advance the country's material interests.

CONCLUSION

This volume makes a significant contribution to the characterisation and assessment of the South African state and its institutions at a time when democracy is being challenged globally, and when huge changes are taking place in the political scene in South Africa, including debates about the value of its Constitution. In addition to considering the performance of the state during three decades of democracy, the chapters shed light on the capacity and capability of the state to deliver on its constitutional mandate and evaluate the ethical underpinnings of the state and its actions.

The fundamental question remains: should the South African state be compared to a glass half full or half empty? The answer depends on an overall assessment of both the state's institutional capacity – its structural frameworks and resources – and its capability to utilise those resources effectively to deliver services and implement policy. The chapters in this volume paint a mixed picture. After colonial and apartheid rule in South Africa, strategic opportunities manifested at global, regional and national levels, leading to a critical opening in which the foundations of a new state were laid. The founding principles of that state – including a unitary state upholding democratic values and fundamental human rights – also laid the basis for the transformation of the lives of many citizens. A state in which all people enjoy the right to vote and the results are generally accepted by all parties; in which the media is free to report; in which the courts operate independently; and a social wage protects the population – especially its most vulnerable members – is not to be scoffed at.

These are freedoms and rights that distinguish the democratic South African state from its colonial and apartheid predecessors, and from many postcolonial states. However, the point of this book is not to glorify South Africa's achievements, but also to shine a torch in the darker corners, and to detect the strains and fractures. Rakabe (Chapter 15), in asking how South Africa can move towards a performing state, provides an overview of what is wrong with state capacity and why the state is failing to deliver on complex tasks. His analysis lends weight to Haricharan's argument (Chapter 6) that complexity calls for new leadership models fit for the 21st century. To achieve the societal transformation envisioned in the Constitution, the public service must be professionalised, which will require transformational leadership.

A state is meant to represent the values of the society it holds together and serves, but South Africa remains a deeply fractured society. The intersections of race, class and gender with the reproduction of deep economic inequalities have led many to ask whether the state requires a more radical, interventionist agenda. For some, this means deepening state capacity and adopting the mantle of a developmental state, with a greater sense of purpose. For others, the fundamental problem is the structure of the economy; they argue that the state needs to intervene directly to place the economy in the hands of the Black majority. Some of the interventions proposed in political manifestos include nationalisation of key institutions and resources such as the country's central bank and mineral wealth, expropriation of land (without compensation to owners) for redistribution to the poor, and measures to ensure that state-owned enterprises are not privatised. Such measures, it is argued, will begin addressing the economic imbalances of the past.

The fact that these policy options for the South African state are given voice in noisy political party contestation suggests that informed policy debate is lacking. Part of the reason for this is the marginalisation from discussion of those who do not have access to the resources that powerful interest groups do – which Friedman also points to with regard to debates about the judiciary. These discussions are unfolding at a time when authoritarianism is on the rise globally, and the attractiveness of populist promises is becoming harder to counter as people do not see meaningful improvements in their own lives (Van der Westhuizen et al., 2023). This has led to tensions between state actors and citizens, especially when the latter organise themselves to oppose policy or long-established edifices of power. Incumbent governments are ambivalent about being pressured by citizens, even though they attained their positions on the back of citizens' support.

This has been evident in how the South African state has responded to protests – especially small, uncoordinated service delivery strikes by communities for whom the protest is the only language the state understands (Brooks et al., 2023). It is also evident in broader, national initiatives like the student-led 'Fallist' movements. A show of force by the state has all too often been the default, as it attempts to stamp its authority on society. But the use of violence, often under executive direction, can backfire and erode trust and even state legitimacy, as pointed out by Africa in Chapter 11. The police's killing of 36 protesting miners at the Marikana mine in 2012 became symbolic of the state siding with the rich and powerful against the poor and exploited working class. On the other hand, the state's failure to prevent the loss of lives and destruction in the July 2021 unrest after the jailing of former President Jacob Zuma exposed weaknesses in its capacity to provide security guarantees to citizens in the event of looting and bedlam. Moreover, the capacity of the security sector to guarantee South Africa's sovereignty, and to play an effective role in peacekeeping on the continent, has been undermined by inadequate state funding, fuelling an erosion of South Africa's regional stature.

Civil society activism has a crucial role in deepening democracy. Heywood and Levy (Chapter 16) discuss the role of civil society in participatory democracy through the lens of two important civil society campaigns, the Treatment Action Campaign (TAC) for the provision of antiretroviral drugs, and the push to improve education outcomes. They argue that the activism described illustrates the possibilities for two different aspects of mobilisation. They point to an adversarial style of activism when pressure is applied on the state to live up to its responsibility and a participatory coalitional style which entails civil society cooperating with the state to deliver on its goals. There are, of course, also sections of civil society that remain marginalised by the state and various political and even society elites. The question of how civil society organisations – usually representing the most impoverished parts of South African society – access the spaces needed to pressurise the state to address their demands is an ongoing challenge. The lesson to draw from their experiences is that the state remains a site of struggle and will be moulded by those who are most effective in leveraging its institutions: be it courts, elected bodies, the executive or independent entities.

This volume's unique contribution lies in its ability to offer a comprehensive understanding of the South African state and its ongoing evolution. It acknowledges the progress that has been made, but also critically engages with the structural and institutional challenges that continue to hinder the state's potential, and points to resistance to the state where sections of the citizenry protest against the state's non-performance. This book also provides invaluable insights into the complexities of governance, state capacity and the role of civil society, encouraging reflection on how best to navigate the tensions and struggles that will shape the future of South Africa. The state's journey towards a fully realised democracy remains unfinished, and the work presented here serves as both a testament to the state's resilience and a call to action for those seeking to engage with and shape its future.

REFERENCES

Ansari, S. 2021. *Neoliberalism and Resistance in South Africa. Economic and Political Coalitions.* London: Palgrave MacMillan.

Anugwom, E. 2023. 'Beyond the debate: Decolonisation, decoloniality and the reframing of development in Africa'. *Politikon,* 50(4), 419–437.

Barbara, J. 2008. 'Rethinking neoliberal state building: Building post-conflict development states'. *Development in Practice*, 18(3), 307–318, http://www.jstor.org/stable/27751926, accessed 14 January 2025.

Beall, J., Gelb, S. and Hassim, S. 2005. 'Fragile stability: State and society in democratic South Africa'. *Journal of Southern African Studies* 31(4), 681–700.

Bond, P. 2014. 'Constitutionalism as a barrier to the resolution of widespread community rebellions in South Africa'. *Politikon,* 41(3), 461–482, https://doi.org/10.1080/02589346.2014.975931, accessed 14 December 2024.

Brooks, H., Chikane, R. and Mottiar, S. (eds). 2023. *Protest in South Africa: Rejection, Reassertion, Reclamation.* Johannesburg: MISTRA.

Ebrahim, H. 1998. *The Soul of a Nation: Constitution-Making in South Africa.* Oxford: Oxford University Press.

Falola, T. 2022. 'Walter Rodney's *How Europe Underdeveloped Africa.* Its relevance to Contemporary Issues 50 Years later'. *African Economic History*, 50(2), 58–63.

Fine, B. 2014. 'Politics of neoliberal development: Washington Consensus and post-Washington Consensus', in Weber, H. (ed.), *The Politics of Development: A Survey.* London: Routledge.

Gasa, N. 2011. 'The Traditional Courts Bill: A silent coup'. *South African Crime Quarterly*, 35, 23–29.

Mkhize, G. and Vilakazi, F. 2021. 'Rethinking gender and conduits of control: A feminist review'. *Image & Text*, 35, 1–22, https://doi.org/10.17159/2617-3255/2021/n35a10, accessed 14 December 2024.

Mpofu-Walsh, S. 2021. *The New Apartheid. Apartheid Did Not Die. It was Privatised.* Cape Town: Tafelberg Books.

Ngomane, T. and Flanagan, C. 2003. 'The road to democracy in South Africa'. *Peace Review,* 15(3), 267–271.

Pillay, D. 2011. 'The enduring embrace: COSATU and the Tripartite Alliance during the Zuma era'. *Labour, Capital and Society / Travail, Capital et Société*, 44(2), 56–79.

Southall, R. 2024. 'South African democracy at 30: Election leads to formation of a Government of National Unity'. *Australian Outlook*, https://www.internationalaffairs.org.au/australianoutlook/south-african-democracy-at-30-election-leads-to-formation-of-a-government-of-national-unity, accessed 14 January 2025.

Terreblanche, S. 2010. 'The British Empire and unification: 31 May 1910'.

Unpublished paper, https://www.ekon.sun.ac.za/sampieterreblanche/wp-content/uploads/2018/04/SJT-2010-The-British-Empire-100-years-after-unification.pdf, accessed 14 January 2025.

Van der Westhuizen, C., Dube, S. and Jolobe, Z. 2023. 'Beyond democracy's travails towards just inclusion: Remembering the *Demos'*, in Van der Westhuizen, C., Dube, S. and Jolobe, Z. (eds), *The D-Word. Perspectives on Democracy in Tumultuous Times*. Gqeberha: Mandela University Press.

INDEX

402

www.ingramcontent.com/pod-product-compliance
Lightning Source LLC
Chambersburg PA
CBHW060019030426

42334CB00019B/2098